HISTORY AND MYTH IN ROMANIAN CONSCIOUSNESS

Lucian Boia

Central European University Press
Budapest

First published in Romanian as *Istorie și mit în conștiința românească* by
HUMANITAS, Bucharest, 1997

English edition published in 2001 by
Central European University Press

Nádor utca 15
H-1051 Budapest
Hungary

400 West 59th Street
New York, NY 10019U
USA

An imprint of the Central European University Share Company

Translated by James Christian Brown

Distributed in the United Kingdom and Western Europe by
Plymbridge Distributors Ltd., Estover Road, Plymouth, PL6 7PZ
United Kingdom

ISBN 963 9116 96 3 Cloth
ISBN 963 9116 97 1 Paperback

Library of Congress Cataloging in Publication Data
A CIP catalog record for this book is available upon request

Printed in Hungary by Akaprint

Contents

Three Years on: an Introduction to the Second Romanian Edition

THE STORY OF A BOOK

Only this new introduction distinguishes the second edition from the first. Much could have been added, modifications and refinements could have been made, but I considered that the text ought to be left unchanged, just as I saw fit to write it three years ago. All the more so as the book has become almost a classic: I have the feeling that it is no longer really my property any more. So I shall rely on this introduction to say all that I have to say about the book, its history, and the historical and cultural controversies to which it has given rise.

In writing it, I was convinced that I was laying myself open to attack on many fronts. I had had a foretaste only a short time earlier, when, together with my students, I published the collection *Romanian Historical Myths* in a limited print-run at the Bucharest University Press. The armed forces television program *Pro Patria* (now discontinued) did me the honor of making a veritable "soap opera" out of the issue, which was broadcast at peak viewing time on the national television channel. Military and civilian commentators outdid one another in talking about me (in my absence) in less than pleasant terms. I had struck, it would appear, at the foundations of national ideology and Romanian identity—by relativizing what my accusers "knew" full well to be the one and only history of the nation. Just one more step—and a short one at that—and it would have been a matter of high treason. The military had become a tribunal of historiography: what could be more telling both for the confused state of Romanian democracy and for the contempt in which professionalism was held? Some newspapers gave me a similar treatment. The students, too, had their share of troubles at the hands of certain professors—scarcely to the credit of the latter. I realized then what it means to find oneself isolated in such a situation, even in what I must recognize was a self-cultivated isolation. Adversaries are usually quicker off the mark than supporters. The fact is that at the time no one leapt to my aid. And I must confess that I had not expected such an uproar. My aims had been purely professional; I had never sought to gain cheap publicity or to scandalize public opinion. I was caught red-handed in my own naivete: I should have known—it was, after all, the very thesis I had always propounded!—that history cannot be isolated from society, from ideologies and politics. So much the better: I now had the opportunity to test the degree of social sensitivity to history by my own experience.

Life is full of surprises. One of the least expected—for me—was the exceptional reception which the present book enjoyed on its first publication in May 1997. It became the favorite topic of discussion in intellectual circles. Its praises were sung by personalities of the highest standing in Romanian culture. It was clear that it responded to a deeply felt need. Something was not quite right with the history which had been taught for generations. But what, exactly? It was, of course, the task of a historian to identify the ideological pitfalls in our reconstruction of the past. When people speak about history they are really speaking about the present, about themselves. However, the book had reached even further than I intended. It was not just history that was under discussion but Romanian culture as a whole, and the Romanians' sense of who they were. Among the many reviews the book received, which repeatedly highlighted the novelty and the necessity of the project, I was particularly impressed by Mircea Iorgulescu's article in *Dilema* (15–21 August 1997), under the title "At last!". The critic insistently repeats these same words: "At last." "At last", he stresses, "we have the first radical and systematic critique of the Romanian culture of today." Less enthusiasm was shown by historians (with a few exceptions, mainly among the younger generation), and it is easy enough to see why. A relativistic perspective on history, according to which history is inevitably seen from the present and is impossible to separate from the social and cultural environment in which it is produced, is not the sort of thing likely to delight professional historians. They would rather believe in a scientific and objective history—something with which to justify their own professional status. All I ask them to do is to explain how it is that this scientific and objective history is always different. I am not the one who makes history relative! History *is* relative: all I am doing is noting the fact.

The most curious thing, however, was the almost complete absence of the sort of attacks which had been so frequent a short time before. I am not sure if it was entirely to its advantage, but the book was met with much praise and very little controversy. When hostile voices could be heard at all they were timid and isolated, perhaps because of a general strategic withdrawal after the elections of November 1996, which had deprived the forces of aggressive nationalism of the levers of power that they had previously held. Will there be a belated reaction after the elections of 2000, I wonder? Such politicization is, in any case, the last thing I want; I wrote an honest book about history, not a partisan intervention.

The critical success I have mentioned was matched by the book's success with the general public. Four successive print-runs of 9,000 copies, which sold out in two years (a considerable figure for the Romanian book trade), are proof that *History and Myth* has itself entered into "Romanian consciousness". I am glad the book has been successful; it remains for me to get used—though I doubt I ever shall—to being a "public figure", a strange role which I do not, and never did, desire for myself. Out of the same reticence I appear on television as seldom as possible. Would it not be wonderful if we could separate the book from the author!

DEMYTHOLOGIZING?

It is not for me to assess the extent to which *History and Myth* had an unleashing role. I like to think that I did not write in vain, and that at least a few of the new historical–cultural approaches of the last two or three years can be traced back directly or indirectly to the book. Perhaps I have put an end to a state of innocence and raised questions which can no longer be avoided.

I have followed with interest, and often with amazement, the career of the word *myth*, a word rarely encountered before 1997, which has slipped rapidly from the cover of my book into fashionable circulation, at the risk of a veritable inflation and a pronounced unscrupulousness in the way it is used. Demythologizers are now in full swing. Against them, no less active and vehement, are arrayed the upholders of national mythology, in whose vision the myths express our Romanian essence and are to be left untouched. This new line of defense is an interesting one. Of course, there are still intransigent upholders of an unblemished Romanian historiography, in which everything is true and nothing is mythical. More subtle minds, however, do not dispute the existence of a dose of mythology: they just say that it is not a good idea to demolish it! Such an attitude is no longer scientific: it is almost mystical.

"The hunting down of myths", writes no less a cultural authority than Eugen Simion, president of the Romanian Academy, "is a risky activity, because myths are part of the cultural identity of the nation."[1] Are we to understand that we do not need intelligent historians—that patriotism is sufficient? To mix things up even more, there is an easy slippage from "myth making" to "mystification", and vice versa. Thus Eugen Simion sums up my argument in a spirit which I do not recognize as my own: "In short, the history of the Romanians would appear to have been abusively mythologized, and, by mythologizing, mystified. What is needed is to demystify it and judge it lucidly..."

We ought, however, to make a distinction between the two words and concepts. Mystification is a crude process (though it can sometimes be an efficient one), which has nothing to do with the subtle substance of myth. Mystification is a matter of lying, deception, and deliberate misinformation, while myth is something quite different, defining or illustrating a great belief which animates a people. It is, of course, possible to mystify on the basis of certain myths—to take advantage of what people like to believe, of their prejudices, hopes and illusions—but it is not permissible to confuse the two concepts. I for one do not waste my time hunting down lies: I try to unravel the great mythical tendencies which are inherent in the human soul and in the consciousness of communities.

None of those who have written in the last few years about myths, demythologizing and demystification have sought my opinion, and indeed there is no reason why they should. I am not, and I do not aspire to be, the leader of a school. I am responsible only for what I write and for my own ideas. For this reason I feel the need to make two things clear.

Firstly, the adaptation, deformation, and mythologizing of history is inscribed within a universal typology. There were those who believed that I had identified it as something peculiar to the Romanians! Hence some were furious—how could the Romanians be treated with such a lack of respect!—while others rejoiced—at last someone was showing the Romanians the mistakes they had made and the right way forward. Both sides should have been more moderate in their sorrow or joy. It is not just the Romanians who treat history this way: everybody does it. So, to avoid any confusion, and to carry the idea through to the maximum degree of generalization, a year after *History and Myth* I published *Playing with the Past: History between Truth and Fiction*.[2] It would be a good idea if the two books were read together, perhaps in inverse order of their publication.

Secondly, I do not recall using the concept of demythologizing. I would like it to be clearly understood that I have not declared war on myths. For a long time I have been dealing with the imaginary—not only, or even primarily, with the Romanian historical imaginary—and I am well aware that we cannot live outside the imaginary and mythology. It is this that makes us human, rather than animals or robots. Never for a moment did I propose the abolition of myths: all I wanted was for them to be interpreted historically. I know we cannot live without myths, but nor can I, as a historian, justify my existence if I do not try to understand. Some may say that a myth once interpreted will crack and crumble. So be it, but what are we to do then—stop interpreting? Once again, do we want an intelligent history or (to speak euphemistically) an unintelligent one? And are we really incapable of looking from two points of view at the same time, both "poetically" and rationally? Must we sacrifice our intelligence to save our poetry? Can we not keep both?

In an article entitled "A Fashionable Toy: Demythologizing"[3], the critic Alex Ştefănescu presents the case against rational research into myths, while at the same time apparently putting all attempts at demythologizing under the sign of my method: "The historian Lucian Boia has rapidly made a name for himself by submitting the myths of history to an analysis lucid to the point of cynicism." The argument is that we cannot rob people of their illusions. I would urge him to relax a little: no one will ever succeed in robbing people of their illusions! Love, too, is an illusion, explains Alex Ştefănescu, so why not accept it as such? Of course we accept it—indeed we do!—but does the author of the article think that the physiological and psychological aspects of attraction between the sexes are not to be spoken of? Are we to tear pages from the anatomy textbook? Do we throw Freud's works in the bin? This is how Alex Ştefănescu would have it with the "thousand-year unity" of the Romanians: even if there was no such thing in fact, it exists for us, and that is sufficient. So what are historians to do: knowingly tell a lie, lest they awaken the Romanians from their beautiful dream? I do not share the demythologizers' intolerance of myths, but nor can I understand the anti-demythologizers' intolerance of an absolutely normal scientific project.

EMINESCU

Spirits got heated almost to incandescence around the figure of Eminescu. It is true that no other Romanian myth carries a higher emotional charge than that of the national poet. He is perceived not only as a poet of unparalleled value—which would already be claiming a lot—but as a symbol of the Romanian nation, the supreme, concentrated expression of Romanian-ism. It is no use—or is it?—saying that he was not seen this way during his lifetime and that perhaps he will no longer be seen this way at some point in the future. The myth was the creation of the period around 1900, and, like any myth, it produced a transfiguration, which may or may not correspond to the sensibilities of today or tomorrow. A rather puerile, and certainly unfair, game is played around Eminescu. Some try to find all sorts of flaws in him, intellectual and even physical, while others cannot agree to bring him down by even a single step from the heights of the myth, and seek to convince us that we have no right to break away from Eminescu.[4] I gave my point of view in an interview in the Chişinău periodical *Sud-Est* (1–2/1999). Perhaps it is worthwhile reproducing the relevant passage here:

> Where Eminescu is concerned, there are two aspects to consider. There is Eminescu the poet, and there is Eminescu the ideologist. Many of those who are revolted by the "attacks" on Eminescu are admirers not of his poetry but of his ideology. It is an autochthonist and xenophobic ideology. In fact this is no fault of Eminescu's. He was not, strictly speaking, an ideologist. He had the right to have any ideas, but these need to be related to the cultural and political context of his period, not glorified or condemned from our late-twentieth-century perspective. As an ideologist, Eminescu was "discovered" by the nationalist wave after 1900. And nowadays he is still promoted by nationalists. It is a manipulation: this is what the national poet said, so this is absolute truth before which we must all bow down. On the other hand, there is the poetry of Eminescu, which has no need of ideology to be admired. However, it remains to be seen what the future will bring. I, personally, am a great admirer of Eminescu—the poet Eminescu, not the ideologist. I believe I can feel his poetry, and I know many of his verses by heart. But I sometimes wonder if my generation is not the last really to savor Eminescu. Tastes evolve. The day young people no longer recite his poems by moonlight (and perhaps that day has already come), Eminescu will remain a great name in the history of Romanian literature but he will no longer be among us. It is stupid to say that this must not happen. What will be will be. Paradoxically it may be that Eminescu the ideologist will stand up better to time than Eminescu the poet: there will always be nationalists to wave him as a banner.

THE INTERWAR YEARS AND THE COMMUNIST PERIOD

The tendency to see things in black and white is not a specifically Romanian one. This sort of polarizing is a feature of the imaginary in general. But the more conflictual a society—and the Romanian society of today is highly conflictual—the greater the risk of extreme solutions, without half measures. The interwar years and the communist period—that is, recent history, in relation to which interests and ideological options are manifested directly—are fully at the mercy of such contradictory assessments and are obsessively invoked as mythological models.

The years between the two world wars continue to be discussed endlessly.[5] Was this the golden age of Romania, of Romanian culture, of Romanian democracy? Or, on the contrary, a society which, behind the façade, concealed a serious backwardness and all sorts of deviations from democratic principles? The opposing judgements are both just and unjust at the same time. Romania then was Romania then. The world then—everywhere—is no longer the world of today. Interwar Romania, with all that was good and bad in it, can no longer be a useful model. But over-severe critiques are also out of order. They define present options and err in their lack of historical sense. Deficient democracy, nationalism, and anti-Semitism are characteristic of the period in general, not of Romania in particular, and it is not fair to judge such dysfunctionalities or attitudes exclusively in relation to current norms (which are themselves more ideal than effective). Romania at the time was a contradictory society: on the one hand there was an elite of European character (thought not completely free of autochthonous reflexes and prejudices) and a modern cultural and institutional framework, and on the other, an indisputable historical time lag in the deeper reaches of the country, in spite of a relatively sustained rhythm of modernization (a proportionately large rural population, a low literacy level, and traditional demographic patterns: a high birth rate, a high mortality rate, and the highest rate of infant mortality in Europe).[6] This "primitivism" of deeper Romania was what justified and permitted the authoritarian deviations. It was also the base on which Romanian communism was constructed and the source of many of the latter's aberrations: the almost complete disappearance of a too small elite, of cultural and political traditions, and of a whole way of life, the uprooting and manipulation of disoriented masses. Out of all these contradictions of the time, as with those of our own time, only multiple and contradictory images can result.

It is the same with communism. Some condemn it with no appeal, but there are also attempts at rehabilitation, if not global (everyone at least pays lip service to democracy and repudiates communism as a system) then segmental, on the principle that "it wasn't all bad". (If we put together all the segments which have been "rehabilitated" by one group or another—from cultural life to industry or international politics—it would seem that more things were good than bad; indeed we might ask ourselves why communism fell at all.) It would be an illusion if we were to imagine that the majority of Romanians rose up in 1989 against communism as a system—from philosophical motives, as it were. They rose up against the consequences of communism, refusing to go on accepting the total degradation of their conditions of life. And nowadays these same people are no longer ready to accept poverty out of love for democracy. According to opinion polls, at least half the Romanian population consider that they had a better life before 1989. Such nostalgia is fed not only by poverty but also by lack of adaptability to an open society (as proved by the fact that we find it also in the eastern part of Germany, which is far from poor). A correct intellectual approach ought to dissociate the historical and moral judgement of communism from an assessment of people's attitudes to communism. It is one thing to arrive at the conclusion that it was an immoral and harmful system, and quite another to consider that all Romanians would have made the same judgement. There was indeed an anti-communist resistance: some would minimize its importance or even dispute its existence, while others, in contrast, give it a greater significance than it really had. There was also, even without open resistance, a degree of intellectual and individual non-adherence to communism. The "Romanian resistance" is a chapter of our history which has its share of truth but also of mythology. In general, "resistances" are amplified in the imaginary. Westerners have done the same thing in reconstructing the story of "anti-fascist resistance". In fact in any society those who resist are in the minority compared with those who submit, accommodate themselves, or even profit. The Romanians who joined the *Securitate* were certainly more numerous than those who resisted in the mountains.

The mythological temptation can be glimpsed again when we hear of "resistance through culture", a subject dear to the hearts of Romanian intellectuals. It would be unjust to say that all writers, for example, were no more than docile servants of the authorities. But, on the other hand, they went on publishing their texts in conditions of censorship. There was no clandestine publishing in Romania. The writer tried to push things to the ultimate permissible limit, and the reader was urged to read between the lines, to imagine the unspoken but suggested message. It was a game played between the writer and the authorities: who could outwit whom? Each agreed to make certain concessions to the other. The result: a confused message. Who outwitted whom?

To give one well-known example, no literary work enjoyed more fame than Marin Preda's novel *The Best-Loved of all Mortals* (1980). It was a critical portrayal—severely critical by the standards of the time—of the 1950s. But the criticism was of abuses, not of the system (and even then, not of all abuses, not of the most serious). Ceauşescu, too, had distanced himself from such abuses in order to define his own brand of "communism of humanity", in contrast to the dark years of the Gheorghiu-Dej regime. Preda went somewhat further than Ceauşescu, but not much further, just as far as the limit beyond which one could not go. He could have gone beyond that limit and published a clandestine text, but he did not. Nor did other writers. Today it is somewhat embarrassing to read the novel. The Romanians have no Solzhenitsyn, no Havel.

Many, on the other hand, joined up. Communism brought about an overturning of society, to the disadvantage of some but to the advantage of others. Some were put out of their jobs and their houses; others took their places. Today's Romanian elite, with the exception of a few survivors, is the creation of communism. Many of its members, even if they do not admit it or admit it only partially and indirectly, know only too well that without communism they would not be what they are now—even if they show no hesitation in invoking the interwar period by way of an alibi or legitimizing procedure, identifying themselves in the imaginary with a quite different elite. And even people lower down the scale, for example peasants who were moved into towns and installed in districts of apartment blocks, accept this change of condition as a social advancement. An article by Daniel Barbu[7] provoked a lively discussion, complete with vehement protests, with the claim that the beneficiaries of communism were more numerous than its victims: "The proportion of those for whom the totalitarian regime represented a permanent threat, a burden, or an immediate or virtual danger, is between 4 and 8 percent, while those for whom communism meant a positive change in their lives, a stable and rising income, increasing access to higher education, and a closer connection to the state, can be placed somewhere between 20 and 70 percent." It must be emphasized that Daniel Barbu is not making communist propaganda, merely proposing an explanation, although it is probable that his formula contains an element of exaggeration and idealization. It should also be made clear that what is under discussion here is less the objective condition of people than their image of their own condition, which is not quite the same thing. (Ultimately, however, it is what counts! It is no use explaining, with the aid of a virtual history, that without communism Romania would have been modernized anyway, and in even better conditions, just like Greece and Portugal, countries that were no more advanced than Romania in the interwar period.) Essentially, however, I think Daniel Barbu is right; a good many Romanians—it is hard to say just how many—have nothing much to reproach communism for, while, on the other hand, they feel that they are indebted to it for their social advancement—just as some of them have come to consider after 1989 that they are "indebted" to democracy only for a fall in their standard of living.

Neither the interwar years nor the communist period can be represented in a single, coherent image. Each of us has our own personal relationship to recent history. We can only try to get as close as possible to the truth, but our judgement of that truth will never be a single one.

The Kosovo Syndrome

The crisis in Kosovo and the NATO attacks on Yugoslavia proved once again how divided the Romanians are, how inclined towards extreme judgements, and how ready some, or even many, of them still are to indulge in anti-Western propaganda on any pretext. They took up their positions without reserve, some on the side of Milošević, some on the side of the West, and so defined their own options. In fact, justice and injustice in this crisis were very much shared between the two camps. Even if we were inclined towards one solution or the other there were plenty of reservations that could have been expressed, yet these were scarcely heard. The most characteristic phenomenon was the slipping of a section of the political class, the press, and public opinion from the Western to the Serbian side. At first the percentage of those opting for NATO and the European Union was among the highest, if not indeed the highest, in this part of Europe. Almost all Romanians had followed with bated breath the country's unsuccessful attempt (but with the promise of a re-examination in the near future) at integration in Atlantic structures: it was a veritable national obsession. Then suddenly, with Kosovo, the percentage of Romanians in favor of NATO dropped by some tens. When it came to a choice, many Romanians preferred Orthodox, nationalist and authoritarian Serbia to the democratic and cosmopolitan West.

As always, when we speak about the "other" we characterize ourselves. It has become clear that for many Romanians attachment to the West has nothing to do with Western values but only with the wealth and power of a world to which we strain to attach ourselves out of purely material considerations. In addition, the difficulty with which Romanian legislation adapts itself to European legislation—with step-by-step resistance in some cases, as in the interminable discussion about the normalization of the legal status of homosexuals—illustrates the lack of real adherence to many Western norms. Economic inefficiency already keeps Romania far from Europe: if we also have a state of mind to take into account.

We Are a Nation, Not an Orthodox Nation

The mixing of politics and religion is another archaic feature of Romania (found also, it is true, in Greece, another Orthodox country and a member of the European Union). For a considerable number of Romanians it seems that it is not liberalism or democracy, but a rather vague, yet insistently affirmed, religious ideology that has occupied the place left free by the ideology of communism. This means that the unanimist and authoritarian logic of the past has not yet been left behind. Fortunately we are far from fundamentalism, for the political-religious equation also includes a fair dose of traditionalism, convention, and political demagogy. But this only makes the notes sound all the more false. The students of the University of Bucharest take sides over the building of a church (Orthodox of course) in the university precincts: some support the project, others oppose it. The former brand their opponents atheists and communists, while they in turn are branded Legionaries. At a moment of major crisis—the miners' march towards Bucharest—prime minister Radu Vasile found no other mediator than the church, and chose the Cozia monastery as a place for talks. Finally, an immense Cathedral of the Salvation of the People is to be erected in the heart of Bucharest. Meanwhile, politicians compete to be seen in churches and at religious events. Even Ion Iliescu, until recently a self-confessed "free thinker", has started making the sign of the cross. The current seems irresistible.

"Is the Romanian nation an Orthodox nation?" I asked, in a recent article from which I shall quote some extracts here.[8]

"Of course", some will reply. "Since the vast majority of Romanians are Orthodox the nation cannot be otherwise than Orthodox." It seems elementary, but it is not quite so simple. There are, after all, plenty of citizens who belong to other traditions. Do we want to say that they are second-class Romanians, obliged in religion as in other matters to submit to the will of the majority? What about the more than a million and a half Hungarians, who, naturally enough, are not Orthodox? Do we tell them that they must belong to another nation, the Hungarian nation? What about the Uniates, who are pure-blooded Romanians and who at one time were even the initiators of Romanian national ideology? Do they belong to the Romanian people or not? What about the Baptists, whose numbers have increased among the Romanians in recent decades? And, since we have mentioned ex-president Iliescu, what about free thinkers? Are you still allowed to present yourself as an atheist (as so many Romanians did until about ten years ago, at Party meetings anyway), or at least as a skeptic in matters of faith?

This may be how things are with us here, but there is another dimension of the problem to be considered. It seems that we are liable to forget that not only Romanians are Orthodox. Confessions are generally transnational and do not follow the political-national divisions of the day. If we attribute to religion a meaning which lies outside its specific message and give it the mission of structuring national spaces and civilizations, not only from a historical point of view but also in terms of current projects, then, as a logical consequence, we ought to associate ourselves with Orthodox Europe, alongside the Russians and Bulgarians, and keep well clear of the Catholic and Protestant, and, more than anything, secular West.

In fact, modern nations are not identified with a particular confession, even when it is that of the majority, for the simple reason that the nation is something different. The French, for example, are no less Catholic than the Romanians are Orthodox, but the French nation cannot be defined, and indeed is not defined, as a Catholic community.

Germans may be Protestants or Catholics, but the German nation remains one. In modern societies there is a separation between the sacred and the profane, between the religious and the civic or political space. And this does not necessarily mean an alienation from religious values—although the last two or three hundred years have seen a process of desacralization, first of all in the West and then in the rest of the world; it is simply a matter of separating sets of values which are distinct and should remain so. The nation is, in any case, a secular creation, quite different in its nature and its objectives from the universalism of religion. If religion alone had counted in the modern age then the Romanians would have been lost in the Slav mass—and who knows which way the Uniates of Transylvania would have gone? The Romanian national state was built on the basis of national ideology and liberal and democratic political principles, not religious criteria. It is normal that we should all share the same civic values, without which the national community would fall apart. But faith (or the lack of it) remains a matter of personal choice. We would do well to protect this area from any authoritarian principle and any form of discrimination, which would not only fail to consolidate the national organism, but might even threaten its cohesion.

The temptation to fuse nation and church has its own historical mythology. The first axiom is that "the Romanian people was born Christian" and has gone on to identify with Orthodox Christianity throughout its history. Leaving aside the fact that the "birth" of a people is a highly mythological concept, in the face of the paucity of source material we ought to be more cautious. There is no incontestable evidence of Christianity in Roman Dacia. Such evidence does exist from the fourth century onwards (both in Dacia, and, more extensively, in Dobrogea, which had remained a province of the Empire), but its frequency is not sufficient to support a coherent and certain history of Christianity north of the Danube. The claim—which has become insistent in recent years—that the apostle Andrew preached in Dobrogea, is based only on a late legendary tradition. (In any case, the tradition refers to Scythia—southern Russia—and not specifically to Little Scythia—Dobrogea. That is why Saint Andrew is the patron of Russia; he is also, at the other end of Europe, patron saint of Scotland; and now he is starting to be venerated as patron saint of Romania.) It is interesting that all this is a recent development. Around 1900, religious belief and practice were certainly much more alive in Romania than today; but Orthodoxism,[*] as an ideology, is much more ambitious and aggressive in its manifestations nowadays.

---

[*] Here and elsewhere in the present book, "Ortodoxism" (adj.: "Orthodoxist") is to be understood as referring to a political ideology which makes the Orthodox faith a mark of national identity, and should not be confused with "Orthodoxy" (adj.: "Orthodox"), the transnational Orthodox faith itself, which resists identification with any modern ideological "-ism". *Trans.*

THE FEDERALIST "THREAT"

The Romanian nation, like any other, is less unitary in reality than in the imaginary. It was assembled from distinct parts, welded together by the ideology and centralizing force of the unitary national state (a process made easier by the fact that Romanians were in the majority in all its regions), but even today we cannot talk of complete homogenization (which would, in any case, be impossible). For a number of years there have even been signs, generally discreet but sometimes more emphatic, of a desire to mark regional identities. In Moldavia there is now a Party of the Moldavians, although it is hard to say what its political chances may be. In the lands beyond the mountains, regarded in the Romanian imaginary as more civilized, more dynamic, and closer to Central Europe (Hungary!), we are starting to hear voices raised against making sacrifices for the sake of the other regions. There is nothing dramatic yet, but all the same it is something new for a Romania in which the mythology of the thousand-year unity of the Romanian people and the unitary national state has for so long covered over the inevitable diversity. A "provocative" article by the Transylvanian columnist Sabin Gherman, entitled "I Have Had Enough of Romania", caused a sensation and aroused the indignation of many. The fear—undoubtedly exaggerated—is beginning to take shape that Romania may disintegrate. Even federalism is looked on with suspicion. So, in fact, is any kind of decentralization. I repeat here what I wrote in an article on this theme:[9]

> The minds of many Romanians are imprinted with the idea that federalism is a risky invention, a first step towards the dismemberment of the nation. The best solution in their view is, of course, right at the opposite extreme from federalism and from decentralizing processes in general: the *unitary national state*. The last thing I want to do is to turn things round and say that the federal system is best. There is no universal model, applicable everywhere and in all conditions. But we need to know what we are talking about, and above all we should not rush to proclaim our prejudices to be immutable general truths.
>
> The model which the Romanians imitated, when they constructed modern Romania, was France. That meant a highly centralized political and administrative system: like the French *departments*, our counties are closely dependent, through their prefects, on central government. In the case of Romania, the centralizing process seemed all the more necessary as the country, which did not exist before 1859, was made up of "bits" which had to be welded together. Or at least that was what was thought best at the time. What would have resulted from a federal solution we cannot know, since we cannot remake history. What is certain is that uniformity was preferred to the acceptance or even cultivation of the historical and cultural differences between provinces—real differences

which are still visible today in spite of a history that has adapted itself to the political discourse and that tells us of an imaginary, centuries-long (or even millennia-long) unity of the Romanian space.

The federal solution, whatever the Romanians may think (and we are not the axis around which the world revolves), is not exactly an aberration. The United States, Germany, Switzerland, and nowadays even Belgium, are federal states, and they seem to be getting on not so badly! Moreover, all sorts of intermediary solutions can be imagined (and indeed have been imagined) between federalism and out-and-out centralism. The most interesting tendency of the last few years is, in fact, an evolution towards decentralization and the re-invigoration of historical provinces, with varying intensity, of course, from one country to another. Spain has been divided into seventeen autonomous provinces. Likewise, there is regional autonomy in Italy. And in Britain, Scotland has recently voted for autonomy.

We may, if we like, consider that the best variant for us is still that which corresponds to the expression "unitary national state", but let us not pretend that this is nowadays the dominant solution in the world, or in Europe, because it is not: *not any longer*! The French example deserves to be invoked again. France has doubled its system of *départements* with a parallel system of regions—broadly corresponding to the historical regions which the French Revolution hastened to abolish and which we now see returning after two centuries. The regions enjoy a certain degree of autonomy, limited in the case of France, but nevertheless effective: elected regional councils, their own budgets, etc. It is exactly what would happen here if, alongside the system of counties, we also divided the country into its historical provinces: Moldavia, Muntenia, Oltenia, Transylvania, Banat, etc. Even the thought of such an organization would call up the specter of national disintegration for some. But it is not even a federal solution. It is the solution adopted in France, which, nevertheless, remains the most centralized political organism in the whole of Western Europe. The Romanians were once imitators of France: now they are more French than the French!

What needs to be discussed in our case is not federalization, but how we can get beyond a strict centralization, which once played a historical role but was never uniformly beneficial and today is effectively a hindrance. Like Paris, Bucharest pulled too much towards itself. The country was divided, polarized between a capital and the rest: the provinces. In the nineteenth century, from an intellectual point of view, Iaşi, and Moldavia in general did not lag behind Bucharest and Muntenia; quite the contrary, I would say. The balance has been upset. Moldavia is now the poorest province in the country (according to all indicators: per capita production, unemployment, etc.). It is re-emerging as a province, but in what conditions?

In the more prosperous region of Transylvania, in the Banat and Crişana, some, and not only Hungarians, are starting to look over the western border. This is partly, though not only, the negative effect of an excessive centralization. The solution does not lie in more centralization (dictated, perhaps, by the unfounded fear of secessionism), but in seeking ways of revitalizing local and regional life. Not in a federal direction—which would be hard to promote here, taking into consideration our whole tradition and present context—but in a less centralizing direction than hitherto. In any case, the real risk we run is not federalization but becoming locked in an outdated form of political behavior, insensitive to recent evolutions. Let us not make the federalist threat an alibi for immobilism!

FROM THE "GETO–DACIANS" TO THE "MEDIEVAL ROMANIAN NATION"

The Dacians, too, seem to be casting aside that seamless unity which has characterized them for decades. In *History and Myth* I raised the question of what a "Geto–Dacian" people could mean. A specialist in the field, Alexandru Vulpe, recognizes that archaeologists have been somewhat exaggerating "where the common history of different tribal groups in the Danube-Carpathian space is concerned". The uncritical interpretation of ancient sources has been a veritable tradition in this country! When Strabo says that the Getae and Dacians spoke the same language, Romanian historians take him at his word, without stopping to wonder if the Greek historian, or his source, Poseidonius, had any competence in the field of Thracian dialects! Of course they had none! Alexandru Vulpe's conclusion is that the notion of "Geto–Dacians" must be taken to refer to a fragmentary space "and not a historical-social and political unit, not a common language, and not necessarily a common material and spiritual culture".[10] In a paper entitled "The Material Dimension of Ethnicity" (in course of publication in *New Europe College Yearbook*, 1997–98), Alexandru Niculescu attempts to theorize ethnic divisions in the spirit of modern anthropological concepts. He considers the summary identification of archaeological cultures with ethnic groups to be outdated: an ethnic group is not characterized by cultural uniformity, and its identity references are more symbolic than material. The whole issue of ethnicity in the Dacian space thus needs to be re-evaluated, with more professional refinement than before and leaving nationalist prejudices behind.

The fictive unity of Dacia is fading and giving way to effective diversity. The Getic and Dacian tribes are not alone. Celts and Scythians, and later Bastarnians and Sarmatians, complete a varied ethnic and cultural landscape. Indeed, a mixture of populations and cultures, not Daco–Roman purity, more correctly characterizes the Romanian space, from antiquity to the modern period. The tendency to eliminate the "others" from the Romanian equation—marginalizing the Slavs and other "migratory" peoples (who, once they had settled in the territory, ceased, in fact, to be migratory), along with later ethnic and cultural infusions—and to insist on a twofold Daco–Roman purity, reflects and sustains attitudes of rejection which belong to the present, not just to the interpretation of the past.

While some historians are breaking away from the mythology of unity, or at least proposing a more nuanced view, others prefer to go the opposite way, probably in the illusion that a Romanian nation which has always been united will continue to be so for ever. The upholders of this thesis now have a new text to refer to: *The Medieval Romanian Nation* by the Cluj-based historian Ioan-Aurel Pop. The book is subtitled *Romanian Ethnic Solidarities in the 13th to 16th Centuries.* Right from the title page we find the confusion, frequent among Romanian historians, between ethnicity and nation. In the author's vision all sorts of local solidarities, especially among the Transylvanian Romanians, support the existence of a Romanian nation: "Large and small groups of Romanians acted in solidarity in the Middle Ages... They manifested themselves by ethnic *solidarity.* From the totalizing of these solidarities, and the interaction between them, in the thirteenth to the sixteenth centuries we can obtain the image of the medieval Romanian nation."[11]

However, the nation manifests itself precisely as a *greater solidarity,* which contains and subordinates other solidarities, and not as an amalgam of lesser solidarities. The latter are as old as the world itself: indeed, without solidarity there could be no human society. This sort of argument would lead us to look for nations even in prehistory. Of course, medieval people were aware of the languages they spoke and of the ethnic groups to which they belonged, as they were of the fact that others were "different". To insist on these points is to force an open door. But the nation is something else: it is a unique and all-encompassing solidarity, willed and created, not historically given. Ioan-Aurel Pop does indeed make a distinction between the medieval nation, "passive and relatively fragmented", and the modern nation, "active, unitary, conscious of its role and mission". I fully agree with these characterizations. The question is, however, whether a passive and fragmented nation, lacking a consciousness of its role and mission, can still be called a nation! Such a concept recalls the famous "non-organized state" identified by the "Romanian Communist Party Program" in the period after the Roman withdrawal from Dacia. The nation is a state of consciousness, and where there is no consciousness there can be no nation, since it has no way of existing.

The isolation of a few segments or moments of unity cannot cancel out a whole mass of concrete, ideological, and mental structures which do not support in any way the idea of an effective Romanian unity in the period, even at the level of an ideal. The author himself involuntarily lets slip counter-arguments to his own thesis: "The name of Iancu of Hunedoara has not remained in the Romanian public consciousness of the Middle Ages as that of a Romanian sovereign or of a sovereign who supported the Romanians, and that of Mathias even less so; indeed nor could they, as their ideals were different and *the ethnic aspect was of secondary importance at the time.*"[12] Is it just my impression, or was the book not trying to demonstrate precisely the opposite? Of Michael the Brave we find out (as was well enough known anyway) that he did not leave very many memories of a "national" order in the consciousness of subsequent generations. This is curious, all the same—indeed inexplicable—if he was then, in 1600, giving life to Romanian aspirations! Well, the Braşov chroniclers of Şchei seem to have had no idea of this. Our author prudently does not mention the Moldavians: they would have had nothing good to say of Michael anyway. On the other hand, he gives a forced interpretation of a passage in the *History of Wallachia*: "And the Christians, and especially Wallachia, were left without him. But for this all Christians should curse the Hungarian people all the more, for they are evil and sly, by their very nature." The author comments: "As we can see, for the time being the general Christian ideal is combined with the ethnic one, but the cliché of the 'evil and sly' Hungarians who put the innocent Michael to death is fully active. Only one more step remained to be taken before, following the erudite works of the scholars of the Transylvanian School, the romantics would set Michael among the precursors of modern Romania..."[13] It remains to be seen now who inspires more trust, the Muntenian chronicler or the historian from Cluj, for the two are definitely not saying the same thing. Where does the historian see the chronicler combining the general Christian ideal with the ethnic one? The fragment cited has nothing to do with ethnicity. It is talking about Wallachia, not about Romanians in general, and in any case not about Transylvanians or Moldavians (who continued to call themselves Moldavians and not Romanians well into the nineteenth century). We are left with the evil and sly Hungarians, but I am not sure that such labeling was sufficient for the coalescing of the Romanian nation. Disliking Hungarians is not enough to make one automatically a Romanian patriot: at least it certainly was not in 1600. (Nowadays, who knows?) And only one step from this to the prefiguration of modern Romania? It seems a rather big step. What is the point of citing sources if one is only going to put a false interpretation on them?

As far as I am concerned, discussion of the issue of the nation is closed. I have expressed my point of view in an essay entitled *Two Centuries of National Mythology*[14], in which I tried to show how the nation was invented in the years around 1800, as a supreme form of solidarity (above all other solidarities) in the modern imaginary. Of course, I have no illusions that I have solved the problem, since no problem is ever finally solved. Interpretations go on to infinity. All I can do in my books is to say openly what I think.

OPINION POLLS

I must confess that I love opinion polls. I know they are often contested. They may be approximate, even downright wrong, and they may be willfully distorted; they can be used to manipulate, too. But whatever their deficiencies it is better to have them than not at all. What would I not give to have such information for certain periods and key moments in history! (A poll, for example, to tell us how the Romanians of around 1650 saw Michael the Brave and the union of 1600.) In their absence, we use fragmentary material to try to identify all sorts of attitudes and states of mind. Can we be sure we are not wrong? Might we not be treating our sources as more representative than they really are?

So let us take advantage, at least for very recent history, of the polls which are available. For an interpreter of Romanian historical consciousness there can be nothing more interesting than an enquiry into the rating of historical personalities. In June 1999, the National Institute for the Study of Opinion and Marketing (Insomar) released the results of a poll[15] in which 1,200 individuals all over the country were asked to choose "the most important historical personalities who have influenced the destiny of the Romanians for the better". The responses (the top ten figures and their respective percentages) were as follows: Alexandru Ioan Cuza—24.6; Michael the Brave—17.7; Stephen the Great—13.4; Nicolae Ceauşescu—10.3; King Michael I—5.2; Vlad Ţepeş—4.1; Nicolae Iorga—3.1; King Carol I—3.1; Nicolae Titulescu—2.3; Ion Antonescu—2.2.

The classification says a lot, not about the past but about how Romanians relate to the past, in other words, about how they think nowadays.

Out of the ten chosen personalities Cuza takes first place, well ahead of the next in line. He seems posthumously, and decisively, to have won his mythological confrontation with Carol I. Before communism the relationship was the other way round: the kings appeared at the top of the hierarchy, leaving Cuza more or less in eclipse. In the meantime, royalty has almost been wiped from the collective memory of the Romanians, and this, together with the insistence on the idea of national unity (both before and after 1989) explains the placing of Cuza in the highest position. These are the effects of historical propaganda in the communist period (and of course no fault of Cuza's!). Moreover, in the time of Ceauşescu the gallery of great statesmen stopped at Cuza (with a minor concession in the case of Titulescu, which explains his presence, when other statesmen are absent, in the "memory" of the Romanians), before jumping over a century to the figure of the dictator himself.

Next in the top ten of the heroes of national history appear the traditional pair who have featured in all ideologies, Michael the Brave and Stephen the Great (with the former rated higher, as a symbol of national unity), and immediately after them, surprisingly but quite explicably given the general orientation in Romanian public opinion, is Nicolae Ceauşescu. King Michael gets only half the score of the late dictator. Vlad Ţepeş is also well placed, the authoritarian and relentlessly just ruler of whom, or of whose solutions, not a few Romanians dream nowadays. Among modern political figures, while Iorga, Titulescu and Antonescu are remembered, the Brătianus, King Ferdinand (who was, after all, sovereign at the time of the Great Union of 1918) and Queen Marie, for example, are not.

It is easy to decipher all this. We are looking at a pantheon that was largely set in place in the "Ceauşescu era"—many Romanians still imagine that what they learned at school then is "what history is all about"—with, understandably, a few amendments and new accents: a limited recognition of the kings or an inclination towards authoritarian solutions like those of Antonescu or Vlad Ţepeş. It is the choice of a society predominantly oriented towards the left, which feels closer to communist mythology and its representations than to what was before communism. Opinion polls dealing with current politics confirm this shift, or rather "return", of the electorate, the result of the tarnished image and failures of the present government. But the way the Romanians look at their history expresses something more profound than the present political conjuncture, namely, a structurally dominant leftist sensibility, which, of course, constructs its own historical mythologies. In a strictly mythological sense, Cuza, the peasants' ruler and great reformer, is felt to be more "left-wing" than Carol I; in addition, he symbolizes more powerfully and directly the idea of national unity; and finally, he was a native Romanian, not a ruler from outside. On the other hand, the relatively modest score obtained by Antonescu would suggest that the fears sometimes expressed in the West regarding his ascent in the political imaginary of the Romanians are not justified. Much more disturbing remains the shadow of Ceauşescu.

There are accents which take us beyond simply noting a leftist sensibility, which would be perfectly legitimate in itself. It is, in fact, a leftist culture with an attraction towards nationalism and authoritarianism—far from what a modern left would stand for. And it is not just the selection and ordering of historical personalities that justifies such a diagnosis. We can continue to look at all sorts of choices. The credit accorded to the various institutions of the state has remained constant for a number of years. At the bottom (with 15 percent and 20 percent respectively) are the political parties and Parliament, exactly the structures that are indispensable for democracy. And it cannot be said that they are placed so low because they have not done their duty. Those that receive a higher rating have not behaved irreproachably either. No, it is simply that this is how the Romanians want to see things. At the top of the list are the Church and the army (with 88 percent and 75 percent respectively), institutions which are no doubt essential (though it is curious, and significant, that the Church is considered an institution of the state) but which, by their function, embody the principle of authority rather than that of democracy.

The polls also allow us to follow other recent evolutions and tendencies. I shall limit myself to noting here (following on from what is said in the book about the traditional competing models, French and German) the new configuration of foreign reference points in the imaginary of the Romanians. Around 1900, France would have won outright in any poll, followed, at a safe distance, by Germany; there were no other significant models. However, the disappearance of the old elite and the opening after 1989 to a world politically and culturally dominated not by France but by America, have had a strong erosive effect on the French myth and French reference points. Already young people express themselves more readily in English than in French, which is a quite new phenomenon in Romania, long the principal bastion of French culture in Central and Eastern Europe. Nowadays not only the United States, which easily dominates, but also Germany seem closer and more interesting to the average Romanian than France. A questionnaire on "the countries the Romanians appreciate most" gives the following percentages: USA—26.9; Germany—18.8; France—8.8; Italy—6.8; Switzerland—5.2; Britain—3.2.[16] The predominantly French age is over for most Romanians. It is in the past along with the old Romania, the "world we have lost". But the new reference points are more indicative of the prestige enjoyed by certain countries and the opportunities they offer to Romanians than of a well-defined set of values; they are still far from being true models, like the French and German models of the past (albeit at the level of "forms without substance"). Romanian society today suffers from an acute lack, or confusion, where values and models are concerned—hence the illusory parallel solutions: isolation in a mythologized history, the attraction of Orthodoxism...

And finally, returning to the rating of personalities, we cannot ignore an extremely significant recent poll (November 1999). In answer to a question about the leaders who have done the most harm and the most good to Romania in the last century, Ceauşescu appears in the first place in both lists, the good and the bad, with the same rating in each: 22 percent. What could be more illustrative of the division in Romanian society and its great confusion of values?

THE TEXTBOOK SCANDAL

Without wishing it, I returned abruptly to the foreground of things with the "textbook scandal" of October 1999. It would appear that in the imaginary of some people (nationalists with an inclination towards conspiracy theories), I am the "man in the shadows" who has been working, through his disciples, on the demolition of Romanian national history. I do not know to what extent my historiographical criticism contributed to the decision radically to restructure the history curriculum with textbooks to match. Preoccupied as I was with my own projects, I certainly had no idea what was being prepared; indeed, I had no idea that anything was being prepared at all! I did not expect a change in history to take place so fast. If I stimulated it in any way, then I must confess that I am glad. But I was certainly not consulted by anyone when the curriculum was under preparation. (There is no point in trying to answer the question "Why?": perhaps they wanted less controversial personalities to be involved.) None of the textbook authors asked me a single question, and, as far as I know, not one of them has claimed to be my "disciple". If I had written a textbook it would certainly have been different from those that were published. Indeed, I wonder what it would have been like. There are rules and limits that must be respected in conceiving such a text, however open and nonconformist it may be. As far as I am concerned, I have opted for complete liberty, so there is no way I could write textbooks.

That said, the changeover (slow enough, after ten years) from the single textbook, a communist inheritance, to the system of parallel textbooks, in line with European education and Romanian tradition (five were approved by the Ministry of National Education for the "History of the Romanians" in the twelfth grade), was clearly a step forward. The concept behind the new curriculum, and implicitly behind the textbooks, is certainly more modern than that of the single textbooks previously in use. Some would say it could hardly fail to be! The textbooks which we are finally laying aside have contributed to the unofficial (but very real) status of history in Romanian education: the least liked subject! It had become a discipline in which young people learned what they had to, but from which they came away with nothing; an undigested mass of information, without meaning or finality, excused by a few worn-out patriotic clichés.

The approach has now changed in at least three essential aspects. Factual ballast has been given up in favor of a synthetic treatment, problematized and open to discussion with the pupils; there is a more pronounced accent on civilization, culture, and mentalities than on events and personalities; and recent history is given an appreciably greater weighting in comparison to earlier periods. The communist period, on which the previous textbooks were almost silent, at last gets an appropriate treatment (at least in terms of the number of pages, but also in terms of interpretation in most of the textbooks). It is understandable that such a re-centering creates imbalances in its turn. No one has yet invented, or ever will invent, "incontestable history"! "Structural" history is not necessarily more true than "factual" history; it is simply another sort of history. A better balance could have been sought. The Middle Ages should have been given more space. The sacrifice of "heroes" and of many events, in the spirit of the "new history", was certainly not the most inspired solution. I would plead for an intelligent treatment of personalities (in a different sense from that of the "heroic" history which has prevailed up till now), not for their abolition or diminution. It may be that history is not made by personalities, but people believe it is made by personalities. And what people believe is, in a sense, more important, even for history, than anything else. It is here that myths and symbols are born, which in their turn create history. Michael the Brave did indeed unite the Romanians, not in 1600, but posthumously in 1918. We ought, in general, to free ourselves from the rigidity of "formulae", and not abandon one formula only to enter into another.

One textbook chose to go further than the others along the road that was thus opened. This was the already celebrated textbook coordinated by Sorin Mitu and published by Sigma. It bore the brunt of all the fury provoked by the new orientation. First of all it was the Romanian Senate that began to boil. And the senator who expressed himself most vehemently was Sergiu Nicolaescu, a director of historical films in the "age of Ceauşescu"—films like *Michael the Brave* and *Mircea the Great*, vehicles not only for patriotic pride but also for the message of unity around the great leader. Now he found the saving solution: the textbook should be burned in the public square. The education committees of both chambers then held meetings. For more than a month (October to November

1999) the matter seemed to be the main preoccupation of Parliament. Finally, a motion calling for the withdrawal of the textbook came to the vote. It was rejected (not out of appreciation for the "new history" but out of government solidarity). With only a little exaggeration we might imagine Parliament abandoning current legislation to debate and vote on history textbooks, paragraph by paragraph. Or even a government falling because of history!

Attacks multiplied from various directions. Like any society in crisis Romania today has its "prophets", who know what is good and what is bad and who are called to set the nation on the right road. A popular show on the television channel *Antena 1* staged a trial, which turned out to be more of an execution. Such summary judgements multiplied. Apart from principles ("patriotic", of course), there was no shortage of personal attacks, including the insinuation that Hungarian interests and even money might be involved. Public opinion was overcome by emotion. We even heard of family rows (as in France, at the time of the Dreyfus affair): for or against Michael the Brave; for or against Sorin Mitu.

I rarely make public statements except in writing. But in those days, as a totally senseless hysteria swept the country, I felt it only right to make clear my point of view (all the more so as my name had been invoked). I was given a few minutes on the national channel's evening news program, in which I tried to get the essential message across. I also participated—as an *ad hoc* expert for the Ministry of National Education—in the meeting of the parliamentary committees, where I was able to express myself more fully. Here, in brief, is my argument:

The necessity for a pluralism of textbooks is almost unanimously recognized. So, if we agree that there should be more than one, let us not ask that they be identical—perhaps with different covers and illustrations! The elimination of a textbook on the grounds that someone does not like it is called censorship, and it would be the first measure of this kind in Romania since the fall of communism. A single history is a utopia. Even in communism, where a single ideology functioned and precise instructions were given in historical matters, history was not chanted with a single voice. The limits were narrow, but some historians, to their credit, managed to express themselves with a small measure of liberty (while others, on the contrary, went even further in their conformity than they were asked to). If that is how things stood in a totalitarian system, what can we expect nowadays, in a democratic and pluralist society? When we look at the Romania of today, which we know well, certainly better than its distant past, is there a single option, a single interpretation? Of course not. It is the same with history. If you can criticize presidents Iliescu and Constantinescu without mercy, are you not permitted to say something a little unconventional about Vlad Ţepeş or Michael the Brave?

The shift in accent, which is so new to many Romanians, is no more than a normal adaptation to the orientations of contemporary historiography. In the nineteenth century, if we may simplify what is without doubt a more complex picture, history was treated in terms of events, with an accent on national values and political authority. Today, history has shifted from events to structures, and from nationalism and authority to another combination of values. National identity remains, of course (Europe will not come into being without or against the nations), but alongside it we have European identity and democratic principles, including the respect due not only to the community but also to the individual. The nation, Europe, and democracy make up one body. None of these points of reference is more important than the others: all three must be equal for us, if we really want to go forward. We cannot progress in the spirit of a nineteenth-century history (and still less in the spirit of a nationalism taken over from the nineteenth century and exacerbated in the Ceauşescu period).

But the polemic, it has been said, concerns not just any books. These are school textbooks, aimed at pupils who are at risk of being disoriented by all sorts of "relativizations". These pupils, however, are young people in their final year of high school, preparing to enter into the wider world. It is not with prejudices, with ready-made ideas, and with an outdated way of looking at the world that we should be equipping them, but with the capacity to think critically and to make choices. What are we doing? Playing a hypocritical game? Is there a history for adults, in which anyone is free to say anything, and another, not exactly true but "reassuring", for the use of adolescents? In the past it was sexual hypocrisy that worked that way. Now young people know all about sex; do they not have the right to know just as much about how Romania was made?

For the time being the maneuver has not succeeded, but the opponents of the "new history" have shown that they are still powerful, probably more powerful than the upholders of the modern current. All the more so as they build on a widespread inclination—easy to stimulate in a traumatized society—towards nationalism and authoritarianism. The dispute has also illustrated the division in the intellectual community, historians included. In the case of the contested manual, the Group for Social Dialogue and the History Faculty of the University of Bucharest (by a majority of its members) pronounced in favor of respecting professionalism and the right to uncensored expression. The Romanian Academy, on the other hand, issued a communiqué (disavowed, however, by some members of its own History Section) in which it aligned itself with the chorus of denigrators. It is not the first time that the Academy has appeared as a conservative forum. Moreover, the "conservatives" also voiced the idea that from now on textbooks should be approved by the Academy! "The wisest among us", in other words. Falling back on authority as usual!

To return to the incriminated text, a prime motive for the hostility is immediately evident: the uncompromising treatment of the communist period (and of communist survivals after 1989) and an unconcealed position against the Iliescu regime and in favor of the Democratic Convention. The second motive is the demolition, more radical here than in other textbooks, of national-historical mythology. That is what determined a severe judgement from those who, regardless of their political orientation, see in history the principal ingredient of national identity. "Anti-Mitu" reactions were thus not restricted to the zone of the nationalist left. The textbook passes rapidly over the heroes of history (somewhat too rapidly, it is true). About Michael the Brave there are just a few words, and a summary (if true) characterization of him as the "favorite figure of Romanian historians". Vlad Ţepeş (the last great love of over-heated minds) appears only as the prototype of Dracula, giving an excessively Anglo-Saxon color to a mythology which, in its Romanian aspect at least, does not highlight the vampire but rather the relentlessly just prince who struggled for his country's independence. Indignation was also aroused by the observation that the obsessive problem of the origin of the Romanians is principally a matter of mythology and ideology (and not of incontestable scientific reality); I have no more to say on this subject, as it is precisely the thesis which I developed myself in *History and Myth*... They do not like to see the history of the Romanians relativized. And we do not like nationalist propaganda and authoritarian attitudes.

There was a lot of fuss, too, about the claim that the nation was "invented". How could the Romanian nation be invented? And yet so it was, like all others (and historians who find such an affirmation strange could do worse than glance at the recent bibliography of the subject). Another reproach was that the union of Transylvania in 1918 was not properly presented; the emphasis on the presence of the Romanian army and on high-level political decisions pushed the enthusiastic participation of the masses and the "plebiscitary" character of the action into the background. However, if we want to be correct we must accept that the union of 1 December was the direct consequence of the defeat of Austria–Hungary in the First World War. There was no referendum to allow the freely expressed vote of all the inhabitants of the province, and indeed no such referendum could have been organized in the confused conditions prevailing at the end of the war. Only Romanians participated at Alba Iulia. It is hard to believe that the Hungarians would have declared themselves in favor of separation from Hungary! We have to get used to the idea that Transylvania (like any other territory, anywhere) belongs equally to all its inhabitants, regardless of ethnicity. These considerations— motivated strictly by respect for truth—do not change the fact that the Romanians were in the majority and really did want union with Romania (nor the fact that nowadays they are even more in the majority and the union has proved viable).[17] In any case, no other European nation-state (with the occasional exception) was constituted by "universal vote".

Unfortunately, this textbook, which has many good features and calls many things by their true names, also has plenty of vulnerable points. Such a new approach calls for an argumentation to match. The text is, however, too summary in relation to what it seeks to demonstrate. Serious and complicated matters are treated in a familiar and simplified style (giving the impression of an "adaptation" for children, although the concept is in fact more subtle than in the other textbooks). To give a single example, obviously related to my own approach, the question "What is myth?" gets a simple, far too simple, answer: "A myth is a tale." A little further on it is stated, in addition, that every myth "conceals a solid grain of historical truth". Neither of these two formulations seems adequate to me.

And, in any case, they are contradictory: a "tale" is usually thought of as something "untrue".

I do not intend to make a comparative analysis here. I simply note that some of the other textbooks, those published by Humanitas, Rao and All, are more complete but also "better behaved" than that coordinated by Sorin Mitu. They are not without their own errors and contradictions either. (For example, the Humanitas version, while it is, overall, a convincing and elegant publication, gives a confused presentation of Michael the Brave, who, from one sentence to the next, is, and then is not, inspired by the Romanian ideal; nor does the author of the same chapter hesitate to bring in the text of the capitulation—those capitulations again!—concluded in 1393 between Mircea the Old and the Sultan Bayazid, a document long ago proved to be inauthentic!)

I shall pause, however, to consider the only textbook that was conceived in a different spirit, that produced under the direction of Ioan Scurtu, a professor in the History Faculty of the University of Bucharest, and published by Petrion. Scurtu has criticized Mitu severely, accusing him of politicizing history (and, more than that, of "adopting the viewpoint of those in government"). I do not believe that the political options of the "Mitu team" can be denied. However, Ioan Scurtu politicizes history just as intensely, though in the opposite direction. In his book we meet again the old, well-known nationalist clichés. First, the Geto–Dacians: "a powerful ethnic, linguistic, economic and civilizational entity" (p. 6)—a true nation, it might be said! Then there is the Michael the Brave episode. Apparently his death was arranged by the "powers of the time" (p. 33): an unfounded accusation and a vague and generalized formulation, suggesting the involvement of the whole of Europe and channeling the attachment that the Romanians bear towards the voivode in an anti-European direction. The conclusion, contrary to real evolutions before the nineteenth century, is that "the idea of state unity has accompanied the history of the Romanians, affirming itself as one of their fundamental aspirations" (p. 95). For the period after 1989 there is an uncompromising judgement of the anti-Iliescu orientation, the Democratic Convention, and the government set up in 1996 (why such annoyance, then, when others express their own political options?). The treatment of communism offers some telling pages. Everything that is nowadays possible is done to partially rehabilitate it, by making it banal—the idea being that it was really neither better nor worse than other periods or governments. Here is a sample: "The life of the village goes on at heightened rhythms compared with the past, and people are more present in its social activity. Homes have been modernized and new houses built on completely modern lines, with or without upper storeys, impossible to distinguish from town villas" (p. 133). Is this a Swiss village? No, it is the Romanian "socialist" village. With luxurious villas, and probably without dust and mud, with running water and everything else one could wish for!

In spite of the desire, legitimate up to a point, that the attitudes expressed in the school textbooks should be brought closer together (since it is not a good idea to give pupils histories which are radically at odds with each other), this "polarizing" seems to be inevitable for the time being. I wrote in *History and Myth* that in the traditional Romanian historiographical discourse "differences of interpretation and accent, such as we find, for example, in the school textbooks, do not affect the overall coherence of the model. We are far from the French model, which is characterized by a high degree of polarization between the historical reference points of the two Frances..." However, it seems that this is what we have come to: a model similar to the old French model (albeit structured on other criteria). As in France a century and more ago, these are the aftereffects of a revolutionary trauma: a fissured society, with reference points not only different, but actually opposite. As far as history is concerned, the confrontation is being played out, and will probably continue to be played out for a long time to come, around two contradictory "ideal models": one nationalist and authoritarian, and the other European and democratic (with, of course, all sorts of nuances and combinations in between). Moreover, and on a more general level, there is a process of relativization of values and cultural diversification going on in the world today; consequently history, too, is becoming multiple and diversified.

WHAT I BELIEVE

I want to say in conclusion, succinctly and unequivocally, what I believe about a number of important matters.

I believe, above all, that a patriot is someone who does something for their country today. To speak fine words (all too often untrue or at least exaggerated) about the past is the simplest (and often a very cheap) way of showing one's patriotism. I am not inclined to judge the patriotism of deputies and senators by the way they judge the history textbooks or their appreciation of Michael the Brave. To prove their patriotism they are called on to pass the laws which Romania needs so badly, and which they are somewhat slow to pass.

At present, patriotism means not the noisy affirmation of nationalism, but, on the contrary, putting a damper on it. It means a new and positive attitude towards Europe, and towards minorities. Above all, however, it means a new attitude towards ourselves, in a world which is changing at a dizzying pace and into whose rhythms we need to enter if we do not want to remain isolated, condemned to backwardness, and, in the end, to collapse. The so-called patriotic discourse, with its insistence on our "uniqueness", has all too often served as an excuse for an accumulation of delays. Such "patriotism" is in fact directed against the interests of Romania.

We have still not truly come out of the nineteenth century! The two great projects of that century, nationalism and communism, survive in an amalgam of concrete and mental structures: excessive centralization, a weighty and uncompetitive economy, insufficient openness towards the world, too great an accent on the collectivity and not enough on the individual, not to mention the whole array of outdated mythological images. Let us at least settle into a twentieth-century pattern, though it would be better to take a leap into the century that is about to begin.

We are too laden with frustrations and complexes, and hence with feelings both of inferiority and superiority that are as damaging as they are contradictory. This explains our far from normal attitudes to the "other". We over-dramatize our relations with "foreigners" and with ourselves. We ought to "normalize" ourselves, to realize that we are neither worse nor better, neither more capable nor less capable. We are, quite simply, a European nation like all the others—on the one hand more different among ourselves than we like to recognize, and on the other, closer than we believe to people everywhere.

Perhaps we can try, not to forget history, but to be a little less obsessed with it. We look towards the past too much (a past mythologized with ease), and too little towards the present and future. We have nothing to learn from Stephen the Great and Michael the Brave, nor even from the politicians of the interwar period. The problems of the present must be solved with the means of the present and from the perspective of the present. Almost two centuries ago, when they decided to play the card of modernization, of Westernization, and of the national state, the Romanians did not place themselves in continuity with an old tradition; they broke with it. Now we are entering a new world, and we need a new beginning. We cannot remain prisoners of the past. We must show that Romania means something, *today*.

(November–December 1999)

Introduction to the First Edition

Any intellectual project presupposes a prior definition of the concepts with which we are operating. In the present work we are dealing with history and historical myths. Let us be clear, therefore, about what we understand by history, and what we understand by myth.

The word *history* has two distinct meanings, which the general public, and indeed many professionals, often tend to confuse. *History* refers both to what really happened and to the reconstruction of what happened; in other words, it is both the past in its objective unfolding and *discourse* about the past. These two histories are far from being equivalent. The first is cancelled out as one event succeeds another, while the second lacks the means to "resurrect" events in all their fullness. What we usually call history is our discourse about history, the image, inevitably incomplete, simplified, and distorted, of the past, which the present never ceases to recompose.

In relation to real history, history as discourse presupposes a drastic filtering of the facts, their ordering in a coherent whole, the "dramatization" of action, and its investment with a well-defined sense. Real history is an unordered and inexhaustible deposit. Out of this deposit the historian (or, more generally, anyone who speaks about history), selects and orders. Historians are untiring producers of coherence and significance. They produce a sort of "fiction" out of "true" materials.

The same historical processes and the same facts are treated differently, often very differently, according to the standpoint from which they are observed. School textbooks published in different parts of the world amply demonstrate the impossibility of history being the same for everybody. Many things contribute to the differentiation of the discourse: the zone of civilization, the cultural inheritance, the mental context, the historical circumstances, the training of the historian, and, decisively, the spectrum of ideologies. Ideological and political pluralism is inevitably translated into historical pluralism.

Let us grant—for the sake of the demonstration—that it might be possible to establish the "absolute truth" of facts. Even then, their selection and their organization in hierarchy and sequence would still remain open to a variety of solutions. In reality, "facts" are themselves constructed by the historian, detached from a much broader context and set within an explanatory schema elaborated by the same historian.

It must be understood that *objective history does not exist*. Indeed, not only does it not exist; it cannot exist. This is the end of an illusion that has been sustained and amplified by the scientism of the last two centuries. The "critical school", convinced as it was of the historian's ability to squeeze out of documents what Ranke called "history as it really was", and Marxist theory, with its impeccable setting of all phenomena in a complete schema of human becoming, are the two extreme points attained by the myth of a perfect and objective history. "The historian is not the one who knows, but the one who seeks", said Lucien Febvre. His effervescent dialogue with the past cannot possibly crystallize into a single truth, which would, in fact, mean the end of history.

Indeed, the time for absolute truths has passed even in what were previously considered exact sciences. Contemporary epistemology has seen an appreciable infusion of relativism. It would be strange if history, which is in any case a less structured discipline than physics, were to continue to claim an access to the "absolute" which physicists no longer invoke.

There is something else which sets history in a place apart. Physics is the exclusive domain of physicists; the gifted amateur who may occasionally stumble on a new theory generally counts for little in the dynamics of the science. But that is not how it is with history. History is not just the work of historians. It represents a privileged expression of the self-consciousness of every community or social group. Everyone participates, in one way or another, in the elaboration and endless adaptation of the stock of history which is imprinted in the collective consciousness. Oral tradition, literature, school, church, army, political discourse, press, radio, television, cinema—all are sources of history that act, sometimes in contradiction and with variable intensity and effects, on the historical consciousness. The professionals of history are themselves caught within the net. Their influence should not be underestimated, but nor should it be rated too highly. A historical novel or film may often prove to be more influential. A school textbook has an impact on an incomparably larger public than a masterpiece of historiography addressed to an elite. Nor should the resistance of historians to mythology be overestimated. Historians cannot detach themselves, at least not completely, from the "historical environment" in which they have evolved, with its stock of traditions and with the prejudices and constraints that it implies. The historian is fed by the ambient mythology and is, in turn, a producer of mythology.

There is thus, at all levels, an inevitable process of *mythologizing of history*. Now that we have reached this point, it remains to clarify the second concept, by answering the question: What do we understand by myth?

Myth is a fashionable word. Its ever more frequent use, and often abuse, conceals a high degree of ambiguity. Current usage and dictionary definitions suggest a wide range of meanings. Basically anything which deviates to a greater or lesser extent from reality seems liable to be called myth. All sorts of fictions, prejudices, stereotypes, distortions, and exaggerations can be brought together under this convenient label.

However, this is not my conception. First of all, I do not see any inherent contradiction between the imaginary (in which myth my be subsumed) and reality. To distinguish, in the case of myths, between the "true" and the "untrue" is the wrong way of looking at the problem. Myth presupposes a certain *structure*, and it matters little, fundamentally, whether this structure incorporates material which is true or fictive, or a combination of the two. All that is important is that it arranges it according to the logic of the imaginary. There is a myth of Napoleon, and a myth of Michael the Brave. It would be ridiculous to reproach someone for using the concept on the grounds that Napoleon and Michael the Brave really lived! The mythologizing of these figures can be seen in the setting of real facts within a model which belongs to the imaginary (historical or political). When Michael the Brave appears as the forger of "national unity" we are in the presence of a process of mythologizing, for the simple reason that onto his real actions there is being projected the ideology of the national state, an ideology of the last two centuries that did not exist in 1600.

The definition of myth which I would propose is the following: an imaginary construction (which, once again, does not mean either "real" or "unreal", but arranged according to the logic of the imaginary), which serves to highlight the essence of cosmic and social phenomena, in close relation to the fundamental values of the community, and with the aim of ensuring that community's cohesion. Historical myths, of course, involve the treatment of the past in the way described in this definition.

As a result, not every distortion, adaptation, or interpretation is a matter of myth. Myth presupposes the extraction of an *essential truth*. It has a profoundly *symbolic* meaning. It offers both a system of interpretation and an ethical code or model of behavior; its truth is not abstract but understood as the guiding principle in the life of the community in question. The *myth of the nation* and the *myth of progress*, to name two fundamental myths of the contemporary world, offer in equal measure a key to historical becoming and a system of values which create solidarity and shared projects.

Myth is highly *integrative* and *simplificative*, having a tendency to reduce the diversity and complexity of phenomena to one privileged axis of interpretation. It brings into history a principle of order, attuned to the necessities and ideals of a particular society.

My field of research here is the Romanian society of the nineteenth and twentieth centuries. I am interested in the way in which the ongoing elaboration of the historical discourse, examined at all levels so as to embrace (making appropriate distinctions but without any exclusion or artificial separation) historiography, school textbooks, literature, and political propaganda, has attuned itself to the evolution of Romanian society itself, with its spectrum of ideologies and projects of all kinds. I do not note every distortion or adaptation, but only those accents of the historical discourse that are truly rooted in the structures of a national mythology, those that give meaning, through the past, to the projects of the present.

Romanian historiography is currently in a phase of necessary critical revisions, in which the relation between the imaginary and history cannot be evaded. The present study may appear unusual. In other historiographies there is no longer anything "revolutionary" about such a treatment of the historical discourse. The problem in Romania lies in the deep-rooted illusion of the objectivity of history, an illusion which communism, as the promoter of the unique and incontestable truth, only served to consolidate. What Guizot knew a century and a half ago—namely, that "there are a hundred ways of writing history"—does not appear at all evident in Romanian culture. A simplistic logic is in operation: either communist ideology did not substantially distort history, in which case there is no reason to give up the existing schema; or it did, in which case our mission is to establish the Truth at last! The fact that distortion is inevitable and truth relative seems to be hard to understand and accept.

My aim here is not to demolish historical mythology. This does not mean that I do not reserve the right to point out the way in which certain historical and political myths are maintained artificially, and even currently amplified, which, despite the declared patriotism of their promoters, serves only to hold us back from what a large majority desires or at least says it desires: that is, the modernization and democratization of Romanian society and the integration of the country into European structures. Nationalist myths which carry an authoritarian and xenophobic message are not the best companions on this road. But, I repeat, there can be no question of the demolition of mythology as such. We cannot live outside the imaginary. The life of any community is organized around certain mythical constellations. Every nation has its own historical mythology. Nothing is more revealing of a society's present and its chosen paths into the future than the way in which it understands the burden of its past.

CHAPTER ONE
History, Ideology, Mythology

THE FIRST ENTRY INTO EUROPE

In the last century there took place something which we are trying to repeat in quite different, and perhaps more difficult, conditions today: the entry of Romanian society into Europe. For more than a century the process of Westernization, affirmed initially among an elite group, made gradual progress, despite being slowed down by material and mental inertia. At least a few more decades would have been necessary for Western values and institutions truly to establish strong roots in Romanian soil. But history was not willing to grant these decades to Romania. The right-wing autochthonist offensive was followed by the far more lasting and transforming solution of the extreme Left. Communism quite simply knocked Romania off the normal path of evolution, totally overturning all its structures and values. However, the construction which it attempted—that of a new type of civilization—has collapsed, requiring us, at the end of half a century of exit from history, to retrace the steps taken a century and a half ago. Once again we are knocking on the gates of Europe and attempting our second entry into the Western world.

Chronological markers are a delicate matter; however, we may consider that the process of the first entry into Europe began to acquire consistency around the year 1830, in the period of the Treaty of Adrianople and the *Règlement Organique*. The alphabet of transition is a perfect illustration of the direction in which Romanian society was moving. Between 1830 and 1860 the Cyrillic alphabet gave way to a mixed form of writing, a combination of Cyrillic characters and Roman letters, with a tendency for the latter to become more prevalent. In 1860 the Roman alphabet was established by law. By around 1830, young aristocrats had already adopted Western clothing. Iconography offers us some amusing images: in the salons of the time, men of more mature years, faithful to the Oriental mode of dress, appear alongside younger men, and women of all ages, dressed in "European" style. Ştefan Cazimir has sketched out an interesting scale of receptivity to Western forms: boyars seem more receptive than the middle or lower categories, the young more receptive than the old, and women more receptive than men. A young gentlewoman—an admirer of French fashions and a reader of French novels—would certainly have felt the pulse of the age better than an elderly townsman! Writing and fashion can be seen as the symptoms of a process which was to embrace, with varying intensity, all sectors of Romanian society.[1]

One idea, which has become deeply rooted as a result of its repetition over almost five decades, must be set aside at this point. In the first half of the nineteenth century the bearers of the notion of progress were neither the lower classes nor a practically non-existent bourgeoisie. The opposition between "old" and "new" did not separate antagonistic social classes, but was, in fact, a division within the Romanian elite of the time. The wearers of new clothes, with ideas to match, were, for the most part, young boyars. The same group could also be found at the head of the revolution of 1848, which communist historiography called the "bourgeois-democratic" revolution; "democratic", granted, but where was the bourgeoisie to make it "bourgeois"? In any case, the social category which we might describe as a somewhat insubstantial middle class, rather than a bourgeoisie in the strict sense, was far from being highly receptive to what was happening in the west of the continent. The chronicle of Dionisie the Ecclesiarch, completed around 1815, seems to be highly characteristic of the culture and attitudes of the "small townsman" at the time when the process of modernization was about to take off. Dionisie transforms the French Revolution into a fantastic novel. He neither understands nor accepts its principles and, given a choice between the French and the Russians, he sides unhesitatingly with the latter, whom he sees as the defenders of Orthodoxy.[2] His notions of European politics prefigure the judgements of a "jupîn Dumitrache" or "conu Leonida", the imaginary, but so real, characters created by Caragiale more than half a century later. It is quite clear that the Europeanization of Romanian society did not start in this social environment.

Communist ideology needed a bourgeois revolution (a necessary moment in the Marxist historical trajectory) and a bourgeois class to implement it. Prior to this, the dominant interpretations of Romanian cultural history had seen modern ideologies and institutions as having been borrowed from the West; this is the thesis on which E. Lovinescu based his well-known theory of modern Romanian civilization. An alternative viewpoint was suggested by Ştefan Zeletin, who argued that the effective development of a Romanian capitalist economy was the starting point for sociopolitical restructuring.[3] But even Zeletin emphasized the importance of the stimulus provided by Western capital and the Anglo-French bourgeoisie (in other words, "external factors"), and his indigenous "bourgeois" category was in fact made up of boyars, who had suddenly become interested in the grain trade after 1829. All in all, whichever particular interpretation we prefer, it is clear that everything started from the top down, from the boyar class and not from the fragile and disorientated "middle class". Moreover, even if we accept that Romanian society was involved—to a limited extent—in the capitalist exchange economy, there is no escaping the fact that *all* the elements of modern civilization, from forms of literature to the constitution, from the university to the financial system or the railways, were imported products. These products could only be "imported" by those members of the elite who had become accustomed to Western civilization. This does not mean that Romanian society as a whole had no part to play. The process of acculturation presupposes the equal participation of two players: the one who offers a model, and the one who takes it up and adapts it. It is not possible for anyone to imitate any model whatsoever. The very act of imitation presupposes a certain degree of compatibility with the chosen model. But there can be no debate about the fact that the Romanians imitated.

NATIONALISM AND MODERNIZATION

The path taken by Romanian society in the nineteenth century can be summed up in terms of three great problems, which also had a decisive impact on the relationship of the Romanians to their own past.

The first is the *national idea*. In recent decades, discussions of the concept of nation have been affected, often in contradictory ways, both by Stalin's famous definition (still repeated today, albeit "anonymously") and by the exacerbated nationalism of the Ceaușescu period. The end result has been a thorough confusion of the concept. The Stalinist definition makes the economic unification of the territory an obligatory factor, and so confers an abusively material dimension on what is, in fact, an eminently ideal project. The nationalist tendency, genuflecting more towards national mysticism than towards economics, pushes the premise of a Romanian nation, if not actually the Romanian nation itself in all its fullness, far back into the past. If we take these two interpretations to their extreme then we must conclude either that we are a nation formed in the modern period for predominantly economic reasons, or that we are a nation as old as history itself!

In fact, what is usually meant by national consciousness, if it is to mean something more than the mere consciousness of an ethnic identity, is the idea of the *national state* or *nation-state*, the result of the will of a community, whether ethnically homogeneous or not, to form itself into a political organism. This does not emerge inevitably from a "unitary economic market" (in 1900 the Romanians of Transylvania belonged to the Hungarian market, not that of Romania), but nor does it arise from some illusory predestination, the irrevocable mark of which may be traced across a history of millennia. The idea of the nation-state is no more than two centuries old, and nowhere is it written that it must endure to eternity. Its origins can be found, on the one hand, in the philosophy of the "social contract", as defined by Jean-Jacques Rousseau, and on the other, in the perception of ethnic communities as living organisms, each with its own spirituality and destiny distinct from those of other ethnic communities (according to Johann Gottfried Herder's interpretation in *Ideen zur Philosophie der Geschichte der*

Menschheit, 1784–1791). Popular sovereignty and the mystique of "shared blood" are thus the contradictory, but also complementary, principles that lie behind the fact of nationhood. The French Revolution, followed by the overturning of the European system by the Napoleonic Wars and subsequent revolutions, hastened the crystallization of the concept and led to the actual or ideal division of the continent into a constellation of nation-states.

Prior to this historical phase the formation and evolution of state organisms bore no connection to ethnic and linguistic borders, or to the expression of the popular will. France, which has come to be seen by many as the model of the national state, began as a conglomerate of disparate territories and cultures; the Provençal language of the south was closer to Catalan than to French, the Bretons were Celtic, and the people of Alsace German. When, as a result of the Revolution, the French became a nation, that nation would be defined not as an ethnic organism but as the outcome of the free option of its citizens. At the opposite pole to this "contractual" understanding of the nation, the German model would insist on ethnicity and history, blood and culture. It is easy to see why the people of Alsace were long regarded, with equal reason on both sides, as both French and Germans. They were French according to the French definition of the nation, and Germans according to the German definition. This theoretical divergence was the source of endless conflicts, which affected not only the two states but the whole continent of Europe.

In the case of the Romanian nation (and the nations of Central Europe in general), the model which is invoked corresponds to the German formula. The Romanians are defined by a common origin (whether Roman, Dacian or Daco–Roman), a unitary language, a shared history, and a specific spirituality. This is why, like the Germans and Hungarians, they cannot accept the division of their people into distinct nations (Romania and the Republic of Moldova), and why they find it hard to consider as true Romanians those whose origin and language are different (like the Hungarians of Transylvania, who, for their part, hold to a similar conception of the nation and so are less than eager to integrate with the mass of Romanians).

The segmentation of present-day life according to the lines of fracture between nations is also manifested in the projection into the past of these real or ideal divisions. Myths of foundation have been elaborated and re-elaborated in such a way as to make the original configuration as close as possible, if not identical, to the present-day national organism. The phenomenon is a general European one. In the Romanian case, the all-embracing symbol of the entire national space became Dacia, at a time when the very name of Romania did not exist. Indeed, we may note the absence, until well into the nineteenth century, of a modern generic term for the whole territory occupied by Romanians. The present name of the country was first formulated by the Transylvanian Saxon historian Martin Felmer in the eighteenth century, and it was again employed in 1816 by Dimitrie Philippide, a Greek historian settled in Wallachia (in his *History of Romania* and *Geography of Romania*). In the middle years of the nineteenth century the term Dacia was frequently used to refer to what we know now as Romania, that is, the entire territory inhabited by Romanians. In their very titles, publications like *Dacia literară* (Literary Dacia), *Magazin istoric pentru Dacia* (Historical magazine for Dacia), and *Dacia viitoare* (Future Dacia) set forth a whole program of national politics. Even somewhat later, when the term Romania had been officially adopted to designate the little Romania resulting from the union of Wallachia and Moldavia in 1859, Dacia continued to serve as a name for the whole national space of the Romanians, the future Greater Romania. The title of A. D. Xenopol's great work of synthesis, *The History of the Romanians in Dacia Traiana* (1888–1893), symbolizes the direct relationship between ancient Dacia and the modern Romanian nation.

The second great challenge of the nineteenth century was the problem of the *modernization*, or rather *Westernization*, of Romanian society. There is no doubt that the giving up of Orientalism and traditionalism in writing and clothing implied an approach towards the Western model, but the hardest step still remained to be taken. The question was how to set in motion a patriarchal and authoritarian system, a society overwhelmingly rural, dominated by landed property, in which the modern stimulating factors of capitalism and democracy were almost completely absent. Within a short space of time, and above all between 1860 and 1870, the young Romanian state adopted almost everything that it could borrow from the European institutional and legislative system: constitution, Parliament, responsible government, legal codes, the university, the academy... For Titu Maiorescu these were "forms without substance", and he was right in the sense that a profound transformation of Romanian society and mentalities required much more than the simple naturalizing of Western institutions through the enthusiasm of an elite. For almost a century, until the course of development was disrupted by communism, the great problem of Romanian society was to be the aligning of the substance with the form. The game was half won, and half lost.

The main contradiction in the project of modernization lay in the very structure of Romanian society. Modern society is the creation of towns and of the bourgeoisie. In the Romanian case, however, the principal groups brought together and set in opposition by the dialectic of social relations were the great landowners and the peasants. Even around 1900, after a period of relative urban development, no less than 81.2 percent of the population of Romania still lived in villages. This massive predominance of the rural population had important implications for a wide range of social and political projects, as well as for the various ways in which the national past, and the spirituality and destiny of the Romanians, were interpreted. The "Romanian model", past, present, and even future, became fixed as a predominantly rural one, and so it has remained in the minds of many Romanians. From such a perspective the town came to seem a foreign excrescence on the healthy body of rural Romania, especially as urban communities were in fact largely foreign, or at least cosmopolitan.

Thus the inherent discrepancies between the village and the town were widened, in the Romanian case, by significant ethnic, religious, and cultural differences. In 1899, Iaşi, the capital of Moldavia, had 76,277 inhabitants, of whom 26,747 were Romanians and 48,530, well over half, were Jews. Even Bucharest seemed a cosmopolitan city. Towards the end of the nineteenth century, out of a population of around 250,000 people, 32,000 were of Catholic or Protestant religion and 31,000 were Jewish.[4] It would thus appear that about a quarter of the population of the capital were of "non-Romanian" origin. This is without taking into consideration the towns of Transylvania, where Romanians were in the minority in relation to either Hungarians or Germans. The opposition between village and town, between the ethnic and cultural purity of the peasant and of the "native" boyar on the one hand, and the cosmopolitan character of the Romanian bourgeoisie on the other, is a common theme in Romanian culture over more than a century. The refusal of modernity—in the urban and bourgeois version which was its only true manifestation—reached such an extent that in the interwar period E. Lovinescu felt obliged to fight a veritable campaign for the rehabilitation of the urban environment in literature. Ştefan Zeletin regarded Romanian culture as quite simply reactionary, "the rebellion of the medieval elements in our soul against the bourgeois order imposed by the invasion of foreign capitalism into our patriarchal way of life". Historians, too, have shown much more interest in rural issues, especially agrarian property relations, than in the evolution of urban life and of the Romanian bourgeoisie. All this suggests a traditionalist and anti-bourgeois sensibility; a mental brake that delayed, even if it could not block, the modernization of Romanian society.[5]

It is certain that in the first phase of the modernization process, around the middle of the nineteenth century, property relations in agriculture appeared to be the most urgent problem facing the country. The question was whether the great landed estates would win in the end, by freeing the peasants from feudal burdens without a substantial transfer of ownership, or whether Romania would move in the direction of a system of small properties. The Rural Law of 1864 was an attempt at a compromise, a partial transfer of ownership resulting in the coexistence of great estates with small properties. Peasant unrest, culminating in the great rebellion of 1907, revealed how precarious the balance was. The new agrarian reform of 1921 would abolish the system of latifundia, transferring most of the land into the hands of small peasant landowners.

Romanian historians took sides in the struggle over property with their own specific weapons. The past was summoned to bear witness for the present and the future. Two tendencies stand out. The first, starting with Nicolae Bălcescu's essay *On the Social Status of the Workers of the Land in the Romanian Principalities in Various Times* (1846), highlighted the primordial character of peasant property, which had been usurped during the Middle Ages by the great estates of the boyars. The other, in contrast, affirmed the pre-existence and permanence of great landed properties.

That the debate was essential for Romanian society is beyond question, but insistence on this issue tended to leave the active forces of modernization in the background. Rural property, whether large or small, was not at the forefront of these. The problem was how to remove Romania from the condition of a predominantly rural country, and the Romanians from their patriarchal mentality. From this point of view, communism can certainly be seen as a specific attempt at modernization. Indeed, the brutality of the solutions adopted achieved a forced break from the rural past, but at the cost of upsetting all structures and knocking together a false modern society, quite outside all that modernity had come to mean by the end of the twentieth century.

The third great problem was that of *models*, of relations between the Romanians and "others". The new ideas and institutions were all products of the Western laboratory. Even the national idea and the nation-state itself originated in the ideological evolution of the West. Up until the nineteenth century the Romanians were integrated in the Eastern cultural space. Much is made of the occasional Western connections made by scholars, like the high steward Cantacuzino who studied in Padua or the Moldavian chroniclers with their studies in Poland, but these were never enough to change the general condition of a society and a culture. It was a culture penetrated by the Orthodox idea, not the national idea. The first important break was made in the late eighteenth century in the work of the Transylvanian School, a group of Uniate intellectuals who had studied in Vienna and Rome and who were guided, sometimes to the point of obsession, by the idea of their Latin origins and the need to re-actualize them. The work of the Transylvanian scholars was an important source for the re-orientation of the Romanian space towards the West, but the tone which they set—as the spokesmen of a peasant society under foreign domination—only began to be manifested on a larger scale once the elites of the two Romanian states decided to adopt the Western model.

The process of modernization and the affirmation of the national idea both led in the same direction. As long as the generally shared values were those of Orthodoxy, the Romanians could feel at home in the East European space. But once the sentiment of national identity had come to the foreground everywhere, things took a radical new turn for them. They suddenly became aware of what they had, in fact, always been, though without necessarily standing out as a result—"an island of Latinity in a Slav sea". The Russians were no longer the great liberating Orthodox brothers. Indeed, their shared religious identity seemed to pose an additional danger, threatening to facilitate the absorption and assimilation of Romania (as had just happened with Bessarabia). Romanian nationalism now stood up against the nationalism of the Slav peoples and Pan-Slavism.

Relations with the Catholic or Protestant Hungarians were no more encouraging. Once Hungary itself (or that part of the Habsburg Empire dominated by the Magyar aristocracy) began to emerge as a national, and thus assimilating, state, the situation of the Romanians in Transylvania became even more delicate. Whether it was a matter of Hungarians or Slavs, the Romanians were surrounded on all sides by national constructions or national projects which contradicted their own project.

The only solution was to look to the West, especially to the Latin idea, and to appeal above all to the great Latin sister: France. The French model, and in a sense the "French illusion", developed into a fundamental reference point for nineteenth-century Romanian society. In yet another dramatic and insoluble contradiction, the Romanians tried to break away from the part of Europe to which they nonetheless clearly belonged, and to set sail, in the realm of the imaginary, towards the shores of the West.

Nor should the opposite reaction be underestimated. The Western model found a less than propitious ground in the rural base of Romanian society and in the rural-autochthonist mentality, which, despite being partially masked for a time by the pro-Western activity of an elite, would remain strong and ready to burst forth when the time was right. The tension between the Western model and indigenous cultural standards was to continue throughout the period which we are considering, and indeed is still in evidence today.

As far as historical discourse is concerned, attachment to the Western model had the effect both of diminishing nationalism and of amplifying it. Set against the brilliance of Western civilization, which had been erecting impressive cathedrals at a time when the Romanians had yet to enter history, early Romanian culture seemed no more than a variety of "Oriental barbarism" (the expression used by Titu Maiorescu). This reaction of astonishment was the dominant one, especially in the first phase of contact. Writing in 1828 to Stratford Canning, the British ambassador in Constantinople, Ioniță Tăutu confesses, with all due humility, that the Romanians are a people "without arts, without industry, without enlightenment". So had their ancestors been before them: "While letters were flourishing in Rome, Ovid, exiled to Dacia, thought that he was in the Empire of Pluto." Referring to the history of Moldavia, another text of 1828, *Nouveau tableau historique et politique de la Moldavie*, which may be attributed to the great boyar Iordache Rosetti-Roznovanu, says essentially the same thing: the past of the country "presents, on the whole, nothing of interest, no act whose memory deserves to be preserved in the annals of the nations".[6]

On the other hand, it was also argued (and with more and more insistence as national projects were affirmed with increasing force) that, on the contrary, the Romanians had once enjoyed those essential attributes of civilization of which the West was so proud. They had lost them, however, because they had been obliged for centuries to keep their hands on the sword rather than the pen, in order to defend Europe from the expansion of Islam. Their sacrifice had contributed to the ascent of the West. For all they were now about to receive, the Romanians had already paid in abundance.

Of course, such complexes could not touch the autochthonist model. Once the Romanians were seen as different from other people the problem no longer needed to be formulated in terms of superiority or inferiority. A discussion that took place within the Junimist circle some time in the 1870s, between the nationalist Eminescu and the skeptic Vasile Pogor, provides a perfect illustration of the opposition between autochthonists and unconditional admirers of the Western model.

According to George Panu, the memorialist of the group, the exchange—and it matters little whether or not it is authentic—went like this:

"What's all this about the history of the Romanians?" exclaimed Pogor. "Can't you see that we have no history? A people which has no literature, art, or past civilization—such a people is not worth the attention of historians... At a time when France could produce Molière and Racine the Romanians were in a state of utter barbarism."

Then Eminescu, who was sitting in a corner, rose, and said, with a violence which was not his usual tone: "What you call barbarism, I call the settled wisdom of a people that develops in conformity with its own genius and shuns any mixing with foreigners."[7]

What we find summarized in these few lines is the great dilemma which has divided Romanian society for the last two centuries.

A NATIONAL MYTH: MICHAEL THE BRAVE

The way in which the myth of Michael the Brave took shape illustrates better than any other historical model the mutations which have taken place in Romanian consciousness. The prince, who managed for a short time (1599–1600) to rule the three territories that were to be united some three centuries later in modern Romania, begins to be perceived as a *unifier* only towards the middle of the nineteenth century.[8] Such an interpretation is completely lacking in the historiography of the seventeenth-century chroniclers, and even in that of the Transylvanian School around 1800. What they emphasized, apart from the exceptional personality of Michael himself, were the idea of Christendom and his close relations with Emperor Rudolf. The conqueror's ambition is likewise frequently cited as a motivation for his actions, occupying in the interpretative schema the place which was later to be occupied by the "Romanian idea".

In the writings of the Moldavian chronicler Miron Costin, Michael the Brave appears in the role of conqueror of Transylvania and Moldavia, "the cause of much spilling of blood among Christians", and not even highly appreciated by his own Muntenians: "The rule of Voivode Michael was hateful to the Muntenians, what with his armies and wars."[9] The perspective of the Muntenians themselves is to be found in *The History of the Princes of Wallachia*, attributed to Radu Popescu, which bundles together all Michael's adversaries without distinction, Romanians and foreigners alike: "He subjected the Turks, the Moldavians, and the Hungarians to his rule, as if they were so many asses."[10] The picturesque flavor of the expression only serves to confirm the absence of any "Romanian idea". Could Michael the Brave, in 1600, have been more "patriotic" than the erudite chroniclers of the later seventeenth century?

Even the Transylvanian School, to which nineteenth-century Romanian consciousness owed so much, did not make the decisive step, however much it sought to affirm the identity of the Romanians and pride in being Romanian. The idea of a single state for all Romanians had yet to be voiced, and it was still not time for the achievements of Michael the Brave to be exploited in this sense. Consider how Samuil Micu sums up Michael's reign in his *Short Explanation of the History of the Romanians* (written in the 1790s): "In the year 1593, Michael, who is called the Brave, succeeded to the lordship of Wallachia. He was a great warrior, who fought the Turks and defeated the Transylvanians. And he took Transylvania and gave it to Emperor Rudolf..."[11] Nowadays, such an interpretation would provoke widespread indignation—yet its author is considered one of the great founding fathers of Romanian nationalism!

In his *Chronicle of the Romanians and of Other Peoples*, Gheorghe Şincai devotes much space to Michael's reign, and especially to his actions in Transylvania. In opposition to Engel, he always sets the record straight in favor of the Romanians. He is determined to defend the personality of the voivode, whom he portrays in a morally positive light in antithesis to the defects of his adversaries. The ingredients of the myth are there, but the myth itself is still absent. Şincai puts an emphasis on national pride, but he does not exploit the idea politically in the direction of national unity.

A few decades later, in 1830, Damaschin Bojincă, a follower of the Transylvanian School from the Banat, published a biography of the prince in *The Romanian Library*, under the title *The Famous Deeds and End of Michael the Brave, Prince of Wallachia*. The national idea is still not fully developed, with the main emphasis being on Michael's struggles against the Turks.

The turning point is marked by Aaron Florian, a Transylvanian who settled in Wallachia and became a teacher at the Saint Sava College in Bucharest. Michael the Brave occupies an essential role in his *Quick Idea of the History of the Principality of Wallachia*. Aaron Florian dwells at length on Michael's personality and his period, to which he devotes considerably more space than the economy of the title might seem to warrant—two hundred pages, amounting to the greater part of the second volume, published in 1837—and at last gives the voivode's actions their place in the foundation of Romanian national unity. He reproaches Michael only for the fact that he was not able to give the unified Romanian territories an appropriate constitution. Only thus might a new era have begun, in which the Romanians would have been able to evolve, united, alongside the other nations of Europe.

This is how the Transylvanian Aaron Florian saw things in Bucharest. Not so the Moldavian Mihail Kogălniceanu. The man who was later to be the great artisan of the union of the principalities gives no signs in his youthful writing that he was at all sensitive to the national potential of the Michael the Brave episode. In his *Histoire de la Valachie*, published, like Florian's volume, in 1837, we find a Michael whose source lies in Miron Costin's evocation. There is not the slightest hint of a project of national unity: rather, Michael's dominant characteristic seems to be the "unbounded ambition" which drives him not only to conquer Transylvania but even to dream of the crowns of Hungary and Poland. "His reign was outstanding in conquests, but fatal to Wallachia", is Kogălniceanu's summing up, and he draws from it a certain historical moral: "The names of great conquerors never perish in the memory of the people, while virtuous but peaceful princes are forgotten."[12] Michael appears as a great warrior, a hero indeed, but certainly not a unifier.

Despite his Muntenian origins, Nicolae Bălcescu gives no signs of any special attraction towards the personality of Michael the Brave in his earliest works— *Armed Power and the Military Art from the Founding of the Principality of Wallachia to the Present* (1844) and *On the Social Status of the Workers of the Land...* (1846)—where he gives him the place and importance which the respective themes call for and no more.

However, after 1840 the irresistible ascent of Michael becomes more and more visible. It is an ascent in which he appears in two different lights, sometimes contradictory but potentially complementary, as both the glorious ruler of Wallachia and the unifier of the Romanians. The former aspect is highlighted by Gheorghe Bibescu, himself a ruler of Wallachia (1842–1848), who liked to present himself as the worthy successor of the great voivode and orchestrated insistent propaganda along these lines. His deposition from the throne in 1848 prevented him from becoming a new Michael, but the vanity with which he assumed his great predecessor's heritage did not pass without an echo. An atmosphere increasingly charged with the memory of the hero of Călugăreni must have made an impression on Bălcescu, despite his opposition to Bibescu's regime.

Even in Moldavia Michael was beginning to emerge as a symbol. In the *Opening Word* of his 1843 course in national history at the Mihăileană Academy in Iaşi, Kogălniceanu approached the Muntenian voivode with noticeably more sympathy than he had shown six years previously. Now Michael was presented as the one who had united the separate parts of ancient Dacia.

The symbol attained its full brilliance and functionality in the last and most ambitious work of Nicolae Bălcescu, begun in 1847 and still not completed when he died in 1852: *The History of the Romanians under the Voivode Michael the Brave*. The evolution in relation to his earlier essays is pronounced, as far as the national idea is concerned. Now the ultimate aim of Michael's actions is clearly proclaimed: *national unity*. "[He] wanted to create for himself a country as extensive as the land of the Romanians", and so achieved "the dearest dream of the great Romanian voivodes", a dream which went back to Mircea the Old, "the first Romanian ruler who fought for national unity". Indeed, these rulers had only been giving expression in their actions to a widely shared sentiment, considering that, from the very beginning, "nothing had been able to wipe from the heart of all Romanians the tradition of a common life and the desire to establish it once again". This explains "the national hatred of the Romanians against Hungarian tyrants". This is why "every time a Romanian flag was seen flying on the summits of the Carpathians all Transylvania trembled: the Romanians with hope, the tyrants with dread."[13]

Bălcescu's book marked a new departure in Romanian historiography. For the first time the medieval history of the Romanians, of the three Romanian lands, was explicitly treated as *national* history, as the history of a national desideratum which had never ceased to be manifested throughout the centuries, the history of an ideal Romanian state, complete and unitary. The influence of the work on Romanian national consciousness was considerable, despite the delay in its publication (a partial edition in 1861–63, followed by the first of many full editions in 1878). Thanks to Bălcescu, Michael the Brave was set up decisively and definitively as the first founder of modern Romania.

In the years leading up to the union of the principalities in 1859, there was a growing interest in the figure of the voivode, in Moldavia as well as in Wallachia, paralleled by a tendency to attribute a unifying role to certain Moldavian rulers, above all to Stephen the Great. Together, Michael and Stephen came to symbolize the separate yet shared history, which had led in any case towards unity, of the two Romanian sister lands.

Thus we can observe Michael the Brave undergoing a process of transfiguration between 1830 and 1860, with a notable intensification at the time of the 1848 revolution and again at the time of the union. From being a warrior and Christian hero he becomes a symbol of Romanian unity. These are the years when the ideal of union in a Romanian state, an ideal Romania prefigured in consciousness, came to be projected onto the historical past. This national, political, and historical orientation belongs essentially to a single generation, the generation that carried out the 1848 revolution and later achieved the union of the principalities and the foundation of modern Romania. We have seen also how Dacia is frequently invoked in this same period as the expression of the primordial unity of the Romanian land. The two symbols point towards a great aspiration: *ancient Dacia*, resurrected for a moment by Michael the Brave and destined to be re-embodied in the Romania of tomorrow.

DIFFERENT PROJECTS, DIFFERENT HISTORIES

Just as the national idea sought a justification and model in the historical past, so too did the modernization of Romanian society. If the national project was broadly similar for all Romanians—a single nation in the homeland of ancient Dacia—the transformations which were thought necessary to propel Romanian society into the modern age naturally reflected ideological divergences and the specific interests of social groups. Compared with the relative homogeneity of the national discourse, when we turn our attention to the great problem of reform, and especially to the question of property, the historical evocations become contradictory. Towards the middle of the nineteenth century the past was restructured according to three distinct political-historical sensibilities: *democratic*, *conservative*, and *liberal*.

The democratic solution—in fact a rural-democratic solution adapted to the profile of Romanian society—found in Nicolae Bălcescu its great historian and a politician of uncommon consistency. For Bălcescu, the principal question was not liberty as such, but property, from which everything else derived. When the Romans colonized Dacia "they shared the land among the colonists according to their custom". Romanian society was originally, and had long remained, a society of landowning freemen. The usurpation had come later, after the foundation of the principalities. "Interest, need, and force" had led to the ruining of the small properties and their incorporation into large estates, resulting in "the social monstrosity that an entire country is enslaved to a few individuals". Michael the Brave made the peasants serfs, by his famous "bond", and the country was divided into "two hostile camps with conflicting interests". This unhappy evolution brought with it the decline of the Romanian lands. Only the emancipation of the peasants and their endowment with property could remedy the situation. Otherwise, the very existence of the Romanian nation was under threat. If the national revolution was to be victorious, it had to be sustained by a social revolution.[14]

What emerges from Bălcescu's study is the *illegitimacy of the great estates*. Carried to its full consequences, the transposition of his historical demonstration into social reform would have meant the restructuring of Romanian society as a society exclusively of *small properties*. Clearly, things could not go quite so far. However, in 1848, Bălcescu defended the most radical point of view expressed in the Property Commission, advocating policies which would have led to a partial but significant expropriation and the creation of substantial small peasant properties. It was also he who upheld the notion of universal suffrage.

At the other extreme, the conservative thesis upheld the historical land rights of the boyars and the indispensable role of this class in the present as in the past. From being a moderate revolutionary in 1848, Ion Heliade Rădulescu later shifted towards an uncompromisingly pro-boyar stance. Far from being the subjugators of the peasants, it was the boyars, argues the great scholar in his *Balance between Antitheses*, "who, together with Radu Negru, founded our princedom on the basis of institutions so humane and egalitarian that the laws of Numa, Lycurgus, and Solon cannot stand comparison". Moreover, the boyar class here "was not hereditary, but was open to all the sons of the fatherland". The Romanian boyars had even anticipated, and in a much more reasonable way, the democracy of the French Revolution: "The old boyar class had nothing to fear in the French Republic, which brought down the sons of nobles; for the old boyars created new boyars out of the sons of their servants, making them family members and giving them their daughters and nieces in marriage."[15] The democratic spirit of the age—imported from the West—demanded it! Romanian history proved to be profoundly democratic: democratic in Bălcescu's peasant variant and democratic, too, in Heliade Rădulescu's boyar variant.

Barbu Catargiu, the prime minister assassinated in 1862, was a skilled upholder of boyar property rights, who invoked historical arguments among others. He, too, set out to de-dramatize the situation by improving the image of the boyars and restoring the legality of the great estates. "Feudalism never existed in Romania", he affirmed in June 1859. The system was only established in the West, as a result of Germanic conquest. This was why revolutions had been necessary in the western part of Europe, to remedy what had been a usurpation there. Here, however, the Roman colonists had remained masters of their own land. Catargiu's starting point is the same as Bălcescu's, but his conclusion is different. There was no usurpation of any kind, he tells us. The present owners hold the land by inheritance from the earliest times (the Roman period), or have bought it with all title deeds in order. Thus the great estates are fully justified historically, not to mention their economic justification.

All the same, the historical arguments invoked by Barbu Catargiu carry a limited weight in his political discourse. While offering a necessary sacrifice to the game of history he insistently draws attention to the fact that what counts in the end is not the past, but the present. The skepticism which he manifests as far as historical models, more or less imaginary, are concerned deserves to be noted. "Public opinion", he points out, "is formed, and may very easily be inflamed, by the pompous words of sentimentalism and patriotism about Trajan, Mircea the Voivode, and even Decebalus. [...] Let us not be led astray by speeches. [...] Let us deal with each question from the point of view of law and political economy."[16] Barbu Catargiu's thinking was basically reactionary, but his logic was, in essence, more modern than that of the revolutionaries!

We might perhaps have expected that it would be conservatives who would be more susceptible to the siren song of the past. However, that is not how things generally are in fact. The past is more often invoked, and invoked in the most imperative terms, by those who want to break away from it. The logic of the imaginary has its own rules. The French revolutionaries invoked Sparta and republican Rome. Any project or ideology needs models. Even when it is the future that is at stake, the models are taken from the past. Ultimately there is no other reality than the past. The more transforming an ideology aspires to be, the more radical the project, the more it appeals to the past: to a past restructured according to the necessities and ideals of the present. The boyars, too, could invoke history, and they did not hesitate to do so, but the existing state of things both in fact and in law was on their side anyway. It was those who sought to modify this state of things who were compelled to appeal to history, to a history that could set an idealized past against the corrupt present. The road to the future presupposed a re-actualization of origins.

This is just what we find in liberal ideology. What could be more modern than liberalism? However, its references to the past, to a clearly outlined historical model, are extremely frequent and significant. Alecu Russo's *Song of Romania* (published in 1850 and 1855) could be appreciated as a veritable hymn of liberalism. If the supreme values for Bălcescu were property and the nation, for Russo individual liberty is the fundamental historical and political principle from which all others flow.[17]

The *Song of Romania* is a poem. However, the writings and speeches of I. C. Brătianu belong to the genre of political discourse and their author counts as one of the principal founders of modern Romania, which he set on the path of liberalism. In comparison with the "rural" Bălcescu, Brătianu comes across as an urban bourgeois figure, in mentality at least, if not in his boyar origins. He was a pragmatic politician, but none the less visionary for all that: the two facets are not necessarily antithetical. What is impressive is his passion for history and the way he understood how to draw from the national past the elements of a liberal doctrine, which had in fact come not from the Roman colonists but from the nineteenth-century West!

And indeed the Roman colonists are set to work once again. From an article published by Brătianu in *Republica română* (November 1851) we learn that the Romans who settled in Dacia preserved their republican spirit intact. They had not come from Rome, where the flame of liberty had been extinguished, but from rural areas, where the old beliefs and virtues were still strong. Thus we are told that "the colonization of Dacia was carried out in the name of, and by, the power of an idea." Those who settled here were a kind of political refugees and refugees of conscience. Hence there is a resemblance between the founding of the Romanian nation and the creation of America, both nations being equally devoted to the religion of liberty: "[...] just as the Puritans of England did, as we know, in 1660, by their emigration to America after the fall of the English Republic, so all the evidence allows us to say that the democratic and free population of Italy, in order to escape from the fiscal yoke, from the insolence of favorites and the threat of being disinherited, took the plowshare in one hand and the sword in the other and came to plant the iron of liberty in a new land, a young and powerful land, far from the infected atmosphere of decaying despotism [...]." Within the new Roman colony "democratic traditions were preserved with holy and pure reverence". The Romanian nation "not only has a mind and soul prepared for democracy, but has preserved it unceasingly in its heart and in its customs".[18]

Even later on, when the revolutionary plotter had become a responsible statesman, I. C. Brătianu lost no occasion to justify the laws and acts of modernization in terms of historical models and precedents. What could be more normal, as the nineteenth century progressed, than the development of avenues of communication? However, here again we find an invocation of the Romans, the great road-builders: let the Romanians prove worthy descendants and "build highways, lay railways, channel rivers, construct harbors, and organize navigation companies".[19] Likewise, respect for private property was affirmed by a recourse to origins. Among the Slavs, joint ownership predominated, while "the Romanians borrowed the idea of individual property from the Greeks and Romans". The aim of the government in 1883 was no more than "to constitute property as it was before in Romania, and as it is everywhere in the Latin and Greek nations".[20] As for the constitution and political system, it sould be known that "Romania has a past, and while in other states there was the most absolute despotism, here there was a regime, which, according to the conditions of the time, was very liberal and,

I might say, parliamentary".[21] When the Law of Communities came under discussion in 1878, Brătianu pointed out that the aim was basically no more than the revival of a Roman tradition that had long been maintained here: "These Communities existed in Romania too, and it was only later, when our strength was exhausted by the struggle against barbarian invasions, that foreign rulers came and abolished the Community [...]."[22]

More generally, the great politician never ceased to affirm the necessity of studying the origins of the Romanians if their national identity was to be marked and their present interests upheld. He himself published essays and gave lectures on this theme. For any political "mutation", history offers precedents and lessons. Sometimes these can be unconsciously humorous. When, in 1883, Romania joined the Triple Alliance, Brătianu could not miss the chance to announce that Stephen the Great had been the "oldest friend" of Austria![23]

Thus the liberal program, though it was the closest of all to the Western bourgeois model, was presented, almost point by point, as the re-actualization of a transfigured past which extended from ancient Dacia up to the decline of the Romanian lands in the late Middle Ages.

History thus provides *equal* justification for the essentially rural democracy of Bălcescu, the bourgeois liberalism of Brătianu, and the conservatism of Barbu Catargiu. There is nothing strange in this: *History always justifies everything.*

THE GLORIFICATION OF THE PAST

Another aim pursued by means of history was the demonstration of noble origins and of a glorious past, more capable than its less than splendid image in the present of ensuring the Romanian nation a respectable place in the concert of European nations.

Towards the middle of the nineteenth century the question of origins appeared to have been clarified, in the most favorable version from the point of view of promoting Romanian interests. The Romanians were descendants of the Roman colonists, with perhaps some minimal concession to the native Dacians. As a Latin nation by origin and vocation they could hardly do otherwise than integrate into the European community of the Romance-speaking peoples.

The extreme expression of this interpretation is to be found in the Latinist school, the exacerbated prolongation of the Transylvanian School into the second half of the nineteenth century. In 1853, the undisputed leader of this Latinist current, August Treboniu Laurian, linguist and historian and one of the most respected Romanian scholars of the time, published his *History of the Romanians*, a work of synthesis which began, without more ado, with the foundation of Rome in 753 BC. The history of the Romanians is presented as a continuation of Roman history. Indeed, any difference between Romanians and Romans disappears. They were the same people, and their history is one and the same. The chronological system adopted by Laurian carries the integration of the Romanians into Roman history to its logical conclusion: as all dates are recalculated from the foundation of Rome, the reader will be surprised to discover that Tudor Vladimirescu's revolution took place in the year 2574!

Despite Laurian's optimism there remained large unknown spaces in the early history of the Romanians, especially during the "dark millennium" between the Aurelian withdrawal and the founding of the medieval principalities. With the launch of the immigrationist thesis in the late eighteenth century, in the works of Franz Joseph Sulzer and Johann Christian Engel, a major problem confronting Romanian historians was how to demonstrate Romanian continuity north of the Danube. But this was only a minimum requirement. To sustain the significance of Romanian history at a European level, something more than an affirmation of indigenous origins in terms of mere ethnic survival was called for. Thus, even while trying to combat immigrationism, Romanian historians were tempted to emphasize and amplify the phenomenon of Romanian presence south of the Danube, which was better attested in the sources and capable of being integrated into a greater history. First Şincai, and later Laurian, developed a theory according to which the Bulgarian tsardoms were in fact mixed Romanian–Bulgarian states, with the Romanian element even dominant in certain periods. In a manner which could, however unintentionally, serve immigrationist schemes, the center of gravity of Romanian history for over a millennium was shifted south of the Danube. The Romanians thus integrated themselves with greater history again and avoided the marginalization to which a withdrawal within the strictly defined space of ancient Dacia would have condemned them.

As far as the continuity and historical affirmation of the Romanian people in the actual space of Dacia and modern Romania was concerned, the starting point towards the middle of the nineteenth century was almost zero. The archaeological study of the issue, and the invocation of linguistic arguments, were still in the future, and the external data—generally late, limited in quantity, and vague—left the ground free for all sorts of hypotheses. The "filling in" of this millennium became a favorite theme of the Romanian historical imaginary.

For a while, in 1856, it was possible to believe that the whole question had been miraculously solved. In that year, Gheorghe Asachi's printing house offered to the world the *Chronicle of Huru*, presented as a translation made by the high sword-bearer Petru Clanău in the time of Stephen the Great, of a Latin original compiled by Huru, the great chancellor of Dragoş Vodă, which was itself derived from a much older text written by the *campodux* Arbure. The chronicle covers the entire dark millennium from the Aurelian withdrawal in 274 down to 1274 (the supposed reign of Bogdan Dragoş). The document provoked a considerable historiographical and political stir. The ruler of Moldavia, Grigore Ghica, set up a commission of specialists in literary and historical matters to check the authenticity of the source. Opinions were divided. Many found the document suspect from the start, but its partisans included some distinguished scholars, notably Gheorghe Asachi himself, who published the text, and Ion Heliade Rădulescu, who would exploit its historical significance to the full.

When the Roman withdrawal was announced, so the *campodux* Arbure informs us, people began to gather in Iaşi, where a great assembly took place. They decided to stay where they were and resist the barbarians. Here, at last, was the much sought after testimony to Romanian continuity! The state was organized as a sort of republic, on Roman lines—a federative Moldavian republic (the document refers strictly to the area between the Carpathians and the Dniester). A number of objectives were thus attained: the demonstration of state continuity, evidence of old indigenous democratic institutions, and the underlining of the identity of Moldavia and of the fact that Bessarabia had belonged to it from the earliest times. The message needs to be seen in the context of the moment in which it appeared: this was 1856, the year of the Congress of Paris and of the decision to consult the principalities about their possible unification. An accent was put on the historical rights of Moldavia over Bessarabia, which had been seized by the Russians in 1812. At the same time there was an affirmation of Moldavian distinctiveness, in line with the orientation of the minority—including Gheorghe Asachi—who were less than enthusiastic about the prospect of union with Wallachia.

There is no need to repeat here that Arbure the *campodux*, the great chancellor Huru, and the high sword-bearer Clanău are completely imaginary figures and the *Chronicle* a forgery, the product of the "document factory" of the Sion family. This was also the source of the *Archondology of Moldavia*, written by Constantin Sion, with its numerous fictitious or semi-fictitious genealogies, which were even supported on occasion by the *Chronicle of Huru*. It is worth mentioning that the author of the *Archondology*, who was also author or co-author of the *Chronicle*, campaigned in 1858 for Grigore Sturdza as candidate for the throne of Moldavia, thus setting himself against the national party and the union, which he saw as a "fools' project". The political meaning of the forgery thus becomes clearer: the document testified to the continuity of the Romanians in general, but even more to the rights of Moldavia as a state in its own right.[24]

The controversy around the *Chronicle of Huru* did not die down easily. The famous linguist Alexandru Philippide still found it necessary, in 1882, to test his powers in a detailed study to prove it a forgery. The document provoked more of a stir than the modest ability of the forgers deserved, for the simple reason that it filled in a gap and gave material substance to the illusion that Roman history had continued, through the Romanians, at a high level of political organization and civilization.

The projection into the foreground of world history with respect to a period in national history about which nothing was in fact known was also a chief preoccupation of Heliade Rădulescu. Inspired by the *Chronicle of Huru*, but stimulated even more by his own convictions and fantasies—an amalgam of national messianism, Christian spirituality, conservatism, and democracy—the father of modern Romanian culture cast his own light on the continuity issue in his synthesis *Elements of the History of the Romanians* (1860 and 1869), and in various chapters of *The Balance between Antitheses.* Following the Aurelian withdrawal, Dacia remained "autonomous and Christian", "Organized according to the institutions of the primitive ecclesia, it was constituted and continued to govern itself in ecclesiae, or Christian democracies, autonomous and confederate [...]. Their civil code was the Pentateuch [...]." At the other end of the controversial millennium, the constitution of Radu Negru, in 1247, organized Wallachia on the lines of biblical Palestine, in twelve Christian democracies or autonomous counties. In any case, the Romanian political tradition was republican, with rulers being elected and originally holding power for only five years (a "historical precedent" made up-to-date in the revolutionary program of 1848). All this was proof of the fact that "Europe, in its institutions concerned with liberty, equality, and fraternity, and in those concerned with the brotherhood and solidarity of peoples, has not yet caught up with the first Romanians."[25]

The Romanians were thus proved, in one version or another of this fictive history, to be the undisputed repositories of the values of the two great models of world history: the Roman and the Judeo-Christian.

The later phase of Romanian history, beginning with the *real* foundation of the principalities in the fourteenth century, was, of course, better known. But even this history, no less than the unknown history which preceded it, lent itself to an appreciable process of amplification. There is a particular manner of highlighting the excellence of the Romanian past that we find in the historians of the 1848 generation, including the greatest among them, M. Kogălniceanu and N. Bălcescu. In their respect for the concrete data of history they are far from the fantasies of Heliade or the forgeries of Sion, but they manifest, to the same extent, the desire to occupy a privileged place in European history—a desire which is perfectly understandable and in full agreement with the political project of affirming the nation in the community of Europe.

Two themes, which were to have enduring echoes in Romanian consciousness, now crystallized for the first time: on the one hand, the role of the Romanians in defending European civilization; and on the other, the antiquity, and even priority, of Romanian achievements in a wide variety of fields. The two registers combined in a contradictory relationship–sacrifice for the sake of Christian Europe resulted in the wearing down of a remarkable civilization.

In his introduction to the French edition (published in 1845) of extracts from the Romanian chronicles, Kogălniceanu captured in a striking synthesis these characteristics of a national history abruptly thrust into a greater European history. The Romanians, he writes, "are one of the peoples who distinguished themselves the most in the Middle Ages by military virtues and by the activities of the spirit. They were the first in Europe to have a regular army; for centuries they were the defenders of religion and civilization against Islam and Asiatic barbarism. [...] They were among the first to establish religious tolerance and liberty of conscience, to embrace the advantages of printing, and to adopt the national language for use in the church, the chancery, and in schools."[26] According to Kogălniceanu, the Romanians were also among the first peoples to write their history in their national language—a surprising claim, given that the earliest chronicles written in Romanian date only from the seventeenth century. In France, Villehardouin was already writing in French at the beginning of the thirteenth century.

Bălcescu, in *Armed Power...*, expresses an identical point of view:

> "The Romanian army was the first standing army in Europe. [...] Already in the fourteenth century, when all of Europe was sunk in barbarity, the Romanians had institutions with which they would have gone on to become a powerful nation in Europe, if unity had prevailed among them."[27]

And some decades later, in 1889, Kogălniceanu, speaking in the Chamber of Deputies about the adoption of the principles of "great 1789", did not hesitate to identify again "their beginning right here in our country", as the Romanians could invoke "many examples which were later imitated by countries more advanced than ourselves".[28]

From the pupils of the West, the Romanians were becoming its defenders, and, in many respects, even its precursors. We are clearly witnessing a nationalist amplification of history. However, the phenomenon must be understood in a particular context, and especially in relation to two essential coordinates.

The first of these is the spirit of romantic historiography in general. The highlighting and amplification of specific national values, the valorization of origins, a pronounced taste for an idealized and "heroicized" Middle Ages, a historical discourse suffused with patriotism, and even an inclination to patriotic falsification, are all characteristic of the romantic and nationalist tendency of the times. The Romanians were doing no more than adapting the general formula to their own history. The excessive exaggeration in the Romanian case reflects the extreme disproportion between reality and ideal. When Michelet places France— as other historians and ideologists place Italy or Germany—at the head of the peoples of the world, his pretension may seem less flagrant than the invocation of the various Romanian "firsts", but the logic of the predestination and privileging of a certain nation is exactly the same in both cases.

Secondly, and paradoxically, the nationalist amplification of the past did not in any way serve an autochthonist project, but rather the bringing of Romanian society closer to Western civilization and the acceptance of Romania as a state with full rights among the other European states. Historians and politicians (and some of them, like Kogălniceanu and Bălcescu, were both historians and politicians) set out to demonstrate that the history of previous centuries, a history of subjection, decline, and unwanted integration into the Oriental world, was only a historical accident, and that once the effects of this were cast aside, Romania would be able to return to the normal pattern of its evolution, a pattern marked by its Latin origins and by a destiny in no way inferior to that of the Western, Latin branch. Behind the nationalist discourse we can clearly read the desire for integration with Europe.

From Romanticism to the Critical School

The nationalist-romantic formula in Romanian historiography long outlasted the chronological limits of European romanticism. The strength and persistence of the current find their justification in the general conditions of Romanian political and intellectual life.

A first explanation lies in the way in which the national problem became more acute in the last decades of the nineteenth century. The national objective became a priority for the Romanians, in the conditions of discrimination to which they were subjected and in the resulting intensification of national movements in the territories under foreign rule: Transylvania, Bukovina, and Bessarabia. The historical discourse continued to be profoundly marked by the ideal project of a unified nation. National antagonisms were supported by historical arguments. Far from having exhausted its political-historiographical resources, the problem of continuity took on highly conflictual accents following the publication of Robert Roesler's *Romanian Studies* (*Romänische Studien*, 1871). His revitalization of the immigrationist thesis came at just the right time to serve the Hungarian political project—the dream of a Greater Hungary and a fundamentally Hungarian Transylvania in which the Romanians had appeared relatively late. The Romanian response, insisting, with a few exceptions and nuances, on Romanian continuity on the former territory of Dacia, evidently served a no less clearly defined political and national goal. Through history, the Hungarians and Romanians were tracing the ideal frontiers of the present or future. The implications at an emotional level, with a strong echo in public opinion, of divergent national projects, posed a challenge to historiography. Was it possible to reconcile the demands of research with the requirement to adhere to a particular national program? Could the historian be a patriot while speaking *in any way* about the past of his nation? He could, of course, but in less favorable conditions than would have been offered by a society unaffected by conflicts and projects of this sort.

Secondly, we must note the slow pace at which Romanian historiography went through the process of professionalization. The professional is not beyond all mythological temptations, as indeed this book itself demonstrates. However, he is capable—at least theoretically—of avoiding simplistic and infantile forms of mythologizing. However daring his constructions may be, they are built on a real foundation of verified facts. A step had to be taken towards the "disciplining" of historical studies and their bringing into line with the methodology and institutional system of Europe. The beginning of this process had taken place in the German universities in the eighteenth century. Around 1800 there were a dozen university chairs of history in the German space; by 1900 their number had increased to 175. Germany had become the undisputed world center of historiography; here it was possible to acquire the norms of a history based on the rigorous study of sources, a history that at last sought to be free of fantasy. France lagged behind, but professionalization had also made great progress in its universities—there were 71 chairs of history by the end of the nineteenth century.

The first two Romanian universities, at Iaşi and Bucharest, were founded in 1860 and 1864 respectively. In principle, these dates could mark the beginning, albeit modest, of the professionalization of history. The reality, however, was somewhat different. The theory of "forms without substance", formulated by Maiorescu and developed by E. Lovinescu in a more optimistic direction (with the forms gradually creating their own substance), could be applied here with ample justification. The four chairs of history (History of the Romanians and World History, in Iaşi and Bucharest) were occupied for decades by people who had little to do with the profession of historian. Petre Cernătescu, professor of World History in Bucharest until 1892(!), made his reputation with a textbook of world history to which he had added only his name, the rest being no more than a Romanian version of Victor Duruy's synthesis. His opposite number in Iaşi, Nicolae Ionescu, was a politician and an admired orator of his time, but in no sense a historian. Meanwhile, Andrei Vizanti was teaching the history of the Romanians in Iaşi; he became well known not for the few booklets of little value that he published, but for the more spectacular fact of his fleeing the country, under accusation of embezzlement, to escape the rigors of the law. Only V. A. Urechia, professor of the History of the Romanians at Bucharest University from 1864 to 1901, proved to be a hard worker, although his industry was not matched by his competence. His extensive papers are rather compilations than original works, and his passionate, if naive, patriotism places him among the discoverers of all sorts of autochthonous "firsts".

Until almost the end of the century it was not the chairs of history that would promote the norms of the erudite and critical school which characterized contemporary European historiography. Unconstrained by such a discipline, historiographical romanticism had free rein. The principal historiographical personality of the 1860s and 1870s was Bogdan Petriceicu Hasdeu (1838–1907), an autodidact with an immense body of knowledge—especially in the field of linguistics, philology, and history—a sparkling mind, a genius even, but with fantastic inclinations and a tendency towards the most unexpected intellectual constructions. In 1874 Hasdeu became professor of Comparative Philology at the University of Bucharest. Before this date, as for some time after it, his influence on history was enormous, and not in terms of the disciplining of the field! His solid contributions, including the publication of an impressive number of Slav documents and old Romanian texts, and his fertile ideas, such as those concerning the role of the Dacians in the formation of the Romanian people, his theory of the circulation of words, or, on a larger scale, his project of interdisciplinary research, bringing together history, linguistics, anthropology, economics, etc., combined with an attraction towards arbitrary elaborations and pure intellectual exercises, are seductive and misleading.

As a nationalist of liberal political sensibility (he was elected deputy on the Liberal Party lists in 1867 and 1884), Hasdeu did not hesitate to infuse history, sometimes in defiance of the evidence, with the values in which he believed. His monograph *Ioan Vodă the Terrible* (1865) presents the ruler as the most brilliant

European political mind of the sixteenth century and Moldavia as in many ways a modern country, with an electoral system which anticipates universal suffrage. The reforms of Ioan Vodă, as the historian interprets them, actually anticipate the reforms of Cuza, which were being implemented as the work was published. The Moldavian prince secularizes the wealth of the monasteries and thinks of a very intelligent fiscal reform, capable of improving, almost miraculously, the situation of the peasantry. Hasdeu would even recommend that law makers give consideration to indigenous laws and institutions in the process of modernizing Romania, stressing the "character of the Romanian nationality as the basis of its legislation".[29]

In his later works—the most important of which is his *Critical History of the Romanians* (1873 and 1875)—Hasdeu strove to highlight the value of the old Romanian civilization, the strength of the Romanians in the Middle Ages, and the political continuity from Dacia, through the Roman Empire, to the Romanian principalities. While he was an opponent of pure Latinism and argued for the importance of the Dacians in the Romanian synthesis, he tried to minimize the importance of the Slav element in the Romanian language and in old Romanian culture: although he was a Slavicist he was also a Bessarabian, an opponent of Russia and a partisan of Latin solidarity. The prestige of Hasdeu, coupled with his undoubted knowledge and other merits, were to further complicate the path towards the affirmation of critical norms in Romanian historiography.

In these conditions, the process of professionalization did not begin to take shape until the 1880s and became firmly established only in the 1890s. A. D. Xenopol began his career as professor of the History of the Romanians at the University of Iaşi in 1883. There is no doubt that he was a historian in the most complete sense of the word, and even a great historian, but, inclined as he was towards the theory of history and towards great works of synthesis, he did not fully meet the requirements of the time, which were direct knowledge of the sources and immersion in strictly specialized research. Hence the reticence of the "critical school" where Xenopol's work and general approach are concerned. We may consider as a key moment the publication of the first fundamental study by Dimitrie Onciul in 1885. (This was a "critical appraisal" of Xenopol's work *The Theory of Roesler*.) Onciul, a product of the Austrian school, an extension of that of Germany, became professor of the History of the Romanians at the University of Bucharest in 1896. Ioan Bogdan, a Slavicist with an identical methodological background, came to the chair of Slav Languages in 1891, and, on the death of P. Cernătescu, the chair of World History went, in 1894, to Nicolae Iorga. The leap from Cernătescu to Iorga is a significant, even symbolic, indication of the radical restructuring of Romanian historiography. It was a remarkable beginning, but only a beginning, limited to the contribution and example of a few historians. Only in subsequent years and decades would professionalism acquire a solid base through the arrival on the scene of new generations trained in the spirit of a demanding methodology.

THE JUNIMIST PARADIGM: DETACHMENT FROM HISTORY

It is now time to deal with the *paradigm change* attempted by the Junimea group in Romanian historiography and the way in which the Romanians in general related to their past. Onciul and Bogdan were Junimists, and Iorga was, for a time, a "fellow traveler" of the movement.

Junimea was founded as a cultural society in Iaşi in 1863–64. From 1867 it published the journal *Convorbiri literare* (Literary conversations), which moved to Bucharest, where the most important members had by then settled, in 1885. Those who set the tone of the movement in its formative years, foremost among them being Titu Maiorescu (1840–1917) in cultural matters and Petre P. Carp (1837–1919) in political matters, were young men with a solid background of study in the West. They were the exponents of a modern-style conservative doctrine, inclined not to traditionalism but to the gradual, organic evolution of Romanian society along the lines offered by the Western model. The key to their philosophical, political, and cultural conception was *evolutionism*; they did not believe in reactionary immobilism, but nor could they accept liberal voluntarism. They believed in the necessary solidity of a construction that could not be improvised. They felt no need to refer to the past, either to uphold their privileges like old-style conservatives or to radically change Romanian society by invoking fictive historical models like the liberals. They could look at the past with detachment, and this in itself was a very important change of paradigm, something quite new in the nineteenth-century Romanian context! It has remained to this day the only notable attempt in Romanian culture to detach the present from the past, to bring current problems under discussion without the obsessive need to refer to real or imagined historical precedents.

This programmatic detachment from history coincided with the Junimists' conception with respect to the methodology of historical research. Having been trained in the spirit of the times at the great European universities, and particularly in the German environment in the case of the leaders of the current, they promoted an objective history, reconstructed strictly on the basis of meticulous and rigorous documentary investigation. Starting from German methodology, "history as it really was"—in Ranke's famous formulation—was to spread all over Europe as the historiographical ideal of the "critical school". From this point of view, Junimism was perfectly synchronized with the movement of ideas in the West. The model, which was of course an ideal one and, like any ideal, unattainable, was that of a history reconstituted with scientific coldness, unaffected by the pressures of politics and ideology. This translated into a 180-degree turn, the result not only of conviction but also of a polemical spirit, not without its share of exaggeration, such as is inevitable in the affirmation of any new current.

Of course, criticism did not appear out of the blue in Romanian culture. Polemical attitudes towards nationalist amplifications can be found before

Junimea, too. The Latinist school, for example, had come in for harsh criticism. In his 1843 *Opening Word*, Kogălniceanu took a stand against "Romanomania", the temptation to add to the virtues and deeds of the Romanians those of their Roman ancestors. Alecu Russo, too, was scornful of this tendency. Even Hasdeu, nationalist as he was and ready in his turn to amplify Dacian roots, consistently ridiculed the Latinist mania. With or without Junimea, Latinism would have left the stage anyway, as indeed it did in the 1870s after the publication of Laurian and Massim's uninspired dictionary.

A critical tradition was, therefore, in existence. However, Junimea developed it and generalized it, giving it the strength of a veritable filtration system capable of separating the true from the false, and authentic values from pseudo-values.

Everything is there, firmly and even aggressively expressed, in the extraordinary programmatic article published by Titu Maiorescu in 1868 under the title "Against Today's Direction in Romanian Culture". History up to the beginning of the nineteenth century is dismissed in two words: "Oriental barbarism." Nor are books from the beginnings of modern Romanian culture rated more favorably. It is worth quoting in its entirety the passage referring to Petru Maior (to whom Titu Maiorescu was actually related!) and to history in general: "In 1812 Petru Maior wrote his history of the beginnings of the Romanians in Dacia (we shall pass over the compilation of quotations made uncritically by Șincai). In his inclination to demonstrate that we are the uncorrupted descendants of the Romans, Maior maintains in his fourth paragraph that the Dacians were totally exterminated by the Romans, so that there was no mixing between the two peoples. To prove such an unlikely hypothesis our historian relies on a dubious passage in Eutropius and a passage in Julian, to which he gives an interpretation which it is impossible for anyone in their right mind to accept, and thus the historical demonstration of our Romanity begins with a falsification of history."

The next comment concerns Maiorescu's contemporaries: "[...] what is surprising and saddening about these products is not their error in itself, for that can be explained and sometimes justified by the circumstances of the times, but the error in our judgement of them today, the praise and satisfaction with which they are regarded by intelligent Romanians as valid scholarly achievements, the blindness of failing to see that the building of Romanian nationality cannot be based on a foundation at the center of which lies untruth."[30]

In the same year his article "Against the School of Bărnuțiu" highlighted the ridiculousness of obsessively referring the present to the past. Bărnuțiu and his disciples were maintaining that Romanian laws and institutions should simply be those of Rome. "Alas for our nation", exclaims Maiorescu, "if its leadership is ever inspired by such principles. Against them we must summon unswerving truth and say that our regeneration cannot begin unless it is in the spirit of modern culture..."[31]

In various texts Maiorescu never tired of amusing himself and the reader with a whole collection of nationalist "gems", intended to highlight all sorts of

Romanian superiorities and priorities. Perhaps the most successful page is that in which he ridicules the parallel between Goethe and Ienăchiță Văcărescu, with reference to the poem "In a Garden". On the basis of this poem V. A. Urechia had proclaimed the superiority of Văcărescu, making Goethe a "practical German", a "gardener from Erfurt", while the Romanian was a "sublime poet". All this, of course, delighted the critic immensely.[32]

The following lines from the periodical *Adunarea națională* (National Assembly), perfectly illustrate the sort of discourse which Maiorescu confronted with an intransigent refusal:

> Two of the greatest events in the history of Europe have received their direction, or have at least been born, at the signal given on our land: the French Revolution and the national unifications of Italy and of Germany.
>
> The French Revolution is only the continuation of the revolution of Horea, with the sole difference that Horea's had a national direction as well as a social one. Indeed, even the failings and errors of Horea's revolution can be seen in the French one.
>
> At the cry of the herald, announcing the union of Moldavia and Muntenia, Garibaldi and Bismarck were aroused [...].
>
> Less noisy, but with no less profound results, was the revolution of the Romanians in the direction of liberalism and democracy. The constitutions which we have produced in these last years are also a foretaste of the new spirit in Europe. After us Austria will return to parliamentarism; after us Spain will have its revolution; after us France itself will take a few steps forward in the direction of democracy.

Here is what Maiorescu has to say: "Following on from these words, the page in question advises us: 'Let no one smile as they read this.' Honorable *Adunarea națională*, this goes beyond a joke! We should at least be forgiven a smile! For one of the happiest resources of the human race, a means of defense against many hardships in social and literary life, is precisely that movement, half of the body and half of the soul, which begins with a mere smile and ends in an explosion of delight, and which, in recognition of the liveliness of the ancient genius, we designate as Homeric laughter."[33]

George Panu, the author of three historical studies published in *Convorbiri literare* between 1872 and 1874, follows a pure Maiorescian line with strict application to history. The young author had no special training in history, but, armed with some quick reading, with the liveliness of his own mind, and with Junimist polemical verve, he manages to demolish almost the whole of Romanian historiography and even to tarnish the hitherto almost intact prestige of the great B. P. Hasdeu.

In "Studies on the Political Dependence or Independence of the Romanians in Various Centuries"[34], Panu appreciably diminishes the originality and greatness of the Romanian past. He insists on foreign, and especially Slav, influences, which can be identified on a massive scale in the Romanian language, in institutions, and in customs. The Slav contribution is no longer seen as something additional but as an important constitutive element of the Romanian synthesis. Panu also considerably limits the sphere of political action of the Romanians, insisting on the far from merely formal relationship of vassalage which bound Moldavia to Poland and Wallachia to Hungary. Even the great heroes of the Romanians are characterized in a visibly provocative manner, starting from the situation of a history which is certainly not "imperial", but rather limited and dependent on the interests of the great powers. Thus Stephen the Great becomes a "Polish vassal", and Michael the Brave a "German general"!

With the same lack of complexes, Panu reviewed Hasdeu's *Critical History of the Romanians* in 1873, seeing through the astonishing play of artifice to grasp the weakness of many of the author's demonstrations. In Hasdeu's vision, fourteenth-century Wallachia had become almost a "great power", prefiguring, in its extent, modern Romania, with borders extending over the mountains and into Moldavia as far as Bacău and Bîrlad: the young Junimist demolished all this with critical arguments. A year later, in 1874, Panu, in his "Study of History among the Romanians", sketched out an ample panorama of the distortions, exaggerations, and downright inventions of all sorts which had been developed in order to ensure for the Romanians a privileged position in the history and civilization of Europe.

The tone of Junimist historical criticism was set by Maiorescu, and after him by Panu. However, it was to be a few years before a true historical school emerged based on these principles; when it did, it was due in particular to the contributions of Dimitrie Onciul and Ioan Bogdan. In them we can see a fusion of the critical spirit with historiographical professionalism. Onciul "complicated" the continuity thesis, integrating some of Roesler's arguments in his own theory of "admigration": it was basically a solution of compromise between two rival positions. He it was, too, who demolished the myth of Negru Vodă, painstakingly reconstituting a "real" model of the formation of Wallachia. Meanwhile, in a spirit close to Panu's suggestions, Bogdan, the first great Romanian Slavicist, arrived at the definition of important Slav components in medieval Romanian culture and even in the process of the formation of the Romanian people and language.

All this, of course, was contrary to the historical prejudices of the nineteenth century. Onciul and Bogdan were not opponents of Romanian national identity and unity, nor were they advocates of the integration of Romania in the Slav space. Their model was the Western one, and they went so far as to apply this within the field of historical studies. Quite simply, they sought to separate the contemporary political project from the realities of the Middle Ages. The fact that the Romanian national state—real or ideal—occupied a well-defined territory did not mean that this national configuration had to be projected back a millennium or a millennium and a half into the past. The fact that the Romanians were trying to break away from the Slav mass and to turn towards the West did not mean that the very real presence of the Slav factor throughout medieval Romanian history had to be minimized.

Did the Junimist "new history" succeed in clearing mythology out of the discourse about the past? There is no doubt that such was its aim, but the result was not quite as intended. The demolition of one mythical configuration gives birth to "countermyths". The imaginary and ideology cannot be driven out of the historiographical project. A professional historiography is generally free of "elementary excesses", of pure falsehoods and fables. The imaginary may be cleared of fiction, but this does not mean that its logic does not continue to work upon "real facts". The factual material in question becomes more secure, but the guiding lines of the discourse are still determined by the same mental mechanism.

When Maiorescu speaks of "Oriental barbarism", the countermyth appears no less flagrantly than the myth that he is setting out to deny—that of a brilliant Romanian history and civilization of quasi-Western character. "Oriental barbarism" was, after all, a system of civilization too, as valid in itself as any other. The amplification of Slav influence, which could go as far—in the interpretation, favored by Junimea, of Alexandru Cihac—as the identification of the Romanian language as more Slav than Romance, clearly bears the same mark of countermyth, contrasting with the dominant myth of the pure Latinity of the Romanians.

Nor could detachment from the present, however much it was willed and programmatically defined, be taken the whole way. In a generally mediocre synthesis of the history of the Romanians, Onciul gives a clear expression of his dynastic conception and of the supremacy which he attributes to political institutions by the way in which he organizes the whole of Romanian history around rulers, starting with Trajan and ending with Carol I. Maiorescu's remarkable *Contemporary History of Romania* inevitably offers a Junimist-conservative perspective on the building of modern Romania, a process which most historians are more inclined to see in terms of the ideology and political action of the liberals. Here indeed is a question *any* answer to which presupposes a sliding towards myth: Who made Romania? The liberals? The conservatives? Cuza? Carol I? Kogălniceanu? Brătianu? The people? The European conjuncture? Or if we say that it was all of these, then in what order of importance?

Whatever prejudices the Junimists may have transposed into their historical discourse, and however inaccessible the historical objectivity which they sought, the critical intransigence of the movement infused Romanian culture with a spirit that every culture has an absolute need of. Any system of convictions, even—indeed especially—if it is considered beyond attack, has to be subjected to questioning. To succumb to the temptation of unanimity around certain untouchable "truths" is cultural suicide. The great merit of Junimea does not lie in the "rightness" of the solutions proposed, which is always debatable, but in the fact that it dared to put a question mark over many comfortable convictions of the Romanians. It is also to its great credit that Junimea then represented the European moment, in history as in other fields, more than any other cultural direction. The problem is not, ultimately, one of an illusory absolute rightness, but of the synchronizing of Romanian culture with European evolutions.

THE AUTOCHTHONIST REACTION

A new direction emerges immediately after 1900. It is the reaction of the national spirit. The new nationalist orientation presents itself in a quite different way from the nationalist manifestations of the nineteenth century to which I have so far been referring. They had aspired to align the old civilization and history of the Romanians to Western values, precisely so as to justify and hasten the European integration of Romania. After the turn of the century, Romanian nationalism came to insist more and more forcefully on the individuality, specific culture, and distinct destiny of the Romanians. Nationalism with a European finality gave way to autochthonist nationalism.

These two divergent faces of the national ideology had also co-existed during the nineteenth century, but the aspiration towards modernization and Westernization had been more powerful than the resistance to this process. Only in this way could modern Romania be built. However, important figures in Romanian culture were already expressing a distrust of Western civilization and a fear of invasion by foreign values. Simion Bărnuțiu did not hesitate to identify the enemies of Romanian nationality, who were, in his view "a) the foreigners in our midst, b) the egotistic and materialistic civilization of Europe, c) Romanians educated abroad."[35] Indeed, he considered that the coming of a foreign prince was a danger to Romanian nationality itself. (It is worth quoting here Maiorescu's reply: "Our only fear today is not that we will ever become German, which is impossible, but that the German prince might become too Romanian."[36]) Hasdeu also took a stand against cosmopolitanism.

No one, however, would express this state of mind better than Mihai Eminescu, the great national poet but also the great nationalist columnist and prophet. Eminescu expressed reserve, at the very least, and often overt hostility, where Western values were concerned. He dreamed of a pure Romanian civilization, untouched by foreign influences and still less by the effective presence of foreigners. ("He to whom foreigners are dear / Let the dogs eat his heart [...]."*) His theory of "superposed layers" distinguishes between an authentic, pure Romanian class, which is essentially circumscribed by a rural setting, and the layer of foreign origin, of those who live, ultimately, by exploiting the labor of the peasants.[37] Eminescu's ideas were not totally new; what set them in relief was the systematic spirit and the vehemence of his language. A few decades earlier, Bălcescu had sketched out the village/town opposition, seeing the urban environment as an imported structure. The cliché even appears unexpected but justified to the extent that it serves the critique of the forms without substance of

---

* The quotation is from Eminescu's poem "Doina". *Trans.*

the elite, in Titu Maiorescu's writing: "The only real class in our country is that of the Romanian peasant, and his reality is suffering, under which he sighs as a result of the phantasmagorias of the higher classes."[38]

After 1900 all these rather disparate manifestations came together in an expanding ideological constellation centered on the affirmation of the specificity of Romanian civilization, which was seen mainly, or even exclusively, in terms of the rural store of values. The signs of the new tendency are numerous and diverse. In the last decades of the nineteenth century, public buildings in Bucharest had generally been designed in the Parisian style of the time, first by French architects and later by their Romanian pupils. After 1900, a change of style is evident, with the emergence of the neo-Romanian architecture promoted by Ion Mincu and his school. In 1903 the journal *Sămănătorul* (The sower) appeared. The *"semănătorist"* current that surrounded it, and the parallel current of *poporanism*, the former patriarchal and the latter more social, illustrate this shift towards rural values opposed to Western urban civilization. In his *Romanian Culture and Politicianism* (1904), Constantin Rădulescu-Motru denounces the phenomenon of cultural mimicry, which he sees as leading to the alienation of the Romanian soul from its past. He foresees an exit from the phase of the "negative criticism" of national values and the picking up of the thread of the old traditions once again.

A symbolic event took place on 13 March 1906. A veritable street battle broke out in the square by the National Theatre, as a sign of protest at the staging of plays in French. From this beginning the "struggle for the Romanian language"— as Nicolae Iorga termed it—acquired a more general orientation, becoming directed against the abuse of foreign influence and the cultural alienation of the elite. Iorga was indeed the hero of the moment and the "instigator" of the disturbance. In his lecture on 13 March 1906, the starting point of the events mentioned above, the great historian raised the question of national solidarity. How could the great victories of Stephen the Great be explained? By the fact that "in the sword of the voivode lay the feeling of security that started from the true unity of the whole people. Those who made up that people were not isolated in hostile classes, since an enemy class had not been formed by another cultural ideal and speaking another language." How, on the other hand, could the failure of Michael the Brave be explained? By "the disappearance of social solidarity, the disappearance of the unity of consciousness of the Romanian people", and by "the chasm which opens up between those who take a certain foreign culture for themselves and those who are forbidden any right to culture". This sort of social and cultural division was continuing to deepen. In Iorga's opinion the Romanian elite had become de-nationalized, had "thrown itself into the arms of foreign culture", manifesting "a sentiment of contempt multiplied tenfold, a hundredfold, a thousandfold, towards us" and towards the real country.[39] What was needed, therefore, was a radical change of direction.

It was, in fact, only natural that once the essential elements of the Western model had been adopted the autochthonist spirit would demonstrate its resistance and vigor. There was a line beyond which things could not go. The Romanians could not become French or German. National specificity had to be preserved, respected, and integrated harmoniously with the European model.

This was the direction in which social and cultural evolution was leading. The revolution of the nineteenth century had been the work of a restricted elite, strongly marked by Western values. In each generation, however, the ranks of those who were beginning to have access to culture and to a say in social life were growing. The new movement was fed by layers closer to the base of society. The middle class in particular, which had been almost nonexistent when the process of modernization first got under way, had gradually grown and become consolidated. It was inevitable that autochthonous values would acquire a heightened force. After the First World War the rhythm of these changes intensified. Universal suffrage and the agrarian reform of 1921, which meant the almost complete dismemberment of large properties, brought about a radical change in the rules of the social and political game. Meanwhile, there had been a considerable growth in literacy and in the extent of involvement in the cultural process. Western influence continued to be active, but its impact on a much expanded public opinion could not match its seductive appeal to the restricted elite of former times. In the political sphere, nationalist discourse became much more profitable than the invocation of foreign models. Politics had entered the phase of the "masses". A century before, Tocqueville had warned against the possible turning of democracy into authoritarianism. This is exactly what happened in the interwar period. Almost everywhere in Europe the "democratic" manipulation of the masses was to ensure the triumph of totalitarian and nationalist solutions (generally in combination: totalitarianism and nationalism fed on the same ideal of unity). The Romanian excesses in this direction were in conformity with European evolutions.

The vitality of the nationalist sensibility closely reflected the dynamic of Romanian history itself in the first half of the century. It was stimulated initially by the movement for the liberation of the Romanians who were under foreign rule, and the creation of Greater Romania. However, the attainment of this ideal in 1918 did not exhaust the resources of nationalism. The construction of a national state of all Romanians fed the feeling of identity and of a specific destiny, which was also sustained by the fear of possible attack and of the dangers which threatened the national construction (fears which proved well founded in 1940, when the country was partially dismembered). In addition, there was the minority phenomenon, appreciably amplified by the inclusion, within the enlarged borders of the Romanian state, of a considerable number of people belonging to various ethnic minorities. The more or less conflictual relations of the Romanians with these "others" (Hungarians, Germans, Jews, Ukrainians, etc.) helped to maintain a marked sense of Romanian specificity, which could, in its extreme manifestations, go as far as the utopian ideal of a purified national organism, homogeneous from an ethnic, cultural, and religious point of view.

Such an ideal formula is to be found in the Orthodoxist ideology that developed between the two world wars as a major component of Romanian nationalism. Nichifor Crainic and Nae Ionescu—to mention two influential "leaders of consciousness" of the time—superposed Orthodoxism and Romanianism; the Legionary movement took up this amalgam.

This transfer from the religious to the ideological and political deserves a more detailed commentary. We may note, firstly, that the identification of Romanian culture with Orthodox spirituality marginalizes in a quite unjustified way the Greek Catholic (Uniate) Church, to which about half the Romanians of Transylvania belonged; the paradox is all the more striking as Romanian nationalism had its origins in the activity of the Transylvanian School, an ideological and cultural current which was almost entirely Uniate. Thus, against the evidence of history, a view of Greek Catholicism as "other" took shape. The forced abolition of the Uniate Church in 1948, by communist decree, only carried to a logical conclusion the identification of the national concept with a restrictive religious concept.

A second, and even more serious, paradox concerns the apparent limitation of Orthodoxy to the Romanian space. Orthodox Christianity is characteristic of the whole eastern part of Europe, from Greece to Russia. It is not national, but trans-national, like any other religion. Moreover, for two centuries the Orthodox idea was the principal propaganda argument of Russia in its policy of expansion towards Constantinople and, of course, over the Romanian space.

The fact that a majority of Romanians are Orthodox is beyond any doubt, and nothing is more natural than that they should feel attached to their religion. However, the problem is not one of religion but of the distortion of the meaning of religion by its transfer into ideology. The ideological compartmentalizing of Orthodoxism means a clear delimitation from the Catholic and Protestant West, but since "splendid isolation" is not an option, the inevitable consequence is integration, or reintegration, into the Slav and Orthodox East. This is the situation that the nationalists of the nineteenth century had tried to get beyond, not by giving up their ancestral faith but by adopting the cultural and political models of the non-Orthodox West. The nationalists of the interwar period were, of course, sincere in their approach. They wanted an independent Romania, built on indigenous values. But what were these indigenous values? Could they offer a complete and viable political model? Would peasant tradition and religious morality have been enough? The project was vague and utopian. Its only practical outcome would, I repeat, have been a breaking away from the Western model and a "return" to an Eastern space dominated by a single great power—Russia.

The interwar atmosphere cannot, of course, be reduced to the exclusive attraction of autochthonism. From the "European idea", itself compatible with moderate versions of Romanian nationalism, to nationalist exclusivity, the ideological picture of the period is far from uniform.

A perfect antithesis to cultural isolationism was offered by E. Lovinescu's *History of Modern Romanian Civilization* (1924–1925), a demonstration that the institutions and cultural forms of contemporary Romania were purely Western in origin and adopted by a simple process of imitation. Lovinescu goes further than Maiorescu, justifying the "forms without substance" that the great Junimist had condemned, by seeing in them a natural stage in the process of Westernization, a necessary pattern for the later coalescence of the modern substance of civilization. He was vehemently opposed to the "peasantism" of the time, against which he upheld the urban values that alone could promote modern civilization. Likewise, although coming from a different direction, Ştefan Zeletin argued in *The Romanian Bourgeoisie: Its Origin and Historical Role* (1925) for the inevitability of a Western type of capitalism and the forms of civilization that this brings with it.

Thus the picture appears to be complex, with room for all shades of opinion. However, it is no less true that the national-autochthonist idea continued to affirm itself strongly and the theme of the "Romanian specific" was invoked ever more insistently, with notable extensions into the ideology and political life of the time (for example, the project of a peasant state with an economy based on small rural properties, promoted by the peasantist ideologists Virgil Madgearu and Ion Mihalache). On the eve of the Second World War, traditional rural civilization was the object of a very special interest. This was the time when Dimitrie Gusti's sociological teams were at work, with pioneering results in rural sociology but also with implications on the cultural and national level. The Village Museum, opened in 1935, remains a symbol of this attempt to reintegrate the village and rural traditions into modern Romanian civilization. It was a perfectly futile project; not because it might not, theoretically, have borne fruit, but because, to put it simply and crudely, communism ended it all, striking without discernment at all that represented authentic peasant culture in the Romanian space.

IMPOSSIBLE OBJECTIVITY

It remains for us to trace the connections between historiography and this flourishing nationalist and autochthonous sensibility.

After 1900, Romanian historians generally followed the pathway opened up by the "critical school". The methodological norms of a professional historiography were now well defined and historical research fitted within the European model of the time. But historiographical discourse does not depend only, or even primarily, on method. A method does not in itself produce obligatory answers and interpretations. Very different methods can lead to similar solutions (the rigorous Onciul and the extravagant Hasdeu more than once arrived at similar conclusions), while by using the same set of methodological norms it is possible to reach the most diverse interpretations. A method can help towards a more adequate definition of problems and events, but the logic of history and its meaning—which are ultimately all that really matter—depend more on the historian and less on the method.

In Romanian historiography, the introduction of critical method is, in the first place, the work of Junimea. Succeeding generations inherited the methodological norms but not necessarily the spirit of Junimist interpretation. The full momentum of the negative criticism of Maiorescu and Panu could not be maintained beyond 1900, while even the critical approach initiated by Onciul and Bogdan was to undergo more or less significant modifications. Junimea remains, in the end, an almost unique phenomenon: the most accentuated phase of demythologizing—even if some of its emphases were, of course, incorrect or debatable—that Romanian historiography has ever known. On the other hand, the romantic nationalism of the nineteenth century, free of criticism and control, was no longer current in the interwar period. Nationalism was now expressed in more reasonable and subtle historiographical forms, and with varying intensity from one historian to another and from one phase to another.

In any case, the relation of history to politics remained close. The historian continued to be perceived as a spiritual guide, who, from the experience of the past, had a clearer understanding of the imperatives of the present. Iorga caught this idea in a memorable characterization. "The historian", he said in his reception speech to the Romanian Academy in 1911, "is an old man with the experience of his nation." It is his duty to be "a tireless recaller of national tradition, a witness to the unity of the folk over and above political and class barriers, a preacher of racial solidarity and discoverer of ideals towards which he himself should advance, giving an example to the youth who come after us."[40] We are, it is easy to see, far from the cold Junimist approach. We still find here the typology, which is not only Romanian but Central and Eastern European, of the historian as political figure and history understood as a *decisive* argument in the defense of political rights and the achievement of national aspirations.

Even in the interwar period, when history and politics became clearly separate professions, the list of historians who were political figures, or who were attracted at some time or other to enter politics, is impressive: Iorga, above all, who crowned an important career in national politics by heading the government in 1931–32; Alexandru Lapedatu, Ioan Lupaş and Silviu Dragomir, leading exponents of the Cluj historical school and ministers in various cabinets; Ioan Nistor, professor at the University of Cernăuţi, historian of Bukovina and Bessarabia, with a long ministerial career in Liberal governments; and, in the younger generation, G. I. Brătianu, party leader, C. C. Giurescu, minister and royal resident during the dictatorship of Carol II, and P. P. Panaitescu, whose career alongside the Legionaries came to an abrupt end with their removal from power in January 1941.

The problem, however, is a more subtle one. How far are the national ideology, the convictions, and the political action of each of these historians reflected in their historiographical approach?

With Iorga, the accent falls strongly on the unity of Romanian civilization, the aim of the historian being to present "the nation itself as a living being" and to follow its "inner movement".[41] The idea of a distinct evolution in relation to the surrounding peoples was given a concrete form in his theory of the "popular

Romanias"*, signifying the autonomous organization of the indigenous Romanian population in the face of the barbarian invaders of the first medieval centuries. *Semănătorist* ideology, and a general predilection for national unity over and above class differences, led Iorga—in accordance, in fact, with the older thesis, promoted by Bălcescu, of a free rural society—towards a patriarchal vision of the early and central periods of the Middle Ages; these were "times of a harmonious common life, in which the classes did not regard each other with enmity, in which the country was strong through its unity, from the lowest peasant to the highest, the crowned lord of the peasants".[42] Iorga's "peasant state" suffered a merciless blow when the tomb of Radu I was discovered in the Princely Church at Curtea de Argeş in 1920. The treasure that was brought to light and the refinement of the adornments did not seem characteristic of a peasant, even a crowned one. The historian was forced to modify his theory, proving yet again the dangers of projecting present utopias into the past.

On the other hand, Iorga underlined the role of the Romanians in the southeast of Europe as the inheritors of "Eastern Romanity" and of the historical and political tradition of Byzantium (the latter idea being reflected in his *Byzance après Byzance*, 1935). The civilization specific to the Romanians thus combines with their European mission. Although a nationalist and autochthonist, Iorga was in no way an isolationist. He was a European in his own way, but for him Europe meant a combination of nations, each of which had its own spirit. His attitude to "others" comes across as nuanced and variable. His pointing out of interdependencies and reciprocal influences is a counterbalance to his attraction towards cultural autochthonism. It was the nationalist Iorga who rehabilitated the Phanariots in Romanian historiography. Iorga was a complex and often contradictory historian, who offered each reader what they wanted to take from him. In a simplified version, his nationalism and "peasantism" could become a source for the Legionaries, just like Eminescu's nationalism. It is, of course, necessary to make a distinction between the intellectual approach of the great historian and the primitivism of autochthonist and xenophobic outbursts. But Iorga remained overall a right-wing nationalist, whose social and political ideas (unity and national specificity, social solidarity, monarchical regime, and European mission) can be traced in his historical discourse.

An interesting case for our demonstration is that of Vasile Pârvan. Unlike Iorga, the great archaeologist and historian of antiquity was not a national prophet. He was never tempted, like other historians, by the world of politics. His attitude during the First World War could be considered equivocal, or at any rate lacking in commitment. It is certainly hard to count his name among the great fighters for the unity of the Romanians. Pârvan is considered the founder of the modern Romanian school of archaeology, a rigorous researcher, trained in the

---

* *Romanii populare*: the difference between Iorga's term *Romania* (a space of continuing Romanity) and *România* (Romania in the modern national sense) is quite clear in Romanian, but impossible to convey in English. *Trans.*

spirit of the German school. His great work, *Getica* (1926), brings together a multitude of archaeological and literary sources and passes them through the filter of a minute exegesis. And yet here is the conclusion that he formulates at the end of his research, in perfect keeping with the tone of the national-autochthonist and even Orthodoxist ideology of the time: "The Geto–Dacians were a *people of peasants*: settled, stable, subject, and fearful towards their god, harassed by their neighbors in endless wars and raids, and rendered savage themselves much of the time by the wickedness of these others, and yet happy and good-humored in peacetime, furious and cruel only in war, but usually ruled by good sense, and always turning back to their ancient optimistic faith in gods and men."[43]

I shall return later to this characterization. For the moment let us only note that for Pârvan, Dacia and Romania make up a whole, a trans-historical civilization whose religious, cultural, and moral features are those of the idealized autochthonous peasant synthesis.

The question of politics and nationalism in history was vigorously and even passionately debated in the context of the offensive launched by the "New School" of history, gathered from 1931 around the journal *Revista istorică română* (Romanian Historical Review), against the "Old School", which was reduced basically to Nicolae Iorga and his *Revista istorică*. The young historians, who were scarcely thirty years old, and foremost among them G. I. Brătianu (1898–1953), Petre P. Panaitescu (1900–1967) and Constantin C. Giurescu (1901–1977), called for a return to the methodology, "detached" from politics and passions, of the great Junimists Dimitrie Onciul and Ioan Bogdan. The attack was unleashed by C. C. Giurescu in an extensive review—published in 1931–32 under the title "A New Synthesis of Our Past"—of Iorga's book *The History of the Romanians and their Civilization*. Discovering numerous errors and risky affirmations, the young historian presumed to give the master a lesson in *elementary* methodology: "Any affirmation in a historical study must be based on conclusive evidence, on a document which is beyond discussion. And when documents are not available or are not conclusive, the results of research should be presented as *hypotheses* or *suppositions*, not as truths gained for scholarship."[44]

There followed harsh reviews by Iorga of the first volume of C. C. Giurescu's *History of the Romanians* (in 1935) and of P. P. Panaitescu's monograph *Michael the Brave* (in 1936). The quarrel over Michael the Brave is significant in defining two distinct historical sensibilities. From Iorga's point of view, Panaitescu's interpretation meant bringing the hero down from his pedestal. The accent was shifted from the hero to the dominant social class of the time: the boyars. "Michael the Brave", claimed Panaitescu, "was the arm that struck, the victorious and glorious captain, but behind him and in the shadow of his glory stand the boyars, who gave political directives and made decisions with or without the will of their master. [...] Michael's lordship meant the triumph of the boyars over the other classes, and their social and economic strengthening."[45] Panaitescu even dared to claim that Michael was not the son of Pătrașcu the Good, which for the dynastically minded Iorga amounted to an act of *lèse majesté*.

From methodology there is an inevitable slide towards ideology. The programmatic article of *Revista istorică română* stated the young historians' position plainly: "History should not be shifted onto the level of political and social struggles. It ought to illuminate these, not to be in their service. Only a perfectly objective attitude can guarantee incontestable scholarly results. From the national, as from the individual point of view, the truth can never harm; on the contrary, it is always of real use. Between patriotism and objectivity there is no antinomy."[46]

The Junimist mirage of the objectivity of history and its loosening from political-national issues was taking a new shape. In a series of articles published in 1936, Iorga called the young men a "school of negation" and a "rationalist generation", who were setting themselves against "the national interest". He saw in them the continuation of Junimea, passing over the fact that he himself had gone alongside this current for a time (without, it is true, becoming fully part of it). In C. C. Giurescu's reply, *For the "Old School" of History: An Answer to Mr. N. Iorga* (1937), the great historian is accused of making research into the past an instrument, a weapon of war. According to Giurescu, Iorga is not preoccupied with the truth, only with the result, the political finality of the historical discourse. The comparison of the "New School" to Junimea is not only accepted, but taken up with pride. Their only preoccupation, Giurescu affirms yet again, is "with the *truth*".[47]

But Iorga, too, was seeking the truth. All historians—at least all historians worthy of the name—have been seeking the truth since history began. It is not "truth", a very fluid concept, that is ultimately under discussion, but the differentiated reception of truth, according to the "observation point" of each historian.

The new generation was in a sense less nationalist, less "militantly nationalist", than Iorga. The messianic nationalism of those who had fought by means of history too, indeed largely by means of history, to bring the national ideal into existence, seemed outdated now that Greater Romania had become a reality. And the evolution of historical studies called anyway for a more reserved attitude, more professional and less emotional. However, the differences seem to me to be more of tone than of message. The willed and sometimes even forced detachment of the Junimists from current national mythology did not recover all of its former vigor through the "New School".

Paradoxically, the most virulent critic of Iorga, C. C. Giurescu, was the closest to him in the profoundly national sense of his historical discourse. His tone is intended to be precise and neutral, but an emotional wave runs through it from time to time, as in the memorable and powerfully actualized evocation of Michael the Brave: "Ever more strongly shines the face of Michael the Brave; ever more alive and luminous is the memory of his action. The more documentary information is added, the more we know of the struggle, triumph, and fall of this great captain, this fearless fighter for the Faith and eternal founder of the country of today, the more admiration grows in our souls. Alongside Stephen the Great, Michael the Brave is the embodiment of heroism, the wellspring of power, of belief, and of pride for the Romanian people."[48] The call for "detachment" addressed to Iorga does not seem to be followed by Giurescu, certainly not in this passage, anyway. *The History of the Romanians*, his great work of synthesis, tends to highlight the idea of political solidarity and of the respect due to the state and its leader as the exponent of national interests. The political career of C. C. Giurescu during the period of royal dictatorship can be seen to be closely bound to this principle, which is strongly emphasized in his historical work.

As for the more general significance of Romanian history, here is what the same historian wrote in 1943:

> [...] *we are one of the oldest peoples of Europe and the oldest in the European southeast.* [...] *"We are from here"*, while all our neighbors came later into the lands which they now occupy. [...] *The Dacians or Getae were also an elite people of antiquity*, mentioned with praise right from the beginning by the "father of history", Herodotus. The *Dacian religion* was always a source of admiration for writers of the Greco-Roman world, as were the heroism and contempt for death shown by the Dacians. *Then we are the oldest Christian people in the European southeast.* All our neighbors, absolutely all, were Christianized long after us. We are, finally, the only people in this part of Europe that has managed to have *a political life without interruption*, from the founding of the state to the present day.[49]

It might be pointed out that the Greeks are actually older than the Romanians; that nowadays (though not, it is true, in 1943) the concept of an "elite people" has an uncomfortable sound; that the information and evaluations provided by ancient authors who knew little about the Dacian space have themselves an inclination towards myth and should be judged in relation not to our patriotism but to their ideology; that, given the paucity of sources, the Dacian religion and the Christianization of the Daco-Romans remain matters on which no definitive answers are possible; and finally, that the continuity of the Romanian states does not change the fact that they were in a subordinate position, nor that they were the last to be founded in this part of Europe (Hungary, Poland, and even Bulgaria were "great powers" in the region at a time when the Romanian principalities did not yet exist). The infusion of patriotism is unmistakable and is further amplified by the moment of publication, in the crisis years of the Second World War. For Giurescu, the purpose of history was to confirm the "sentiment of *national pride* and *absolute faith* in the future of our people and our state".

G. I. Brătianu, too, who is in many ways the closest to Iorga among the group of young historians, does not hesitate to place history in direct relation to the political conjuncture. As both a historian and a politician, the inheritor of the Brătianu tradition, he also saw how to look after Romanian interests through history. The national sense of his historical discourse became accentuated on the eve of, and during, the Second World War, as Romania passed through critical moments. He produced a firm rebuttal of immigrationist theories, denouncing the anti-Romanian aims of "neighboring" historians (*Une énigme et un miracle historique: Le peuple roumain*, 1937), and in 1943, as a response to the breaking up of Greater Romania, he published *Origines et formation de l'unité roumaine*, in which he presented the road of the Romanians towards unity, presupposing the existence, even before national consciousness took shape, of an *instinct* of unity.

Beyond doubt, P. P. Panaitescu was closer to the Junimist sense of criticism and reconstruction. He was, in fact, the only member of the "New School" who systematically placed a question mark over major elements of Romanian historical mythology. His conception and method, which gave a privileged role to material, social, and cultural structures, were essentially opposed to a heroic and personalized history. The demythologizing of Michael the Brave fitted naturally into this project. "Why did the Turks not Conquer the Romanian Lands?" is an article published in 1944, in which he challenges the heroic edifice of medieval Romanian history. It was not the struggles of the Romanians with the Turks—a dominant theme in national historiography—which saved the existence of the principalities, but their position away from the central line of Turkish advance into Europe, coupled with the greater advantages, for the Ottoman Empire, of indirect exploitation rather than effective annexation. Like Ioan Bogdan before him, Panaitescu gives the Slavs an important place in medieval Romanian history, going so far as to consider the indigenous boyar class to be of Slav origin. On the issue of continuity he adopts the thesis of Onciul, taking a reserved attitude towards the idea of a continuity over the whole Romanian territory.[50]

And yet this historian, whose discourse, in specialist works and even in school textbooks, is anything but nationalist, attached himself for a time to the Legionary movement, the extreme expression of Romanian nationalism and autochthonism. Regardless of the personal calculations that can be suspected, and the mysteries of the human soul, Panaitescu's Legionary episode shows us the "virtues" of double-talk in all their splendor. The newspaper *Cuvîntul* (The Word), which was under the direction of the short-time rector of the University of Bucharest in the autumn of 1940 and early 1941, abounds in historical-mythological constructions in the most autochthonist spirit imaginable. Here is a representative passage: "We are Dacians! In our physical being, in the being of our souls, we feel ourselves to be the descendants of that great and ancient people who were settled in the Carpathian mountains centuries before Trajan. We have no beginning, we have always been here. [...] We are not only the sons of the earth; we form part of a great race, a race which is perpetuated in us, the Dacian race. The Legionary movement, which has awakened the deepest echoes of our national being, has also raised 'Dacian blood' to a place of honor [...]." And here is another, which highlights the same type of historical continuity as a justification of the Legionary phenomenon: "Like Stephen of Moldavia, whose name is awakened by the great horn sounding on the hills of the Siret; like the Voivode Michael, for whom the bells of the monastery on Tîrgoviște Hill weep; like Horea, for whom the great oak tree still grows in the Apuseni mountains, they [the Legionary heroes] are the great protectors of the whole folk, over whom they keep watch from another world."[51] The author of these emotional evocations is P. P. Panaitescu, otherwise the great demolisher of myths—when he was not writing for *Cuvîntul!*

I can only repeat what every page of this book illustrates: History can keep itself free of a particular ideology but it cannot keep itself free from ideologies in general, and often it cannot escape the more concrete and more direct demands of the political moment either.

COMMUNIST DISCOURSE: THE ANTI-NATIONAL PHASE

As it was constructed in the course of the nineteenth century and in the first decades after 1900, Romanian historical ideology was organized around national values and the relations between national culture and the (West) European model. The controversy which is so characteristic of Romanian society in the first half of the twentieth century was about what exactly the appropriate balance was, in the modern synthesis of civilization, between these two cultural sources: indigenous tradition and Western values. For a time, communism put a stop to these prolonged debates with a decision apparently beyond appeal: neither the West nor tradition.

The model now invoked and applied was a completely new one: that of Soviet communism, which Romania adopted in an even more servile and complete way than other countries of Central and Southeast Europe. The change was all the more brutal as the revolutionary Marxist Left had occupied a quite peripheral area of the Romanian ideological spectrum. The Communist Party, which was largely made up of non-Romanian ethnic elements and acted on the orders of Moscow, had generally been perceived by public opinion in the interwar period as hostile to national interests. Even the Social Democratic Party had played little more than a symbolic role in the political life of the country. The political sensibility of the Romanians was more inclined to the Right; even some "leftist" tendencies (Poporanism, the peasantist ideology) breathed a pre-capitalist rural air, expressing the ideal of a society of small producers, not the mythology of a post-capitalist future forged by the working class. In other words, even the majority of the Left were guided by ideas that may be considered somewhat "rightist", or at least to correspond to a certain traditionalism with roots in "peasant democracy".

In this context, the material, social, and mental restructuring imposed by communism appears all the more radical. The mechanisms of Romanian society were smashed to pieces and replaced by completely new structures and mechanisms. The elite was pulverized and its members perished in prison, resigned themselves to exile, or ended up blending into the new social mixture and disappearing. The peasantry, which up to 1944 had been considered the fundamental class of Romanian society and the depositary of the national spirit and traditions, was dismembered by collectivization. Massive industrialization filled the urban space with an uprooted and easily maneuvered mass. The center was shifted effectively, but above all symbolically, from the village to the town. The workers became the most representative class, the so-called leading class—in fact the ideological alibi of the Party aristocracy, which, by a process of "spontaneous generation", formed the new elite of the country. The thread of tradition was broken. A new history began, not only different but totally opposed to the old; a new culture, too, had to be born—a Romanian version of Soviet culture.

After the short transition of the years 1944 to 1947, which still allowed some manifestations of the "old" historiography, the "new" Marxist, or basically Stalinist, history took over the whole field. Some professional historians aligned themselves with the new imperatives, but the great university professors, with a few exceptions, were reduced to silence, thrown out of their posts, and in many cases imprisoned; some, like G. I. Brătianu, were to die in prison. Their places were frequently taken by improvised "historians", among whom should be mentioned the conductor of the new historiography and little dictator of the history of the late 1940s and early 1950s, Mihail Roller.

The earthquake in historiography was no less powerful than that which shook all the structures of society. There was no Marxist tradition in Romanian historiography. The few contributions which can be considered Marxist were occasional and insignificant. Those that are most worth mentioning are Constantin Dobrogeanu-Gherea's *Neo-serfdom* (1910); the flagrantly mediocre works of Petre Constantinescu-Iaşi, the only Marxist historian in a university post (but completely marginal in the field, as professor in the Faculty of Theology in Chişinău); and the similarly modest contributions of Lucreţiu Patraşcanu. Without intending to be paradoxical, it could be said that the interpretations of the "Legionary" P. P. Panaitescu, with the centrality that he accords to economic and social structures, were in a sense closer to a Marxist spirit than the undistinguished writings of the declared Marxists.

In the space of only a few years the reference points of Romanian history were turned upside down.[52] The guiding thread had been the national idea. What emerged in its place was the internationalist spirit, which meant, in fact, an attempt to wipe out all that was nationally Romanian. *The History of the R.P.R.*, published in numerous editions under the direction of M. Roller—from 1947, when it was still called *The History of Romania*, to 1956—illustrates in its very title the direction of this new reconstruction of the past. Romania had become the "R.P.R."*, an anonymous set of initials after the model of the Soviet republics. Any reference to the national significance of the history of the previous century was done away with or turned upside down. Here, for example, is the interpretation of the union of 1859: "The ruling classes managed to ensure that the union would be carried out primarily from above by an understanding between the bourgeoisie and the boyars; those who benefited from it were bourgeois elements and the commercial boyars, and not the broad masses of the

---

* *Republica Populară Romînă* (Romanian People's Republic). *Trans.*

people."[53] In other words, it was an act of class politics, not a national act. All the same, the 1859 moment enjoyed a certain weighting in the economy of the book. The reader will be unable, on the other hand, to find a chapter or subchapter referring to the creation of Greater Romania in 1918. The union of Bessarabia with Romania appears under the title "Imperialist Intervention against the Socialist Revolution in Russia", and deals, of course, with the *occupation* of the province in question; as for Transylvania and the symbolic date 1 December 1918, we find them in a subchapter called "Intervention against the Revolution in Hungary".[54] Far from being a natural result of history and an incontestable right of the Romanian people, national unity is inscribed within an expansion of imperialist type.

The place of national solidarity, so much invoked in pre-communist historiography, was taken by its contrary, *class struggle*, which was considered the motor force of historical evolution. From antiquity to the overturning of the "bourgeois-landlord" regime, history is punctuated by social conflicts of all kinds. In some cases these are quite simply invented (the rebellions and other protest movements in Roman Dacia, for example); more often, they are taken out of context and amplified, whether in the case of peasant rebellions in the Middle Ages or of more recent workers' movements. History took its shape around the great "class battles", and the heroes of these replaced or devalued the great traditional figures, who were guilty, in general, of belonging to the "exploiting classes".

A major branch of pre-communist historiography was concerned with relations between the Romanians and the West. Here, too, the shift was radical: the "Latin island in a Slav sea" was obliged to go back to where it came from. Period after period in "Roller history" was marked by connections between Romanians and Slavs, from the cohabitation of the two ethnic groups and cultures in the first centuries of the Middle Ages down to the "liberation of Romania by the glorious Soviet army" on 23 August 1944. The result is a powerful anchoring in the Slav world, the political significance of which is too evident to need comment. At the same time, no occasion is missed to strike at all that is meant by the West and Western values.

The role of the church in national history was also diminished and distorted. In promoting atheism in a brutal form, again closer to the pure Soviet model than the relative compromise that was attempted in Central Europe, the communist regime in Romania proceeded to secularize official history with a flagrant disregard for the real importance of religion and the church in the history of the Romanians, especially in the Middle Ages but also in the modern period. Militant atheism remained to the end a characteristic mark of Romanian communism, although this did not prevent certain maneuvers to attract the clergy, particularly the Orthodox clergy. The Uniate Church, which was no less Romanian than the Orthodox, was dissolved in 1948 and its bishops and priests imprisoned. Its relations with Rome, and so with the West, could not be tolerated. The regime succeeded in striking a double blow, cutting spiritual connections with the West while offering a present, albeit not without strings attached, to the Orthodox Church. It is in this context, in the years 1950 to 1955, that the first Romanian saints were canonized. There was a certain small satisfaction in this for the Orthodox Church, which, however, adopted in its turn new criteria in assessing the merits of the persons sanctified. Stephen the Great's time had not yet come. The new saints combined religious merits with well-defined sociopolitical orientations. Among them were Sava Brancovici, the metropolitan of Transylvania, appreciated for his relations with Russia, and the monk Sofronie of Cioara, who led an anti-Uniate movement around 1760.[55] All this, however, went on in an undertone, never transgressing the limits of what was strictly ecclesiastical or affecting the promotion of atheism, through history as by other means.

COMMUNIST DISCOURSE: RECOVERING THE PAST

Towards the end of the 1950s the national factors in Romanian history gradually returned to center stage, and the process was accentuated in the first part of the following decade in parallel with a diminishing of the Slav, Russian, and Soviet element. It was a slow but steady evolution, culminating in April 1964 in the famous *Declaration* of the "independence" of the Romanian Workers' Party. Romanian communism had abandoned "internationalism", which was in fact a disguise for anti-nationalism, and had opted for nationalism. It was, at least as far as discourse was concerned, a 180-degree turn.

All sorts of interpretations have been proposed to explain this remarkable shift. It must be said at the start that the phenomenon is not essentially a typically Romanian one but characteristic of the evolution of communism in general. Communism everywhere displayed the tendency to slip from "internationalism" to nationalism, in forms that were sometimes extreme and at other times relatively discreet.[56] The champion in all categories must be Russia under Stalin, which, under the misleading label of the U.S.S.R., promoted Russian nationalism in the most aggressive and aberrant forms. China monopolized communism in its turn, giving it a specifically national coloring. Romania, Albania, and North Korea belong in the same company. But nor did countries like Hungary and Bulgaria hesitate to re-adapt their history to fit a nationalist discourse. The case of the G.D.R., the so-called Democratic Germany, is quite characteristic. As an invented country, a relatively prosperous colony of the Soviet Union, the eastern part of German territory guarded itself for a long time against any manifestation of national spirit. However, towards the end, incapable of imagining any other valid argument for its own existence, it had to fall back on the same historical–nationalist rhetoric. Frederick the Great, king of Prussia, previously denounced as the father of Prussian militarism and the adversary of Russia, was rehabilitated, becoming one of the founding fathers of the G.D.R.

The phenomenon is thus general and can be explained, on the whole, by the isolationist character of utopias (regardless of what they proclaim) and by the incapacity of communism to offer people anything more than an, at best, mediocre existence. There had to be something to compensate for the long series of shortages and frustrations. The "radiant future" no longer worked, but the past could still work. The nationalist discourse was the simplest, most frequent, and often most efficient diversion in the face of the accumulation of real difficulties. The slide towards this type of discourse was also necessary in order to legitimize power. In countries where it had been imposed by an occupying force, communism could not carry on the internationalist argument for ever; for the effective validation of the system indigenous values could not be ignored.

Seen against this general background, Romania, it is true, went further than others. It is probable that the traditional force of the nationalist discourse, covered over by the anti-nationalism of the 1950s but not annihilated, counted here. The feeling of Romanian individuality, that syndrome of the "Latin island in a Slav sea", may also have counted. Nor should it be forgotten that the Communist Party, initially a handful of people, most of whom had nothing to do with Romanian culture, had become a mass party and so had gradually been "Romanianized", just as its leadership had been Romanianized with time. (In 1964, four out of nine members of the Political Bureau were still of "non-Romanian" origin.) Not only were the new leaders Romanians, they came largely from a rural background, like Ceauşescu himself, and so were, by virtue of their very origins, more inclined towards autochthonism and isolationism. Even the old intelligentsia, to the extent that it was recuperated, brought with it a wave of nationalism, additionally motivated and amplified in reaction to the anti-nationalist terror of the 1950s. The controversies which followed with the Soviet Union and other neighbors served only to accentuate this nationalist coloring, while the final crisis of the regime after 1980 quite simply exacerbated it; the nationalist discourse offered the only way of escape from reality.

The passage from one system of values to another and the modification of power relations within the ruling elite produced a certain relaxation of the communist regime; the phase of relative calming of tensions can be situated broadly between the years 1964 and 1971. The regime began to treat its own citizens better (the political amnesty of 1964 being symbolic in this respect), and to renew relations with the West (symbolic also being the visit by the prime minister, Ion Gheorghe Maurer, to France in the same year). National values began to be rehabilitated and reintegrated in Romanian culture, while nationalist excess was not yet the order of the day. Historians were able to benefit from the same openness, which allowed them the luxury of introducing a degree of nuance and even, up to a point, diversification into their interpretations. It is significant that towards the end of this period no less than three syntheses of national history appeared, which, while not radically different, nevertheless presented certain differences of interpretation (*The History of Romania*, edited by Miron Constantinescu, Constantin Daicoviciu, and Ştefan Pascu, 1969; *The History of the*

Romanian People, edited by Andrei Oțetea, 1970; and *The History of the Romanians from the Earliest Times to the Present Day*, by Constantin C. Giurescu and Dinu C. Giurescu, 1971: it is worth noting that C. C. Giurescu was brought back to the university in 1963 and was to remain, until his death in 1977, one of the leading representatives of a historiography free of any anti-national coloring).

Some Romanian historians began to be able to travel beyond the borders of Romania, and Romanian participation in international gatherings increased, involving more and more individuals. Foreign historians came to Romania, too, and it was easier for Western historiographical productions to penetrate. Given their traditional cultural affinities, Romanian historians were especially close to the *"Annales* school", the French "new history", which could indeed, with prudent treatment, be reconciled more easily with Marxism than any other current. (This was due to the importance that it gave to structures and mass phenomena in general. This sort of history could, however, also illustrate a resistance to the political, event-based, and nationalist re-elaboration of the past that was beginning to be seen.)

Although some have not hesitated to speak of a "liberalization", it was in fact far from being any such thing. There was liberalization, it is true, in comparison to the 1950s, to the extent that former political detainees had more liberty outside prison, under more or less discreet surveillance, than within its walls. The chain had been loosened by a few links, just enough for some no longer to notice it, or to want no longer to notice it, but it had not been broken. The "liberty" of Romanian society between 1964 and 1971 was limited and controlled. The Romanians, as most political scientists recognize, did not experience a true process of de-Stalinization. The Party and the Securitate kept the process under control the whole time, and when the degree of "liberty" granted began to seem disturbing, they had no difficulty in turning the process back again.

One observation is necessary with reference not only to the sub-period under discussion but also to later history, concerning the reconsideration of Romanian historical and cultural traditions. Year by year, and name by name, the communist regime integrated into its value system a substantial part, indeed the greater part, of the national inheritance. All the great historians were recuperated in the end, Iorga in the first years of the "new wave", and G. I. Brătianu, whom the communists could not so easily forgive for his death in the prison at Sighet, closer to the end. Many of their works were republished. Between killing a man, physically or morally, and publishing his books, there is undoubtedly a difference. But the recuperation was at the price of sacrificing the spirit of Romanian culture, which was profoundly incompatible with communism and yet was now obliged to fit into its schemas. Writers, scholars, and politicians, who not only had had nothing to do with communism but had utterly detested it and in some cases been among its victims, were posthumously obliged to uphold the communist project. In taking possession of the "cultural heritage", communism sought to legitimize itself even at a price, that price being the distortion of the authentic repository of national culture.

Let me illustrate this by two examples.

E. Lovinescu's *History of Modern Romanian Civilization* was republished in 1972. It was the recuperation of one of the most original ideological constructions of the interwar period, but editing was turned into "critical takeover". Whatever was inconvenient was taken out of the text (respecting, it is true, the convention of suspension marks). Among the passages removed were some in which the essential message of the work is made explicit: the refusal of totalitarianism, whether communist or fascist, and belief in the triumph of democracy on Western lines. In addition, the introductory study is careful to underline that Lovinescu did not set out "to elaborate a work of anti-Marxist polemic" and that he even had points in common with historical materialism.[57] This is just too much! Even if Lovinescu's work was not intended as an anti-Marxist polemic (and why should it have been?), it is fundamentally *anti-Marxist*: the text is the most profoundly different from Marxism and the most clearly anti-communist (from a democratic perspective) in our culture. That is what should have been said, but of course it could not be said. The choice facing the editor was a simple one: to publish the book in "adapted" form, or not to publish it at all. I make no comment on the solution; I merely note it.

Nicolae Iorga is another interesting example. He was, as we have seen, a right-wing nationalist, opposed in every fiber of his being to the communist model. The fact that he fell victim to the Legionaries "threw" him into the "anti-fascist" camp (even though the historian had shown sympathy towards Italian fascism and other similar political experiments). There is, of course, nothing about the stands he took against communism in the texts devoted to him in the communist period. Anyone leafing through school textbooks, for example, will immediately notice the amalgam: Iorga and other "bourgeois" but "anti-fascist" politicians are mixed in with all sorts of names out of the working-class pantheon.

Here are a few sentences which deserve to be reproduced from the school textbook on the "contemporary history of Romania". "In order to achieve a broad front of anti-fascist forces, the Romanian Communist Party gave great attention to the use of progressive, democratic intellectuals. Alongside a series of intellectuals who were communists or sympathizers with the Communist Party [...] a series of leading politicians and intellectuals of other political orientations were also engaged in this action, such as: Nicolae Titulescu, Nicolae Iorga, Grigore Iunian, Virgil Madgearu, Dem. Dobrescu, Petre Andrei, Grigore Filipescu, Mitiţă Constantinescu, Traian Bratu, etc. All that the detachment of patriotic intellectuals in Romania had that was most valuable, in these years, was strongly enrolled in the democratic, anti-fascist movement."[58] Pupils were to remain with the impression that Iorga, Titulescu, and the rest, "enrolled" in a "patriotic detachment", were basically following a policy set by the Communist Party! Having become a sort of "anti-fascist fighter", Iorga joined the ranks of those who contributed, evidently without so wishing, to the legitimizing of the communist regime, in whose prisons the Legionaries had not given him the chance to die.

Communist Discourse: The Exacerbation of Nationalism

The year 1971 saw the unleashing of the Romanian "cultural revolution". "Liberalization" and "openness" were put an end to once and for all. Year by year, until its fall in December 1989, the Ceauşescu regime would accentuate the totalitarian pressure, at the same time isolating Romania from the rest of the world (a relatively slow process in the first decade, then in continuous acceleration after 1980).

Nationalism became the decisive historical and political argument. United throughout their whole history, united around the single party and the Leader, the Romanians were infused with the vocation of *unity*, in other words, the subordination of the individual in the face of the national organism and, at the same time, a strict delimitation of their own nation in relation to others. As a political instrument of legitimization and domination, nationalism gained advantage from the amalgamation of the authentic nationalist tradition and the specific aims pursued by the communist dictatorship. It seemed like a recuperation, when in the first instance it was actually a *manipulation*.

Such a re-elaboration of history presupposes an attenuation of the mechanism of class struggle. However, the two divergent interpretations—the nationalist interpretation and the social conflict interpretation—continued to coexist, taking advantage of the capacity of communist dialectic cheerfully to harmonize contradictions of any sort. The Romanians needed a history of great achievements, and they had one.

The evolution in interpretations of the interwar years is characteristic. Initially, every evil imaginable was attributed to this period—logically enough, since it was in the bankruptcy of the bourgeoisie that the origins and justifications of proletarian revolution were to be found. In the new phase, the interwar years were appreciably improved. The merits (relative, it should be understood) of bourgeois democracy; the importance (for all its limits) of the agrarian reform; the increase in production, especially industrial production; the successes of Romanian foreign policy; and the remarkable level of scientific and cultural creation were all highlighted. Another motive for pride was the Romanian resistance to fascism. Romania had succeeded for a long time in preserving its democratic system, while in most European states dictatorships of fascist type were being set up. References to the extent of foreign capital, the exploitation of the workers, and the difficulties of the peasants had the role of diminishing the positive aspects, but the overall picture tended to become more and more favorable. (In some interpretations it might be noticed that the dictatorship of Carol II became an "authoritarian regime", in contrast to the dictatorships in other European countries, and the Antonescu government was sweetened by a blurring, or even elimination, of its fascist characteristics.) How could this ever more favorable perspective on the interwar period be squared with the imperative necessity brutally to overthrow its system? How could an appreciation, albeit with reservations, of the democratic regime be squared with the installation of its perfect antithesis—communist totalitarianism? Of course they could not be, but the logic of double-talk is at the very heart of communist ideology.

Everything grew to the same rhythm: the virtues of interwar Romania on the one hand, and the virtues of overthrowing the interwar system on the other. The king's coup d'état on 23 August 1944, which had subsequently become "the liberation of the country by the glorious Soviet army", passed through the variant "armed anti-fascist insurrection" to be apotheosized finally as "revolution of national and social liberation, anti-fascist and anti-imperialist", carried out, of course, under the leadership of the Communist Party. From a military point of view, the "two hundred days earlier" theory places Romania among the principal victors of the Second World War, which the intervention of the Romanian army is said to have shortened by at least six months.

It is interesting that, in parallel with these remarkable re-elaborations, there took place a "semi-rehabilitation" of the Antonescu regime, the overthrow of which was nevertheless the starting point of the mythologizing of the communist revolution. The 1950s, the "heroic" phase of the revolution, even attracted "severe" looks, with the highlighting of certain exaggerations and abuses, but without, of course, touching the foundations of the communist system itself. The "obsessive decade" permitted Ceauşescu to draw the line between himself and state terrorism and pro-Sovietism, in the name of a "communism of humanity" (an expression apparently inspired by the "socialism with a human face" of the "Prague Spring", which unfortunately corresponded little to the Romanian case), while the gentler treatment of Antonescu was in line with the nationalist discourse and detachment, at least formally, from the Soviet Union.[59]

The Ceauşescu era was, however, characterized by a notable shift from the contemporary towards origins. That was where legitimacy and unity had to be sought above all. The ridiculous attained dizzying heights when the "Institute of History of the Party", which specialized in monographs on labor struggles and heroes of the working class, turned its attention towards antiquity and devoted itself especially to the issue of Dacian origins. Ancient history became even more politicized than contemporary history. The great event took place in 1980, when everything available was put together to confection the 2050th (?) anniversary of the founding of the "unitary and centralized" Dacian state under Burebista. Burebista offered Ceauşescu the supreme legitimization, as the ancient king's state prefigured in many ways (unitary, centralized, authoritarian, respected by the "others", etc.) his own Romania, as the dictator liked to imagine it. Verses like this resounded in the great stadium:

> The land had sworn him fealty, and would follow him in all things
> Fifteen years had passed since first at its head he stood
> His face, his name and destiny for ever are encrusted
> In the eternity of the land, and of the lion's brood.

It was not, in fact, Burebista that was magnified, but his successor centuries later. All the more so as there appeared a feminine double, who could not be identified in ancient Dacia.

> Beside him, in the country's profoundest admiration
> Stands the comrade of his life, and of his vibrant ideal:
> 'Tis Elena Ceauşescu, noble soul of a Romanian
> Good mother, politician and scholar of renown.[60]

One commemoration followed another, all organized according to the same pattern. Regardless of who or what was being commemorated, they would start with origins, underline *continuity* and *unity*, and end with the present, the Ceauşescu era. Everything announced the supreme fulfillment of Romanian history, the dictator finding himself again in his forerunners. This is why, in 1986, when the commemoration of Mircea the Old generated a veritable psychosis, the prince was required to give up being "old" and become, or become again, "the Great" (any deviation from this epithet being considered a serious political error). History was thus abolished; the same Romanian history, always the same as itself, was perpetuated throughout the millennia.

No less interesting from the point of view of the national-communist actualization of history was the question of the *capitulations*. These treaties, allegedly concluded by the Romanian lands with the Ottoman Empire, were cited towards the end of the eighteenth century and in the nineteenth century as legal arguments for autonomy and in support of the revival of rights that had not been respected by the suzerain power. Applying the demystifying principles of the "critical school", Constantin Giurescu demonstrated in 1908 (in *The Capitulations of Moldavia with the Ottoman Porte*) that the texts in question had been no more than patriotic forgeries. Not that this deterred Nicolae Copoiu, a prominent member of the Institute of History of the Party, from republishing the documents as if they had been authentic. Suddenly the capitulations became a matter of political dogma. They "proved" that the Romanian lands had treated with the Ottoman Porte *as equals*, just like Ceauşescu with Moscow and Washington. Anyone with the slightest idea of medieval history knows that relations then were fundamentally hierarchical and far from our current principles of "equality", real or formal. Our historians can look as much as they like in the Turkish archives for Romanian–Ottoman bilateral treaties. At best they will find unilateral "privileges" granted by the sultans to princes much lower than themselves in the hierarchy of the time.[61] But Ceauşescu and his people could not allow his predecessors to make even the slightest abdication of dignity and national sovereignty.

The nationalism of the Ceauşescu era also manifested itself in a specific manner in the curious, but not entirely unprecedented, form of *protochronism*.[62] What was probably the most virulent strain of the disease had broken out in Stalin's Russia in the middle of the nationalist phase of the 1940s and 1950s. The conclusion then had been that almost every valuable achievement in human culture science, and technology had been the work of Russian minds. Anyone who proclaimed that Marconi rather than Popov was the inventor of radio risked years of imprisonment (not just in Russia, but in Romania too). The Romanian protochronist model followed the same line, not in imitation but as the product of a similar logic. (In a way it can be seen as a re-actualization, but in a highly amplified manner marked by autochthonism, of similar patriotic attempts in the nineteenth century.)

The concept was launched in 1974 by Edgar Papu, an intellectual trained in the interwar period, who had spent several years in a communist prison. It was yet another illustration of the attraction held out to certain exponents of Romanian culture, who were allured by the rehabilitation, and even exacerbation, of national values. Of course Papu, whose proposal was limited to a number of cultural "firsts", had no way of foreseeing the huge expansion of his "discovery". Once the affirmation of Romanian values had become confused with patriotism, there followed a veritable competition among "patriots", each hoping his discourse about the past would improve his present position in the cultural and political hierarchy.

As there was no longer a Titu Maiorescu to mock at overheated minds, the revolution of Horea posed once again as precursor of the French Revolution. As an anteriority of five years did not mean very much, the Bobîlna uprising, too, was metamorphosed into a revolution towards the end of Ceauşescu's rule, by the authority of the dictator himself. Ceauşescu never explained his profound thinking, so it remained for historians to take the idea further and show how the Transylvanian peasants had had a revolution in 1437, three and a half centuries before the French. By a similar logic it was possible to conclude that the Romanians had also invented the modern nation and the national state, a fact demonstrated by the union under Michael, and even by the multiple manifestations of Romanian unity before 1600, at a time when no one else in Europe was thinking of cutting borders according to ethnic criteria.

Turning to cultural achievements, it was just as easy to demonstrate the superiority of the *Teachings* of Neagoe Basarab to Machiavelli's *Prince*, in a fascinating text, Paul Anghel underlines the universal, almost cosmic, sense of the Romanian ruler's work, in comparison with which the Florentine secretary's effort seems much less inspired: "The *Teachings* are a book of initiation. Their equivalent cannot even be found in Byzantium"[63]—perhaps only in ancient India. In his turn, the sociologist Ilie Bădescu took it upon himself to demonstrate how Eminescu revolutionized world *sociology*. Meanwhile, Ion Creangă, in the interpretation of Dan Zamfirescu, became the equal of Homer, Shakespeare, and Goethe—or even their superior—as the creator of Ivan Turbincă, a hero "more contemporary than Hamlet, Faust, Don Quixote, and Alyosha Karamazov" and quite simply "the character who dominates world history in our century".[64]

From 1971 to 1989, the general tendency was a gradual accentuation of isolationism and cultural megalomania. But this tendency, in which orders issued from above joined hands with personal initiatives (including some of the craziest protochronist discoveries), does not in any way account for the entire Romanian cultural and historiographical spectrum. Especially among writers and critics there was a notable opposition towards aggressive autochthonism and the protochronist phenomenon, nor did historians recite a uniform litany. On the contrary, divergent points of view never ceased to multiply, broadly separating those who were determined to maintain a certain professional standard from those ready to apply promptly (often adding something of their own) any orientation dictated by political considerations.

The limiting of freedom of expression could not do away with the real diversity of points of view and sensibilities. These were expressed within the space that remained free, however small it might be, where they found indirect or disguised ways to manifest themselves, focussing on details of little apparent relevance but which could come to symbolize real divergences. Given the limited space available these contradictions could become remarkably concentrated. Katherine Verdery has given a very suggestive definition of the different orientations in Romanian historiography, starting from the name used for the Horea episode: *uprising* or *revolution*. Party historians, military historians, and autochthonists opted for the latter formula, which was considered to give enhanced value to the national past.[65]

The "Party line" was followed especially closely by historians in positions closer to the center of power and to the condition of activist. This was, in the first place (though not, of course, exclusively), the case of the Institute of History of the Party and the Center for Military History. The latter, which was patronized by Ilie Ceauşescu, brother of the dictator general, and "historian", gained appreciably in influence after 1980. A tendency to "militarize" history took shape (both in the interpretation of the past and in the organization of research, the publication of results, and participation in international gatherings). It is significant that the only major synthesis of history published in the time of Ceauşescu was the *Military History of the Romanian People* (six volumes, 1984–1989), which came to be a "substitute" for the ever-postponed synthesis of national history.

More reticence in the adoption of official slogans and the excesses which accompanied them was shown by university historians and researchers in the "civilian" institutes (though here, too, there were marked differences from one individual to the next and between different fields, the worst affected being contemporary history). It is certain that the result was not the often invoked "historical front" so much as a disordered and inefficient historiographical movement. For this reason the great planned historiographical synthesis of the Ceauşescu era, a ten-volume treatise on the history of Romania launched as a project in 1975, never reached the printers. The previous synthesis, also conceived in ten volumes, had come to grief after the appearance of volume IV in 1964 (it had got up to 1878). This time things got so complicated that not even one volume could appear. In the first case the stumbling block had been the last hundred years of history. Now the project got bogged down in the first millennium. The pure, hard Dacianism of the Party and military historians came up against the more balanced position of the university historians and professional archaeologists.

All these divergences, compressed into a limited problematic and dampened by the totalitarian atmosphere, gave a foretaste of the much clearer divisions that have emerged since 1989 in matters of professional competence, political orientation, and interpretative inclination alike (including the famous Romanian dilemma of the relation between autochthonism and Europeanism).

The dominant, even in a sense the sole, discourse in the time of Ceauşescu was that of nationalism. I say "sole" because it could be sidestepped but not counteracted, fought with explicit arguments or matched by another coherent discourse. And if historians sometimes managed to find safety in less exposed areas or by making use of professional subtlety, the population as a whole was subjected—through the current propaganda channels—to a virulent nationalist demagogy.

Not enough emphasis has been placed on the role played by this type of historical discourse, obsessively repeated, in the consolidation and prolonging of the Ceauşescu dictatorship, in as much as the communist-nationalist image of history corresponded to a traditional mental pattern (Daco–Roman origins, continuity, struggle for independence, the role of the Romanians in defending Europe, the victimization of the Romanians at the hands of the "others", etc.) and seemed to offer the most appropriate reaction to the anti-nationalism of the preceding period and the imperialism of Moscow. The adoption and amplification of a nineteenth-century national mythology, even in a distorted manner, bestowed credibility and legitimacy on the regime and an aura of patriotism on the dictator—at least until the Romanians began to suffer from hunger and cold. The glorious shades of the past could not prevent economic disaster and the explosion of social tensions. But the historical mythology accumulated in the Ceauşescu era has outlived the dictator himself. Mental constellations have a longer life than material structures. Thanks to the communist regime, a historical mentality which has been long outdated in Western Europe continues to affect Romanian culture and society to the full.

CHAPTER TWO
Origins

Having surveyed the stages through which Romanian historical ideology has passed, I now propose to analyze one by one its fundamental components, the great mythological configurations around which the national consciousness has crystallized and evolved.

It is natural to start with beginnings, not just out of respect for chronological criteria but above all because of the exceptional significance of *foundation myths*. Each community, from the tribe to the modern nation, legitimizes itself in terms of its origins. In all times and all cultures these have been invested with great value and have been continually remembered and commemorated. Nothing is more contemporary, more ideologized, than a beginning. Foundation myths are a condensation of the community's own consciousness of itself.

Origins are not self-evident, not objective facts. We can invoke the founding of Rome or the Cucuteni culture; the Getae of Herodotus or the emperor Trajan; the first flint tools or the "dismounting" of Negru Vodă, Burebista or Cuza. In each case there is a choice to be made, and it is made not according to any objective scientific standard but on the basis of the ideological resources and present projects of the community. It is worth noting that foundation myths tend to multiply like links in a chain; the *first* foundation must be ceaselessly renewed and consolidated, giving birth to more and more new founding moments, which are, in fact, reiterations of the original foundation, links which bind it to the present.

Thus, choosing from among the multitude of possibilities, we might recognize as a founding event the Daco–Roman synthesis on the territory of Dacia, identified with the Romania of today, and see this initial foundation as being re-actualized and consolidated by new founding events: the formation of the principalities, the union of 1600, the union of 1859, the creation of Greater Romania in 1918, or, more recently, the revolution of December 1989, to the extent to which we consider this a fresh beginning, the birth certificate of a renewed, yet eternal, Romania.

For Bishop Chesarie of Rîmnic, writing two centuries ago, the founding phases were four in number: the wars of the Dacians and Romans, and especially the work of Trajan, later consolidated by Saint Constantine (the emperor Constantine the Great); the building of the monasteries of Cîmpulung and Curtea de Argeş (symbolizing the foundation of Wallachia by Radu Negru); the translation of books from Slavonic into Romanian (under Matei Basarab, Şerban Cantacuzino, and Constantin Brîncoveanu); and—somewhat surprisingly, but the present time imposed its obligations—the reign of Alexandru Ipsilanti, under whom Chesarie was writing. (See the services for November 1778 and January 1779, reproduced by Ioan Bianu and Nerva Hodoş in *Bibliografia românească veche*). The distance in time and the difference of mentality allow us, in this case, to perceive more clearly the ideological sense behind the systematization of history in terms of founding moments. The erudite cleric's scheme relates only to Wallachia, and places religious and cultural events in the foreground. It is neither correct nor incorrect; like any other scheme it reflects a particular vision of history based on a particular view of the present.

Romanian founding myths are simply one individual case of a quasi-universal mythological category, which, regardless of space or time, seeks to justify the present with reference to origins and to link the two ends of history by means of intermediary markers.

That these myths fit into a wider typology can be seen, too, in the slide from traditional to modern forms. The former tend, in general, to place a high value on *external* interventions, capable of propelling a previously empty or amorphous space into history. We find creations *ex nihilo*, creations of something fundamentally new. It can likewise be observed that the foundation is personalized, with an exceptional personality being central to the founding act. All this gives the new structures a nobility and a transcendent sense; indeed, the archetypal essence of the foundation myth is inseparable from the notion of the *sacred*. Even in its later, apparently secularized, forms, foundation retains a mystical significance that places it in the zone of the perennial, above the contingencies of history.

The foundation myths of the Romanian principalities, as they are recorded in the chronicles—the "dismounting" of Negru Vodă in Wallachia and the double "dismounting" of Dragoş and Bogdan in Moldavia—fit perfectly within the traditional typology. In the same period the French and the English were dignifying their origins with invented peregrinations, bringing their founding heroes, Francus and Brutus, all the way from the far-off city of Troy.

Modern foundation myths place a higher value on indigenous origins, in line with the "scientific", nationalist, and democratic phase of historical discourse. The foundation is no longer perceived as a rupture, as an act attributed to an exceptional hero; it takes its place within the organic development of a community or civilization. *Roots* become more important than nobility of origins—a translation that we shall be able to trace in the Romanian historical consciousness too.

ROMAN TIMES

The modern period opens under the sign of the *Roman foundation myth*. This is made the real foundation, with the "dismountings" in the Romanian lands seen as belonging to a later phase, as repetitions of the first creation, the "dismounting" of Trajan. The attempt by some researchers to connect this myth to a Roman consciousness, preserved uninterrupted in Romanian society, seems to me to be illusory.[1] In this case, why was an uninterrupted Dacian consciousness not also preserved? In fact, the invocation of distant origins cannot be a matter of popular consciousness but of intellectual combinations with a well-determined ideological and political purpose. Regardless of their Latin origins, the Romanians evolved until around 1600 in a predominantly Slavonic cultural environment. Their historical curiosity went no further back than the founding of the Romanian states. It was Westerners who first noted the connection between Romanians and Romans, for the simple reasons that, with their knowledge of Latin, they could observe the similarities between Romanian and the ancient language, and had access to historical texts referring to the conquest and colonization of Dacia.

In Romanian historiography it was Grigore Ureche, towards the middle of the seventeenth century, who first noted that the origin of the Romanians was in "Rîm". A few decades later, Miron Costin composed the first "monograph" on the Roman origins of his people, under the title *About the Moldavian People*. Both chroniclers had studied in Poland and knew Latin, so they were able to use sources and secondary works written in that language. Certainly nothing in their arguments concerning Romanian origins can be linked to any earlier indigenous source. At that time, in the seventeenth century, Romanian historiography was emerging from its Slavonic phase, not only in the fact that the chronicles were now compiled in Romanian, essential as this was, but in the sense of a shifting of cultural and historical reference points. The starting point became Rome, the conquest and colonization of Dacia. The principle of "external intervention" still applied, indeed with intensified force. Roman origin made a strong mark on the individuality of the Romanian lands, giving them nobility and prestige. Latin was the language of culture throughout most of Europe, and the Roman imperial tradition survived both in the Holy Roman Empire and in the desire of Russia to be considered the "third Rome".

Purity of origins was not in question. With the exception of the high steward Constantin Cantacuzino, who accepted a Daco–Roman mixing in his *History of Wallachia*, the chroniclers and later historians, from Dimitrie Cantemir to the Transylvanian School, would agree to nothing less than a pure Roman origin, with the Dacians exterminated or expelled to make way for the conquerors. For the Transylvanian scholars, having recourse to a Roman origin, and as far as possible a Roman origin without the slightest foreign mixture, was even more essential than for their precursors in the principalities. As campaigners for the emancipation of the Romanians of Transylvania, who were kept in a condition of clear inferiority by the Hungarian ruling elite, they used their origins as a weapon. As descendants of the masters of the world, whose language was still the official language of Hungary and Transylvania, the Romanians could not go on for ever accepting the supremacy of a people inferior to themselves—according to the standards of the time—in "race" and origin.

The main difficulty for the Transylvanian scholars was explaining the disappearance of the Dacians, or at least their non-participation in the formation of the Romanian people. Solutions invoked included extermination, expulsion from the land of Dacia (Budai-Deleanu saw, in Dacians forced to leave their country, the ancestors of the Poles) or, quite simply, an incompatibility in civilization that prevented the two peoples from blending together. The most elaborate demonstration is that of Petru Maior, who, in his *History of the Beginning of the Romanians in Dacia* (1812), brings together all these arguments. Many Dacians, "unable to escape before the Roman advance, killed each other", while others, "with all their women and children, fled from Dacia and went to their neighbors and friends, the Sarmatians". Maior takes pains to demonstrate that the war was not a conventional one, but one of extermination. This is how he deals with the question of whether the Romans might not still have married Dacian women. Such marriages could not have taken place because, firstly and most importantly, there were neither men nor women left in Dacia. And even if some women had survived—Maior concedes the possibility only to reduce the hypothesis to the absurd—"the very excellence of the Roman blood was nevertheless sufficient to prevent the Romans from marrying such barbarians as the Dacian women were". Moreover, "among the Romans it was shameful to marry women of any other people", let alone the "savages" of Dacia. The habit of "not marrying women of another language" has, Maior emphasizes, been kept by the Romanians too; this explains the survival of the Romanian people and the Romanian language. The contrast with the Hungarians is striking: "When they came to Pannonia [...] they did not even have women of their own people" and so "were forced to marry women of other peoples: Russian, Slav, Romanian, Bulgarian, Greek and others."[2] The nobility and purity of the Romanians thus emerge with enhanced value in antithesis to the Hungarian mixture.

It may be noted that around 1800, historiography in the principalities, which had entered a phase of Greek influence with the period of Phanariot rule, treated Daco–Roman fusion as a natural phenomenon. This is a point of view which we find in Greek historians settled in the Romanian lands—Dimitrie Philippide (*History of Romania*, 1816) and Dionisie Fotino (*History of Old Dacia*, 1818–1819)— but also with the Romanians Ienăchiță Văcărescu and Naum Rîmniceanu (the latter in an essay called *On the Origin of the Romanians* and in his introduction to the *Chronology of the Lords of Wallachia*). The 1828 *Tableau historique* of Moldavia, mentioned in chapter one, is not even shy of affirming the Dacian origin of the Moldavians.

However, the Romanian historiography of the nineteenth century evolved along the national lines marked out by the Transylvanian School, and the more cosmopolitan products of the Phanariot period could not compete with the purely

Romanian project of the scholars on the other side of the mountains. The Romanian national movement that emerged after 1821, the shift towards the West and towards the Western model of civilization, and the complexes of a small country that aspired to play a role in Europe by the restoration of old Dacia (Roman Dacia, it was understood), all contributed to the highlighting of the Roman model. The excellence of the foundation myth guaranteed the excellence of the Romanian future, in spite of the mediocrity of the present. Through the Romans, the Romanians could present themselves to the West as the equals of anybody, and the phenomenon of acculturation no longer meant borrowing, but rather a return to the source, to a ground of civilization shared with the civilization of the West.

This is why, in the period between 1830 and 1860, interpretations which do not uphold the Latin purity of the Romanian nation are rare. Differences of interpretation exist, but these do not so much concern the nature of the origins themselves as their relation to the present, the degree to which they can be actualized.

The *Latinist school*, represented primarily by Transylvanians but not restricted to Transylvania (since Transylvanians already occupied important positions in the cultural system of the principalities and later of united Romania), sought to carry to its ultimate conclusions the Latinism established by previous generations of the Transylvanian School. If the Romanians were pure Romans, then their history was simply Roman history, the prolongation of the history of Rome. This is what decided August Treboniu Laurian, the mastermind of the tendency, to begin the history of his people as naturally as possible with the foundation of Rome (just as Samuil Micu had done previously). If the Romanians were Romans, then they should remain Romans and cast off all foreign influences, perhaps even where the institutional organization of modern Romania was concerned (this was the viewpoint of Bărnuţiu, opposed by Maiorescu) and certainly in the area of the Romanian language, the "purification" of which was to bring it as close as possible to the original Latin.

The outstanding monument of this tendency was the *Dictionary of the Romanian Language*, published in two volumes and a glossary by Laurian, in collaboration with Ioan Massim, between 1871 and 1876. The appearance of this work demonstrated the key positions occupied by Latinists in Romanian culture, including the Academic Society (founded in 1867 and known from 1879 as the Romanian Academy), which had commissioned the project. The result was far beyond expectations. Once it had been purified of non-Latin elements (listed in the glossary, with a view to their elimination) and an etymological spelling system had been adopted, the language as reworked by Laurian bore only a vague resemblance to authentic Romanian. The dictionary was both the highest expression of Latinism, and its swan song. The attempt to create an artificial language only provoked laughter and permanently discredited the Latinist school. Even such bitter enemies in other issues of national history as the Junimists and

Hasdeu joined forces to denounce the sacrifice of the Romanian language on the altar of an imposed Latinity.

However, the opponents of Latinism were basically Latinists themselves, in the sense that for them the Romanians were descended from the Romans. Until about the middle of the century there was near unanimity on the Latin affiliation of the Romanian people. Kogălniceanu, one of the most severe critics of Latinist abuses, makes a clear-cut affirmation, in his *Histoire de la Valachie*, of the Roman background of his people, which can be traced even in the web of Romanian folklore: "Our peasants have preserved a multitude of Roman superstitions; their weddings include ceremonies practiced by the citizens of Rome [...]." The preservation of undiluted purity seemed to him an essential feature of Romanian history, from the Romans onwards: "The Romanians have never wanted to take in marriage women of another folk. [...] The Romanians have always remained a nation apart, preserving their ways and the customs of their ancestors, without losing anything of the daring and courage of the citizens of Rome."[3] Bălcescu, too, in *The Romanians under the Voivode Michael the Brave*, mentions as a fact needing no further comment that Dacia was colonized by the Romans "after the annihilation of its inhabitants".[4]

All the same, there were differences between the Latinists and those who were content simply to note the fact of Roman origin. These can be summed up in three main points.

First, the critics of Latinism did not agree with the abusive actualization of origins, that is, with the transforming of contemporary Romanians into Romans with the consequences that we have already seen (with respect to the Romanian language, for example). In opposing "Romanomania" in his 1843 *Opening Word*, Kogălniceanu pointed out the necessity of distinguishing between Romanians and Romans, between origins and present. The Romanians had to prove themselves alone and not rely for ever on their Roman ancestors for "assistance".

The second point concerned the purity of Roman blood. For a long time this was almost a "taboo" subject. The famous passage in Eutropius, in which all claims concerning the colonization of Dacia found their support, actually states perfectly clearly that the colonists came "from the whole Roman world" (*ex toto orbe romano*). Şincai, without basing himself on any supplementary information, expanded this expression in his own way: "[...] they brought very many settlers into Dacia from the whole Roman world, but especially from Rome and Italy", and "not just the low-class mob" but "also leading families were brought or moved to Dacia".[5] An aristocratic colonization indeed! In order to explain the regional variants of the Romanian language, Maior admitted the presence in Dacia of dialectal varieties, but argued that these were strictly of Italian origin. In contrast, Alecu Russo, an adversary of Latinist purism, could accept without complexes a mixing of colonists coming from the most diverse provinces of the empire; the particular profile of the Romanian language could be explained precisely by the input of these different elements.[6] Even without invoking the Dacians, "purity" was a thing of the past; we could not be pure Romans.

Thirdly, and lastly, the Dacians began to be perceived other than as a burdensome barbarian element, capable only of upsetting the schema of Romanian Latinity. Their never-contested love of liberty and spirit of sacrifice seemed, to the romantic revolutionary generation, to be virtues worthy of admiration and imitation. What could be more noble than sacrifice for one's country and death in preference to slavery, symbolized by the heroism of Decebalus and the pathetic scene of collective suicide? "Decebalus", exclaimed Kogălniceanu in his famous speech of 1843, "the greatest barbarian king of all time, more worthy to be on the throne of Rome than the rascally descendants of Augustus!"[7] Alecu Russo, attempting to draw a parallel between Decebalus and Stephen the Great, expressed himself as follows: "The one and the other both had the same aim, the same sublime idea: the independence of their country! Both are heroes, but Stephen is a more local hero, a Moldavian hero, while Decebalus is the hero of the world."[8]

This admiration did not necessarily modify the Latinist interpretation of origins. Kogălniceanu spoke in his *Opening Word* of "the Dacians, whose soil we have inherited"—soil, let it be noted, not blood. Russo went one step further: while only Roman colonists appear in the essay to which I have already referred, in another text (*The Stone of the Lime Tree*—accounts of travel in the Moldavian mountains), he sees in the race of mountain people, and even in their speech, the result of a Daco–Roman fusion. For all the concessions made towards them, the Dacians appear in the romantic period—until after 1850—more as mythical ancestor figures, sunk deep into a time before history, in a land which still recalled their untamed courage. Although they only rarely kept them as a founding factor, the romantics contributed to the consolidation of the theme of the Dacians, preparing the ground for the coming re-elaboration of origins.[9]

DACIANS AND ROMANS: A DIFFICULT SYNTHESIS

It would soon be time for a more complete and nuanced synthesis. The inferiority complex which had promoted the Romans was no longer so justified after the foundation of Romania, the gaining of independence, and the proclamation of the kingdom. The Romanians could now become themselves. Purity and nobility of blood ceased to be decisive considerations (although they continued to have a certain force in the arsenal of national arguments). The fact that Dacia had been colonized not only, and not even primarily, by inhabitants of Rome and the rest of Italy, began to be recognized and de-dramatized. The Dacians in their turn began to be recognized, first by a few non-conformists and later by Romanian historiography as a whole, as a founding element of the Romanian people. It was basically a combination, characteristic of the phase that Romanian society had reached in its evolution, of Western sources (the Romans and kinship with Latin sister nations) and sources of an indigenous nature (the Dacians). In any case, the acceptance of mixing meant that complexes had been at least partially healed.

Indeed, the progress of research and of historical conceptions no longer permitted the ignoring of the native population or the illusion of an exclusively Italian colonization. By 1870 it was hard to go on claiming, with Maior's nonchalance, that the ancestors of the Romanians had come from Italy while the Dacian men had been exterminated and their womenfolk disregarded by the conquerors. Maiorescu put a lid on the matter, pointing out that "no one in their right mind" could believe such a thing. A more adequate interpretation of the literary sources, supplemented by linguistic deductions and archaeological investigations, was opening the door towards a gradual affirmation of the Dacians.

As we have seen, the phenomenon fits within the typology of the evolution of foundation myths. The French, too, had begun, as early as the Renaissance, to put more of an accent on their Gaulish base (so much so that the French Revolution could be schematized as a confrontation between the Gaulish people and an aristocracy of Frankish origin, with the former taking a long overdue revenge on the latter), and in Russia the traditional version of the founding of the state by the external intervention of the Varangians came to be opposed, in the name of Russian patriotism, by an emphasis on the native Slavs.

We may note the intervention in this question of a politician, even before the historians. In 1857, I. C. Brătianu published a series of articles in the newspaper *Românul*, under the title *Historical Studies on the Origins of Our Nationality*. While in the already-mentioned text of 1851 this statesman, so preoccupied with origins, had been content to invoke the multitude of Latin colonists and the transmission of their virtues to the Romanians, now the picture appears more complex. The Romanians are not just descended from Romans, but from Thracians, Celts, and Romans. Thus "we are three times stronger and more powerful", a claim that clarifies the purpose of this approach.[10] The Thracians, and thus the Dacians, symbolized rootedness in the soil of the land; the Romans the political principle and civilization; while the Celts, an unusual presence in the Romanian mythology of origins, deserved to be invoked since through them we could be more closely related to the French. The role of France in the coming union of the principalities seemed overwhelming, as was the French model of civilization. A connection to the Celts, thus to the Gauls and, through them, to the French, completed the profile of a Romania that should at the same time be itself, the inheritor of old Rome, and the eastern replica of the French model. It is a remarkable piece of advocacy, clearly illustrating the mechanism of the actualization of origins and the political charge carried by foundation myths.

The Celts did not manage to impose their presence in Romanian consciousness, but the Dacians proceeded to install themselves permanently on the scene. In 1860, Hasdeu published in *Foiţa de istorie şi literatură* an important study entitled, somewhat provocatively given the predominance of the Latinist current at the time, "Did the Dacians Perish?" The young historian demonstrated that the Transylvanian School and its epigones had erected their whole scaffolding on a forced interpretation of the ancient sources. The "reduction of the menfolk" mentioned by Eutropius had been abusively amplified into the extermination of a whole people. The Dacians had not perished, Hasdeu concluded, and the colonization had not been an infusion of pure Romans but of people from the most diverse origins. Thus, "our nationality was formed out of a number of elements, none of which was predominant". The myth of purity was cast to the winds. The Romanians appeared as a "chemical composition", in which diverse constitutive elements gave birth to a fundamentally new synthesis.[11]

In his numerous later works, including the *Critical History of the Romanians*, Hasdeu continued to attempt, despite the paucity of documentation, a reconstruction of the old Romanian civilization, which, without any diminishing of the importance of the Romans, he saw as descending to a considerable extent from the civilization of the indigenous Dacians. He had a special faith in the historical virtues of linguistics, believing that the origin and evolution of words could offer a faithful mirror of history. He carried out a veritable "hunt" for Dacian words in the Romanian language, managing to identify a total of eighty-four, plus fifteen place-names. This was a decisive argument in favor of the survival of the Dacians and their contribution to the Romanian synthesis. Significant in this connection is Hasdeu's article "The Origins of Shepherding among the Romanians" (1874), in which he demonstrated the Dacian origin of the words *cioban, baci, stînă, urdă* and *brînză.** Thus shepherding terminology confirmed Daco–Roman continuity, both from an ethnic point of view and in terms of the perpetuation of ancient practices. It is hardly necessary to say that all too few of Hasdeu's etymologies have stood up to more recent research. The truth is that in the question of Dacian etymology it is possible to affirm almost anything, given that we know next to nothing about the essential evidence, the Dacian language itself.

In "Stratum and Substratum: The Genealogy of the Balkan Peoples" (his introduction to the third volume of *Etymologicum Magnum Romaniae*), Hasdeu takes up the problem of the Dacian–Roman–Romanian connection again, this time as part of an overall perspective. He shows that the peoples of the Balkan Peninsula were formed by the superposition of successive strata: the original "Pelasgians", then the Thracians, overlaid by the Romans, and finally the Slavs. The ultimate predominance of one of the elements should not lead us to ignore the presence of deeper layers. Underneath present linguistic differences can be seen the relatedness of the Balkan peoples (the Thracian-ness of the Bulgarians, the Dacian-ness of the Romanians, etc.). The Dacian substratum of the Romanian people is thus placed within a general schema of historical and linguistic evolution.

While Hasdeu was doing battle with words, an amateur archaeologist was turning the country upside down in search of ancient Dacian material remains. In 1858 Cezar Bolliac (1813–1881), journalist, writer, and politician, published in the newspaper *Românul* a veritable manifesto under the title "About the Dacians", in which, two years before Hasdeu, he took issue with the Latinist doctrine, unable

---

* *Cioban*: shepherd; *baci*: head-shepherd; *stînă*: sheepfold complex with summer huts for shepherds; *urdă* and *brînză*: varieties of cheese made from ewes' milk. *Trans.*

to hide his enthusiasm at the antiquity and achievements of Dacian civilization. One sentence is worth repeating: "Our nobility is as old as the soil." It was the Dacians who aroused in Bolliac the passion for field research. "Our mission, the mission of the Romanians, in archaeology, is above all to define what the Dacians were, what their beginning was, what their beliefs were, what level of civilization they had reached when the Romans conquered them and took their country, and finally, how they lived on with the Romans in their country, what they borrowed from the Romans and what the Romans borrowed from them."[12] Over two decades, from 1860 to 1880, he undertook countless journeys on the Danube and to the hills and mountains in order to answer these questions. On one occasion he thought he had discovered a Dacian alphabet, and another time he identified "prehistoric pipes", the conclusion being that the Dacians did not despise the art of smoking. This made him the object of Odobescu's irony in *Archaeological Smoke Concocted from Prehistoric Pipes by a Man Who Does Not Smoke*. What interests us here is not the real value of the research of this enthusiastic dilettante. The important thing is that he "stirred up" the Dacian substratum, which had hitherto been hidden in Romanian consciousness by the brilliance of the Romans.

Etymology and archaeology were joined by poetry. The Dacians are invoked repeatedly in the verses of Mihai Eminescu, the great national poet of the Romanians, generally in texts which remained in manuscript, in various stages of completion, such as the poems *Memento Mori* and *Sarmis,* and the historical drama *Decebalus.* Like Hasdeu, Eminescu invoked Dacians and Romans alike with equal pride. His Dacia is imagined as a primordial, ahistorical world, expressive, like his other incursions into the past, of an ideal of regression and the nostalgia of beginnings still under the sign of the golden age. There is in these verses the starting point, though not yet sufficiently crystallized, of a national mythology, the expression of the nationalist and autochthonist basis of the poet's ideology, which was to produce an echo in the nationalism and autochthonism of later generations.[13]

Dacia was also the subject of a doctoral thesis, *Dacia before the Romans,* defended by Grigore Tocilescu in 1876 at the University of Prague and awarded the Academic Society's prize. Published in 1880, it was the first synthesis in Romanian historiography concerned with the history and civilization of the Dacians.

Around this time, in the 1870s, there took place an essential reworking of the question of origins. From Romans (first pure Romans, later "mixed" Romans) the Romanians became *Daco–Romans.* It was a formula which seemed closer to the truth but which in fact turned out to be more fragile and unstable than the exclusive affirmation of one or other of the component elements. The stress would always fall on either the first or the second term of the expression. Who was greater: Trajan or Decebalus? In which of them do we primarily recognize ourselves? Such questions may seem puerile, but in mythology nothing is puerile; everything is invested with meaning.

The Latin idea remained very present in Romanian society. If "pan-Latinism" (regarded coldly by France) was never affirmed to anything like the extent of pan-

Germanism or pan-Slavism, this was not the fault of the Romanians. The "Dacianist" Hasdeu called imperiously in 1869 for a "pan-Latin congress in Paris", and in 1878 Vasile Alecsandri was awarded a prize in Montpellier for his *Song of the Latin Race*: "The Latin race is queen / Among the great races of the world [...]." The poet put his literary triumph and the glory recently won by Romanian soldiers at Grivitsa on the same level, a sign not just of his own vanity but of the intensity of the Latin myth.

The dominant discourse continued, in varying degrees, to favor the Romans. Among those who proved unwilling to grant the Dacians more than was absolutely necessary we even find the author of *Dacia before the Romans*. In his textbook on the history of the Romanians, Tocilescu observes that after the wars with the Romans Dacia was left *almost* without inhabitants. The phenomenon that took place was not a simple process of *Romanization*, as in France and Spain, but a massive Roman *colonization*, in which various provinces took part (Italy to a lesser extent). The Romanian people is, essentially, a *Roman people* (in contrast to the French, who are Gallo–Romans, or the Spanish, who are Ibero–Romans). Dacians entered into the synthesis too, the historian recognizes, but on a limited scale.[14]

Dimitrie Onciul expresses a similar point of view. He considers that the Romanian people was born "especially from the Roman colonists, who, on the conquered territory, absorbed the remains of the Dacian population after the latter had been largely exterminated here in battle, as the Roman authors say, or forced to withdraw to the north and east. The opinion that the Daco–Romans are to be seen more as Romanized Dacians is not confirmed by the historical sources. The Dacians remained in the non-colonized parts, as a population distinct from the Roman population and often actually hostile to the empire, until the end of Roman domination, only to disappear then in the wave of invaders."[15]

Other historians are more generous. In his *History of the Romanians in Dacia Traiana*, the first volume of which appeared in 1888, A. D. Xenopol assembles a number of proofs and arguments in support of Dacian continuity. In a notably balanced presentation, he brings the indigenous and colonizing elements face to face. Taking account of the general prejudice in favor of the Romans, he feels the need to convince his readers that there is no loss in being descended also from the Dacians: "[...] the root of the Romanian people is to be identified in the historical layers in two branches which are both equally energetic, enduring, and full of virtue. Let us not therefore be offended if the blood of the Dacians turns out to be mixed into our nationality." However, for Xenopol, too, the colonization and Romanization were decisive and were on a greater scale than occurred in other provinces of the empire. The Roman element seems to have been larger than that of the Dacians, "so that the finest examples of the Romanian race of today do not come from the Dacian character but from the Roman". We are Daco–Romans, but more Roman than Dacian![16]

Nicolae Iorga, in his numerous works of synthesis, on a greater or smaller scale, affirms in his turn the Daco–Roman fusion, but within the broader framework of the whole of eastern Romanity and with an insistent underlining of a substantial demographic current coming from Italy even before the incorporation of the provinces in the Roman state. "A people", he considered, "does not come to speak another language unless a large number of people come over it who speak that language and have similar activities to its own." The Thraco–Illyrian mass of farmers and shepherds could only be de-nationalized as a result of a massive emigration of the Italian peasantry. The process then continued in Roman Dacia, where the number of Dacians who remained "in the midst of the other Romanized Thracians was not very great, for the folk had suffered much in previous years".[17] The balance was thus tilted towards the Romans and, at least for the initial phase of the Romanization of the Balkans, even towards the pure Italian element.

Roman symbols, and above all the face of Trajan himself, long remained dominant. Decebalus may stand beside him, but in general Trajan is preferred, defining the founding moment par excellence as that of the conquest of Dacia by the Romans. On the occasion of the inauguration of the Romanian Athenaeum in February 1888, Alexandru Odobescu gave an erudite lecture in which he set out to underline the relationship between the new building in Bucharest and circular-domed Roman buildings; the Athenaeum thus symbolized the Roman origin of those who had erected it. In order for the Romanian–Roman connection to be even clearer, the distinguished archaeologist proposed that a bas-relief should be placed on the façade representing "the Transfiguration which took place here in Romania when, from under the harsh and dark overlordship of the Dacian Decebalus, our land, through its happy conquest by Trajan, entered rapidly and easily into the luminous and blessed dominion of the Latin folk". The fresco in the great circular hall was to present first of all the barbarism of prehistoric times, then the Daco–Roman wars and the triumph of Rome. Decebalus's image was not to appear at all; on the other hand, the "noble and gentle figure of the emperor Trajan, with his gray hair and his prophetic gesture, will preside over his whole army. [...] He, to whom we, here, owe both our birth and our name, both our life and our faith. He will shine in this place, like the sun at noon."[18]

The fresco which Odobescu sketched out as an ideal project would be made reality half a century later, in the years 1933 to 1937, by the painter Costin Petrescu. By this time the major role of the Dacians in the Romanian synthesis was recognized (and, as we shall see, sometimes even exaggerated). And yet, faithful to a persistent tradition, the founding scene presented by Costin Petrescu completely ignores Decebalus. We see only the victorious Trajan contemplating the Dacian disaster. Apollodorus of Damascus likewise appears, a more representative symbolic figure than Decebalus, in that the bridge which he built united Dacia with the rest of the empire. The mixed origin of the Romanian people is not, however, ignored; it is illustrated by the idyll of a Dacian woman and a Roman legionary. The man is of course Roman; it is he who will give the offspring their name and legitimacy.[19]

It is in Dimitrie Onciul's synthesis, *From the History of Romania* (editions published in 1906, 1908, and 1913), that we find the most concentrated expression of the Romanian pantheon. The work has only two illustrations. The first shows the emperor Trajan, "the founder of the Romanian people"; and the second, King Carol, "the founder of the Romanian kingdom". The linking of these two founding moments, ethnic and political, appears insistently in the climactic phase of Carol I's reign, the period marked by the jubilee of 1906. The king of Romania and the Roman emperor are represented together on a number of plaques and medallions, with inscriptions such as: "Fathers of the Romanian folk, 106–1906–1866."[20] As well as nobility of blood, Trajan also symbolized a political project: the imperial glory of Rome re-actualized in the reign of Carol I.

While they could be accepted, more or less, as a population that had undergone Romanization, the Dacians could not offer the kingdom of Romania a sufficiently attractive political symbol. Between their barbarian monarchy and the Roman imperial insignia the choice was self-evident. The political leaders of 1900 were certainly less inclined to admire Decebalus than the revolutionaries of 1848 had been.

For all that, the ground won back by the Dacians continued to be consolidated. The autochthonist wave after 1900, amplified in the interwar period, directly or indirectly favored Dacian roots. We have seen how Vasile Pârvan sketched an image of Dacian civilization remarkably similar to the image (as it was perceived at the time) of traditional Romanian civilization. The work of Pârvan, a historian respected for the solidity of his documentation (both literary and archaeological) and considered to be unassailable from a methodological point of view, established the Dacian factor in a position from which, practically speaking, it could not be dislodged. It was possible to go further than the conclusions of the great archaeologist, much further even, but none of the ground won for the Dacians would henceforth be given up. They now appeared as a numerous and powerful people, the forgers of a remarkable civilization, and alone among the Thracian peoples in being the founders of a state. Pârvan himself sums up the essential features of the Dacian space at the moment of the Roman conquest as follows: "First of all, Dacia was a great kingdom based on a solid and homogeneous ethnic foundation: its historical traditions were already old, its social and economic structure was well marked, and it possessed an advanced culture, which, influenced at first by the forms of Celtic civilization, had for two centuries before Trajan felt the impress of the Roman. Here was a worthy rival even for Rome. This was no mere agglomeration of a number of savage 'tribes with a shifting population, scattered loosely over an extended territory with a complete lack of political and national cohesion such as the Romans had found in Dalmatia or Thrace or Pannonia or Moesia; here was a nation, organized, powerful, conscious of itself."[21]

"A nation conscious of itself": the formula is an anticipation of Romanian national consciousness, and, in the context of 1926, makes ancient Dacia equivalent to united Romania. The role of the Romans is not diminished as that of the Dacians is affirmed. Pârvan presents a long process of Westernization, of "pre-Romanization" we might say, beginning long before the conquest of Dacia.

He believes that in the Roman province of Dacia, with a thinned indigenous population and in conditions of massive colonization, the Roman element was dominant. The process of Romanization was also felt in the rest of Decebalus's Dacia, the parts that were not annexed by the Romans and continued to be inhabited by Dacians. "Not only the Banat and Oltenia, but also Muntenia and Moldavia, through connections of ethnicity and interest with Roman Dacia on the one hand and Getic Moesia on the other, gradually received the Roman form of life. [...] The solidarity of interest of pre-Roman Dacia was remade: the Dacians of greater Dacia contributed with their race to the preservation of what the Romans in Roman Dacia had created with their culture."[22]

Pârvan succeeded, by his genius, in fixing the Daco–Roman synthesis in a perfect balance. The Romanians are, to the highest degree, both Dacian and Roman, and pre-Roman Dacia, Dacia of the Roman period (whether included or not in the empire), and modern Romania appear as historical entities which can be perfectly superimposed and which echo each other across the millennia.

A decade later, in the *History of the Romanians* by C. C. Giurescu (first volume, 1935), the "biological" weighting of the Dacians in the formation of the Romanian people is affirmed even more strongly, and they end up by becoming a majority even in Roman Dacia: "For all the losses they had suffered in battle, and the emigrations of tribes which, unwilling to submit to the empire, withdrew into the northern mountains, we believe that the population that remained was considerable in number and constituted the *majority* of the inhabitants of the new province. [...] *Romanism was victorious in Dacia because it won over the natives.*"[23]

The Romanians could thus be defined as *Romanized Dacians*, having first been pure Romans, then Romans more or less mixed, and later Daco–Romans.

THE DACIANS GET THEIR OWN BACK

But things did not stop here. The next move, somewhat inevitably given the logic of nationalism, was to be the exclusion of the Romans from the Romanian mixture. Autochthonist nationalism returned to the theme of the purity of the race, just like the first nationalists, only this time the purity was to be Dacian, not Latin. The Roman infusion had attached the Dacian space to an indisputable center of the world: Rome. Now the center was simply to be in Dacia, an eternal Dacia outside time, around which the rest of humanity would gravitate. The concept of *center* emerged from this about-turn consolidated, not weakened. We may observe that the shift to the center of a peripheral space, which has been in all ages on the margin of the great units of civilization, has been, and still is, the major preoccupation of Romanian nationalism.

In 1894 the archaeologist Teohari Antonescu (1866–1910), Odobescu's disciple and future professor at the University of Iaşi, published an essay entitled "Dacia: The Primitive Fatherland of the Aryan Peoples". The author was a Junimist, and the text appeared in *Convorbiri Literare*, a periodical oriented towards the critique of nationalist phantasms but sufficiently open and tolerant to accept any original contribution. By way of a chain of deductions, starting from linguistic material, in a way that recalls Hasdeu's method, Antonescu actually did no more than find a new fatherland for the Aryans, who had already been trailed by their researchers and admirers all over Asia and Europe. Dacia now became the starting point of a brilliant history.

But the great discoverer of a world with its center fixed in Dacia was Nicolae Densuşianu (1846–1911), a Transylvanian settled in Bucharest since 1878, an erudite historian and fiery nationalist. He made himself noticed by a work which was appreciated at the time, *Horea's Revolution* (1884), in which he attributed to the "revolution" in question the aim of founding a "Romanian political system". But for Densuşianu the "Romanian political system" and the history of the Romanians in general could be traced far back, very far back. In his passion for the question of origins he left Hasdeu far behind, believing that he could truly arrive at the earliest beginnings. His method, basically Hasdeian but without the professionalism that, at least from time to time, tempered the fantasies of the author of the *Critical History*, brought into play elements of archaeology and folklore, linguistics and mythology, which he combined at will. The result was *Prehistoric Dacia*, an immense work of 1,200 pages, which appeared posthumously in 1913 through the efforts of an admirer, C. I. Istrati (himself a fascinating character: doctor and chemist, professor at the University of Bucharest, conservative politician, and, on top of all that, spiritist!). Vasile Pârvan regarded it as a "fantasy novel"; it is, at any rate, the expression of the strongest dose of the imaginary in Romanian historiography. It was also a truly influential book, if not at the time of its publication, when the securely installed principles of the critical school left little room for alternative theories, then certainly in the later manifestations of Dacianist autochthonism.

Densuşianu reconstructed the history of a supposed "Pelasgian Empire", which, from beginnings in Dacia around 6,000 B.C., allegedly succeeded, under two great rulers, Uranus and Saturn, in extending its rule over Europe, the Mediterranean, Egypt and North Africa, and much of Asia. This prehistoric equivalent of Romania had united around itself a universal empire, certainly the greatest that ever existed. It was from here, between the Danube and the Carpathians, that civilization poured forth through the other parts of the world. It was from here that the ancestors of the Romans set out for Italy. Dacian and Latin are only dialects of the same language, which indeed explains the lack of "Dacian" inscriptions in Roman Dacia: the two peoples were of the same speech. Among the arguments put forward by Densuşianu we also find a reference to the representations on Trajan's Column, where Dacians and Romans engage in dialogue without interpreters, proof that they could understand each other very well, each speaking their own language! Thus in contrast to the other Romance peoples, which are the result of a mixing process, the Romanians are a pure race, the descendants of the ancient inhabitants of this land, and their language owes nothing to Latin, having been transmitted from time immemorial. This also explains its differences from the western Romance languages.

C. I. Istrati, who prefaced *Prehistoric Dacia* with a long text about the life and works of its author, closes his enthusiastic evocation with a remarkable parallel: he finds the "times of unknown glory [...] which were planned and enacted around the Carpathians, and especially in the Bucegi mountains", re-actualized on the occasion of a visit to Peleş. Dacia, center of the world; the Bucegi, center of Dacia; and Peleş in the heart of the Bucegi: here is a symbol that is both cosmic and political at the same time. King Carol I appeared to Istrati as "a new Uranus and Saturn"![24] What was Trajan beside these emperors of the earliest times, who had molded history into its first forms?

In the interwar period Densuşianu's thesis was taken up and developed by a number of amateur historians, intoxicated with nationalism. The increasingly violent clash of ideologies and the affirmation of the autochthonist spirit offered them a space for maneuver which the professionalization of history had seemed, for a time, to be eliminating. In the eyes of some, the intuition of the non-specialist even became a virtue; to go beyond rationalism was a fundamental desideratum of the nationalist Right. Mircea Eliade called for a "new dilettantism", on the basis of the observation that "dilettantes have always had a feeling for history and understood it"; the deeper meanings and the great synthesis are more accessible to them than to the professional.[25]

The dilettantes were not slow to come forward. Their favorite battleground became the question of origins; even today they still make a point of glory out of the original and "patriotic" resolution of this question. One of them was General Nicolae Portocală, who published in 1932 *From the Prehistory of Dacia and of the Ancient Civilizations*. The enthusiastic military man broadly follows Densuşianu and is harshly critical of Pârvan, accusing the great promoter of Dacian civilization of an abusive insistence on foreign influences! The most remarkable part of his demonstration concerns the impossibility of the Dacians being Romanized. Who was to Romanize them? "Foreign and uncultivated legionaries, whose knowledge of Latin may have been limited to military commands?" And how could the half who lived in territory unoccupied by the Romans be Romanized? The conclusion could only be that the Dacians had always spoken "a rustic Latin language". Romanization did not go from the West to the East, but from the East to the West. It was not the scholars who were right, but the Romanian peasants, with their saying: "Italians speak Romanian too, but messed up." Romanian is not "messed up" Latin: Latin and its descendants are "messed up" Romanian![26] What the Roman conquest actually did was destroy a flourishing civilization and remove the Romanians from history for a thousand years.

Portocală was followed by a certain Marin Bărbulescu, whose name was suggestively extended to Bărbulescu-Dacu, author of *The Daco–Thracian Origin of the Romanian Language*, published in 1936. The conviction that the Romanian language is nothing other than ancient Dacian took hold of the writer Brătescu-Voineşti, who, before and during the Second World War, became a great admirer of the solutions and mythologies of the extreme Right. "We are not neo-Latins, but proto-Latins", he wrote in *The Origin of the Romanian Folk and of our Language* (1942, new edition 1943). "The Others" speak a language similar to ours, simply because *they* are descended from our ancestors. The Romans are, like the Romanians, the descendants of the Thraco–Geto–Dacians. "Latin was the literary form of the language of the Geto–Dacians. The same language, when it reached France, became first the language of the Gauls, and with time French."[27] According to Brătescu-Voineşti these are axioms which no longer require demonstration; let those who maintain the contrary do the demonstrating!

And so, we do not originate from "Rîm": the Romans, the French and all the rest come from the Bucegi!

The Dacianism of the amateurs denied (and still denies) what is evident—the Romance character of the Romanian language—for the sake of a fictive Dacian language similar to Latin. This is, of course, not the approach of the professionals, even those attracted towards the same Dacian horizon. They do not deny linguistic Latinity, but consider that the essential lies deeper than the Roman crust. Biologically and spiritually the Romanians are Dacians, not Romans or even Daco–Romans.

Also invoked towards this end is the cult of Zalmoxis, in which the Geto–Dacians allegedly foreshadowed the Christian religion, so that they were more prepared than other peoples to receive it. Since the Romanian nation is in the first place Orthodox Christian, the connection is made to the Dacian supreme god, not the Roman pantheon. Zalmoxis offers a remarkable model of mythological logic. The starting point, in fact the only certain starting point, is a succinct and obscure passage in Herodotus (who also provides the information, evidently passed over by nationalist exegetes, that Zalmoxis was a slave of Pythagoras). It is hard to say to what extent these lines tell us of the authentic religion of the Getae and how far they are simply the projection into the Getic space of Pythagorean doctrine. Furthermore, Zalmoxis never appears in representations of any kind, either in the pre-Roman period (figurative representations are, in any case, no more characteristic of the "oral" civilization of the Dacians than is writing) or in Roman Dacia, rich as it is in all sorts of divinities. It was on this fragile axis that the ancients themselves developed the myth of Zalmoxis, which was subsequently taken over and amplified in Romanian culture, especially in the interwar period and in right-wing circles. Gradually, those few lines of Herodotus became a whole library.[28]

Lucian Blaga noted the "revolt of the autochthonous layer"; it was he, too, who published, in 1921, the play *Zamolxe*, in which the Dacian space appears as "a means of capitalizing on the ethical and metaphysical values of existence", to quote Mircea Eliade. Eliade himself was a great promoter of the Dacian layer. This was certainly what attracted him to B. P. Hasdeu, whose *Literary, Moral, and Political Writings* he edited in 1937. In his introduction to this collection he insisted on a general orientation—anticipated by Hasdeu—towards appreciation of the value of autochthonous roots and reduction of the significance of borrowings. He also cites Camille Jullian, who had demonstrated, in the case of Gaul, "that the much-praised Roman civilization was no more than a brutal militarism, which destroyed the beginnings of a promising culture". Unamuno's "desolidarizing" of Spanish thinking from Latinity went in the same direction. "Today", concludes Eliade, "the fascination with the Dacians goes beyond scholarly interest; everything encourages us to believe that the thirst for the 'originary' and 'local' will deepen in Romanian spirituality."[29]

In 1943 in Madrid Eliade published in Spanish a synthesis of the history of the Romanians: *Los Rumanos. Breviario histórico*. The first chapter of the book was given the suggestive title "Under the Sign of Zalmoxis". Where origins are concerned, the author distinguished between Romanization and... Romanization. The phenomenon followed a different course in Dacia than in Spain and Gaul. "Here, unlike in other regions, the Romanization did not mean a radical change of the autochthonous ethnic substance. The Dacian learned to speak Latin, but he preserved his customs, his way of life and ancestral virtues. The new towns worshipped the gods of the empire, but in villages and in the mountains the cult of Zalmoxis perpetuated, even if, later on, under a different name. That is why, when the first Christian missionaries arrived to bring the new faith to the Daco–Romans, the latter embraced Christianity at once and before others did so: Zalmoxis had paved the way for the new faith for centuries."[30] We need hardly state that none of these affirmations have the slightest documentary basis.

For the Legionaries, Zalmoxis had a special appeal. Their foundation myth was the Dacian myth. Indeed, P. P. Panaitescu, who had become, in the autumn of 1940, one of the leading personalities of the Legionary regime, put it in so many words in the text quoted in Chapter One, which begins: "We are Dacians!"—an assertion made on the basis of "race" and "blood".[31]

Ethnic purity—whether in the Latin or the Dacian version—belongs to a traditional tendency in Romanian culture, but the stronger accent put on *race* and *blood* cannot be separated from the context of 1940. At a time when the Nazis were claiming the superiority of the Germanic race, the exponents of the Romanian nationalist Right were not shy of invoking a similar model. All the more so as, between the Germanic tribes and the civilization of the Dacians, the reference to earliest times might even be to the Romanians' advantage.

The years of the Second World War, a period marked by the trauma of territorial dismemberment and the hope of rebirth within restored or even enlarged borders, were marked by an instinctive appeal to Dacian permanence. Here are a few lines which appeared in the first issue (April 1941) of a literary journal with the symbolic title *Dacia Rediviva*: "From far off there appears, shining, the eternal archetype of Dacia. In its profile, which corresponds precisely to ourselves, we find again our whole dimensions."[32] And in 1945, a certain G. Ionescu-Nica tried to resolve the border issue by recourse to the same mythical space of ancient Dacia as a decisive argument for the perennial outline in which Romanian territory was inscribed.[33]

CLASS STRUGGLE IN DACIA

The first phase of communism meant a retreat both for the Dacians and for the Romans. Daco–Roman origins were not actually contested, but the problem of origins as such no longer had the same importance as before. Communism had other foundation myths. Revolts and revolutions, the founding of the Communist Party, the Grivița strike and the liberating action of 23 August 1944 became more significant points of reference than the remote Daco–Roman synthesis. Moreover, the class principle was set over and above the ethnic principle. The dividing line did not so much run between Dacians and Romans or between Daco–Romans and the others, as within Dacian and Roman society respectively. It was no longer possible to treat a certain ethnic element as a block. Under Burebista, and even more under Decebalus, the Dacian state had become a slave state. With the Roman conquest, "the rich social layer in Dacia aligned itself with the Roman invaders", according to Roller's textbook. On the other side were "free but poor people, and especially slaves".[34] Social struggle was combined with the struggle for liberation from under Roman domination. The Dacians formed the great mass of the oppressed, just as the oppressing class was principally Roman (or Romanized).

The model projected onto Dacia was that of liberation struggles in colonies or in the "third world", struggles supported by the Soviet Union and the "Socialist camp", while the Romans came closely to resemble Western imperialists. Through perseverance in forcing the interpretation of sources, the class struggle took on unsuspected proportions, not least in the form of revolts combined with attacks by the free Dacians.[35] The file on the "latrones" is particularly significant and amusing. *Latrones* in Latin simply means brigands. A number of funerary inscriptions from Dacia refer to the killing of inhabitants of the province by so-called *latrones*. The monuments are erected in memory of well-off people, and hence the idea took shape that they were killed not in the course of common robbery, but as an expression of class struggle. The *latrones* became outlaws, the avengers of the oppressed many. One historian went a step further and identified an actual institution of *latrocinia* among the Dacians, a term translated as *partisan struggle*.[36]

Thus there was little thought given, in the 1950s, to the *ethnic*, Daco–Roman substratum of the Romanian synthesis. Of the two elements, however, the less favored were the Romans. They were consistently referred to as *invaders*, and their departure from Dacia was seen as a *liberation*. Even without an explicit formulation, the Romanians appeared to be rather the Romanized descendants of the Dacians, identified largely with the oppressed mass of the people of the Roman province. Beyond that it was not possible to insist. Denunciation of the Romans fitted in with the anti-imperialist and anti-Western project, but too much insistence on autochthonous roots would have given the historical discourse a nationalist tinge, and this was not, of course, the desired goal. Nationalism was to be combated just as much as Westernism. With this end in view a third element was added to the Dacians and Romans; further on we shall pause to consider the development of the problem of origins in the "internationalist" ambience of the time.

THE DACIAN MOMENT OF COMMUNISM

The gradual shift from the historical mythology of class struggle to nationalist mythology was to restore the traditional foundation myth to its former status. Already in 1960 the first volume of the treatise *History of Romania* proved to be much more conciliatory towards the Romans. The influx of Roman colonists and the process of Romanization are henceforth no longer automatically devalued by an insistence on the unjust character of the conquest. The Romans continue to be criticized—no good communist could agree with the annexation of foreign territory—but only up to a point, and with a compensatory underlining of the elements of progress which they brought. The Communist Party's *Program* of 1975, phrased in somewhat vague terms so as to please everybody, refers to the "negative aspects" of Roman rule, but also to the "new socioeconomic flourishing" in the period, emphasizing too that the Romanians appeared "from the blending of Dacians with Romans".[37]

All the same, the rehabilitation of the Romans did not go all the way, and in particular could not keep up with the relentless consolidation of autochthonous roots. Whether good or bad—generally bad at the beginning and good later on—they only represented one episode in a history that stretched over millennia. The nationalist ideology could find support here in a wealth of archaeological discoveries. In their own right, and quite apart from any ideological exploitation, these represented perhaps the most productive sector of historical research in the communist years. Archaeology was, however, stimulated precisely because it was through it that a solution could be sought to certain historical problems in the sense pursued by ideology. The Romanian past was thus considerably deepened, with the Dacians themselves supported by a much earlier history, from the Stone Age to Neolithic and Bronze Age cultures. However significant the "seal of Rome" might be, it could now only give a certain coloring, limited in time, to an independent history that had its own specific features and belonged to a specific space.

If professional historians continued to pronounce—with inevitable nuances, of course—in favor of the Daco-Roman synthesis, around the middle of the 1970s a far from negligible current, made up of non-specialists but influential on a political level, took over the Dacianist thesis of Densuşianu. The historical obsessions of the "extreme Right" on the eve of the Second World War were thus transferred to the "extreme Left", which says much about the common inclinations of the totalitarian phenomenon, especially where the nationalist variant of communism is concerned. The offensive was launched by the Institute of History of the Party, which, having falsified the recent history of the country, turned with similar intentions towards a history thousands of years old, offering it the competence of its specialists in the history of the working-class movement.

In issue 4 (1976) of *Anale de istorie*, the journal of the above-mentioned Institute, there appeared a most remarkable article (unsigned) under the title "The Beginnings of the History of the Romanian People"—conceived as a support to those who had to teach and study the course on "Fundamental Problems of the History of the Nation and the Party".[38] This text claims, not as hypothesis but as fact, the pre-Romance or Latin character of the Thracians' language. The demonstration, since we are offered a "demonstration", is a telling illustration of what a lack of basic professionalism and a straightforward contempt for the truth can mean. The line followed is that of Densuşianu's work, which, from a "prehistoric fairy tale", has become an "authorized source". As the bibliography nevertheless needed bringing up to date, there is a reference to the "French academician Louis Armand", who apparently *showed* that "the Thraco–Dacians spoke a pre-Romance language". If an academician says it, and a French one at that, then it must be true! The casual reader might be led to believe that the individual cited is a great historical and philological authority (we lay aside for the moment the elementary principle that appeal to authority cannot be admitted as a procedure in historical argument). In fact, Louis Armand was an *engineer* who held senior positions in the French railways and nuclear energy industry! Returning to Densuşianu, what the Party researchers retain from his tortuous presentation is the story, with all its humor, of the missing interpreters: "In support of this conclusion [the Latinity of the Dacian language] we have the bas-reliefs on Trajan's Column. One of these shows a delegation of peasants discussing directly with Trajan, without interpreters, and when he replies it is similarly without interpreters." This is the lowest point of the profession (since the authors had the status of "professionals"), the bottom limit reached by history under the communist dictatorship: a sign of the impertinent conviction that ultimately we can make what we want out of history.

The elimination of the Romans from national history thus returned to the agenda (with or without a denial of Romanization). The Institute of History of the Party and the Center for Military History were at the forefront of this tendency. If Nicolae Ceauşescu continued, in his various historical invocations, to plead on behalf of Daco–Roman synthesis, his brother Ilie Ceauşescu lost no occasion to denounce the Roman invaders, even suggesting that the Romanian people had been formed before the Roman conquest. The period of Roman domination is judged harshly in the first volume of the *Military History of the Romanian People* (1984). Negative consequences of the conquest are pointed out, while the positive aspects are no longer mentioned. It is true that a "weaving together of Dacian and Roman civilization" is accepted, but it is carefully stressed, without fear of contradiction, that "the Dacian people successfully preserved its ethnic being".[39] There was no biological blending with the Romans, just the adoption of their language; at least the Latinity of the language was recognized!

The identification of the Romanians with the Dacians led to an insistent foregrounding of the originality and values of the civilization of the latter. Nothing could be more natural (in mythological terms): the Romans had no need of such an amplifying operation, but the Dacians could only gain by retouchings and additions. Here again, a notable role was played by historians of the category mentioned above, to whom must be added some authentic professionals, such as Ion Horaţiu Crişan, the author of a monograph which enjoyed considerable publicity: *Burebista and his Age* (1975, new edition 1977). Crişan's method is not without interest: he first makes an apparently correct analysis of the sources, and then advances conclusions which have nothing to do with those sources. The use of writing by the Dacians thus appears, for Crişan and other authors, to be a feature indicative of the high degree of evolution of Dacian civilization. It had become almost a political error to claim that the Dacians did not practice the art of writing, although in reality the sources do not demonstrate very convincingly that they did. But writing was not enough. By writing and other methods the Dacians must have expressed ideas of the highest possible level. The idea was launched that the history of Romanian philosophy should begin with Dacian philosophy. The essential references to the "philosophical preoccupations" of the Dacians are to be found in the sixth-century historian Jordanes, the author of a work on the Goths, whom he sought to elevate by assimilating them to the Getae, attributing to them, moreover, all sorts of intellectual aptitudes and curiosities. The fable-mongering of Jordanes or of his model Cassiodorus, who could not even distinguish Getae and Goths, can in no way be considered a source for a history which they knew only in a vague and distorted form, unless we are going to accept anything as a source. Crişan, being a professional, does not hesitate to note the exaggerations of the text, before going on to draw an unexpected conclusion—the necessity of "including in the history of Romanian philosophy a chapter dealing with the philosophy of the Daco–Getae, which ought to be researched and made the subject of a monograph".[40] It is an astounding statement. Granted, a few considerations might be possible, if we agree to be caught up in Jordanes's game, but a *monograph* on the history of Dacian philosophy, when we do not even have three words written in Dacian!

There was a certain agitation, too, around the insoluble question of the Dacian language. Whether it was a "Latin" language or different from Latin, it demanded to be reconstituted and perhaps even established as a subject in the university curriculum. At one point it was suggested that a Department of Dacian Language should be set up in the University of Bucharest. I do not know whether it was intended that Dacian philosophy should be taught in Dacian; what is certain is that all these fine initiatives collapsed in the face of one unavoidable obstacle: the non-existence of the object of study. The enthusiasts keep marching on, however. For several decades a whole "amateur movement" has been invading the territory of linguistics, imagining fantastic etymologies capable of restoring to us the language of our ancestors. This sort of "para-linguistics" with ultra-nationalist accents seems to have become a veritable social phenomenon in Romania.

More prudent, but likewise pursuing the goal of consolidating the Dacian heritage, have been a number of academic research projects along the lines inaugurated by Hasdeu. The dedicated specialist in this direction is I. I. Russu, the author of *The Language of the Thraco-Dacians* (1959 and 1967). He succeeded in identifying—although his findings are considered debatable by many linguists—no less than 160 words belonging to the Dacian substratum, which, with their derivatives, could represent around 10 percent of the basic word stock of the Romanian language. The language we speak would thus have a perceptible Dacian coloring.

We should also recall in the same context the far from negligible influence exercised by the scholarly ramblings of the highly controversial businessman settled in Italy, Iosif Constantin Drăgan. A legionary in his youth, Drăgan was later close to the Ceauşescu regime, a characteristic transition where Dacian mythology is concerned. As the author of *We, the Thracians* (1976) and editor of the periodical of the same title *(Noi, tracii)* that was launched in 1974, he was the leading figure of an entire movement aimed at amplifying the role of the Thracians in European history, a movement supported by all sorts of amateurs (even a lawyers' group!) but also by some less than scrupulous professionals (among them the archaeologists Dumitru Berciu and Ion Horaţiu Crişan). In the periodical *Noi, tracii* it was possible, for example, to claim that the ancestors of the Romanians lived 100,000 years ago[41], eloquent proof that the Romanian people is the oldest in the continent, if not in the world. As for the extent of the Thracians' territory, Drăgan generously allows them almost half of Europe, centered, evidently, on the present-day space of Romania. It is interesting that the volume *We, the Thracians* contains arguments and whole passages (for example those referring to the "Latinity" of the Dacian language) identical to the formulations which appeared almost simultaneously in *Anale de istorie*. It matters little who took the information from whom; what is significant is the identification of the Institute of History of the Party, an organism invested with scholarly and ideological authority in communist Romania, with the sort of approach practiced by Drăgan.

But even if we leave fable-mongering and irresponsible exaggerations to one side, it is clear that the Dacians have ended up by imposing themselves in Romanian consciousness. It seems that they have, in the end, won the war with the Romans. The series of busts displayed in front of the National Military Museum in Bucharest is telling in this respect; Dacians outnumber Romans by three to one, the former being represented by Dromichetes, Burebista, and Decebalus, the latter by Trajan alone. We have come a long way since the Athenaeum frescoes!

Indeed, the identification of the Romanians with the Dacians seems to be on the way to becoming a matter of European renown. According to accounts in the press, the president of Italy, Oscar Luigi Scalfaro, on a visit to Bucharest, thought fit to offer the Romanian people apologies—somewhat belated—for the conquest of Dacia by the Romans. Authentic or not, the anecdote is significant for the logic of historical mythology. In fact, the relationship between the Italian president and Trajan is just as mythical as any special relationship linking President Iliescu with Dromichetes or Decebalus.

THE SLAVS, AN OSCILLATING PRESENCE

The ongoing match between the Dacians and the Romans was somewhat complicated by the additional involvement of the Slav factor (other ethnic elements, being less substantial and more rapidly assimilated by the Romanians, could not claim to have participated in the Romanian foundation story). The Slavs, as is well known, had a significant influence on the Romanian language, as well as on early Romanian institutions and culture. In fact the appreciation of their role has also swung between extremes, according to the changing ideological and political conjuncture.

In the Latinist phase, and in nineteenth-century historiography in general until quite late on, the Slav factor was eliminated or drastically minimized. The tendency is easily explained in the context of the process of modernization of Romanian society and the desperate attempt (with partial and temporary success) to escape from the Slav space of the continent. It is worth noting that up to B. P. Hasdeu, modern Romanian historians did not even know Slavonic or the various Slav languages, a paradoxical situation given the Slavonic packaging of medieval Romanian culture. Hasdeu himself, who was educated in a Slav environment and who could be considered the first Romanian Slavicist, did not prove to be an upholder of Slav influence. While he sought to moderate Latinism by recourse to the Dacian substratum, where the Slavs were concerned he strove to limit their impact on the Romanian synthesis. Hasdeu considered that the Romanian people had been fully formed when it entered into relations with the Slavs. Slav words had come into the Romanian language not by ethnic contact but through political, religious, and cultural links over some seven centuries, up to the time of Matei Basarab and Vasile Lupu.[42]

The reaction towards rehabilitating the Slavs and Slavonic culture in Romanian history came from the Junimists of the late nineteenth century as a reply to Latinism and, in a sense, as an exercise in rising above national complexes. I have already mentioned Panu's suggestions in this direction. What caused a sensation, however, was the *Etymological Dictionary* (1870–1879) of Alexandru Cihac, a close associate of Junimea. The etymologies established by Cihac led to the unexpected conclusion that the lexical base of the Romanian language was more Slav (and of other origins) than Latin: two-fifths Slav elements, one-fifth Turkish, and likewise one-fifth Latin. Romanian became a mixed language in which Turkisms and words of Latin origin had about the same weight. The almost simultaneous publication of the dictionaries of Laurian and Cihac illustrates the extremes between which the interpretation of the Romanian language, and of origins and influences in general, was evolving (with the necessary observation that Cihac's work is appreciated by specialists as being far superior to Laurian's linguistic fantasies).

This etymological Gordian knot was cut by Hasdeu with his seductive theory of the *circulation of words*. The structure of a language—Hasdeu shows—is not given by the mere number of words but by their circulation. Some words are almost forgotten, preserved only in dictionaries, while others are in constant use. Their value is thus very different. "It is true that Slavisms and even Turkisms exist in no small numbers among the Romanians; in circulation, however—that is, in the most vital activity of Romanian speech, in its most organic movement—they lose out almost completely in comparison with Latinisms." It is possible to formulate complete sentences only with words of Latin origin, but no sentence is possible using exclusively words of other origins. Hasdeu's demonstration turned the relationship round again, away from the emphasis on Slav influence.[43]

The Slav factor, however, was forcefully highlighted by Ioan Bogdan. For him, the Slavs became a *constituent element* of the Romanian synthesis: "The influence of the Slav element in the formation of our nation is so evident that we may say without exaggeration that we cannot even speak of a Romanian people before the absorption of Slav elements by the native Roman population in the course of the sixth to tenth centuries."[44] In the Romanian language there are "an enormous number of Slav elements", adopted either directly, through cohabitation, or through political and literary contacts. The Slavonic language was used in the church and the state, and even in "the day-to-day business of the Romanians" until the sixteenth or seventeenth century; and in the life of the state "almost all our old institutions are either of Slav origin or contain, alongside a few elements inherited from the Romans, a greater number of Slav elements".[45] Romanian-Bulgarian relations in particular are treated by Ioan Bogdan in a manner which Romanian nationalism could not fail to find disagreeable. While we, the Romanians, "were departing more and more from Roman culture and becoming savage", the Bulgarians, "who came like barbarians over us, took from their Byzantine neighbors, under the protective wings of an organized and powerful state, a civilization which was then advanced, that of Byzantium, which was none other than the continuation, in a Greek form with oriental influences, of the old Roman civilization".[46] For three centuries the Bulgarian tsardom ruled north of the Danube; this is the period in which many Slav elements of culture and political organization penetrated Romanian society. To a large extent the Slav influence was thus Bulgarian influence.

Ioan Bogdan represented the most advanced point reached in the affirmation of Slav influence prior to the advent of communist historiography. His contemporaries and historians of the next generation had varying points of view on the issue, but there was no return to the denial or ignoring of the Slav factor. Even if the former Junimist A. D. Xenopol did not go as far as Bogdan, he allowed a considerable weight to the Slav influence and believed, like Bogdan, that the Bulgarian state also ruled over Romanian territories (a point of view which he formulated in *The Theory of Roesler*, and later in *The History of the Romanians in Dacia*

Traiana). Iorga, while close to Bogdan in other respects, was far more Latinist in his unraveling of Romanian origins. He did not accept Bulgar domination north of the Danube and tended to place limits on the extent of the influence which resulted from Romanian–Slav cohabitation: "From all the life of the Slavs who were in these parts there have remained only many words that have entered our language, but more for secondary ideas and for articles of trade bought from markets on the right bank of the Danube: where principle ideas are concerned we can express ourselves completely in words which come from the old Roman inheritance. Then they have left behind certain elements of folk mythology, certain institutions, and that is all."[47]

The "New School", which took Ioan Bogdan as a model, was critical of Iorga for, among other things, underestimating the extent of Slav influence, though their conclusions tended to be more moderate than those of Bogdan himself. C. C. Giurescu and P. P. Panaitescu insisted on the many Slav elements that had penetrated Romanian language, culture, and political organization, while still considering them as secondary additions to the Daco–Roman base. All the same, as far as language is concerned, Giurescu underlines that "the influence of the Slavs is greater than the influence exercised by the Germanic peoples on the languages of the Gallo–Romans or the Italians". He accepts, but with nuances, Bogdan's claim that we cannot speak of a Romanian people prior to its mixing with the Slavs: "This claim must be understood as meaning that the Romanian people acquired its full composition, its complete ethnic characteristics, only after the Slav element had been added to the *essential* Daco–Roman element, which is the *foundation*. In other words, we are not dealing with *equal* parts, either quantitatively or qualitatively, and the greater accent must still fall on the former two elements."[48] A conflictual note, which must be seen in the context of Romanian–Russian and Romanian–Bulgarian relations in the interwar period, is also added to the Slav penetration. "The Slavs", insists Giurescu, "came to Dacia as conquerors." And they showed even more brutality than the Germanic peoples or the Huns. The conquest also explains the *Slav origin of the Romanian boyar class*, a thesis encountered in several authors, but systematized by P. P. Panaitescu (in his article "The Problem of the Origins of the Boyar Class").[49]

The key moment in the integration of the Romanians in the Slav space was, of course, the pro-Soviet phase of Romanian communism. As we have seen, the Dacians and Romans remained in their founding position, though evoked with no enthusiasm. However, Slav influence was emphasized as much as possible. In Roller's textbook there is no reference to the Latin origin of any word, but tens of Slavonic words are mentioned, demonstrating a powerful influence "in all branches of our economic, social, political, military, and cultural life". If the accent had previously been on the southern Slavs (the Bulgarians), now the Kievan state moves into the foreground, with its essential role in the formation of the Romanian states "lying at the base of the Romanian–Russian relations which have developed over the centuries".[50]

The directives issued by Mihail Roller in 1952 concerning the orientation of historical research express eloquently what was being prepared: the fusion of the history of the Romanians with that of the Slavs, and of the eastern Slavs in particular.

> Without for a moment losing sight of the existence of the Romanized native population (Daco–Roman), the problem of whether the process of formation of the eastern Slavs also took place partially or not at all on part of the territory of our country should be studied [...]. The existence in the vicinity of our country of the powerful feudal state of Kiev, with its advanced civilization, which cast reflected light throughout the east of Europe; the struggles of the Kievan state against the reactionary citadel then represented by Byzantium; and the subsequent inclusion of part of the territory of our country within the feudal state of Kiev contributed to the development of feudal relations and hastened the process of feudal organization in our country. The extension of the Bulgarian feudal state of the ninth and tenth centuries over the territory of our country is an indisputable fact and contributed to the development of the country. This influence of the southern Slavs completed that of the eastern Slavs, which preceded it and again followed it in the eleventh and twelfth centuries, when part of the territory of our country was included in the *cnezate* of Halich.[51]

If ethnically and linguistically the Romanians remained basically Daco–Romans (but with notable Slav influences), the *political foundation* tended to become purely and simply Slav. The distribution of influences is worth noting: Russia first of all, then Bulgaria in second place, while Byzantium appears as "reactionary" (Greece, which Stalin had coveted at one time, had ended up in the Western sphere).

The orientation of communism towards national values led to an ebbing of Slav influences. Without entering into the details of this issue—in which there are differences of accent from one author to another—we may note that in general the political distancing from the Slavs was translated into their exclusion from the ethnic composition of the Romanians. The strategy was simple: it comprised the pushing back in time of the "moment" when the Romanian people was formed. The tenth century—proposed by Ioan Bogdan, accepted by the interwar generation, adopted with a slight shift back to the end of the ninth century in the 1960 *History of the Romanians* and again in Constantin Daicoviciu's compendium of the same title of 1969—meant accepting that the Slavs were a founding element, albeit in a secondary role to the Daco–Romans, and that without their assimilation there could be no talk of a "Romanian people". What was sought in the phase of national communism was not only the lessening of Slav influences, but even more their placing beyond the threshold of the formation of the Romanian people. Slav elements had to have been adopted by a Romanian people *already formed*, or at least crystallized in its essential structures.

Historians proceeded to identify *proto-Romanians*, and a *proto-Romanian* language, starting from the sixth century, on the basis of political calculations that were presented as the fruit of objective research. The record again goes to the *Military History of the Romanian People*, in which the Romanians are already Romanians in the year 271, if not long before, with the role of the Slavs (not to mention other contributions) being proclaimed insignificant. Particularly amusing from an arithmetical point of view is the claim that "the Romanian people dates back over 2,000 years to the time when the Dacian people adopted the Latin language and Latin spirituality".[52] (In passing we might ask how it is possible to adopt a spirituality.) Subtracting 2,000 (to say nothing of "over") from 1984, the year in which the volume appeared, we arrive at the year 16 B.C., some 120 years before the conquest of Dacia by the Romans! The explanation of the "calculation" does not lie in any new theory about Romanization, but simply in a reference by Ceauşescu to the Romanians' antiquity of more than 2,000 years, an idea enthusiastically picked up by Ilie Ceauşescu and the authors of the *Military History*.

What is meant by proto-Romanians? What is meant by a people formed or approximately formed? On the basis of what arguments could one claim that around the year 600 people spoke *proto-Romanian*, when for the period under discussion and even for many centuries later we do not have a single sample of Romanian or "proto-Romanian"? Is it possible, in general, to date the formation of a people—a phenomenon even more complex and harder to define than the formation of the respective language (since it presupposes a certain cultural community and self-consciousness)? When were the French, the Italians, the Germans, or the English "formed"? The exceptional insistence of Romanian historiography on this question—which has been given the scholarly designation "ethnogenesis"—is a national particularity. Any periodization of this sort responds to ideological requirements, and the requirements of communism were first of all the formation of the Romanian people alongside the Slavs, and later its removal from the sphere of Slav influence.

THE NATION: BIOLOGICAL ORGANISM OR SOCIAL COMMUNITY?

Readers may wonder what my own opinion is concerning the relative weighting of the various elements composing the Romanian people. The answer is that I have no answer, for the simple reason that, put in such a way, the problem is formulated in strictly mythological terms. By way of response I could only align myself with one or other of the foundation myths in circulation. The Romanians are Romanians, not Dacians, Romans, or Slavs. Insistence on autochthonous roots puts a value in the first place on the biological stock of origins. But where is this manifested? In blood? In genes? Is there such a thing as Romanian blood? Is there a gene that is specifically Romanian, or Dacian, or Daco–Roman? The only indisputable connection to origins is ultimately that offered by the language. The Roman essence of the Romanian language, as well as the very name *Român*

(Romanian), would tend to tilt the balance towards the Romans; perhaps in the end, although not in the way that they believed, the historians of the Transylvanian School were closer to a certain truth (at least to the only truth that can be demonstrated) than the promoters of Dacianism.

But it is a very long way from this to the claim that we are actually more Romans than anything else. How much did the Romanians of the Middle Ages have in common with Dacians and Romans? Did their Slavonic culture and Orthodox religion not bring them much closer to Byzantine–Slav civilization? What, for example, is more important for defining the Romanians: Dacian origin or Orthodox religion? (The difficulty is resolved for those who see in Zalmoxis a precursor of Christ!) And nowadays, whom do the Romanians most resemble? The Dacians? The Romans? The Slavs? Or the peoples of contemporary Europe? An Arab proverb quoted by Marc Bloch says that "People resemble their time more than they resemble their parents."[53] The saying can be applied equally well to individuals as to nations. However different the Romanians may be from, let us say, the Germans, they are far closer to the latter *today* than to their Dacian and Roman ancestors. These ancestors belonged to "traditional" civilizations with a completely different register of mentalities and behavior than we have in our predominantly technological and urban world. We are brought close to the Dacians and Romans, of course, by all that brings us close to our fellow humans in general, regardless of time and space. Otherwise, when we turn to a more precise inventory, all we can produce are platitudes along the lines of: "We have inherited the courage of the Dacians and the rational spirit of the Romans..." A nation is not a *biological organism* but a *social organism*; it does not present itself as a simple aggregate of individuals (each with their multitude of ancestors) but as a cultural synthesis. Whatever backwardness they may have accumulated, the Romanians nevertheless present the spiritual profile of a people of the twentieth century.

I am not at war with foundation myths. Every nation has its own, which it cultivates with care. The Romanians will go on evoking their history of the earliest times, and it is normal that they should do so. But what must be understood, not in order to blow up the whole mechanism but to penetrate the logic of its operation, is the process of actualization, in mythological terms, of originary foundation or successive foundations. We live in the present but we relate to our origins; we have an indisputable identity but we valorize it through the identity of our ancestors. That all this belongs to the realm of the historical and political imaginary does not mean that it is without significance: quite the contrary. In strict reality we are separated from the distant past, but by its imaginary actualization the past becomes a great force in the present.

CHAPTER THREE

Continuity

A HISTORIOGRAPHICAL PARADOX: THE AREA WHERE THE ROMANIAN PEOPLE WAS FORMED

An exceptional insistence on the "formation of the people" gives a particular character to Romanian historiography and historical consciousness. This question is doubled and amplified by that of the *space* in which the Romanian people and language were formed. It is here that we come up against the famous issue of continuity, which, along with "ethnogenesis", has contributed to the creation of a veritable "national obsession", kept alive by the play of ideology and politics. The problem of continuity is no more than the extreme manifestation of a more general lack of clear knowledge concerning the geographical setting of the beginnings of the Romanian people. Once again we find ourselves confronting a situation which is peculiar in European historiography. According to the various divergent foreign and Romanian theses, the Romanians were formed either on a territory corresponding to modern Romania or in a limited zone within that space, very limited in some variants; or in a region stretching far beyond the present geographical extent of the Romanian people to include a large part of Central and Southeastern Europe; or, finally, somewhere south of the Danube, completely outside the country where they now live.

Three principal factors lie behind this highly paradoxical situation.

First, there is a certain disaccord between the effective process of Roman expansion and Romanization and the present ethnic configuration of Southeastern Europe. The northern half of the Balkan Peninsula formed part of the Empire for some eight centuries, a period long enough to allow the installation and consolidation of a thriving Roman life. To the north of the Danube, on the other hand, on the present territory of Romania, the Romans effectively ruled only half of Dacia. Moreover, the province of Dacia belonged to the Empire for only 165 years, which may raise questions about the extent of Romanization there, while the un-annexed part of Dacia logically had no way of being Romanized at all. However, the result turns out to be the opposite of the starting point: Romania, the successor of Rome in this part of Europe, lies to the north of the Danube and not to the south.

Second, the most varied hypotheses have free rein, given the paucity of sources for the area north of the Danube during the millennium that separates the withdrawal of Roman rule in the year 271 from the founding of the Romanian states in the fourteenth century, and especially the complete lack of internal written sources. Where some historical aspects are concerned, archaeology has proved capable of filling in the gaps. We now know that the territory of Dacia continued to be densely populated; we can reconstruct the way of life of the people who lived here. Unfortunately, the archaeological material cannot *talk*. It cannot tell us what language was spoken by the makers of objects from a particular century and a particular corner of present-day Romania.

The last consideration, but by no means the least important, is that ideological and political factors have intervened in the game, greatly complicating the variants. The denial of Romanian continuity and the bringing of the Romanians from south of the Danube obviously corresponded to Austro–Hungarian objectives in the eighteenth and nineteenth centuries. It continues to be a point of dogma in present-day Hungarian historiography, where it serves to ensure chronological primacy in Transylvania for the Magyars. However, similar arguments have been used, paradoxically, by both immigrationists and Romanian nationalists. The same historical premises can justify one theory or its opposite. The notion of the extermination of the Dacians, invoked by Latinists obsessed with the nobility and purity of Romanian blood, served the immigrationist thesis equally well. What argument could be better than the emptying of Dacia of its native population? Conversely, the notion of the non-Romanization of the Dacians, a tenet of the nationalist extreme of pure Dacianism, only provided further arguments for the hypothesis that the Romanians and the Romanian language had expanded from outside the present space of Romania, given that all serious linguists consider Romanian to be a Romance language.

NORTH AND SOUTH OF THE DANUBE: A POSSIBLE COMPROMISE?

According to the Transylvanian School version, which was adopted by Romanian historiography as a whole around the middle of the nineteenth century, the initial Romanian space included both Dacia and the area south of the Danube. The Romanians appear as the successors to the Romans in this part of Europe. As information about the territory north of the Danube is scanty, their history in the centuries following the Aurelian withdrawal unfolds more in present-day Bulgaria than in Romania. "The Romanians were united to the Bulgars from the time of the arrival of the latter", says Șincai, "so that not only did the Bulgars fight the Greeks but in larger numbers and more often the Romanians fought them under the name of Bulgars, Kumans, and Pechenegs." In the year 963, with Samuil, who was *Romanian*, "kingship passed from the Bulgarians to the Romanians".[1] The first Bulgarian tsardom was thus Bulgarian–Romanian, and the second Romanian–Bulgarian; the "Romanian–Bulgarian Empire", founded by Petru and Asan,

Vlachs from south of the Danube, and raised to its apogee by Ioniţă, was to represent an important chapter in Romanian history down to the phase of communist historiography. Kogălniceanu makes the kingdom of the Transdanubian Vlachs continue to the year 1394, when it was destroyed by the Turks (he is referring, of course, to the Bulgarian tsardoms). He also claims that the Romanians of the Balkans provided numerous emperors for Rome and Byzantium. Laurian, likewise, refers to the "Bulgarian–Romanian Kingdom" (the first tsardom) and the "Empire of the Romanians and the Bulgarians" (the second tsardom, which lasted until the end of the fourteenth century).

We may note that the shifting of the principal scene of Romanian history for several centuries from north to south of the Danube might suggest a scenario similar to that maintained by the immigrationists. However, the Romanian historians presented themselves as partisans of continuity. Romanity south of the Danube was simply more active, more "visible" than the Romanity of former Dacia.

In contrast with this generous expansion of the initial Romanian space, Hasdeu set out, in his *Critical History of the Romanians*, to impose severe limits on it. The lack of Germanic elements in the Romanian language made him withdraw the Daco–Romans from the regions on either side of the Danube, where the presence of migrating Germans was attested. The space in which the Romanian people and language were formed thus becomes even narrower than the frontiers of Roman Dacia. The "ethnographic map" of Romania from the third to the sixth century extends, according to Hasdeu, "from Severin to Haţeg, from the Temeşiana mountains to the Olt, far from the Goths and Gepids". Thus, "the Romanian nationality was born and developed in Oltenia, as far as the Haţeg Valley". From Oltenia the Romanians spread into Transylvania, Muntenia, and Moldavia, by a prolonged process which began in the sixth century and continued until the fourteenth. Hasdeu insists on the "Oltenians' force of expansion".[2] For him, Oltenia was, and remains, the nucleus of Romanian nationality. It is certain that the nationalist Hasdeu was impressed by the "ethnic cleanness" of Oltenia, which, out of all the Romanian territories, was the province with the lowest proportion of foreign elements.

We encounter another sort of territorial limitation with Xenopol. His aim was to dismantle, point by point, the demonstration of Roesler, who had published his *Romanian Studies* in 1871. In support of his thesis of the Transdanubian origin of the Romanians, Roesler invoked the similarities between Daco–Romanian and Macedo–Romanian speech[*], two dialects of the same language which are found nowadays at a great distance from each other, and the south Slav influence in the Romanian language. Xenopol's response appeared in 1884 under the title *The Theory of Roesler: Studies of the Persistence of the Romanians in Dacia Traiana* (and in French in 1885: *Une énigme historique. Les Roumains au Moyen Age*). His tactic is to

---

[*] Daco–Romanian: the Romanian language as spoken in Romania itself; Macedo–Romanian: the dialect of the Aromanians of the Balkans. *Trans.*

concentrate on two objectives: first, to separate, from the very beginning, the Romanians north of the Danube from the Macedo–Romanians; and second, to explain the south Slav influence otherwise than by the Romanians having lived south of the river. According to Xenopol, Moesia was weakly Romanized in antiquity, so the Romanians could not have been formed there. The Romanic element is not found in Moesia but further south in the Balkan mountains. There is thus no direct link between the two Romance branches of the East: "The Daco–Romanians and the Macedo–Romanians are two distinct peoples from their origin, who owe their striking similarities to the circumstances of their having emerged from the same mixture of elements."[3] In order to distance the Romanians further from the Balkan sphere, Xenopol separated them from the Danube, too, and pushed them towards the mountains. In the age of migrations, he argues, the Romanians withdrew within the "fortress" of the Carpathians, into the area of Transylvania; this explains the remarkable unity of the Romanian language and the existence of words of Hungarian origin in the speech of all Romanians. It also lies behind the "dismountings" of Negru Vodă in Wallachia and Dragoş-Bogdan in Moldavia. After the last wave of migration, that of the Tatars, the Romanians (realizing that the migrations were over?) came down to the foothills and plains and founded the two principalities. The formation of the Romanian people and Romanian continuity are thus limited to Transylvania, and took place within the shelter of the Carpathian arc.

As far as clarifying the Slav influence is concerned—the other essential point of Xenopol's demonstration—here, too, we are invited to observe a complete overturning of Roesler's arguments. Once the evolution of the Romanians south of the Danube is no longer accepted, the opposite solution remains: expansion of the Slavs from south to north of the river. Xenopol considers that the first Bulgarian tsardom extended over the entire territory of today's Romania. For several centuries "Romania" was part of Bulgaria. Hence the Slav rite in the Romanian Church and Slavonic political and cultural influence in general.

How would a Romanian nationalist today regard the limitation of Romanian continuity to Transylvania and the subordination of the first Romanians to the Bulgarian tsardom? And yet Xenopol pursued his arguments out of pure nationalism, with the intention of bringing down to the ground the whole scaffolding constructed by Roesler. The pathways of nationalism are varied and sometimes unexpected.

Hasdeu placed the "cradle" of the Romanian people within the bounds of Oltenia. Xenopol expressed his preference for another of the Romanian provinces: Transylvania. Onciul went beyond these limitations. In a text which was conceived as a review of Xenopol's book but which developed into a significant work in its own right, one of the fundamental monographs on the issue ("*The Theory of Roesler: Studies of the Persistence of the Romanians in Dacia Traiana* by A. D. Xenopol: A Critical Appraisal", in *Convorbiri literare*, 1885), he opted for the whole space of Roman Dacia: Oltenia, the Banat, and the western part of Transylvania. According to Onciul, the area in which the Romanian people was formed also extended beyond the Danube. Moesia, which was only superficially Romanized according to Xenopol's thesis, became, for Onciul, a powerful focus of Romanity. The Danube disappeared as a border. Originary "Romania" included about half the present territory of Romania, but also a large part of present-day Bulgaria and Serbia.

We have seen that there was already a tradition in the national historiography of including Romanity south of the Danube in Romanian history. Onciul was referring, however, not only to a common territory of the Romanians and the Balkan Vlachs but to a feeding of Romanity north of the Danube with Romanic waves from the south, which brought him, in part, close to the immigrationists. His theory, which he termed "admigration", is a synthesis or compromise solution between the strict thesis of continuity and the no less strict thesis of immigration. From Onciul's point of view the Romanian people was formed from both the continuity of the Daco–Roman element in the province of Dacia and a considerable input of Romanized population from south of the river. In the first centuries of the Middle Ages the Roman element in the Balkans, claims Onciul, was actually stronger "than it could have been in Dacia Traiana in the time of the invasions. This Roman element in the Balkan countries is beyond doubt identical to the Romanian element, and thus our early history unfolded especially in the Balkan Peninsula, beginning with the Roman conquest of the Thraco–Illyrian lands and their Romanization. It would be very wrong to give up this history and to limit our past only to Dacia Traiana, where it seems that we will look for it in that time in vain, to know it and understand it."[4]

For several centuries from the seventh century onwards, following the Slav invasions south of the Danube there was considerable movement from the Romanic "reservation" of the Balkans into the area north of the river, the Romanity of which, although it had survived, had nevertheless been considerably diminished by a series of barbarian invasions. Like Xenopol, Onciul argued that the territories on the left side of the Danube had belonged to the Bulgarian tsardom, which would have facilitated the process of "admigration". He even considered—in contrast to Xenopol—that the second tsardom, the Romanian–Bulgarian Empire, had extended as far as the Carpathians, which would further explain the weight of the Romanian element in this political construction. The origins of Wallachia are also to be found here, with Muntenia breaking away at a certain point from the Asan state. The Romanian population spread east of the Olt and the Carpathians—into Muntenia and Moldavia—only from the second half of the eleventh century (following the abandonment of these lands by the Pechenegs). The Romanians thus appear at one and the same time as indigenous (in Roman Dacia), immigrants (from south of the Danube), and conquerors (in the principalities).

I do not wish to discuss the validity of the solution proposed by Onciul, or indeed the validity of such solutions in general. I would merely point out that the admigrationist thesis achieved a skillful combination of continuity and immigrationism, offering plausible answers to all the uncomfortable questions of the immigrationists. If the Romanian element had also formed to the south of the Danube, then the whole immigrationist argument could no longer be used against continuity north of the river.

In his later interpretations Onciul came to put a somewhat greater accent on the area of Roman Dacia and to underline the permanence of the Roman element installed here, assigning only an auxiliary role to the contribution from south of the Danube.

It was along the same line of synthesis between continuity and immigration that the greatest Romanian linguists took their positions. Overall it is possible to note a greater willingness among linguists than among historians to consider Romanity south of the Danube as a founding element. Alexandru Philippide (1859–1933) goes furthest, in his *Origin of the Romanians* (1923–1927), where he argues for a complete (or almost complete) extinction of Romanity north of the Danube after the Aurelian withdrawal, and a re-colonization of the present territory of Romania from the seventh to the thirteenth century by a Romanic population from south of the Danube.[5]

Differentiating himself only partially from Roesler and Philippide, Ovid Densuşianu (1873–1938), in his *Histoire de la langue roumaine* (1902)—a work which enjoyed a large readership in the field of Romance linguistics—took into consideration the survival of a certain Roman element to the north of the Danube, especially in the southwest of today's Romania. However, in his view, too, the Balkan element was more important than the indigenous contribution, although he placed its origin not in Moesia, as was generally accepted, but further west in Illyria.[6] Finally, Sextil Puşcariu (1877–1948) proposed a linguistic synthesis involving to an equal extent the territory of Dacia Traiana and the Thraco–Illyrian provinces of the Balkan Peninsula.

Gheorghe Brătianu also follows the Onciul-Puşcariu line in *Une énigme et un miracle historique: Le peuple roumain* (1937, Romanian edition 1940), in which he engages in a polemic with the immigrationists while still accepting an origin partly south of the Danube for the Romanian language and people and conceding to the immigrationists that "the region to the east of the Carpathians, Moldavia and Bessarabia, was certainly the last stage of Romanian expansion in the Middle Ages".[7] However, the relatively late Romanization of the Moldavian area (in the centuries preceding the formation of the principalities) is not, according to Brătianu, an argument in favor of Slav priority, since the Slavs, who are mentioned by Jordanes and Procopius, had been replaced in the meantime by various peoples of the Steppes, such as the Pechenegs and Kumans. If Moldavia had not originally been Romanian, it had thus not been Slav either.

The idea of a double origin, north and south of the Danube, is expressed clearly by P. P. Panaitescu in his textbook of the history of the Romanians: "[...] from the existence of Albanian elements in the Romanian language and the similarity of the Daco–Romanian and Macedo–Romanian dialects it can be shown that the area where the Romanian folk was formed is the lower Danube valley, on both sides of the river, the whole of Dacia Traiana, and the two Moesias (Bulgaria and Serbia)."[8]

One thing must be noticed in all of this, unexpected as it may be for the Romanian reader of today, who has been subjected during the decades of national communism to a violent anti-Roesler campaign: that is, the fact that many Romanian specialists, historians and linguists, chose a compromise solution between continuity and immigrationism (with a variety of nuances concerning the weighting or extent of the territories north and south of the Danube that were involved in the Romanian genesis).

THE CONSOLIDATION OF ROMANITY NORTH OF THE DANUBE

There are, at the same time, historians who, without in any way ignoring Balkan Romanity, set out in the first place to consolidate and integrate the sphere of Romanity and Romanian-ness north of the Danube. In his *Beginnings of Roman Life at the Mouth of the Danube* (1923), Vasile Pârvan couples the province of Dacia with a second focus of Romanity, which he terms "Scythian Dacia". Under this name he brings together Dobrogea, which was under Roman rule for centuries, Muntenia, and the southern part of Moldavia and Bessarabia. Here then, in as much as Romanian rights were justified in terms of Daco–Roman origins, we have the inclusion in the ideal originary Romanian sphere of a large part of the territory that remained outside Dacia Traiana. Though not officially annexed to the Empire, the plain to the north of the Danube, caught as it was between Transylvanian, Oltenian, and Dobrogean Romanity, was subject to a perceptible degree of Romanization. "Dobrogea is full of Roman towns. Muntenia and Moldavia are full of Dacian villages permeated by Roman life. Between Trajan's Dacia, which only began its new life from the year 107 onwards, and Dobrogea, which had begun it almost a hundred years earlier, numerous roads were opened up, which were well guarded and much traveled, both from Transylvania to the sea and from the sea to Transylvania. In the valleys of the Siret, the Buzău, the Ialomița, and the Argeș, Roman troops, Roman merchants, and Daco–Roman peasants passed up and down, and Dacian life, in its deepest recesses, became, without noise or pomp, Roman life."[9] The whole territory of Romania, all the Romanian provinces, brought their contribution to the formation of the Romanian people. Such is Pârvan's conclusion (which he also expresses clearly in his *Dacia*).

Iorga, too, tends to integrate the complete area of Romania into an early "Romanian Land", even if he does not regard the intensity of Romanity or Romanian-ness as equal from one province to another: "The whole land— Transylvania, where there were many Romanians; Oltenia, where there were a considerable number; Muntenia, where villages were rarer; and Moldavia, where our people were still gradually Romanizing the western Slavs, the little Russians— was called the Romanian Land [...]."[10]

For Iorga and Pârvan, the Romanians are, by virtue of their very survival, in contrast to the greater part of the Latin element in the Balkans, the inheritors and continuers of eastern Romanity in its entirety. Romanity south of the Danube played a significant part in the extension of the Roman element in Dacia, but once implanted north of the river its persistence was principally due to its own vitality. The *Romanian* phase of history unfolds in the first place on the territory of present-day Romania. Referring to what is usually known in Romanian historiography as the "Romanian–Bulgarian Empire", Iorga underlines its fundamentally Bulgarian character; the Romanian founders rapidly lost the consciousness "that they belonged to a folk other than the Bulgarian folk". "Through these scattered Romanians, these shepherds of ours, great and glorious things were achieved, but for *another folk.*"[11]

Nor does C. C. Giurescu invoke any movement of Romanian population from the other side of the Danube in the first centuries of the Middle Ages, although he underlines the presence and vitality of the Balkan Vlachs. He seeks, rather, to integrate the whole territory north of the river in the process of the constitution of the Romanian people. In response to Xenopol's "withdrawal into the mountains", which would have drastically limited the originary Romanian space, he proposes a *withdrawal into the forests* in the face of the various invaders: "The shelter of our ancestors in the Middle Ages was the forest." But since forests covered almost the whole Romanian land, we can hardly speak of a withdrawal or cession of territory at all. "The Muntenian plain and the Moldavian and Transylvanian plateaus were covered with immense woodlands. From the foothills of the mountains one could go to the Danube and the Dniester, and in some places as far as the sea, passing through forests all the way."[12] When the Slavs came, the Daco–Romans were at home in the Vlăsia Forest—the "Forest of the Romanians"—in the Muntenian plain.

For all this gradual concentration on the whole territory of present-day Romania, it can still be said that all historians before the communist period also took into consideration the formation and evolution of the Romanian people *in the Balkans.* The differences in interpretation concern the movement of population, that is, the participation (either massive or limited), non-participation, or negligible participation of Balkan Romanity in the construction of Romanian-ness north of the Danube. The historical demonstration was not without contemporary implications: Romania was seeking to play a role of arbiter in the Balkans and was already establishing itself as the protector of the Aromanians scattered through the peninsula.

THE COMMUNIST YEARS:
IDEOLOGICAL IMPERATIVES AND ARCHEOLOGICAL ARGUMENTS

The communist phase of historical discourse was marked, on the other hand, by the eclipse of Balkan Romanian-ness. In its "internationalist" stage the Slav expansion over the originary Romanian space—Russian in the north and Bulgarian in the south—left no room for any manifestations of Romanian-ness beyond the present borders; those borders were themselves blurred, submerged in the Slav sea. Nor did the following, nationalist, stage prove more favorable to the Romanians "out there". The principle of "non-interference" in the affairs of other states—a necessity if the Ceauşescu regime was to demand non-interference by the "others" in its own politics—was pushed back into the past. The borders of modern Romania were imprinted as an unchanging framework over its entire historical evolution—an eternal Romania, with the outline of the Greater Romania of 1918. (At one time the image of Greater Romania, filled in with a single color, appeared on maps intended for educational use regardless of the period represented. Romania emerged as the only European entity with an invariable outline, even in the Middle Ages, centuries before it was founded!) From this point of view it was no longer possible to talk of a historical "annexation" of the area south of the Danube, just as there could be no "renunciation" (again in a historical sense) of those provinces (Transylvania, Dobrogea, and Bessarabia) that had been included for centuries within other borders. History was rewritten in terms of a Romania which had existed forever, needing nothing from others and yielding them nothing of its heritage.

In the first volume (1960) of *The History of Romania*, a theoretical justification for the renunciation of the Balkan space was found by making a distinction between two stages, the first stage, "*preceding* the formation of the people, in which it is only possible to speak of a Roman or Romanic population", and the second, the "prolonged stage of the formation of the Romanian people itself as a separate people". Thus even if both banks of the Danube could be taken into consideration for the period of Roman rule in Dacia or immediately after, this issue has no connection to the actual formation of the Romanian people but only to the extension of the Romanic element in south-eastern Europe. The Romanian people was formed only after the separation of Balkan Romanity from Romanity north of the Danube following the Slav invasion—more precisely, "in the last centuries of the first millennium of our era, in the area north of the lower Danube, having its territorial nucleus in the hill and mountain lands of Dacia".[13]

The limitation to the area north of the Danube is accompanied by an even more strict limitation, which, for reasons of prudence, is expressed in the wooden language of the time. The phrase "having its territorial nucleus in the hill and mountain lands of Dacia" was intended to mean that the Romanian people was not even born on the whole territory of Romania but only where there had been Roman colonization, in the hill and mountain zone of Transylvania and Oltenia.

This was the opinion of Constantin Daicoviciu, which he later upheld openly with arguments in the years of relative "liberalization". In his contribution to *The History of Romania*, published in 1969, Daicoviciu underlined the fact that the principle of continuity concerned only Roman Dacia, not the entire Romanian territory of today, given that "the Dacian population in Muntenia and Moldavia was Romanized much later". He expressed reservations regarding the tendency to attribute ethnic identity to archaeological material, a method which was used and abused in order to decree the Romanian character of each and every vestige. He even dared to consider the Dridu culture (identified in Muntenia, less present in Transylvania, but highly developed in Bulgaria), which was generally interpreted by Romanian archaeologists in terms of continuity, as "a *Slav* culture (or more accurately, Slavo–Bulgar)".[14] The territory of Romania was thus divided between a Romanized Transylvania and an extra-Carpathian zone marked by a profound Slav imprint.

The Dridu culture was for several decades the focus of a polemic, with most Romanian researchers maintaining its Romanian character while foreigners regarded it as Slav. The stakes were particularly high as the period in question, the eighth and ninth centuries, corresponds to the crystallization of the Romanian ethnic and linguistic phenomenon. In contrast to Daicoviciu, Ion Nestor, an archaeologist otherwise noted for the value and originality of his research, demonstrates in *The History of the Romanian People* (1970) a remarkable degree of conformism. He sees the constitutive elements of the Dridu culture as *"in their majority* of Romanian origin", identifies "proto-Romanians" in the sixth century, and extends the area in which the Romanian people was formed, without much discussion, to the entire territory of the country, with an emphasis on the connections between the provinces.[15]

This version, in which the Romanian people was formed *exactly* on the territory where it now lives, without the slightest fluctuation of borders, was imposed in the 1970s and 1980s, both in the official discourse of national history and in the more or less conformist contributions of many specialists.

Ligia Bârzu's work *The Continuity of the Material and Spiritual Creation of the Romanian People on the Former Territory of Dacia* (1979), a newer version of which was written in the 1980s and published in 1991 (*The Origin and Continuity of the Romanians: Archaeology and Historical Tradition*), offers an overall perspective on the problem and a stimulating starting point for discussion of the relation between archaeology and continuity. Between the premises offered, which reflect an indisputable professionalism, and the already well known conclusions, the ideological grid of "unity and continuity" intervenes. Thus we find, presented as a well-established fact, the parallelism of the process of Romanization in Roman Dacia and outside it: "Taking into account all the possible considerations, it appears very probable that an early date can be accepted for the moment at which Latin came into general use in the territory of the eastern Dacians, in Muntenia and southern Moldavia."[16] It is clear from the context that this moment is prior to the Aurelian withdrawal, or at any rate not long after. For a "non-archaeologist" the difficulty is this: the organized and massive character of Roman colonization in the province of Dacia has generally been advanced in support of its rapid and profound Romanization; however, archaeology shows the survival until much later, after the Aurelian withdrawal, of important elements and "islands" of Dacian civilization. How was it then possible for there to take place a parallel phenomenon of Romanization, of the *imposition of the Latin language*, where the Romans had not settled?

We next find out that after centuries of uninterrupted material continuity there was a complete overturning in the second half of the sixth century and the first half of the seventh, with the settlement of the Slavs on Romanian territory. Everything changed—the form of houses, their contents, and even funerary rituals. We find only cremation burials, "in striking contrast with the preceding centuries": "This is the moment in which antique traditions disappear, when culture returns to prehistoric forms of manifestation, such as the preponderance of hand-worked pottery and the decline of craft techniques and traditions."[17]

The conclusion? We know it already: regardless of the premises, it cannot be other than material and spiritual continuity on the former territory of Dacia!

What we in fact see here is an amalgamation of "continuity of life" with Romanian continuity. Continuity of life is evident, and we scarcely need archaeological arguments any more to support it. Who today can still imagine that the Dacians disappeared, exterminated by the Romans, or that in 271 or at some subsequent date the population north of the Danube migrated to the south? The time is past when Roesler could shift the Daco–Romans to the Balkans while Xenopol crowded them into the mountains of Transylvania. However, the problem of Romanian continuity is not whether people continued to live here, but whether they continued to speak Latin, and later Romanian. Or was Latinity wiped out, as it was in Britain, in Pannonia, in the Balkans, and in North Africa? The archaeological discontinuity around the year 600, reflecting a restructuring which led to the evolution of the Dridu culture, might tend to invite an interpretation in such terms. Archaeology is a two-edged weapon: much depends on who uses it and how it is used. It is more correct and more prudent not to mix things: material arguments have nothing to say about the language or languages people spoke, or about the linguistic amalgam, either in favor of the Romanians or against them.

After 1989 the political reasons for limiting history to present-day borders no longer apply. The Dridu culture can now serve not only to keep the whole territory of Romania "under control", but to extend its area of origin. As nothing expresses the historical ideas in general circulation better than a school textbook, let us consider the map in the *History of the Romanians*, an eleventh-grade textbook of 1992, for an impression of the "new" area of formation of the Romanian people. "The area of the first Romanian archaeological ensemble" (which is of course the Dridu culture) includes the whole of Greater Romania, to which are added almost the entire territory of Hungary and Bulgaria as far as the Balkan mountains.[18] It is a remarkable expansion for a culture which Daicoviciu would not even allow to represent Transylvania! Would it not have been more correct to explain to the pupils that we do not actually know whether Dridu was a Romanian, Slav, or Slavo–Romanian culture? That in fact the investigation of material remains does not allow us to draw conclusions (at least not indisputable conclusions) about the language which the people in question spoke? Can we really say that Bulgaria, precisely in the phase of expansion of the first Bulgarian tsardom, was predominantly Romanian? The Romanians were of course present in this vast area, as were the Slavs; one group cannot be excluded in favor of the other.[19]

THE ROMANIAN STATE DURING THE "DARK MILLENNIUM"

Alongside ethnic continuity, a no less mythologized aspect is *political continuity*. The mere perpetuation of an amorphous Romanian element, subject to various periods of foreign domination, does not seem a satisfactory solution. Whether they admit it or not, what gives the Romanians complexes is the absence, for a thousand years, of a Romanian state, the lack of a political tradition deeply rooted in time, comparable with that of the neighboring nations.

The *Chronicle* of Huru was an attempt, for its time, to fill in this gap, by inventing out of nothing a Romanian republic in the year 271. The common state of the Romanians and Bulgarians might, more credibly, have played a similar role. But with Xenopol and Onciul it metamorphosed into a sort of Bulgarian domination north of the Danube.

Following unbeaten trails as was his wont, Hasdeu reconstructed a wondrous history around the great Basarab family. His essay about them in *Etymologicum Magnum Romaniae*, which was later published separately under the title *The Basarabs: Who? From Where? Since When?* (1896), offers perhaps the most fascinating historical text in all Romanian literature. Piece by piece Hasdeu builds up a scholarly demonstration guided by an apparently impeccable logic, until he succeeds in constructing a splendid imaginary edifice. The conclusion is that the Basarabs were originally a Dacian caste who gave Dacia kings and Rome several emperors. As leaders of Oltenia they then watched over the fortunes of the Romanian people for a millennium, before proceeding to found the Wallachian state. It is a perfect political continuity, already, in some periods, marked by events that are inscribed in the greater history of the world.

After so many attempts, unfortunately imaginary, the field still remained empty. In order to fill it in, Iorga suggested that the natives had organized themselves, after the Aurelian withdrawal, into what he called "popular Romanias", a solution which is not quite explicit but which appeared to many to be the saving version and which has been invoked by many authors down to the present day.

The Transylvanian voivodes Gelu, Glad, and Menumorut, recorded in the Hungarian Chronicle of Anonymus (*Gesta Hungarorum*), play an important role in Romanian history, precisely because they illustrate, alongside ethnic continuity, the presence of certain Romanian state structures at the time of Hungarian expansion. This privileged position tended to put brakes on the normal exercise of critical historiography. Rather than being real people, these three seem, like Negru Vodă, to be symbolic figures, the individualizations of a certain political idea or historical situation (in the case in question, the existence of Romanian formations), although this does not change the basic essence of the problem.

In the last half century there has been an attempt—based especially on archaeological material—to push such political units further back in time. It is indeed hard to conceive of an area the size of Romania without any forms of territorial organization, however summary. But this sort of fragmentation into self-contained mini-states was not enough to satisfy the national-communist ideology, with its emphasis on the complete unity of the country and the no less complete continuity of Dacia and Romania. The state, the whole state, had to continue whatever the price. Thus the Romanian Communist Party's *Program* of 1975, a text with considerable historical implications, mentions a "non-organized state", which remained on the territory of Dacia after the withdrawal of Roman rule.[20] According to all current definitions and interpretations, a state is generally considered to be something organized. The concept of the "non-organized state" was thus, at the time, a highly original contribution not only to the history of the Romanians but to the theory of the state in general. The uninterrupted existence of the state from Burebista to Ceaușescu imposed itself as the dogma of autochthonous national-communism, and so the Romanian state became one of the oldest in Europe.

CONCLUSIONS: ARCHEOLOGY, LINGUISTICS, AND POLITICS

In a rapid and inevitably incomplete overview, we have here the avatars of the originary Romanian space: from Hasdeu's Oltenia to the Romanian–Hungarian–Bulgarian complex of the latest school textbooks; from Roesler's exclusively Transdanubian Romanity to the no less exclusive formation of the Romanian people strictly on the territory of yesterday's Dacia and today's Romania. I shall not permit myself to suggest a solution that would favor one or other of the hypotheses. However, I believe that two observations are absolutely necessary, the first concerning methodology and the second ideology.

Regarding the question of the formation and continuity of the Romanian people, Romanian historians of the last half century have tended to overestimate their own means, showing little interest in the research and conclusions of linguists. As the literary sources have in general been used up, Romanian historiography has come to rely on archaeology. The problem of continuity has thus become an almost exclusively archaeological one. Language has taken second place to "concrete" evidence. It is a curious approach, given that what is called, in a somewhat vague formula, the "forming of the Romanian people" actually means, in more precise and appropriate terms, "the forming of the Romanian language". The Romanians are people who speak Romanian; even if it is not the sole "condition" it is certainly the first and essential condition. I would not go so far as to say that archaeology has nothing to offer in such a question, but ultimately its role is limited. In fact, for decades archaeologists have taken upon themselves the mission of fully clarifying the problem of continuity. Naturally enough they have discovered, in every corner of Romania and for every period under discussion, remains which confirm the continuity of life. But here there has been a confusion; it matters little whether deliberate or not. What is at issue is not the continuity of the population in general, but Roman and Romanian continuity. For the purposes of this discussion, a "Dacian" who did not speak Romanian is of no interest: he was not Romanian.

Nor can the linguists propose an indisputable solution. All they can say is that, to a greater extent than the historians, they feel the need to take into consideration an area south of the Danube *too*. Even in the communist period Iorgu Iordan, a pupil of Alexandru Philippide, was ready to uphold this point of view. We should also note the publication—annotated but uncensored—of Carlo Tagliavini's synthesis *The Origins of the Neo-Latin Languages* (1977), in which the respected Italian linguist, in company with many others, situated the formation of the Romanian language in a restricted area on both sides of the Danube: "Without denying the existence of certain remains of the Roman population north of the Danube, most foreign philologists recognize that the place of formation of the Romanian language must be approximately located in the southwestern borderlands to the north and south of the Danube."[21] In fact, once again, the conclusions of the linguists cannot be considered certain and unanimous either.

The version according to which the Romanian language was formed within a limited space (at any rate perceptibly smaller than that of present-day Romania) both north and south of the Danube presents fewer weak points and explains more than the other versions. It may be considered a cleverer and more logical hypothesis, but it is not necessarily more true. It is hard to suppose that the truth, the complete and perfect truth, will ever be reconstructed. History, even history and linguistics together, cannot offer total reconstruction, especially when the phenomena under discussion lie in the far-off mists of beginnings. It is correct to acknowledge and state without embarrassment that everything in this field is hypothesis, though of course nothing prevents us from considering one or other of the hypotheses to be more "true".

My second observation concerns the ideological basis and political exploitation of the question. The actualization of foundation myths is a mental process which we cannot prevent. In invoking their origins, the Romanians, like any other people, have the feeling that they are affirming their individuality and defending their rights. Anti-Romanian attacks appeal no less to historical schemas. To the extent that Hungarian historiography stands out as the principal adversary of Romanian continuity north of the Danube, it is clear that what is at issue is, above all, the problem of Transylvania. The formation of the Romanian people to the north of the Danube, and actually on the land of Transylvania, legitimizes

Romanian rights over the province. The coming of the Romanians from elsewhere, on the other hand, demonstrates the historical right of the Hungarians. The situation is similar with Bessarabia and even Moldavia. What would happen if we found out that the Romanians came here after the Slavs?

In fact nothing would happen. Without denying the right of the historical imaginary to deploy its resources, it is clear that the real moving force behind territorial evolutions is not the appeal to a distant past. The forcible modification of borders can easily find a historical alibi: History offers everything. Mussolini wanted to remake the Roman Empire. He had, it could be said, every right: for almost a millennium the Mediterranean Sea had been an Italian lake, and Latin was spoken from Spain to Bulgaria and from Libya to Britain. On the basis of history—of immigrationist theory, to be precise—the Hungarians could be sent back to the Urals and the Americans back to Europe, leaving the Indians free in their own land. Let no one say I am proposing a stupid game; we can find the same game in our own history, too. Moreover, history is not a unique and absolute given; it proposes a multitude of sequences, from which each of us can select what suits us. If we place ourselves in the year 800, then we can send the Hungarians back to the Urals; but if we move on to 1000 or 1200 things look different, this time in favor of a historical right which can be invoked by those nostalgic for Greater Hungary. Similarly, the Romanian right to Dobrogea is often related to the rule of Mircea the Old. Dobrogea, however, was not only ruled by Mircea, but also, and for much longer periods, by the Greeks, the Bulgarians, and the Turks.

To the extent that not force—which can always find its justifications, in history or elsewhere—but right is to decide, the past must give way before the *realities of the present* and the *free expression of options*. The rights of the Romanians in Transylvania are only supported in appearance by Dacians or Daco–Romans. However, they are supported effectively by the fact that the substantial majority of the population is Romanian and that, if the occasion were to present itself, most inhabitants of the province would decisively affirm their belonging to Romania. In the event of an inversion of the numerical relation between ethnic groups in Transylvania—a phenomenon which has occurred in various parts of the world—the situation would be different. Who could pretend to return to the borders and ethnic proportions of hundreds of years ago? The case of Kosovo is instructive. Here the affirmation of Serbian antiquity and continuity comes up today against the far more convincing argument of an overwhelming Albanian majority. From this point of view the question of Transylvania is settled. Hungarian or Romanian mythological exercises do not change anything: Transylvania is indisputably Romanian, just as it is also indisputable that a Hungarian minority live there, whose specific rights need to be recognized. Neither continuity nor immigrationism can alter the data of the problem one iota.

In fighting against Hungarian immigrationism, Romanian historians have allowed themselves to be caught up in a race, especially in the Ceauşescu period when insistence on the antiquity and continuity of the folk became the order of the day. Historical right was brought to the foreground, and, since nothing is certain and univocal in matters of historical right—especially in such a complicated question as the origins of the Romanians—a feeble and controversial argument ended up eclipsing the undeniable reality of the predominantly Romanian character of Transylvania, regardless of what might have happened a thousand or two thousand years ago. A fragile argument was put above an unassailable argumentation. The recourse to history can have a boomerang effect. We have just admired the Romanian map of the Dridu culture, but there is a danger that a Bulgarian one will look much the same. What do we do then? Do we include Romania in Bulgaria or Bulgaria in Romania?

The issue that must be addressed is not the giving up of foundation myths but the de-dramatizing and de-politicizing of them. This is valid not just for Romanians, indeed not even especially for Romanians, but for everybody, at least within the Central European space, since the West, learning something from its recent history, has considerably attenuated the conflictual character of the discourse of origins. Europe is being constructed on the basis of present realities, including its present political and ethnographical maps. The implication of the past in the present (which in fact means the projection of the present onto the past) can generate inextricable conflicts. It is natural that each nation should respect and love its history, but it is an illusion (which can become dangerous) that history has already marked out the road which we must continue to follow. The responsibility for today is ours, not our ancestors'; we cannot build the future by looking at the past.

CHAPTER FOUR
Unity

TRANSYLVANIANS, WALLACHIANS, MOLDAVIANS... OR ROMANIANS?

Unity is an essential archetype. We encounter it all the time, everywhere and at all levels. Human beings are tireless seekers and builders of coherence. We try to give unity and meaning to a world which would otherwise disorient us by its heterogeneity and its lack of sure significations. Religion, science, and ideology have as their fundamental aim the bringing of order into the world. From the cosmic whole to the basic cells of society, everything is passed through this unifying treatment.

While the aspiration to unity is universal, the specific manifestations of the archetype vary according to the historical context. The *Empire* and *Christendom* are the most typical political and ideological embodiments of the idea of unity in pre-modern Europe. The nineteenth century saw the outbreak of the national phenomenon. The idea of the nation-state imposed itself as a fundamental historical myth, becoming one of the great secular religions of the last two centuries. As a privileged form of unity, the nation began to be seen (especially by the Romantics of the nineteenth century) as the very key and end of the whole historical process. Intoxicated with national sentiment, historians ended up forgetting that what for the modern world is an essential value, sometimes even the supreme value, fades and disappears if we go back into the past, giving way to other concepts and forms of unity.

We find the ethnic unity of the Romanians, or at least their relatedness and common origin, affirmed as clearly as we could wish starting with Grigore Ureche. However, this recognition did not initially presuppose a common political project, still less any political unity on national grounds, for the simple reason that such thinking was foreign to the spirit of the age. The invocation of the Dacian project of Gabriel Bethlen in recent Romanian historiography leaves to one side the elementary fact that the prince of Transylvania was Hungarian, as was the entire ruling class of his land, so that the project in question can hardly be seen as a Romanian one. (The Hungarians of Transylvania are Romanian citizens today, but they were not Romanian citizens in the seventeenth century, nor had they any way of knowing that Transylvania would be united with Romania in 1918.)

Nowhere in Europe, until around 1800, were borders fixed on grounds of ethnicity and language, even as an ideal project. The Moldavians knew perfectly well that they spoke much the same language as the Muntenians, and they felt close to the neighboring land in many respects, but for centuries this did not prevent them from calling themselves not Romanians but Moldavians (as the Romanians of Bessarabia still do). The generic term *român* (Romanian) was increasingly adopted in the first half of the nineteenth century, but until the middle of the century it did not manage to overtake the designation *moldovean* (Moldavian). As for the political union of these two principalities, it was called for by a number of boyars in memoranda presented between 1772 and 1829, a fact which has been noted and highlighted. But a far greater number of such documents deal with the problems of each country separately, without in any way hinting at a future unification. The project of union must be seen as a process, not as something given and invariable from the beginning. Towards the middle of the nineteenth century it came onto the agenda; this does not mean that it was equally present in 1800. The historian must take into account how representative particular sources and events are; otherwise, by isolating and amplifying a particular document or affirmation, it is possible to "prove" anything, in any period.

The issue of Transylvania and its union with the other Romanian territories is even more delicate. From around 1800, and more and more frequently as the century advances, we find all sorts of "Dacian" projects, aimed at bringing together the whole Romanian territory. A Greater Romania from the Dniester to the Tisza belongs unquestionably to the political imaginary of the nineteenth and early twentieth centuries. However, it was hard to imagine the dismemberment of the Habsburg Monarchy, or of the Hungarian nucleus of this monarchy, as an effective solution. The Transylvanian Romanians sought the autonomy of Transylvania, or an autonomy extended to the whole Austro–Hungarian area with a Romanian population (Transylvania, the Banat, and Bukovina), rather than an apparently utopian union with the two principalities, or, after 1859, with Romania. The federalization of the Habsburg Monarchy seemed a more realistic solution, and it would be incorrect to see it as a mere tactic of the national movements, a step towards a subsequent separation from the empire. In any case, up until the First World War the principle of autonomy within Austria or Austria–Hungary was more often and more explicitly formulated than the remaking of old Dacia. In 1848 there was a proposal for a "Danubian Confederation", a project supported by Bălcescu among others. The idea was likewise put forward that the lands should unite in the opposite direction, by the joining of Romania to a "Greater Austria" (a proposal first formulated in 1848 but reiterated as late as 1918, when it seemed as if the Central Powers were going to win the War). In this way the Romanian nation would have found its unity under the patronage of Vienna. The unification of central Europe on a federal basis comes across as a reasonable and promising solution, and one which prefigures the current European project. The fact that it did not happen in the end does not mean that it could not have happened. The Great Union of 1918 certainly represented the perfect formula from the point of view of the national ideal, but the fact thus accomplished should not lead us to an abusive simplification of previous history, by its reduction to the permanent manifestation of the struggle for unity: people had no way of knowing what the future had in store for them. History follows a single pathway, but its virtual pathways are far more numerous.

In historiography, an important step on the path of unity is represented by Şincai's *Chronicle*, in which, for the first time, Romanian history is no longer recounted separately by states or provinces (Wallachia, Moldavia, Transylvania), but according to strictly chronological criteria. Half a century later, as we have seen, Bălcescu attributes a national sense to the actions of Michael the Brave and, even more, sees a traditional aspiration towards unity as the source of Michael's deeds.

In fact, nineteenth-century historians hesitated between projecting the sentiment of unity into the past and criticizing the past precisely for the lack of national solidarity. In each case the supreme value promoted is the Romanian national idea, which can be valorized equally in terms of its enduring historical roots or through the misfortunes that result when the idea of unity is neglected. It is possible to learn just as well from the mistakes of our ancestors as from their virtues.

If Bălcescu's *Michael the Brave* illustrates the former strategy, the latter is central to Kogălniceanu's demonstration in his 1843 *Opening Word*. According to Kogălniceanu, what has characterized the Romanians, as it did the ancient Greeks, is not unity but division, with disastrous political results for both peoples. "If the Greeks fell first under the yoke of Philip and later under that of the Romans, it is because they wanted to be Plataeans, Thebans, Athenians, or Spartans, and not Hellenes; just in the same way our ancestors wanted to be Transylvanians, Muntenians, Banatians, or Moldavians, and not Romanians. Only rarely did they choose to look on themselves as one and the same nation. In their lack of unity, however, we must see the source of all their past misfortunes."

Kogălniceanu pleaded for Romanian unity and for a national history conceived in the spirit of this unity, but, characteristically, Moldavia maintains a certain degree of individuality in his writing. "Far from sharing a sentiment of hatred towards the other parts of my people, I look on the whole area where Romanian is spoken as my country, and on the history of all Moldavia, before it was partitioned, of Wallachia, and of our brothers in Transylvania, as national history. [...] In expanding more, understandably, on happenings in Moldavia, I will not pass over noteworthy acts of the other parts of Dacia, and especially of the Romanians of Wallachia, with whom we are brothers in the cross, in blood, in language, and in law."[1] It is a history of the Romanians as a whole, but a history of the Romanians seen from Iaşi, with a certain insistence on Moldavia. The border has faded, but it separates entities which, however close, remain distinct.

RIVERS AND MOUNTAINS

The problem of unity also implies a geographical mythology. If nations are predestined then there must be a geographical predestination, a well-defined space, marked out by clear borders, which has been reserved for them from the beginning. Herder, the great prophet of modern nationalism, insistently invokes geography in support of national history. For him, it has marked out from the beginning, with its immutable structures, the direction of the evolution of the various human communities.

A unitary history thus presupposes a unitary geography. The unitary geography of the Romanian people, which has continued to the present day, was elaborated in the nineteenth century in the image of a perfect, almost circular space bounded by three great waterways—the Danube, the Dniester, and the Tisza—a space supported and solidified by the vertebral column of the Carpathians which passes right across it. In the Romanian version, mountains unite while rivers divide.

We find a quite different opinion, expressed in categorical terms, with Xenopol. He notes that in most places the opposite rule applies: rivers unite and mountains divide. Far from having ensured the unity of the Romanians, the Carpathian chain is responsible for the division of the national space. In order to unite, the Romanians are obliged to fight against geography:

> The Carpathians are the decisive factor in the political division of the Romanians. We shall see that the Romanians, after remaining for a long time in the fortress of the mountains, at a certain time began to move out towards the valleys and plains of the Black Sea. Thus were born the two states of Muntenia and Moldavia, while on the other side of the mountains, internal ranges divided the Romanians into a number of different lands: Transylvania, Maramureş, Crişana, and the Banat. [...] This movement of the Romanians out from the fortress of the Carpathians by way of two openings in particular, one in the south through Făgăraş and the other in the north through Maramureş, explains why it is that in the eastern and southern plain, even on a continuous territorial unit, it was possible for two states, Muntenia and Moldavia, to coalesce, instead of there being just one. So strong was the divergent orientation imprinted on them from the beginning that they were to go on living separately, even as enemies, for more than half a millennium.[2]

The Carpathians unite, the Carpathians divide: the divergent interpretations lead us back to the mythological roots of the issue. "Natural borders", one of the key figures of the geographical imaginary, could not fail to be sought at some point by national ideology. In fact, a typology is impossible. The territorial expansion of a language or a nation does not derive from some geographical fatality; the land in itself does not conceal any predestination or laws leading to either unity or division. As for the fragmentation of the Romanian territory in the Middle Ages, subtleties of argumentation are of little use. Why should there have been a united Romania in a Europe itself profoundly fragmented?

HISTORICAL UNITY: EBB AND RE-ELABORATION

The emphasis on the question of Romanian unity in the Middle Ages, or rather political division (the reverse side of the same logic), saw a pronounced ebb towards the end of the nineteenth century. The orientation of historical studies towards criticism highlighted the inappropriateness of transferring modern national sentiment into a past that was preoccupied with other values. A certain political conjuncture also played its part in this process of attenuation. The effective construction of Romania considerably reduced the "urgency" of constructing a historical unity in the imaginary. On the other hand, the progressive consolidation of cultural and spiritual relations between the Romanians on either side of the Carpathians, and the increasing momentum of the Romanian nationalist movement could not, before 1914, lead to an effective political project for integrating Transylvania in the Romanian state. On the contrary, fear of Russia pushed Romania towards Germany and Austria–Hungary, which meant the implicit acceptance of a separate status for the Romanians over the mountains. All that could be insisted on for the time being was their full political and cultural emancipation.

It is sufficient to follow interpretations concerning Michael the Brave and the union of 1600—a sensitive indicator of the nationalism-history relationship in Romanian culture—to observe a clear change of tone from Bălcescu to the historians of the following generation. Already A. D. Xenopol unambiguously states that there was no national sense to Michael's policies:

> [...] so little did Michael think of the union of the Romanians that he did not even conceive, such were the conditions of the time, the administrative unification of the Romanian lands, but only their placing under lords subject and obedient to himself, according to the feudal system, which had still not been uprooted from people's minds. [...] Finally, the most incontrovertible evidence that the idea of union never even entered Michael's head is the fact that when he laid his hands on Transylvania he did not release the Romanian people from the slavery in which the nobles of that country kept it, but, on the contrary, took measures to keep it in that state, guaranteeing the nobles the maintenance of their inhuman constitution. What sort of union of the Romanians did Michael the Brave want if, in the chief of his lands, where he desired to rule himself, he left the Romanian population without rights, subject, in the most degrading slavery, to people of another folk and another blood?[3]

With the characteristic forthrightness of the "critical school", Dimitrie Onciul expressed the sense of Michael's action in a few words, noting the absence of any national project. The union, he shows, "was maintained only by the sword of the conqueror, whose guiding thought was the fight for the Faith. The idea of national unity was not in the political consciousness of that time, which was not yet ready to conceive it."[4]

Of great interest for the relationship between critical methodology and orientation towards Central Europe is the solution proposed by Ioan Sîrbu, a historian from the Banat, trained in the German school. According to his point of view, expressed in *The History of Michael the Brave* (1904–1907), what the great voivode sought, in line with a whole series of Romanian voivodes, was "German sovereignty". Unity thus flows from the need for imperial protection and opens towards the wider space of "Greater Austria": "Michael felt the need, and wanted with all his heart, to come within the German Empire with all his Romanian people." The parallel with the present is brought out strongly: "Today, likewise, we want to strengthen the emperor, but we eagerly expect him to strengthen us too, our whole people."[5]

In the interwar period no responsible historian any longer claimed that Michael had in mind a clear project of Romanian unity. Even in school textbooks the non-existence of such an intention is stated. There are, of course, nuances: P. P. Panaitescu refuses any involvement of a Romanian consciousness; Nicolae Iorga and C. C. Giurescu seem less categorical, but nor do they go as far as identifying a national idea. In any case, further than Iorga in the fusion of history with nationalism it was hard to go (at least within professional historical circles); and here is what Iorga writes about the relationship of Michael to Transylvania: "He saw that this too was a *Romanian land*, with villages inhabited by Romanians, and, without having the idea of *national unity* clearly in his mind as it is today, for those times were not yet fully prepared for it, he told himself that he would be able to rule as lord over the Romanian villages here, just as he was master of the Romanian villages in his own principality."[6] The same Iorga characterizes the sentiments of the Moldavians towards Michael thus: "The conquest of Moldavia was carried out quickly, but we should not imagine that the Moldavians were happy about it. At that time, as we know, each land was used to living according to its own customs, with its own ancient dynasty. [...] Thus many of the subjects of Ieremia Vodă looked on Michael when he arrived not as a braver, more effective, and more glorious Romanian lord, come to fulfill the unity of the people in a single political form, but as a foreign conqueror, ambitious and unruly, who was upsetting the countries around him."[7]

We may say that, having reached maturity, Romanian historiography, although penetrated by an indisputable national spirit, tried to avoid the trap of projecting national ideology onto the Romanian Middle Ages. It is worth drawing special attention to two aspects which lead to this conclusion.

First, there is the treatment, without complexes and even with unembarrassed insistence, of the numerous conflicts which punctuated relations between the principalities, especially between Wallachia and Moldavia. Generations of historians presented the parallel reigns of Matei Basarab and Vasile Lupu, in terms of the struggles between the two rulers, from a perspective which set out to be not only historical but also ethical, with Vasile's ambition and love of pomp crumbling before the wisdom and simplicity of the Wallachian prince. In any case, the inclination towards events of the historiography of the period left not the slightest family quarrel untouched. We sometimes come upon uncompromising moral judgements, as in the case of Stephen the Great's unsuccessful attack on Chilia, upon which Xenopol meditates at length. He holds Stephen guilty, and indeed in somewhat bitter terms, for the disaster suffered by Vlad Ţepeş: "It was not the Sultan Mohamed who determined the downfall of the ruler of Muntenia, but Stephen the Great. We can now only begin to measure the extent of the Moldavian ruler's error. He, whom we shall later see running in all directions in search of allies against the Turks, had now crushed the most precious ally of all, the ruler of a people of the same blood and folk, whose fall before the Turks should have shown Stephen the precipice which awaited him, too."[8] (We may note in passing the particular logic of the historian, who notes, on the one hand, the non-existence of national sentiment in the Middle Ages, and on the other vehemently accuses those who acted contrary to this same sentiment, including Stephen the Great and Michael the Brave.)

The second observation concerns the weighting of the Romanian territories in the historical discourse. For a long time, including the interwar period, Transylvania was given less space in works of synthesis than Wallachia and Moldavia (apart from those written by Transylvanians). This is noted by Ioan Lupaş in *The History of the Union of the Romanians* (1937), in which he proposes precisely the full integration of the Transylvanian past in the national history. The overall impression is of reticence in the face of the ambiguous status of a Transylvania that was both Romanian (in terms of the majority of its population and its present situation) and different from the other Romanian lands in that it had participated in *another* history. In any case, a simple statistical calculation offers conclusive results. For example, in the second volume of C. C. Giurescu's *History of the Romanians*, which deals with the fifteenth and sixteenth centuries, Moldavia has, according to the number of pages devoted to it, a weighting of 48 percent, Wallachia 41 percent, and Transylvania only 11 percent. The extreme solution is found in Dimitrie Onciul's *From the History of Romania*, which deals only with Wallachia and Moldavia, leaving Transylvania completely aside.

The somewhat delicate position of Iancu of Hunedoara (Hunyadi János) is also significant, given that he is a figure "shared" by Romanian and Hungarian historiography. As a historical personality he is no less important than Stephen or Michael. For all that, an investigation into the relative weighting of national heroes in history textbooks between 1859 and 1900 found Iancu in a quite mediocre position (with a percentage of 1.04, compared with 6.83 for Michael and 5.55 for

Stephen, a hierarchy which continues in recent textbooks).[9] Romanian historiography adopted the Transylvanian voivode but was not able to assimilate him fully; at any rate it did not imprint him in the national consciousness to the extent that Hungarian historians did.

We may note, all the same, in the interwar period and the years of the Second World War, an attempt to make a tighter connection between the modern unitary Romanian state and its diverse historical components. Of course, the orientations of the critical school constituted a lasting gain, and among them was the explicit renunciation of a Romanian national idea in the Middle Ages. On the other hand, however, the union of the new provinces, especially Transylvania, required also their organic integration in the national history, while actions from outside aimed at the dismemberment of Romania, based on arguments which included the lack of a fundamental basis for unity, could not be left without a historical answer. The need became even more urgent after 1940, when everything was again put under a question mark by territorial maiming and war.

The solution chosen by some historians, in the absence of a medieval unity of national type, was to highlight the unifying factors (geographical, ethnic, cultural, or concerning various forms of political collaboration), which, having been accumulated over time by an organic evolution, would lead progressively to the modern nation and Greater Romania. Ioan Lupaş's argumentation regarding the "history of the Romanian union" goes along these lines. Before national consciousness, according to the Transylvanian historian, there was the fundamental unity of the Romanian space, bounded by the Danube, the Black Sea, the Dniester, and the Tisza, and structured by the Carpathians, to which he adds the unitary ethnic factor with its specific features and the no less important religious dimension of Orthodoxy. Once again, we are looking at a consolidation of the foundations and in no sense, even with the Transylvanian Lupaş, who perhaps goes further than others, a return to the idea of national consciousness. "In 1600", the historian states, "when the three Romanian lands, Muntenia, Transylvania, and Moldavia, came together under the political scepter of Michael the Brave, it was precisely the lack of this consciousness which was the chief reason for the short duration of this Romanian rule." (The statement is somewhat sweetened by the claim that "the seed of the national idea was not lacking from Michael's acts of rule", although it is left unclear what should be understood, in more elaborated historical terminology, by "seed".)[10]

A suitable approach is proposed by G. I. Brătianu in his *Origines et formation de l'unité roumaine* (1943), a work in which the author explicitly acknowledges a particular political aim. "We cannot be unaware", he says, "that around us the adversaries of Romanian unity are ceaselessly active." In reaction to this it was his duty to highlight "the invariable foundation of our right to unity", the elements of which "have for so long been contested by adversaries, neglected by their own defenders, and unknown to European opinion".[11]

Thus, in the fifteenth century the historian detects "the unity of action which the struggle against the Ottoman invasion imposed to an increasing extent on the two principalities and the Transylvanian contingents".[12]

To return to the test case of Michael the Brave, according to Brătianu he had, "in the absence of a national consciousness", at least "an instinct of unity", and his intention was to rule as hereditary sovereign on both sides of the Carpathians. Even the western border claimed by the voivode corresponded more or less to the present Romanian–Hungarian border. Of course, national and linguistic considerations did not enter into the calculation, but "the coincidence is no less striking".

And here is Brătianu's conclusion: "The political objective of Michael the Brave was not national unity and his action can be sufficiently explained in terms of the logical consequences of his ideas of crusade. [...] But the actual history of his reign and his deeds demonstrates clearly that the historical mission of defending Christendom, which he, following many other Muntenian and Moldavian rulers, took upon himself, was beyond the reduced forces of a single small Romanian state. This mission obliged the prince and the statesmen to overcome particularist traditions and to take into consideration, from an as yet exclusively strategic or political point of view, a greater unity, which could not fail to become national once the times permitted."[13]

Thus there is no national consciousness, but nor is there the complete absence of a historical sense which would lead ultimately to national consciousness and unity. Brătianu liked to invoke the Hegelian triad of thesis–antithesis–synthesis. In this case the thesis was "national unity", the antithesis was its complete negation, and the synthesis, as we have seen, a more nuanced point of view. In the spirit of the same program, Brătianu proceeded partially to rehabilitate Negru Vodă (whose existence had been denied by Onciul) in *The Historical Tradition about the Founding of the Romanian States* (1945). Seeing in the legendary ruler a personification of the southern Transylvanian Romanian element which had played a role in the founding of Wallachia (just like the Maramureş people of Dragoş and Bogdan in the case of Moldavia), Brătianu introduced a new argument for unity, cementing relations between the Romanians on both sides of the Carpathians. It is ironic that the "unitarist" theses of this historian, who died in horrible conditions in communist detention and whose works remained for a long time on the "index", were later taken up by the historiography of the 1970s and 1980s, when they were pushed far beyond the limits which the author, who respected the canons of the profession, would not allow himself to exceed.

We may conclude that the Romanian Middle Ages, in the treatment of historians prior to the communist period, were not abusively invested with characteristics of *full and conscious unity* which they evidently did not have; where there are differences, they concern the degree of emphasis or discretion in identifying starting points and directions of evolution which would later lead towards unity.

The armature of unity proved more powerful at the very foundation of national history, by the equation of Dacia with Romania. Medieval dissentions appeared as a mere transitory phase between a well-defined Dacian space and the present-day Romania that restored its outlines once again. It is interesting to observe how from related but distinct peoples, as they are presented in Grigore Tocilescu's *Dacia before the Romans* (1880), the Getae and Dacians become "two branches of the same people" mentioned separately ("the Getae and the Dacians") in Xenopol, and then, from Pârvan and Iorga to the present, a single people with a single name: *Dacians* or *Geto–Dacians*. Modern national ideology has said its word as far as this matter is concerned; but who can know how much the Dacians were conscious of belonging to a distinct people spread over the entire territory of today's Romania and even beyond it. Did this people have a name? We can be sure they did not call themselves Geto–Dacians!

COMMUNISM: THE MYTH OF UNITY AT ITS ZENITH

The first phase of communism was hardly concerned at all with the problem of national unity. According to the definition of the nation formulated by Stalin, what was essential was the creation of a "unitary internal market", which the Romanian lands had clearly lacked until recent times. In Roller's textbooks, far from any Romanian sense being identified in the action of Michael the Brave, the accent was put on class interests and relations with the neighboring powers, especially the Habsburgs. We learn that "Michael the Brave was used by the Habsburg Empire, with the aim of conquering Transylvania for the Austrians. The voivode Michael became *governor* of this province, and as such was considered the representative of Emperor Rudolf II, who regarded Transylvania as an Austrian province."[14] The relations between the Romanian lands and Russia are sometimes more strongly highlighted than the connections within the Romanian space itself (for example in the cases of Stephen the Great and Constantin Brîncoveanu).

Not only does the union of 1859 not now mark the crowning point of a long history permeated with the spirit of unity (as in nationalist interpretations), it is not even seen, as would have been correct, as the expression of the strong national sentiment characteristic of the period. Everything is reduced to the play of material interests: "The idea of uniting Moldavia and Wallachia in a single state first appeared with the development of capitalism, which needed a well-organized state with a large internal market. The developing Romanian bourgeoisie saw its interests threatened by the Turkish yoke. [...] The great boyars who held high positions in the state apparatus were against the union, fearing that after the union these positions would be occupied by bourgeois."[15] As for the union of Transylvania (not to mention Bessarabia and Bukovina) with Romania, this was placed, as we have already seen, in the context of the aggressive actions of the Romanian bourgeoisie at the end of the First World War.

The nationalist phase of communist ideology, and implicitly of Romanian historiography, turned things round completely. In the spirit of absolute truths propagated by a doctrine which was simplistic in its very essence, the point of equilibrium was quickly left behind in the transition from ignoring any Romanian sentiment to the projection of the national idea over the whole of history. *Unity* became, alongside *continuity*, the guiding axis of the historical discourse. What generations of historians had sought to demolish, or at least to nuance—out of simple respect for their profession and a patriotism correctly understood— became again part of an obsessive, and unfortunately efficient, nationalist discourse. Thus nineteenth-century historical interpretations, especially those of the Romantic generation of the mid-nineteenth century, which were completely outdated in terms of contemporary historiography, were combined with the imperatives of current communist ideology and politics. All totalitarian projects, and communism more than any, put a high value on the idea of unity. The insistent underlining of uninterrupted unity, which became almost a characteristic trait of Romanian being, served, through the intermediary of the past, the political program of Ceauşescu's brand of communism: a uniform society of people thinking and feeling the same, closely united around the providential leader. This was the aim, the only aim—certainly not patriotism or the disinterested search for historical truth.

It is fitting to return here to the Michael the Brave moment, the interpretation of which tells us everything there is to be said about the ideological loading of national history. Here there took place a leap back of over a century, with the accent placed once again on the Romanian, *consciously Romanian*, sense of his action. Where generation after generation of historians had claimed that the voivode showed relatively little interest in the Romanians of Transylvania, it was discovered that, on the contrary, Michael had taken numerous measures in their favor. It was then forbidden to speak anymore of the *conquest* of Transylvania and Moldavia (the term previously used, without any problems of conscience, by all Romanian historians). The Romanian provinces could not have been conquered, but *united*: in fact, they aspired to be united.

A *Dacian idea*—seeking the creation of a single Romanian state on the former territory of Dacia—was likewise discovered to have been present throughout the sixteenth century, demonstrating conscious preparation for the act of 1600, two centuries before the concept of the national state had crystallized in the rest of Europe. Yet another Romanian first! This theory was constructed with indisputable but unconvincing erudition by Ştefan Andreescu, in the two volumes of his *Restitutio Daciae* (1980 and 1989). According to Andreescu, Petru Rareş sought a confederation of Romanian states, while Michael the Brave wanted a centralized state. In any case, the princes seem much more conscious of the national idea than does the great scholar Miron Costin, a hundred years later. As a medievalist with a completely different training and style than the historian-activists of the Ceauşescu years, Andreescu offers the instructive case of a history, which, while apparently autonomous and correctly elaborated, essentially does no more than serve one of the great myths of the regime.

From Michael the Brave, historians moved back into the sixteenth century, and from the sixteenth century, as moving back in time was easy and profitable, they went back to the fifteenth and even to the fourteenth. Stephen the Great, in his turn, was proclaimed "lord of all the Romanians".[16] In this case it is not so much a matter of interpretation (what was in Michael's mind when he "united", not to say "conquered" the Romanian territories), as of pure fabrication, since Stephen ruled only Moldavia, and his relations with Wallachia were at times highly conflictual. Indeed, for a long time the great prince had been a symbol of Moldavian particularism, as he still is in the Republic of Moldova.

If "anything is possible" in the case of Stephen, then why not also for Mircea the Old? The joining of Dobrogea to Wallachia under his rule could be interpreted as the first union in the series of successive unions which founded Romania. One particularly fiery historian does not hesitate to write that in 1386 the struggle for the "final union" of the Romanian space began.[17]

The strategy of unity led also to the retroactive extraction of Transylvania from the Hungarian political space. The autonomy of the voivodate—which perfectly fits the general typology of territorial fragmentation in the Middle Ages— conferred on it a Romanian sense. There was much insistence on the notion that Transylvania had closer relations with Wallachia and Moldavia than with the Hungarian crown (passing discreetly over the detail that the voivode was appointed and revoked by the king of Hungary, indicating a higher degree of dependence than that of the great feudal magnates in France or the German Empire, who were hereditary masters of their lands, in relation to their respective sovereigns).

So here, then, was the solution to the delicate problem of a Romanian medieval period that at first sight seemed more characterized by division than by solidarity. The repeated conflicts between the three countries were cancelled by the application of a twofold strategy. First, despite appearances, these conflicts could in fact mean real attempts at unification, with the princes of Moldavia, Wallachia, and Transylvania trying in turn to impose their supremacy over their sister lands. Stephen, Michael, Vasile Lupu, and as many Hungarian rulers of Transylvania had acted according to the "Dacian plan", with a view to the uniting of all the Romanians. Even so, as these conflicts were too numerous they required to be minimalized and partially eliminated. To give a single example, the classic dispute between Matei Basarab and Vasile Lupu disappeared for a time from school textbooks. In this case, there was a clear falsification of history by omission. The method of eliminating historical facts was preferred to the less certain tactic of transforming the conflict into an attempt at unification (Vasile Lupu did indeed want to place his son on the Wallachian throne).

In a few pages of impeccable logic, a young historian has demolished the theory of an early aspiration towards unity in the Middle Ages. He demonstrates that in the fourteenth and fifteenth centuries not only did Wallachia and Moldavia not work together, they were in fact integrated into divergent political systems, the former associated with Hungary and the latter with Poland. Not only could there be no question of unity, there could be no form of political coordination either.[18]

If the Middle Ages could be "resolved" in such a way, the modern age, the period which witnessed the gradual forging of the national sentiment and of effective national unity, could be maneuvered all the more easily. The year 1848 can provide us with a good example. The three revolutions in Moldavia, Wallachia, and Transylvania had traditionally been presented separately, while underlining, of course, the sharing of values and the relations between the revolutionaries. There followed, however, the phase of full "unification" of Romanian history. Already in 1967, Cornelia Bodea produced a skillful and attractive demonstration of the unitary character of the politics of 1848 (and even the preceding period), centering on a well-defined project of the political unification of the entire national space. Vague suggestions in the documents, and hypotheses of all sorts, coalesced in the image of a Romanian consensus, leaving the less convenient facts to one side (for example, the insistence of Bălcescu—the great historian of national unity!—on establishing close ties between the Romanian and Hungarian revolutions, which could only result in the sacrificing not only of union, but even of the autonomy of Transylvania).[19]

In school textbooks, the revolutionary phenomenon of 1848 ended up by being completely homogenized and presented to pupils in such a way that they could no longer understand anything. As unity had to be manifested, the only criterion was chronology, and the text shifted, without any logical connection, from Iaşi to Lugoj and from Blaj to Bucharest... Particularly abusive was the "integration" without any nuances of Transylvania, where the problems of 1848 were much more complex and largely different than in Wallachia and Moldavia. In the case of Transylvania, the principal issue from the point of view of the Romanians was autonomy within the Habsburg Empire, and certainly not, in the historical context, union with Wallachia and Moldavia, which were themselves still not united. But nor was the territory conventionally named "Transylvania" uniform: the Romanians of the historical principality of Transylvania, those of the Banat, and finally those of the "Hungarian" regions (Crişana and Maramureş) had different aims and tactics. It is certain that in 1848 not only Romanians and Hungarians, but also different groups of Romanians, found themselves in opposite camps, as shown by the dramatic Dragoş-Buteanu episode in the Apuseni mountains. Through all this went the great steamroller of unity. Even a more recent textbook claims nonchalantly that the Romanians put forward a single revolutionary program in 1848, when it is well known that there were several, which were far from identical.[20]

The case of Dobrogea is likewise significant. Here the Romanians were in the minority in 1878 (a *relative* majority of the population being Muslim). In subsequent decades Dobrogea was Romanianized by an exceptional action of colonization and development of the territory. It was a remarkable success, one of the most indisputable Romanian successes, but it is "not the done thing" to talk about it, since all Romanian territories must have been Romanian, without interruption, since the dawn of history.

The final phase—at least in the communist variant—of the myth of unity took the form of a ban on the publication of regional studies and syntheses, or at best their disguising under titles like *The Romanians of the Southwest of the Country* rather than *The Romanians of the Banat*. The culminating point was the elimination from weather bulletins, by a decision of the propaganda section of the Central Committee of the Communist Party, of the names of the regions. Even the wind, the rain, and the snow had to respect the unity of Romania. It was no longer permitted, for example, for it to rain in Moldavia; it could rain as much as it liked, but not in Moldavia, only in the northeast of the country!

A no less spectacular initiative was the "re-baptizing" of the principalities. Not only did they all have to be Romanian: they had to be called Romanian. Why was only Wallachia called "the Romanian Land"?* Were the other lands any less Romanian? Thus some historians began to refer to the Romanian Land of Muntenia,** the Romanian Land of Moldavia, and the Romanian Land of Transylvania. A whole line of Hungarian princes had ruled a state which was now called the Romanian Land of Transylvania!

In fact, regional differences are prominent, even in today's Romania, not to mention past centuries. They ought to be researched and inventoried no less systematically than the elements of unity. From this point of view the case of France—so often invoked in so many contexts in a Romania that remains Francophone and Francophile—is instructive and worth following. After long being marked by a centralizing political and national ideology, French historiography in recent decades has embarked on regional studies, bringing to light another, somewhat unexpected, France, the synthesis of a regional life of remarkable diversity. (For the period around 1800 some parameters suggest a greater distance between the various French *départements* than between France seen as a whole and the rest of the world.[21]) Real history, with the infinite diversity of its manifestations, can no longer be sacrificed on the altar of a national ideology aiming at uniformity. Historians can be patriots without falsifying the past.

The myth of unity, or rather uniformity, is so strongly imprinted in Romanian culture that even specialists, whether historians or sociologists, often hesitate to take into account the regional structures of the phenomena they are studying. It is, for example, more than evident that the Romanians vote differently from one county to another and even more differently from one historical region to another, and yet, in a study published by Pavel Câmpeanu,[22] in which the national elections of 1990 to 1992 are minutely analyzed, there is not even the most summary distribution by counties and historical provinces. What is actually striking, especially following the presidential elections of 1992, is the very pronounced definition of two distinct zones, still divided by the former border

---

* *Ţara Românească*: the usual Romanian name for Wallachia. *Trans.*

** Muntenia, the dominant region of Wallachia, stands here for the whole principality. *Trans.*

between Romania and Austria–Hungary (with further divisions within these zones which also merit comment). Political options reflect a multitude of values, models, and cultural, ideological, and mental reference points. Electoral geography is only one example; any historical or sociological phenomenon can and should be represented and analyzed at the local level. The national dimension is one significant outcome, but not the only one. The Romanian nation of today is certainly unitary, but it is not uniform. The differences which persist, after a number of factors inevitably furthering uniformity have been at work for several generations (political power, administration, education, military service, economic mechanisms), highlight the precariousness of interpretations which see nothing but unity 500 or 2,500 years ago.

However, bibliographical references do not tell us everything; direct contact with people, and especially with middle-level professionals (in our case teachers in pre-university education), illustrates even more clearly the relative success of a political strategy for which history was no more than an instrument. The history textbooks are as they are, but in not a few cases they are outdone by the school. Pupils hear from some of their teachers that the "golden dream" of the Romanians, their ideal over the centuries, was unity. Of course, not all history teachers indulge in this sort of discourse, but I wonder how many would dare today to say openly what was common knowledge in schools in pre-communist Romania, namely, that Michael the Brave's action did not originate in national sentiment. Apart from the question of untruth, and apart from what is, whether conscious or not, a political manipulation through history, there is a serious vice concealed here: lack of responsibility. Teachers "know" that it is best to tell it this way. Regardless of what they really believe, they feel that this way they are covered. An exaggeration in "patriotic" terms seems more convenient than entering the uncertain ground of a critical and intelligent history. Unfortunately, their pupils do no more than memorize an endless litany, when the real vocation of history is precisely the exercise of intelligence. History seems to have remained with the objective of training patriots, not people capable of an independent judgement of the world and events. In fact, not even patriotic sentiments can truly be cultivated by a stereotypic and unconvincing discourse.

In Search of the Romanian Soul

If the Romanians have always been a united nation, this means that there exists— beyond the flow of the centuries and the vicissitudes of history—a Romanian dimension of existence, a Romanian way of being, a Romanian soul. The identification of a specific *national spirit* illustrates one of the most significant manifestations of the myth of unity. From Herder onwards, the "spirit of the peoples" made a profound mark on the Romantic ideology of the first half of the nineteenth century. It was the period when the world was cut up into national spaces, each animated by its own spiritual and moral characteristics and marked by its own destiny. In the second half of the nineteenth century this hypothesis was taken further, in the attempt to set it on the solid basis of science. It was a time when it seemed that nothing would remain outside the scope of a complete and perfect scientific explanation. Thus the Germans Lazarus and Steinthal around 1860 and Wundt around 1900, not forgetting the Frenchmen Fouillé and Boutmy, embarked on the delicate task of defining the psychology of peoples.

The theme could not fail to attract the Romanians. As a nation which had come late to unity (in spite of the mythological discourse of an originary unity), the Romanians felt the need to define the elements of this unity, the characteristics which made them resemble each other and distinguished them from the others. A whole range of complexes were also at play. How was it possible to explain the actual inferiority of the Romanians in the nineteenth century (in relation to the West)? Through what historical circumstances or what flaws in the national soul? What stock of qualities, on the other hand, could be thrown into the scales of history to put things right and ensure a future better than the present, a future to match their brilliant origins? It is certain that for a century and a half, from the beginning of the process of "entering Europe", the Romanians have been in a state of continual agitation, trying to establish their own image and their place in European spirituality.

A publication of 1907, Dumitru Drăghicescu's *From the Psychology of the Romanian People*, is of importance from several points of view. In the first place, it is a first synthesis of the matter. Secondly, it takes advantage of "scientific" literature, especially French, on the issue of the "national spirit", and demonstrates an attempt at "objective" research and at the systematic construction of a field of enquiry. Finally, we are still, here, in the phase of a predominantly critical discourse, which, although starting from the inborn qualities of the nation, deals unsparingly with its accumulated defects and proposes a diagnosis and a therapy to get out of the impasse.

Drăghicescu's method is simple and clear, and very much in the spirit of the 1900s. The inner chemistry of the Romanians, he considers, has taken and combined spiritual elements characteristic of the ethnic groups which participated in the creation of the Romanian synthesis, or at least influenced it. It is sufficient to know (and the psychology of peoples offers quasi-certainty in this respect) what the Romans were like, what the Dacians were like, and what the Slavs were like, and by combining these sources we have before us the Romanians of the tenth century, brought back to life, in spite of the lack of sources, by the pure mechanism of psychological laws. Our ancestors, Drăghicescu assures us, were then "rough and violent. Having an iron will, stubborn, impulsive, sometimes self-controlled, sometimes out of control, changeful, they must have been daring beyond measure, courageous, careless of death and animated by a spirit of freedom and independence, which more often than not divided them and only rarely allowed them to unite. According to the circumstances they could be disciplined and organized or lacking in discipline and anarchic, both these manifestations being rooted in their soul from the cradle, as both were inherited from the different ethnic groups. The intelligence of the Romanians, at that time, must have been rich; certainly it was lively, daring, and sparkling, with a sense of generalization and of organization and an inclination to observation which resulted in humor and mocking satire."[23] A thousand years later there is no shortage of humor, generally unintended, in Drăghicescu's work. What we learn from the proposed reconstruction is not so much what the Romanians were like as what it means really to believe in science, in a science which can give an answer without hesitation to every question you ask it.

Turkish and Greek influence, and especially the loss of independence, have altered the character of the Romanians. The chance of spiritual regeneration lies in the transformation of institutions and society along the lines of the Western model. Beyond any doubt the Romanians have considerable assets at their disposal—the fine qualities which they have inherited, and above all their *intelligence*. This combines the open and lively temperament of the Dacians, the generalizing and abstract spirit of the Romans, and the poetic gift of the Slavs. Apparently few peoples enjoy such a complex intelligence. At their birth the Romanians "must have been a people with a very open and very rich mind, with a lively and ingenious intelligence, and a rather powerful generalizing spirit. Their imagination must have been among the richest. [...] The mentality of the Romanians, like the language they speak, had as its foundation and starting point a material of superior essence: the Roman mentality. In history this appears to us as a great reservoir to which all the peoples of Europe came and deposited part of the contents of their soul."[24] As a people of synthesis, the Romanians seem to be composed of exceptional stuff, seriously altered by the vicissitudes of history it is true, but not beyond repair.

Their defects were few at the beginning, but accumulated over the centuries. Drăghicescu underlines "passivity; defensive, resigned, passive, subject, and beaten resistance; lack of offensive energy [...]. Timidity, paralysis of the will, fear, and lack of courage have dominated, and still dominate the soul of the Romanians." At the same time (and contrary to his own project of defining a national individuality) he detects "the lack of a distinct, unitary, and homogeneous unfolding of our past", whence the powerful effect of foreign influences and "the lack of a distinct, smooth, and clear character of Romanian mentality. [...] The content of our ethnic soul is made up, in the greater part, of fragments and patches borrowed from the neighboring peoples, unassimilated, undigested, and un-homogenized." The influence of the Orient, harmful overall, has as its coordinates "unconcern, physical and mental laziness, that is, lack of initiative, resignation, lack of self-confidence, and above all fatalism, blind belief in luck, in fate".[25]

The formula "intelligent but lazy", or "lazy but intelligent", with which we might simplify Drăghicescu's demonstration into a few words, indeed provides a cliché which many Romanians accept with a mixture of resignation and pride. Even if laziness is not praiseworthy, at least not everyone can boast of superior intelligence.

In any case, Drăghicescu's argumentation has as its firm reference point Western values and especially the French spirituality that he considered to be their highest expression. Thus everything which contrasts with the Western spirit and behavior is a defect. The Romanians must move in the direction of a spiritual formula of Western type. This is in fact the sense of historical evolution. In opposition to the European and Francophile Drăghicescu, however, an autochthonist interpretation of the Romanian spirit was already in existence and was carried forward on the nationalist wave of the years after 1900.

I have already referred to the dialogue between the two Junimists so different from each other, Vasile Pogor and Mihai Eminescu, in which the former maintained the "barbarism" of the Romanians and the latter their specific destiny. It is worth noting not only their disagreement but also the point where, in a sense, they fundamentally agree: the Romanians are on the margins of history—only what Pogor took as a subject for sarcasm was accepted with pride by the great poet. The Romanians have their own specific genius: they are not Western and nor should they try to become Western.

"Semănătorism", and later the interwar autochthonist currents, continued along the line of this assumed Romanianism. The historical and social determinants which we find in Drăghicescu—albeit in a debatable and simplistic manner—faded before an atemporal Romanian soul. Criticisms, too, faded away. What is there to criticize, if that is the way we are? What is there to criticize if we do not want to metamorphose into Westerners anyway, but just want to remain Romanians?

The most elaborated form of the discourse of Romanianism is provided by the nationalist Right of the 1930s. In the course of an indisputably seductive demonstration, Lucian Blaga, in *The Mioritic Space** (1936), defines the characteristics of the Romanian soul, which correspond to a well-defined geographical framework, the central element of which is the *plai* ("a high, open land, on the green mane of the mountains, descending gently into the valley"). According to Blaga, there is "an inalienable stylistic matrix of our ethnic spirit". The Romanian appears more profound and more open to cosmic essences than the Westerner: "In the West, tradition is a matter of the pedantic acquisition of a past, from the ancestral gallery, from the chronicle of deeds, from the roll call of ancestors. [...] Our tradition is by its nature more invisible; it only permits a metaphorical or metaphysical formulation. Our tradition is more atemporal; it blends with stylistic potencies which are creative, untiring, as magnificent as in the first day. [...] Sometimes smoldering but always alive, it manifests itself in time, although, measured by our ephemeral horizon, it is above time."[26]

For Blaga, as for Nichifor Crainic, Nae Ionescu, and Mircea Vulcănescu, the national spirit is identified substantially with Orthodoxy, which marks a clear separation from the Catholic and Protestant West and thus from the Western

---

* *Mioritic*: adjective from "*Miorița*", the well-known Romanian ballad of the shepherd and the ewe lamb; suggestive of an undulating landscape suitable for pastoral life. *Trans.*

models invoked by the preceding generation. Nae Ionescu proposed a subtle dissociation between the concepts of "Romanian" and "good Romanian". A Roman Catholic could be a "good Romanian", in other words a loyal Romanian, but to be *Romanian*, purely and simply, without any other attribute, one had to be Orthodox.[27] The Transylvanians who had launched the national movement were thus, as Greek Catholics, only "good Romanians". (At least it was better than not being Romanians at all!)

All these thinkers identified a Romanian spirituality that was clearly outlined and above all perfectly distinguishable from that of the "others", especially the West. Existence is *something different* for the Romanians. It might be defined, suggests Blaga, by the untranslatable word *dor**: "Existence for the Romanian is '*dor*', aspiration across horizons, existence which in its entirety flows towards 'something'."[28] Mircea Vulcănescu does not hesitate to speak about *Romanian man*, and in an essay entitled "The Romanian Dimension of Existence" he defines no less than seven fundamental and specific attitudes: there is no non-being; there is no absolute impossibility; there is no alternative; there is no imperative; there is nothing irremediable; lightness in the face of life; lack of fear in the face of death.[29]

The intellectuals of the interwar period were quite simply obsessed with the "national specific". The case of George Călinescu is particularly remarkable. I say "remarkable", as the illustrious literary historian had no sympathy with the ideology of the nationalist Right. This ideological divergence did not, however, prevent him from invoking similar concepts, illustrating the remarkable expansion of the cliché of Romanian unity. In concluding his *History of Romanian Literature* (1941), he insists on the existence of a distinct Romanian *race*. Even "our physical type is quite different from that of the neighboring peoples and those of Central Europe", claims the critic, who has suddenly become an anthropologist too, and apparently one contaminated by the racial theories of the time. (Unfortunately he does not sketch for us the physical portrait of his "typical Romanian".) Not everyone who wants to can be Romanian, according to Călinescu; you are born Romanian, and you are born a certain way. "As the specific is a structural element, it is not acquired by conformity to a canonic lifestyle. The only condition for having the specific is to be an ethnic Romanian. All the historian has to do is to follow the intimate fibers of the autochthonous soul."[30]

So the Romanian has become a very different being, of course more profound and more complex than his fellows, and the Romanian space a distinct and homogeneous entity.

The first phase of communism did not want even to hear of such heretical interpretations. It might be argued that Mircea Vulcănescu (who died in prison) and Nichifor Crainic were imprisoned, and Blaga marginalized, for "philosophical"

---

* *Dor* is usually translated as "longing"; it often has connotations of melancholy, as in *dor de casă* ("homesickness"). *Trans.*

reasons, as well as out of strictly political motives. Any nationalist tendency in philosophy, any definition of the Romanians as Romanian, had to be stamped out. The key to historical and cultural phenomena was class, not nation; class spirit and not national spirit.

Things changed with the shift of communism in the direction of nationalism. Of course not everything could be rehabilitated: the Orthodox dimension of Romanian spirituality was too divergent from official ideology. Significantly however, *The Mioritic Space* was reissued in 1969 and 1985, and Blaga was not only rehabilitated but set among the great names of Romanian letters. The destiny of Constantin Noica seems to me to be even more characteristic. Having been close to the extreme Right at the beginning of his career, he experienced forced domicile between 1949 and 1958, and prison from 1958 to 1964. His "recovery", starting in 1970, corresponds to the ideological shift and the new strategy of the authorities. Noica was beyond doubt a complex figure and a complex thinker, Romanian but also European in his nature. Autochthonists and partisans of opening towards the West could both claim him as their own. What interests us here, however, is not his subtlety and multisidedness, but what the official ideology was prepared to tolerate and even to use in his discourse. And *this*, in a period of progressive isolation of Romania, was the definition, following the tradition of the interwar Right, of a specifically Romanian spiritual perimeter. For example, his *Romanian Sentiment of Being* (1978) develops, in a much more elaborated manner, Vulcănescu's already-mentioned essay "The Romanian Dimension of Existence". Once again, Romanian understanding appears more open, more nuanced, richer: "Compared with the complex and fairy-like being of our vision, the neo-positivist perspective of the Western world, with its 'forgetting' of being, or else the reappraisal of being in other philosophies, has an air of poverty."[31]

The Romanians are neither Western nor Eastern. They lie between these two worlds and can be a unifying bond: "We are between the Near and Far East [...] and the West. Neither the one nor the other put its seal on us, but, just as we mediate geographically, could we not also mediate spiritually?" Moreover, tradition represents for us a still active factor, which has been eroded for others "by the number of past centuries". We are well able to combine tradition with modernity, which confers on us *"a greater meeting than others with the values of the spirit."*[32]

Such views can be expressed in a quite different ideological register to the communist one—they in fact correspond substantially to the right-wing discourse of the 1930s. It is no less true, however, that Ceauşescu himself could have felt at home with the idea of Romanian uniqueness, of the combination of tradition and modernity, and of Romania as a privileged place and mediating factor between the civilizations of the globe.

Indeed, Ceauşescu sacrificed more than once on the altar of Romanian spirituality, evidently in a manner rather rudimentary than subtly philosophical. He liked to list the characteristics, without exception positive, which had been inherited from the Romans and the Dacians alike. Thus the Romanian people had preserved "from the Dacians the unextinguished thirst for liberty, the will not to bow down before any foreigner, the determination to remain always themselves, single masters of their life and destiny", and from their other ancestors, "the rational spirit, judgement, and creative passion of the Romans".[33]

The operation of identifying "what it means to be Romanian" seems to be far from having exhausted its resources and arguments. We might say that the first characteristic of the Romanians—if we venture to define one too—is the obsession with their own identity. Since 1989 we have seen a polarization of the discourse; on the one hand, nationalist exacerbation continues to exercise its appeal unrestrained, while on the other hand, less favorable, even downright unfavorable, opinions, can also be expressed openly. For an exegete of Romanian culture like Dan Zamfirescu the Romanians are inscribed among the world's great creators of civilization,[34] while at the other extreme, the reaction against such self-eulogies, accumulated frustrations, and the inevitable comparison with the balanced and performing civilization of the West can generate no less passionate appreciations, as in the essays of H.-R. Patapievici, in which the Romanians are defined as a people without backbone and of an inferior spiritual quality.[35]

A FLUID SYNTHESIS

As we have seen, it is possible to say anything about the Romanians, or about any other people. And whatever is said can be just as easily accepted or contested. Ethnic psychology is a tempting exercise but completely without substance. It can never be a question of "scientific investigation", but only of impressions and judgements which are inevitably partial and subjective. In the end, all the ethno-psychological approach does is to isolate and highlight general human qualities and defects. Can the Romanians be considered more intelligent than other people, for example? Of course not, any more than they can be considered less intelligent. Anyway, how could we seriously calculate the intelligence quotient of a nation? According to current scientific norms, only the identification of a specifically Romanian gene would enable us to maintain the essential individuality of the Romanians among the other peoples of the world.

While there is undoubtedly a Romanian phenomenon, it is not bio-psychological in nature but springs from sociocultural structures and evolutions. The Romanian language is certainly an important factor of cohesion, on condition that we do not absolutize its virtues. Not all Romanians speak alike, even if they all speak Romanian. Not all Romanians think alike, even if they think in the same language. A "Romanian specific" may be approximated to, but not as an originary and transcendent given; rather as a *fluid* synthesis of *diverse* features. In recent times massive social restructuring and the action of the national organism upon its component elements have been continually modeling and remodeling the Romanians. If there is nowadays a particular Romanian way of being (a claim which can only be accepted with considerable reservations), then this is not due to any innate disposition but to a series of acquired habits, infused through cultural contexts, through schooling, through the action of dominant ideologies, through the modeling power of public opinion, and so on. We are born as human beings and then "learn" to be Romanian, French, or Chinese. The impact of communism is revealing from this point of view. Its domination left a profound mark on Romanian spirituality. Due to half a century of communism, the Romanians are different than they were fifty years ago.

In any case, the most summary glance at Romanian culture illustrates the fact that the much-trumpeted national spirit (if we insist on invoking it at all) can only be the product of highly diverse "sectional" characteristics. Let us consider a single generation of classic writers: Maiorescu, Eminescu, Creangă, and Caragiale. Which of them—so different as they are from each other—can be considered representative, or uniquely representative, of the Romanian spirit? Do we really encounter the same elements of civilization and the same mentality from Bukovina to Teleorman? The totalitarian ideologies—first the extreme Right, then communism—went farthest in the direction of a fictive (and even, up to a point, materialized) making uniform of the Romanian space. Other interpretations, in contrast, have not been shy of drawing dividing lines, at least between the great provinces, the classic case being that of the opposition between Moldavia and Muntenia. Garabet Ibrăileanu maintained that there were two distinctive spiritualities, Moldavian and Muntenian, in his book *The Critical Spirit in Romanian Culture* (1909), as did E. Lovinescu in *The History of Modern Romanian Civilization*. While Ibrăileanu put a special accent on historical and social determinants, Lovinescu saw the issue in purely psychological, and ultimately "racial", terms. Starting from the concept of "race", he claimed that the Moldavians, "by their contemplative nature, are inclined to poetic creation", while "by their mobile, comprehensive and practical character, the Muntenians have directed their activities more onto the grounds of politics and economics".[36] From the psychological point of view, the Moldavians and Muntenians can thus appear as two distinct nations. This is the "danger" of ethnic psychology: you can prove anything with it—the inconsistency of the Romanian nation just as much as its homogeneity.

In fact, the issue is predominantly social. The nation is too large and too diverse a conglomerate to be examined in the psychological laboratory. Group psychology, if we want it to be plausible and useful, must be limited to well-defined segments with a minimal level of coherence. The typical Romanian intellectual is certainly closer to European intellectuals in general than to the Romanian shepherd in the mountains or the fisherman in the Delta (and this is just as valid for other categories). The "psychology of the Romanian people" was based on the extrapolation of certain elements of traditional civilization (themselves made uniform and highly simplified). From this point of view the persistence here of certain traditional rural structures, at least in comparison with the dynamic and highly urbanized civilization of the West, encouraged the illusion of a Romania *differently* composed and with a different historical destiny.

It is noticeable that this rural civilization was contrasted not only with the rest of the world but also, indeed primarily, with the other dimension of Romanian civilization: the urban sector. The towns, which were, it is true, substantially populated for a long time by other ethnic elements (Hungarians and Germans in Transylvania, many Jews in Moldavia, etc.) were taken out of the equation by the theoreticians of the national spirit. Their synthesis is no less Romanian than the rural synthesis, but it is Romanian in a *different* way, which upsets the schema of ethnic specificity. Between the rural and urban poles we might add the category, so massively present in modern Romanian history, of the *mahala**, the intermediary zone between peasant culture and truly urban culture, the members of which have long ceased to be peasants without becoming townspeople in more than a formal sense. After being x-rayed by Caragiale at the end of the last century, the *mahala* saw a massive expansion in the communist years (albeit under the new guise of districts of tower blocks) as a result of forced industrialization and migration into the towns. This disoriented population, cut off from tradition but not yet integrated in modernity, represented, and continues to represent, an important mass, vulnerable to political and electoral maneuvering. The village, the *mahala*, and the urban nucleus may be seen as "ideal types", each with its own spiritual, cultural, and behavioral configuration. The only condition is that we do not forget that within these models diversity reigns. The Romanians are Romanians, but beyond that they cannot be reduced to a single human type.

To conclude, ethnic psychology is not something given from the origins, but a fluid amalgam of varied attitudes and behaviors, which have their source in history and evolve according to its rhythms. As European integration proceeds and the social structures are modernized, the differences between the Romanian and Western profiles will be attenuated. But they will not disappear. Neither the West nor the Romanian space is, or will ever be, uniform, and still less Europe as a whole. We may hope, however, that the things which bring us closer to each other will prove stronger than those which separate us, or which we think separate us.

---

* Urban periphery, slums. *Trans.*

CHAPTER FIVE

The Romanians and the Others

"HE TO WHOM FOREIGNERS ARE DEAR..."

The "other" is an omnipresent figure in the imaginary of any community. The game of "alterity" is an archetypal structure. In this respect the Romanians are not, and could not be, exceptional. However, two characteristics of Romanian history have contributed to the placing of the other in a specific light: on the one hand, the reactions of a rural and somewhat isolated civilization, and on the other, the massive and uninterrupted impact of foreign rulers and models. The contradictory and complementary action of these two factors has led to a synthesis bearing clear marks of originality.

According to the national mythology, Romanians are by nature hospitable and tolerant. They are characterized to the highest degree by *omenie**, a word which was heavily stressed and amplified in recent decades (a process not unconnected to the isolationist tendencies of the communist regime) until it concentrated an almost limitless range of meanings. To be human, in the full sense of the word, came to mean practically the same thing as to be Romanian.

In fact, it is not the Romanian as such who is particularly hospitable, but the Romanian peasant, and not just the Romanian peasant but the peasant in general. Traditional civilizations are "hospitable". Townspeople, including Romanian townspeople, are less hospitable than their compatriots in some village lost in the mountains.

Tolerance, which was already highlighted in the last century by various Romanian authors, likewise arises naturally from the needs of a rural civilization, to which "others", without merging into it completely, bring diverse and necessary attributes of civilization. Foreigners settled especially in the towns, and for a long time they fulfilled economic and social roles which the Romanians, whether peasants or boyars, only fulfilled to a small extent. The cosmopolitan town thus fitted into the predominantly rural structure of Romanian society and it certainly

---

* A word suggestive of a complex of traditional virtues: humanity, kindness, generosity, etc. *Trans.*

played its part in the Romanian synthesis, but as a tolerated foreign body. Up until the Second World War an anti-urban mythology was manifested in a whole range of ideologies and projects.

Hospitality is only one side, the more pleasant one, of relations with the other. While tolerance is laudable in itself, it already puts us on the alert: to be tolerated is not necessarily to be accepted, still less integrated. In any traditional civilization the foreigner is perceived with maximum intensity. A *special* behavior towards the foreigner, whether good or bad, stands out by the fact that it is special. The more open and urbanized, and thus the more cosmopolitan, a society becomes, the less the foreigner attracts peculiar interest: he is no longer a special case. Westerners seem less "welcoming" than Romanians precisely because for them the notion of the foreigner has undergone a de-dramatization.

There is no disputing traditional Romanian hospitality. However, it would be incorrect to isolate it from a whole complex of attitudes. It reflects the treatment of the foreigner as foreign. Remaining within the same system of references it has often been claimed that the Romanians do not marry foreign partners (as we have seen, Petru Maior and Mihail Kogălniceanu saw in this refusal the illustration and guarantee of Romanian purity). It has likewise been claimed that the Romanians do not leave their country and cannot bear to live in a different environment. Even when large numbers of Transylvanian Romanians began to emigrate to the United States around 1900, the illusion was maintained that this was a temporary state of affairs which would end in the return of those who had left.

When Eminescu exclaims "He to whom foreigners are dear / Let the dogs eat his heart", these terrible words only express the other side of what is essentially a coherent type of behavior. The distinction between *us* and *others* is felt strongly, in all senses, for better or worse. In the "traditional" opinion of the Romanians, foreigners more often appear in an unfavorable light, sometimes lamentably so. Folklore provides plenty of examples. For the Romanians, the Bulgarians and Serbs are stupid ("A green horse and a Serb—or Bulgarian—with brains, you never did see"); the Greeks are also stupid, or variously greedy, bad, rude, and haughty; the Hungarians are boastful and fearful; while the Armenians are dirty.[1] In fact we find a fundamental rejection, to which tolerance is no more than the complement. Indeed, it can turn to intolerance as soon as the function fulfilled by the foreigner no longer seems necessary, or is felt to be harmful. Such an evolution can be seen both in the nationalist current of the 1930s and in the nationalism of the Ceaușescu period.

Moreover, "foreign" is a generic term, embracing all those, regardless of ethnic composition, who reflect a system of values other than that generally accepted or imposed. We have seen that for Nae Ionescu the non-Orthodox Romanian was not quite Romanian. The Romanian who came back from the West after 1989, who "hadn't eaten soya salami", was not accepted as a Romanian, as a true Romanian, by a far from negligible section of the Romanian population. (In Poland and Hungary, countries in a similar situation to Romania, this did not happen). The communist regime only dramatized the "us/others" distinction even more (whether it was a matter of others within or others from outside). What was foreign, including Romanians "contaminated" by foreignness, took on connotations of maximum alterity. But nor was the opposite tendency completely lacking. The reaction was always in proportion to the pressure. Renowned for their attachment to their native land, the Romanians began, in increasing numbers, to dream of going abroad. Many succeeded in emigrating even before 1989, and after that year Romania provided the largest contingent of emigrants, in relation to its population, in Europe. The stifling nationalist discourse proved its "virtues" by producing the contrary effect to that which its creators had banked on.

At present, the dramatization of relations with others, partly inherited but to a large extent cultivated by the communist and post-communist authorities, meets with an opposite process of getting to know, integrating, and accepting. Some reactions are still those of a traditional society, perturbed by too much openness. An apparently minor, but typical, example is the endless discussion of, and resistance manifested on, the issue of homosexual rights; the removal from the Penal Code of sanctions which are in any case useless has been seen by many as a campaign to promote homosexuality and another good excuse to demonize the perverted West. But there are significant evolutions in the opposite direction, too. The Romanians who "didn't eat soya salami" are starting to be rehabilitated; indeed, someone who has made a fortune in the West is likely to be seen as a positive figure. The authorities do not hesitate to recommend some of these to public opinion, in contrast to the discourse of a few years ago: the manipulation of the "Ilie Năstase myth" in the spring of 1996, with his success in the West emphasized more than his sporting glory, is a characteristic example.

Gradually the Romanians are becoming Europeanized. As time goes on they will become less "hospitable", but also less "scared" in the face of foreignness.

DEFENDERS OF THE WEST

The pressure of foreigners from outside and from within, real up to a point but hyperbolized in the national imaginary, generated the *besieged fortress* complex which is so typical of the Romanian mentality of the last two centuries. The history of the Romanians is understood in strictly conflictual terms, as a continuous struggle for ethnic and state survival. The "struggles against the Turks" were powerfully imprinted on the national consciousness; and once they were over, the privileged role of "hereditary enemy" was taken up by Hungary. As always, history chooses and forgets, amplifies and minimizes. It would be just as correct, and certainly more realistic, to observe that, beyond the Romanian–Ottoman and Romanian–Hungarian antagonism, the Romanian lands were *integrated* for centuries in the Ottoman system, or in the Transylvanian case in the Hungarian space and more generally in that of Central Europe. Such a de-dramatization of the Romanian past and its treatment in a structural manner, less event-centered and warlike, comes up against tenacious prejudice and the remarkable functionality of the myth of the struggle for independence. This fulfills the threefold mission of highlighting the *virtue and heroism* of the Romanians, justifying their *historical late-coming* in terms of the sacrifices imposed by ceaseless aggression, and, finally, attracting the attention of the West to its *debt of gratitude* towards the Romanians who defended it from the Ottoman onslaught.

The image of a West protected thanks to Romanian sacrifice and a Romanian society strained and held back by fulfilling the function of defender of European civilization has become deeply ingrained in the political vision of the Romanians, in their behavior and their reactions. The West has a debt which it has not yet repaid. The Romanians should receive, not give. In view of this debt, any failing of the West is perceived as betrayal. Whatever goes badly in Romania does not result from any wrong orientation or bad management on the part of the Romanians; others are to blame—the others who preyed on us, and the others who did not rush to our aid when it was their duty to do so.

I quote from a speech delivered in Parliament by I. C. Brătianu on 25 February 1879: "We were the advance guard of Europe from the thirteenth century until very recently; we were the bulwark of Europe against the Asian invasions of the past. The European states were able to develop then because others sacrificed themselves in order to shelter them. It is for this reason—despite the ancient remains of Romanian civilization—that we have only recently embarked on the way of modern civilization."[2]

Even a historian like P. P. Panaitescu, who was little tempted by nationalist mythology and demagogy, claims the following: "It is known that the Romanians delayed the Ottoman advance towards the center of the continent. This delay did not only mean, as our historians have said, a weakening of the offensive power of the Turks, which was worn down by the resistance at the Danube. It allowed Western Europe to take up the struggle at a much more favorable time, with other weapons and another military organization."[3]

With the lack of responsibility characteristic of national-communist demagogy, new images were projected and inserted into the national consciousness, according to the principle: "You can say anything as long as it is patriotic." Thus the battle of Rovine—about which we know nothing for sure—is said to have saved the Western world. Some teachers call up before their pupils the image of a West which was able to erect its cathedrals precisely because the Romanians were fighting at the same time on the Danube. Others go even further, claiming that this resistance even made possible the discovery of America! As far as America is concerned there is not much to be said, but things are fairly clear in the case of the cathedrals, which were mostly built well before the foundation of the Romanian states.

In fact, Romanian resistance was not continuous: a few episodes and phases can be picked out, but not enough to hold the Turkish forces on the line of the Danube for centuries. In any case, these struggles only affected the flank of the Ottoman advance. Anyone who looks at a map can immediately see (as Romanian historians seem not to have done for a long time) that the Turkish advance into

Central Europe had nothing to do with the Romanian territories; they are completely peripheral to its main axis. This was proved (if there was anything left to prove) by P. P. Panaitescu himself in his 1944 article "Why did the Turks not conquer the Romanian lands?" The answer to this question lies, substantially, in the fact that the Turkish armies advanced along the line Belgrade–Buda–Vienna. The shortest road to Vienna did not pass through Tîrgovişte, still less through Suceava.

The struggles of the Romanians against the Turks did not save the West, and nor did they irremediably impoverish Romania. The divergent evolution of the West and the East is not to be explained by wars or foreign domination. Nor is the backwardness of Romanian society to be explained in terms of its inefficiency, or, to put it more directly, the "laziness" of the Romanians, which some are tempted to set against tales of heroism and ceaseless struggle, thus responding to one mythology with another mythology. Quite simply, the Romanians belong to an entire zone of Europe which has remained behind. In antiquity, the East was more prosperous and dynamic than the West. Around the year 1000, Byzantium boasted a civilization richer and more refined than Western Europe. Then everything swung the other way: the principal axis of history shifted towards the West, and then towards the Northwest. Wars stained the West with blood no less than the East. But they did not prevent it, divided and torn as it was, from constructing a new technological civilization and becoming master of the world. There were dominated peoples in the West too, but the fact of foreign rule did not prevent social and material evolution. The Romanians were not in the "right" zone of Europe; that they entered the modern period with a handicap is not something that calls for either praise or blame.

Where it becomes a matter of blame, however, is when this handicap starts to function as an alibi, as a permanent excuse for failures. To say that history is pulling you down is incorrect. At a certain point in the middle of the crisis of the Ceauşescu regime someone started to "calculate" the enormous sums which foreign overlords owed Romania as a consequence of the robbery they had practiced throughout history. It was, of course, a diversion. It was not because the Romans had stolen the gold of Dacia that Romanians did not have enough to eat in the 1980s, but because the communist structures were aberrant and the economic policy misguided. History does not mark out a fatal pathway. Around 1900, Sweden was a country of peasants, a poor country with massive emigration; half a century later it had become one of the richest countries in the world. South Korea is nowadays a great economic power, while the level from which it started a few decades ago was much lower than that of Romania. At a time when the crucial issue is the construction of a Romania that performs effectively, Romanians ought to sacrifice less on the altar of historical mythology. Neither the invocation of their ancestors nor reproaches addressed to others will be of any use to them.

SEPARATION FROM THE EAST

The break with the East, for which the nineteenth-century elite opted, took the form of a massive devaluing and inculpation of peoples and cultures which had hitherto offered the Romanians more models than motives of lamentation.

The first victims were the Greeks. After 1821, and especially on the eve of the revolution of 1848, a virulent and almost obsessive anti-Greek attitude crystallized, which was to be manifest for a number of decades and which can only partially be explained by the real circumstances of the Phanariot period and the revolutionary episode of 1821. The Greeks symbolized the East and several centuries of Oriental culture, which had to be given up now in favor of the benign influence of the West, or, for others, the "Romanian specific". Bălcescu set the tone in his article "The Romanians and the Phanariots", in which he underlined the "sorry state" to which the latter had brought the country. Eminescu had a phobia of Greeks: "And if the order and establishment of these lands has been upset, if we have lost provinces, if we have discarded good old customs with ease, if corruption and cowardice have entered the classes of old Romanian society, in every case the source of these evils will turn out to have been a Greek, or a handful of Greeks."[4]

Nor does Drăghicescu, in his attempt at a psychology of the Romanian people, appear much more conciliatory. He admits that the Romanian aristocracy became cultivated and acquired a dose of refinement through its contact with the Greeks. Overall, however, their influence was disastrous. "The most strongly felt inheritances which the Greeks left us, the effects of which we still find it hard to bear today, are the poverty and desolation of the country, the stripping bare and alienation of Romanian fields, and the utter impoverishment of the Romanian population in both lands." The Greeks also left "something of their duplicity, something of their divisive perfidy, with their envious and corrupt equivocation, their lack of worth and their flattery coupled with the well-known sick pride of Byzantium. If the public spirit here suffers from these same moral diseases, then they have their origin in the moral rottenness of corrupt Byzantium, for with them we have been intoxicated by the Greeks who came here, driven by the Turks from fallen Tsarigrad."[5]

So here we have the real culprits: the Greeks and only the Greeks! Around 1900, however, this anti-Greek fury began to die down. In 1898 Iorga delivered and published a lecture under the title *Romanian Culture under the Phanariots*, in which he attempted to rehabilitate the period, and Romanian–Greek relations in general. It was the sign of a progressive normalization. Subsequently, the Greeks were practically to disappear from the gallery of negative communities. They were simply no longer needed.

Anti-Turkish attitudes were less vehemently manifested in this period. The separation from Turkey was self-explanatory. As the Turks were "other" in the strongest sense of the word they seemed less harmful than the Greeks, who were Orthodox like the Romanians and had even infiltrated the Romanian environment. Above all, the Turks provided the elements of a series of *images d'Épinal*, which fed the chronicle of Romanian victories from the Middle Ages to 1877. Turkish domination and influence could only be judged negatively, but, once again, the Greek intermediary seemed even more guilty than the Turkish overlord.

Let us return to Drăghicescu's text, to identify "the soul poison of the atmosphere of the Orient" which was transmitted to the Romanians from the Ottoman source. "Every Turkish custom borrowed, every Turkish fashion imitated introduced into our ethnic soul the seeds of corruption and idleness, which cause peoples to degrade and degenerate." If the Romanians are "lazy", the fault is that of the Turks. As a believer in the principle of "the clothes making the man", Drăghicescu especially denounces the wide Oriental garments that were adopted by Romanian boyars: "The *shalwar*, which, as is well known, is a pair of very wide trousers, the jacket with long floating sleeves over which was worn another jacket with split sleeves, or the coat with wide short sleeves, all bear the stamp of a life of laziness and indolence. This clothing is deliberately made so as to prevent any sort of activity and to accustom one to an empty life of unending rest and torpor, to a life of sleep and light entertainment. In it, one scarcely feels one is alive [...]. Even if our ancestors had wanted to break with their lifestyle of unconcern, of drowsy torpor and indolence, even if they had wanted to wake up and work, to start something, this clothing would have prevented and discouraged them. With long, wide split sleeves, which get in the way of, and paralyze, the hands, it is quite impossible to be active and energetic."[6]

After the Greeks and the Turks it is the turn of the Russians to fall victim to the same attempt to escape from Eastern civilization. Until almost the middle of the nineteenth century they were generally well regarded by the Romanians. As protectors of Southeastern European Christianity, they appeared for a century and a half in the guise of potential liberators. Around 1815, the *Chronograph* of Dionisie the Ecclesiarch expresses the anti-Western and pro-Russian attitude of the "middle class": the good and Christian emperor Alexander was perceived as a protective barrier against the anarchy generated by the French Revolution and the imperial ambitions of Napoleon. Indeed, the first significant stage in the orientation of Romanian society towards the West took place under Russian protection and guidance, during the time of the *Règlement Organique* and the administration of General Kiseleff (1829–1834), when Romanians came into contact with a Slav aristocracy which expressed itself in French. The Russians seemed well on the way to winning the Romanians' hearts. What happened subsequently was quite the opposite, however. The 1848 generation set itself more against Russia than against Turkey, and denounced both the *Règlement Organique*, which was seen as a barrier to progress, and the expansionist tendencies of an empire which threatened to swallow up the Romanian space. In order to converse in French, the Romanians no longer needed, as in 1830, the presence of Russian officers; they preferred to go direct to Paris. Even collaboration with the Russians, which was imposed at times by circumstances, as in 1877–78 and 1916–17, proved frustrating and liable to unforeseen consequences (the loss of the counties of southern Bessarabia in 1878, the lack of any support in 1916, and the disorganization of the front in 1917). It is clear that the cultural orientation of Romania towards the West and in the direction of detachment from the Slav context could only lead to an essential depreciation of the Russian model and of relations with Russia (in spite of the fact that, structurally speaking, Romanian society, being predominantly rural and highly polarized between a rich aristocracy and a subject peasantry, was closer to the Russian than to the Western model).

THE FRENCH MYTH

The ground thus cleared was rapidly taken over by the *French* myth. This had, of course, its antecedents, going back to Phanariot times. But contacts with French culture prior to 1830 were sporadic and largely indirect, through Greek and, as we have seen, even Russian connections, and they cannot be equated, or even compared, with the scale of the phenomenon which broke out in the period between 1830 and 1848. Once launched on the road of Westernization, the Romanian elite threw itself into the arms of France, the great Latin sister in the West. When we speak of the Western model, what is to be understood is first and foremost the French model, which comes far ahead of the other Western reference points.[7] Annexed to it is the model of Belgium, a small country, partially Francophone, monarchical, neutral, democratic, and prosperous, which offered Romania a French-style model that was in some respects better adapted to its own condition. The constitution of 1866 was an imitation of the Belgian constitution of 1831, and the expression "the Belgium of the East", frequently used in the second half of the nineteenth century, illustrates an interesting political myth: the illusion of a Romania destined to become, in every respect, a replica of Belgium at the other end of the continent.

To see what the French myth meant in Romanian society, we have an impressive number of testimonies from which to choose. Here are two of these, which carry things to a point beyond which it would be hard to go (a point hard to imagine nowadays, despite the relative survival of Romanian Francophilia).

In 1907 Dumitru Drăghicescu arrived, by way of a subtle argumentation, at the conclusion that there was no nation on earth more perfect than the French nation and no intelligence more complex than that of the French. The French had reached the highest point that other peoples will reach in an indefinite future: "As the nations of Europe acquire their definitive borders and their social life becomes elaborated and crystallized within the precise limits of these borders, so their spiritual accomplishments will approach those of the French, and the immaterial substance of their souls will take on the luminous clarity, the smoothness and brilliance of the French mentality."[8]

Half a century before this impressive characterization, in 1853 to be precise, I. C. Brătianu addressed a memorandum to Napoleon III. The Romanian politician pleaded for the union of the principalities and sought to convince the emperor that this would be a "French conquest": "The army of the Romanian state would be the army of France, its ports on the Black Sea and the Danube would be entrepôts for French trade." Brătianu then goes even further, and even if we treat the memorandum as a text written to further a precise political aim in the circumstances of the time, the words still remain as they are: "France", he writes, "will have all the advantages of a colony, without the expenses which this implies." France was "our second homeland", and Romania destined to become its *colony*.[9]

Even in 1914, by which time there had been considerable evolution in the direction of Romanian cultural and political autonomy, a number of politicians still showed a visceral attachment to France, deeming that Romania should enter the war not to serve its own interests but to defend the threatened civilization of France. I quote from the memoirs of Constantin Argetoianu: "Lahovari and Cantacuzino—especially Cantacuzino—also wanted immediate entry into the war [...] and they wanted it only for the love of France, which could not be left to perish, as if its fate lay within our power! In their sincerity they hardly mentioned Transylvania, the making whole of the folk, or Michael the Brave, abandoning all the arguments of a national character which drove almost all of us to be against the Central Powers, and calling for entry into the war 'pour voler au secours de la France'!"[10] It was not in vain that Brătianu had promised that "the Romanian army would be the army of France".

At the end of the nineteenth century, in *De l'influence française sur l'esprit public en Roumanie* (1898), Pompiliu Eliade argued that Romania owed its whole modern civilization to France. Before French influence the Romanian lands "did not exist for civilization", nor did they "exist for history". Thanks to France we can see "not the rebirth of a people, but its birth".[11] This opinion, flagrantly exaggerated as it is, bears witness to the contemporary obsession with France. But it is no less true that the French myth did play an important modeling role. Within a generation, starting immediately after 1830, French imposed itself as the language of culture, permanently eliminating Greek, while Oriental costume gave way to Parisian fashion. Young Romanians set out for Paris; for more than a century France would provide or influence the training of the greater part of the intellectual elite of the country. You could not be an intellectual without a reasonable knowledge of French (which was a compulsory language in all eight years of high school until the communist education reform of 1948). French political, juridical, and cultural structures and institutions were borrowed to a considerable degree.

Even the Romanian language underwent a considerable evolution under French influence, a process of modernization leading to the elimination or marginalization of part of its Slav and Oriental component and to what might be called a "second Latinization", largely through the massive adoption of neologisms of French origin. It has been calculated that 39 percent of current Romanian vocabulary consists of borrowings from French or has French as the first language of reference (the second being Latin), and that the frequency of such words in use is 20 percent.[12] Thus in everyday speech one Romanian word in five is of French origin.

The capital of Romania became, in its turn, a "Little Paris". As with any myth, here too there is a mixture of truth, exaggeration, and illusion. Despite a number of Parisian-style buildings from the last decades of the nineteenth century, Bucharest as a whole does not resemble Paris. Something of the Parisian lifestyle characterized the behavior of an elite, and certain corners of the Bucharest cityscape acquired a Parisian atmosphere. However, the greater part of the population lived far from the French model. On the other hand, the "Belgium of the East" and "Little Paris" were powerful symbols, which shifted Romania, in as much as it could be shifted, in the direction of Western civilization, just as "Dacia" and "Michael the Brave" contributed, also through their symbolic charge, to the achievement of national unity.

THE GERMAN "COUNTERMYTH"

Of course, the West did not just mean France. It is worth noting that, at least until the interwar period, the other great Latin sister, Italy, was the object of much less interest, while relations with Spain remained sporadic. There is also the interesting case of Britain. Some Romanians were fascinated by the British model (Ion Ghica, for example, who served as minister plenipotentiary in London from 1881 to 1890), but they can be counted on one's fingers. For the Romanians in general, Britain remained a far-off exotic island, and the spread of the English language as a medium of culture and communication came late (paradoxically, under the Ceauşescu regime).

The French myth was so powerful that there was only room, in the polarizing realm of the imaginary, for a single *countermyth*, antithetical and complementary: the German myth.

The position of Germany in Romania was continually consolidated during the half century leading up to the First World War. By the end of this period Germany had become a formidable competitor to France. The factors in its favor were far from negligible. The Romanians of Transylvania and Bukovina were closer to German culture and mentality than to French civilization; Transylvanian intellectuals often read French authors in German translation. In the Romanian kingdom, on the other hand, although clearly overtaken by French, German was the second language of education and culture (with eight years of French and four of German in school). The economic and political weight of the German Empire in Southeastern Europe was more significant than the relatively modest presence of France. In 1883 Romania adhered to the Triple Alliance structured around Germany and Austria–Hungary. The German origin of King Carol I and his indisputable prestige constituted an additional factor in this process of rapprochement.

Of course, mythical evolutions are never univocal: every myth is closely stalked by its countermyth. So while the German cultural model was dominant for the Romanians of Transylvania, they also looked sympathetically towards France, to the extent of admiring the idealized French model more than the concrete German model. Latin consciousness and solidarity, the national movement which inevitably came up against German interests, and the influence exercised by Romania, all contributed to a degree of equilibrium, at least in the imaginary, in the relationship between these two great Western points of reference. In Romania, too, we can detect a certain slippage in the direction of the "other" model, this time from France towards Germany.

After 1866, part of the Romanian elite proved to be sensitive to the virtues of the German model. Its admirers considered that, now that the political effervescence of the mid-century was over, it was time for a new equilibrium and a better thought out and more organized effort. Renowned for its rigor and effectiveness, German culture could offer solutions more appropriate to the aspirations of the Romanian nation than the French mentality, which was accused of superficiality and even frivolity. For some, the disciplined reason and clarity of the French mind were opposed to German cramming: "[...] the German does not have the ordered, harmonious, balanced, and lucid intelligence of the Frenchman. [...] German intelligence has remained confused, chaotic, disordered, and tangled."[13] For others, on the contrary, the Germans were solidly based, while the French were not completely serious. We are, of course, in the zone of highly mythologized representations, with the characteristic polarization between enthusiastic reception and absolute rejection.

The German myth was the option of a minority, but an influential minority, represented in the first place by the Junimea society, which had a decisive say in the cultural and political evolution of the country towards the end of the nineteenth century. (Even if the majority of the Junimists—like any majority in Romania at the time—had been molded by French culture, it was the "Germanophiles" who set the tone of the movement.) A great cultural personality like Titu Maiorescu, a politician of the stature of P. P. Carp, and the greatest Romanian poet, Mihai Eminescu, all belong within this current. On French civilization, and especially on the effects of Romanian contact with France, Eminescu expressed himself with his usual sincerity: "In Paris, in brothels of cynicism and idleness / With its lost women and in its obscene orgies..." ("Epistle III"). Like Maiorescu, Eminescu had a German cultural education. The most remarkable case, however, is that of Caragiale, who, despite having no knowledge of German, decided in 1904 to settle in Berlin, where he remained until the end of his life. His wish was to live in a civilized country, and that could only be Germany. His confrontation with the incurable Francophile Barbu Delavrancea, who was disgusted at everything around him and all that happened during his visit to Berlin, is a delicious anthology piece, a typical illustration of the Romanians' view of the Western world.[14]

In 1891 Kogălniceanu did not hesitate to state, in an address to the Academy, that "All my life, as a youth and a mature man, I have repeatedly borne witness to the fact that it is largely to German culture, the University of Berlin, German society, and the men and great patriots who accomplished the raising up of Germany again and its unity, that I owe all that I have become in my country, and that it was from the fire of German patriotism that the torch of my Romanian patriotism took its flame."[15] With his political flair, Kogălniceanu, who really owed just as much to French as to German culture, sensed that the hour of Germany had come!

Up until 1914, the position of Germany as a molder of Romanian elites continued to advance. It was already threatening French supremacy in certain areas. In 1892, forty-two professors of the University of Bucharest had studied in France, and only eight in Germany; by 1914 the equivalent figures were sixty-two and twenty-nine.[16] The ratio had gone from five to one, to two to one. Disciplines like philosophy, history, and geography already owed more to the German universities than to the French. The past cannot be remade, but we may still ask ourselves how far this German influence would have gone if the First World War had not intervened to put a decisive stop to it, after providing both Germanophiles and Francophiles with an occasion to manifest to the full their enthusiasm for one or other of the two competing models.

The gulf created by the war—in which Romania, seeking national unity, found itself in the opposite camp to Germany and suffered an oppressive German occupation—made it difficult for relations to continue as before. The intransigence displayed by Nicolae Iorga deserves comment. Before the war, the historian had been very close to the German historical school; his "anti-French" action of 1906 (aimed in fact at the protection of Romanian culture) had enhanced his not entirely deserved reputation as a "Germanophile". But as soon as war broke out Iorga's choice was unequivocal, determined of course by strictly Romanian motives in the first instance, but to a certain extent also by a pro-French and pro-Latin sensibility which now came to light. "Why do we love France?" is the title of an article which he published on 17 August 1914, when France seemed almost beaten. Iorga writes:

> That we love France is beyond doubt, although it is now, they say, defeated by Germany. Just as it is beyond doubt that we respect and admire Germany, although it has, they say, defeated France. [...] But why do we love France? Because our whole upper class has adopted its fashions and luxuries? Perhaps, where that class is concerned. Because we are Latins and we read in French? To a large extent, yes. But above all, for all of us, the non-diplomats, it is for a third reason. What does Germany want? Dominance in Europe, for its national economy, for its political power. What does Russia want? The same dominance in

Europe, and if possible even more. What does Britain want? To keep its control of the seas and the gains this brings. What does Austria–Hungary want? To strengthen and advance Hungarian ambitions in the Carpathians and the Balkans. But what does France want? It wants to *live*. It wants the French state and the French nation to live. To keep its lands and its rights. To avenge its honor.[17]

A splendid page of political mythology! Two years later (on 26 September 1916), Iorga did not miss the chance to stir up the "Latins who are not interested", in other words, the Spanish: "The war which France began without a program of conquest, without any greed for foreign lands or any selfish ambition to grasp from others their hegemony over the world, has been joined by Italy, then Portugal, and finally Romania. Today the Latins are pouring out their blood together."[18] Spain stood accused for not taking part in this brotherly outpouring of blood—although it basically was not in any of its interests to do so. We may note that after the war, Iorga, the "false Germanophile" before 1914, was to refuse systematically any contact with Germany and with the German academic community.

In the Romanian political imaginary, therefore, the interwar period meant progress for France and a withdrawal of the German model. There can be no doubt that these evolutions were relative, given that, on the one hand, the autochthonist wave and the maturing of Romanian society in general limited and filtered elements from outside, especially from French culture; and on the other, even though diminished and unable to offer a coherent model, Germany retained a significant weight. German was still the second foreign language after French; young Romanians continued to study in Germany; and on the eve of the Second World War the Romanian extreme Right, although sprung from autochthonous soil, discovered certain affinities with Nazi ideology. The position of Britain (the great Western ally alongside France) was rising, though cases of "Anglophilia" remained limited to a few individuals. More significant was the rise of Italy, which took its place beside France as a place for the education of elites, especially in the human sciences, not to mention the existence of certain sympathies with Mussolini's sociopolitical solutions.

Thus we can see that there were a variety of Western models on offer, as well as the no less present autochthonous model, which was affirming itself more and more strongly, in spite of its nebulous character (Orthodoxism, traditionalism, peasantism, etc.).

COMMUNIST MYTHOLOGY

What took hold, in the end, through the unexpected turn of history, was the Russian model once again, reworked in the communist mold. Around the middle of the century the myth of the Soviet Union blotted out every other cultural reference point. *Light comes from the East*, the title of a propaganda brochure published in 1945 by Mihail Sadoveanu, who had gone over to the side of the new orientation bag and baggage, illustrates the profound sense of the change.[19] Romania was turning its eyes from the West to the East. What is striking, this time too, is the radicalism of the Romanian solutions of imitation. The French model, the autochthonous model, and the Soviet model were all, in their time and for their adherents, veritable religions. In 1866 the Romanians could think of nothing better than to copy the Belgian constitution; in 1948 they copied the Soviet one. This spirit of imitation highlights the fragility and instability of Romanian society, always looking for reference points that could be easily mythologized. It could, of course, be argued in reply that communism was imposed all over Central Europe by the simple advance of the Soviet steamroller. But this does not alter the fact that the new model was more faithfully adopted in Romania than in the other satellite countries. It can be argued that Romania was a defeated country, but so was Hungary. Moreover, not only was there no attenuation of the Soviet model after the relative "breaking free" from the Soviet Union: it was on the contrary, consolidated.

As in the Soviet Union, the multiparty system disappeared completely in Romania (it was maintained partially and as a matter of form in the other communist countries). All that remained was the Communist Party. Very similar methods of repression were experienced, including the notorious Danube–Black Sea canal, a reproduction of the Soviet canal labor camps. The subordination of the church and the virulence of atheistic propaganda reached levels similar to the Soviet Union, such as were not seen in Catholic or Protestant communist countries. The collectivization of the land was almost total, as in the Soviet Union. Heavy industry was likewise constituted on pure Soviet lines. Here we are at the heart of the communist mythical approach, with its emphasis on heavy industries more characteristic of the nineteenth century than the late twentieth—iron and coal, steel, cement—capable of rapidly transforming economic structures, covering the country with factories and furnaces, raising a numerous working class out of almost nothing, and forcing the process of urbanization, regardless of any principle of efficiency and viability. The mythological sense of this sort of industrialization is even more evident in Romania than in the Soviet Union, for the simple reason that the resources of the country were not suited to such a project. Thus Romania became, after the Soviet Union, one of the largest producers of steel in the world. The annoying difference was that the great neighbor could base its steel industry on immense deposits of iron and coal, while Romania had to import them (from India, Canada, or Australia!) in order to satisfy an ideological fantasy. The preeminence of the proletariat—a requirement of the communist myth—was also translated by an orientation of intellectuals towards technology, towards *production*. The myth of the *engineer* was promoted, a myth of Soviet provenance but taken to its peak in Romania. In the later years of the communist regime two out of every three graduates were engineers, an absolute world record (compared with about 50 percent in the Soviet Union and a mere 7 percent in France and the United States).[20] Thus it can be seen that the Soviet model was followed down to the smallest detail and even outdone in some respects.

After 1964 the Romanian communist leaders embarked on an apparently independent policy. Some superficial observers were prepared to believe that if the Soviet model was not being abandoned it was at least being adapted. All the more so as the history and traditions of the country were—albeit in a partial and distorted manner—restored to their proper place, and certain traditional relations with the West were renewed. It was a deceptive appearance. The real structures remained those of *Soviet communism*. In 1989, at the end of Ceauşescu's rule, Romania was closer to the original Stalinist model than to the Soviet Union itself, which had been set in motion by Gorbachev, not to mention more evolved communist societies like Hungary or Poland. What was added to this model was a considerable dose of Oriental mythology. This was the moment when China became a "traditional friend", as did North Korea. The "cultural revolution" launched in 1971 was not identical in its objectives and its scale with the Chinese phenomenon, but they shared certain common characteristics (the calling of intellectuals to order, in the first place). At the same time, the systematic destruction of Bucharest and its rebuilding as a "utopian city" has its correspondent, and certainly its model, in the reconstruction of P'yongyang, with one difference: the North Korean capital had been flattened by American bombardments, while the Romanians set out to destroy the "Little Paris" themselves.

In as much as Bucharest today looks more like a "post-communist city" than a replica of Paris, it can be appreciated that the impact of the Soviet myth was much greater than the influence of the French (or generally Western) myth. Its transforming action went deeper, radically modifying social structures, the landscape of the country, and the lives of the people. The explanation may be found in the massive character of the crude pressure exerted, in comparison with the slower and more nuanced operation of the mental and cultural mechanisms through which the influence of the West had made itself felt. From this point of view the Soviet myth was a false myth, borne rather than shared, in contrast to the Western myth that had seduced generation after generation. But that is not quite how things stand, even if violence essentially explains the transformations which took place. Wary as I am of the trap of mythologizing, I do not intend to claim that the Romanian people in its entirety was won over by communism, nor that the Romanian people in its entirety showed no adherence to communism. Every myth has its believers, its unbelievers, and those who remain indifferent. Moscow, like Paris, had its admirers and imitators. Force alone cannot radically change a society; there must be an element of belief and an element of participation. While the elite of the nineteenth century looked towards the West, in Romanian society around the middle of twentieth century there were sufficient dissatisfactions, frustrations, and complexes to turn other segments of society towards quite different points of reference. This could be recognized after 1989, when a large part of the population were reticent about breaking with communist structures and mentalities. The return to power of ex-communists in the majority of the Central European countries only recently liberated from communism demonstrates that the phenomenon is a more general one. The welfare state, social uniformity (even if only in appearance), a guaranteed right to a job, and many other things which I shall not list here, are elements of a mythology that it is dangerous to say some people did not, and do not still, believe in, simply because we do not believe in it!

On the other hand—and here again we see the complexity of mythical configurations—the failure of communism, especially in material terms, generated a new process of the mythologizing of the West and indeed of the whole non-communist world. In their relative isolation from the rest of the world the Romanians could invent stories at will. However, the mythical West generated by Romanian communism was different in its nature to the West of the nineteenth-century elite. What counted then was above all the cultural model. What the West offered under Ceauşescu was, more than anything, the products of consumer civilization. For Romanians deprived of the most basic goods, things received "in a package" (second-hand goods, sometimes even damaged) became a symbol of Western-style well-being. After December 1989 it was a surprise to find "stockpiles" of completely banal products (coffee, cigarettes, soap) in the possession of leading members of the communist nomenklatura. The packet of coffee and the Kent cigarette illustrated the virtues of Western civilization: it is a significant degradation of the myth, which had descended to the lowest level imaginable. And there was a further degradation: the myth of the West became the myth of "abroad" in general—all that is foreign is good (in a predominantly material sense). Many Romanians no longer make a clear distinction between Istanbul and Paris. It would be worthwhile studying the impact of the Arab micro-society which existed in Romania in the 1970s and 1980s. The thousands of Arab students who came to Romanian universities precisely because they could not afford to study in the West were able, in an impoverished and isolated country, to play the role of a "middle class", sufficiently cosmopolitan and financially endowed to dynamize the various segments of Romanian society with which they came into contact (by dealing in foreign goods and currency, corruption, prostitution, etc.). *Foreigner* became a generic term, the ultimate expression of the mythologizing process.

POST-REVOLUTIONARY REFERENCE POINTS

Since 1989 a reorientation towards the West can be clearly felt, although it is held back by the resistance of the autochthonists, whose aim, explicit or implicit, cannot be other than to keep Romania in the East. The apparently high percentage of those who currently adhere to the European idea must be interpreted with great prudence. "Entry into Europe" does not mean the same thing to everybody. Many think of the advantages, especially from a material point of view, but prefer to ignore the structural transformations which such an orientation imposes, the need to rethink political and cultural reference points, and the inevitable limiting of national sovereignty. They continue to hope for a Romania integrated, but at the same time "untouched" in its perennial values.

Polls taken immediately after the revolution placed France in the first place in the "Western imaginary" of the Romanians, with the United States close behind. The survival of the French myth—even if it no longer has its former strength—seems to be characteristic of Romania. Here French is, or was until recently, in the first place as a language of culture and communication: a unique situation in a Europe dominated by the English language. But English is well on the way to overtaking it, if indeed it has not already done so. The United States is starting to overtake France in terms of what it offers the Romanians by way of a social and cultural model, and in terms of its effective presence in the Romanian space. Communism "preserved" the French myth; now, in an open world, it will find it hard to resist the massive infusion of American mythology (which can be found at all levels, including everyday life, from American music and films to Coca–Cola and McDonalds restaurants). It is to be expected that Germany will return in force; having been inculpated after the war and then completely evacuated from the Romanian mythical complex, it now has all the necessary credentials to reaffirm its traditional influence in Central Europe. In geopolitical terms at least, Romania does not lie between France and the United States, but between Russia and Germany.

Various other reference points were also invoked in the years after the revolution. On the part of the authorities there was no shortage of clever and hope-inducing references to the Swedish, Austrian, or Japanese models. Those nostalgic for communism follow with satisfaction the current Chinese model, which would appear to demonstrate that authoritarian political and social principles are compatible with a free economy. A new reference point is South Korea, all the more attractive as it combines the image of explosive development with the reality of a massive presence in the Romanian market. Less often invoked, but very visible, is the Turkish model. Turkey is coming back in force to the space formerly dominated by the Ottoman Empire: such a performance by the poorest of the European nations that did not experience communism says all there is to say about the good work done by the communist system. Istanbul is not as far away as Paris, and the general appearance of Bucharest brings it closer nowadays to the condition of a "little Istanbul" than the "Little Paris" of former days.

Reference points, models, myths—we are far from a clear option. Indeed, this is a normal phenomenon. In the course of a century and a half the Romanian nation has been traumatized by three great ruptures: the break with the Orient, then the break with the West through the installation of communism, and finally the break with communism and a hesitant return to the Western pattern. All of these have imposed the presence of multiple and contradictory models, charged with giving sense and coherence to an *endless* transition. Modern Romanian civilization is essentially a civilization of transition: hence both the feverish search for what others can offer and the fear of what might be lost by contact with others; hence, therefore, the amalgam of fascination and rejection, in other words, the *obsession* with the foreign.

Three Sensitive Files: The Gypsies, the Hungarians, and the Jews

When the "other" is to be found within the citadel, he often presents more features of difference and stimulates to a greater extent all sorts of unease than the "other" outside. In such cases the process of mythologizing can go very far. This is what has happened, and continues to happen, in the Romanian environment, with three specific ethnic groups: the Gypsies, the Hungarians and the Jews. Investigations since 1989 have demonstrated that it is especially on them that the frustrations and fears of the majority population are projected in varying proportions.

According to the polls, approximately two-thirds of Romanians do not like Gypsies. This rather high proportion is suggestive of a veritable psychosis, and offers all the ingredients of a political myth. Many things are blamed on the Gypsies, from the insecurity of everyday life (murders, robberies) to the damaging of the country's image abroad. In particular, their appreciably growing demographic, and more recently also economic, weight arouses fear. Their number, officially a few hundred thousand, is amplified by public opinion to the order of millions. Some projections foresee the moment when, due to their high birthrate and the low birthrate of others, Gypsies will come to be in the majority in Romania. The traditional myth of the Gypsy, expressive of a feeling of superiority towards a very different, primitive, and marginal other, but also a certain romantic–humanitarian sympathy and a civilizing intention,[21] is giving way to a mixture of hostility and fear. In these conditions the discourse, which is promoted even on state television, becomes racist, serving to further widen a social fissure capable of generating dangerous situations.

The Hungarians in their turn "enjoy" the unfavorable opinion of about a third of Romanians. Here, too, the extreme opinions acquire mythical dimensions and manifest themselves with the intensity of a psychosis. Of course, history has its share of responsibility: discrimination against the Romanians and a contemptuous attitude towards them in pre-1918 Hungary could not fail to mark Romanian consciousness, as did the dramatic events which followed the cession of northern Transylvania in 1940. Apart from this, however, the resentments are well maintained politically and are systematically amplified (by both sides, but what we are interested in here is Romanian mythology, not its Hungarian counterpart). Explicitly or implicitly, the Hungarian threat provided an excuse for the Ceauşescu regime, as it has done on more than one occasion for those in power after 1989. Internal failures, of strictly indigenous origin, are pushed to the background by imaginary threats, in the face of which the Romanians are urged to be united and to forget their passing difficulties. The Romanians continually hear that the Hungarian lobby is creating international obstacles for Romania, and that Magyar irredentism threatens to tear Transylvania from the body of the country.

It would be naive to consider that there are no elements of reality at the base of these mythical constructions. The propaganda with anti-Romanian accents produced by certain Hungarian groups, and the agitation which goes on around the issue of Transylvania, are not exclusively matters of the imaginary. Where the myth begins is when Hungary becomes the dominant player to which all important Romanian evolutions are subordinated. It appears in the guise of a great power—which of course it is not—capable of outdoing Romania, a country two and a half times larger and more populous. Transylvania, which, together with the Banat, has an area larger than that of Hungary and a population in which Romanians are clearly in the majority, appears in this context as an amorphous entity, capable of being extracted from the Romanian national whole. Even the history of the Romanians ends up being conceived in such a way as not to concede anything to the Hungarian point of view or affirm anything which might be to Hungary's advantage. (It is for strictly "Hungarian" reasons that issues like continuity, the history of Transylvania, the relations between the Romanian territories and their unification can no longer be approached with calm professional detachment). Thus, so as not to lose out before Budapest, the Romanians willingly place themselves in the tow of Hungary, becoming dependent on all that is said and done there. An escape from the mythology presupposes awareness of the fact that the destiny of Romania, for better or worse, lies in Romanian hands. Overestimating one's adversaries provides a convenient excuse, but it does not resolve anything except, at the most, the political interests of the moment.

From the point of view of adversity, the Jews now stand in a rather better position. Only 13 percent of Romanians, according to the responses in a poll, appear to be anti-Semitic. It is a small proportion, if we think of the "Gypsy" or "Hungarian" psychoses, but large enough if we consider that nowadays the numbers of the Jewish minority in Romania are very reduced. In this case the "archetypal" dimension of anti-Semitism is combined with reminiscences of a history which is closed but recent, and the traditional accusations brought against great international financial interests and against Jewish influence in world politics in general.

The historical relations between Romanians and Jews are highly mythologized in both directions. On the one hand, some authors, usually Jewish, highlight an entire tradition of Romanian anti-Semitism. From this point of view, the killing of the Levantine creditors in 1594, the act which launched Michael the Brave's anti-Ottoman rebellion, was simply an anti-Jewish pogrom. Romania is reproached for not granting Romanian citizenship to the Jews until after the First World War, an attitude suggestive of fundamental anti-Semitism.[22] Finally, there is an insistence on the wave of anti-Semitism on the eve of the Second World War, the massacres in the time of Legionary dictatorship, and the (partial) genocide with which the Antonescu government is charged.

At the opposite extreme there are interpretations from a nationalist-Romanianist perspective, which see the nineteenth-century settlement of the Jews, especially in Moldavia, as a veritable invasion, and the refusal of citizenship as a minimum protection measure for the Romanian organism. Certainly there is no acknowledgement of Romanian anti-Semitism. As for Antonescu, far from exterminating the Romanian Jews he saved them from the fate of their co-religionists in Germany or even Hungary. On the contrary, the Jews are reproached for having got rich unscrupulously at the expense of the Romanians—from this point of view the appetite for gain of Jewish leaseholders could be considered the primary cause of the uprising of 1907—and for their lack of patriotism, that is, their non-adherence to the Romanian national idea. The enthusiasm with which the Jews of Bessarabia received the Soviet invaders in June 1940 is also noted (as a justification for the subsequent repression), and the Jews are made largely responsible, along with Hungarians and other non-Romanian groups, for the installation of communism in Romania and for the harshest phase of Stalinist terror. The idea is expressed by Iosif Drăgan, in a few words with no nuances: "With the support of the Soviet army, Party activists were brought in, under new, Romanianized names, people like Ana Rabinovici-Pauker, Leonte Răutu (Rotmann), Mihail Roller, Silviu Brucan, Teohari Georgescu, László Lukács (Vasile Luca) and the Bulgarian Borilă, etc. [...] The leadership of the Party was monopolized by these allogenic elements."[23] Far from being persecuted, therefore, the Jews had repaid Romanian hospitality with a mischievous revenge.

I recognize that it is hard to keep a sense of proportion in a field as delicate and as prone to the temptation of mythologizing as this. On the one hand, it is impossible to deny the existence of Romanian anti-Semitism, or, perhaps more correctly and broadly, of a perception of the Jews as a being invested with a high degree of otherness. The range is very large, from fundamental and violent anti-Semitism to a note of understanding and even sympathy, but sympathy for an "other" who is compartmentalized in a distinct position. Even E. Lovinescu, who promoted literature written by Jews, and G. Călinescu, who took the risky step in 1941 of giving Jewish writers considerable space in his *History of Romanian Literature,* saw in them an element capable of enriching the national culture, but no less a race apart, with immutable features, quite different from those of the Romanians. The goodwill they showed was goodwill to a foreigner. Before being Romanian, the Jew was still a Jew. I believe that Leon Volovici is correct in claiming that "A 'Dreyfus affair' in the Romania, of the 1930s, cannot be imagined."[24] In other words, it was impossible to conceive of the basis of Romanian society being rethought only for the sake of integrating the Jews.

On the other hand, all these attitudes are the result of history, not of any Romanian predisposition. The mechanism which is at work here is one which has functioned, and still functions, everywhere in the world (even in Israel, as is demonstrated by the Arab problem). History shows how difficult it is to harmonize communities of different origins, language, religion, and culture. We have seen what happened in Bosnia, where, seen from a distance, the differences appeared to be minimal. The nineteenth-century expansion of the Jewish population in the Romanian space, and especially in Moldavia and in the urban environment, was considerable. In 1912 Jews made up almost 15 percent of the urban population of the country. In Bucharest the proportion was 13 percent, in Iaşi almost half (42 percent) with similar levels in other Moldavian towns too. It is hard to say where the "tolerance threshold" lies; at the bottom line there can be anti-Semitism without Jews (as is the case in Romania today). The fact that dysfunctionalities and tensions generally result from the interpenetration of distinct communities needs to be taken into account. From a historical point of view, the Romanian–Jewish file is explicable, as is the contemporary Arab–Israeli confrontation (though explanation is not the same as justification). The only way out of the mythology is along a line of historical interpretation—which lifts the blame, historically speaking, both from Romanians and from Jews. Otherwise someone will always be to blame: the Romanians or the Jews.

With Antonescu, likewise, things lie somewhere in the middle. As in the well-known principle of the half-full or half-empty bottle, which is the same in either case, differences are simply a matter of interpretation. Antonescu cannot decently be transformed into a savior of the Jews. He was an anti-Semite and that fact must be acknowledged. But he was an anti-Semite in a particular context, which also requires to be understood. The history of those times cannot be judged exclusively by the norms of today. And of course, Antonescu's anti-Semitism did not go as far as Hitler's. The greater part of the Jewish community in Romania survived. The picture is far from being impeccably clean, but it is not completely foul either.

Nor is it possible to evade the issue of the role played by Romanian Jews in the first years of communism. Passing the blame onto someone else has unfortunately been a habit in Romania in recent decades. Regardless of the role played by Jews (not all, for there were Jews who were persecuted too), the Romanians have to accept their own history, for which they are, in the first place, responsible: this includes communism, if not so much its installation (though the massive joining up after 1944, including some leading intellectuals, cannot be ignored), then certainly the way in which it was applied. That said, it would be incorrect not to note the significant numbers of Jews (and of other non-Romanians) in the political apparatus and the agencies of propaganda and repression in the Stalinist period. At the beginning of the 1950s, out of the four members of the Secretariat of the Communist Party, only Gheorghiu-Dej was Romanian, in a clear minority compared with those from "minorities" (Ana Pauker, Vasile Luca and Teohari Georgescu). The phenomenon is so visible that an honest historian cannot simply pass over it. The "Jewish" moment of Romanian communism resulted from a combination of at least three factors: the predominantly non-Romanian character of the Communist Party before 1944, the shift to the "center" of a hitherto marginalized community, and the offensive against national values which characterized the first phase of the new regime. We need to leave mythology behind in this respect, too: there can be no general inculpation of the Jews (in comparison to an "innocent" Romanian nation), nor can we remove from the equation an important group of Jews who played an undeniable role in the history of the period. The ideal must be to judge both Antonescu and Ana Pauker by the same standards.

FRIENDS AND OPPONENTS: A HISTORICAL GAME

The mythology of the "other" provides political propaganda with a priceless weapon. Once it is possible to choose anything from history, the historical imaginary becomes a support for disinformation and manipulation. Every nation has its stock of traditional friends and hereditary enemies, which can be revised according to circumstances.

A significant section of the Romanian population sympathized with the Serb side in the years of conflict in former Yugoslavia. "Pro-Serbism" is largely, though not exclusively, a reflection of the nationalist, Orthodoxist, and anti-Western inclinations present in Romanian society. In support of this completely explicable attitude, however, a quite different argument was invoked: the tradition of Romanian–Serbian friendship, to the extent of claiming that Serbia (or the present Yugoslavia) was Romania's only good neighbor (a claim actually made by the president of Romania, Ion Iliescu).

Anyone with a little knowledge of the history of Romanian–Serbian relations knows that that is not quite how things are. I have already mentioned the less than favorable opinion of the Serbs expressed in Romanian folklore. In the period of Austro–Hungarian dualism, forms of collaboration developed between the Serbs and Romanians of Hungary (in the context of the national movement of the peoples of the Habsburg Empire). There had, however, previously been tensions between them, generated in particular by the dependence of the Orthodox Romanians on the Serbian metropolitan diocese of Karlowitz (between 1783 and 1864). In 1848 the Romanians of the Banat protested more against the Serbs than against the Hungarians. What is certain is that the two states, Romania and Serbia, had good relations in the last decades of the nineteenth century and at the beginning of the twentieth. At the end of the First World War, however, they came close to conflict, the bone of contention being the Banat, which both countries sought to annex wholly or in its greater part. As a consequence, Serbian troops occupied the present Romanian Banat in 1918–1919, where they left less than friendly memories. Even though armed conflict was avoided, the compromise solution—the partitioning of the Banat in two—failed to satisfy either side completely. The interwar period saw close relations within the Little Entente, but with the whole of Yugoslavia, not just Serbia. The statues of the Romanian kings were commissioned from the Croat Ivan Meštrović. After the Second World War communist Romania stood out in its relentless denunciation of Yugoslav revisionism; the "executioner Tito", with blood dripping from his axe, became a familiar image in the Romania of the 1950s. Then, as the Romanian leaders parted company with Moscow, there followed a normalizing of relations and an ever closer rapprochement between the two countries. No longer the executioner, Tito—who was anyway of Croat, not Serb, origin—became the good friend of Gheorghiu-Dej and later of Ceauşescu.

These are a few summary points of reference. The balance is inclined towards friendship, but we are far from the perfect clarity invoked in propaganda. In any case, political relations are based less on history than on present interests and affinities. Good relations with Serbia can be promoted without rewriting the past to seem more idyllic than it was in reality.

A curious double discourse can be heard where Turkey is concerned. On the one hand, the Turks are our old enemies, who invaded us and oppressed us and whom the Romanian voivodes repeatedly defeated in the Middle Ages. But, on the other hand, the Turks have come back now, with capital, goods, and political projects. The contradictory discourses could fuse (the more so as the common history of the two peoples is a matter of collaboration, not just fighting), but they are generally emitted separately: at school, pupils learn about the Romanian–Turkish conflicts, while politicians try to highlight the tradition of friendship between the two countries and peoples.

THE PLOT AGAINST ROMANIA

The *myth of conspiracy* is one of the best-known figures of the political-historical imaginary. We meet it, of course, among the Romanians too, and even in aggravated forms, given the already-mentioned complex of the besieged citadel and more recently the impact of communist ideology and behavior, which are particularly sensitive to the theme of the plot from outside or within.

Thrown from one side to the other by the waves of history, the Romanians have more than once felt betrayed and find it easy to believe that there are all sorts of obscure calculations and arrangements set in motion by others at their expense. *Plot against Romania* is the title of a book which appeared in 1993, and even if the title turns out to be more radical than the content, it remains representative of a certain state of mind. The authors deal with the events of the years 1940 to 1947, putting the dismemberment of Romania in 1940 and its subsequent entry into the communist sphere, with the confirmation of the loss of Bessarabia and Bukovina, under the sign of an international plot.[25] In fact, what happened in 1940 was that the Soviet Union, Hungary, and Bulgaria recovered territories which they had never ceased to claim as their own, while Germany and Italy punished Romania, the ally up until then of France and Britain. It was a national tragedy, but why a plot? For the simple reason that the theme of the plot has taken root in Romanian political culture.

The great plot that remains beyond any doubt was set in motion at Yalta by Stalin, Roosevelt, and Churchill. The "Yalta myth" has penetrated far into

Romanian consciousness, and not only in anti-Western circles. However, its anti-Western essence is not hard to decipher. Yalta means *betrayal by the West*. In this light, indigenous communists, and even the Soviets, appear less guilty than the hypocritical West, which, while it promised the Romanians liberty, was secretly selling them to Moscow. In vain Western historians have labored to demonstrate that no deal was done at Yalta with a view to sharing out Europe. Who believes them? The notorious percentage proposed by Churchill to Stalin in October 1944 is invoked: in Romania, Russia 90 percent influence, the others 10 percent; in Greece, Russia 10 percent, the others 90 percent; in Yugoslavia, Russia 50 percent, the others 50 percent; in Hungary, Russia 50 percent, the others 50 percent; in Bulgaria, Russia 75 percent, the others 25 percent. This is the document of betrayal, scribbled by Churchill on a scrap of paper. It is taken to be a real secret agreement.[26]

In fact, Churchill was trying to save as much as he could—as significant a Western presence as possible in a region which lay wide open before the Red Army. (By this time Romania was already completely occupied.) A Western presence of 10 percent would have done Romania no harm, compared to the zero which it got in reality. Not to mention countries like Hungary, Yugoslavia, and even Bulgaria, where the West was reserving even more for itself (while Poland and Czechoslovakia were not even under discussion). Moreover, and this is an elementary point, the influence in question concerned the economic, political, and strategic interests of the great powers, not the internal regime of the countries named—unless we want to imagine that Churchill expected Romania to be 90 percent communist and 10 percent pluralist and democratic! The Westerners were naive, without a doubt, but decency obliges us to try to understand what was in their minds. They were thinking in classical, "non-ideologized" terms of spheres of influence. What was to happen on a larger scale in Central Europe was what had happened with Finland. The "Finlandization" of the countries in question would have offered the Soviet Union the guarantee of a strong political, military, and economic position in the zone, without internal structures and normal relations with the West being dramatically affected thereby. Things evolved differently, and the West could not, or did not want to, intervene, but this does not mean that there was a plot or a sellout.

As everything is connected, and the imaginary is surprisingly logical, *Yalta* has its antithetical counterpart (which even rhymes) in *Malta*. The 1989 Bush–Gorbachev meeting on the little Mediterranean island is said to have put an end, by means of a new plot, to half a century of communism and Soviet domination in Central Europe. The disintegration of a system which was no longer able to function, and the revolutionary wave of anti-communist movements, seem to count for all too little in face of the archetypal force of the conspiracy myth. The history of the last half century is reduced to two meetings and resumed in the easily remembered catchphrase "Yalta—Malta".[27]

For some, these are episodes in a general campaign of hostility which the "others" bear towards us. In 1993 Dan Zamfirescu published a volume of essays entitled no less than *The War against the Romanian People*. The Romanians deserved to become one of the great peoples of the world, and if they are not in such a high position today, the fault is not their own (they only have merits) but that of the coalition of forces, visible or obscure, which repeatedly comes together to prevent them. "The plot against Romania" seems to be a historical datum: it is the cross we have to bear.

THE IMPERIAL TEMPTATION

Against the aggressivity and unscrupulousness of others, Romanian historical consciousness sets the wisdom and moderation of a people whose only desire is to live in peace. The numerous wars which the Romanians have fought, generally victoriously, have been forced on them, never sought. The Romanians were only defending their ancestral soil or fighting to free Romanian territories that had been subjugated by others.

The strictly defensive character of Romanian policy became a matter of dogma in the time of Ceauşescu, when, with the absurd minuteness of nationalist–communist paranoia, any word or expression which could suggest even a hint of expansionist thinking was cast out. Thus it was that Michael the Brave no longer conquered Transylvania and Moldavia, but "united" them. Thus Burebista, a great conqueror in his day, now only *unified* the Dacian tribes of Central and Southeastern Europe. The same logic was applied to Romanian involvement in the First World War, which had previously been labeled an "imperialist war" by communist historiography. If, in the 1950s, Romania could not have been any less imperialist than all the rest, in the later phase it became the protagonist of a just war, alongside other small peoples and countries (Serbia and Belgium), the conflict remaining imperialist only for the great powers. The division between the "good" and the "bad" fits perfectly with communist and nationalist Manichaeanism. It is interesting that Romania's allies were still in the bad camp, including France, which was likewise seeking to liberate Alsace and Lorraine, and Italy, which had similar aims to those of Romania in relation to Austria–Hungary.

A small and peaceful people, obliged to defend itself: this is a dominant theme of Romanian historical discourse and national consciousness. On the other hand, however, the modesty presupposed by such a vision generated inevitable frustrations and dreams of expansion, projected either into the distant past or into the future. Insistence on Roman origins proved to the Romanians what Octavian Goga expressed so suggestively:

> That they are of an imperial race
> From a land far away,
> That all the circle of the earth
> Was theirs upon a day.

A glory long past, which could yet be re-actualized in days to come:

A future of gold awaits our country,
And across the centuries I see its rising. (D. Bolintineanu)

Behind the image of a small country, subject to the vicissitudes of history, there survives in the background of Romanian consciousness the nostalgia of a great destiny, an imperial dream.

The role of the "Romanian–Bulgarian Empire", which for some nineteenth-century historians became more a Romanian than a Bulgarian empire, was to give the appearance of reality to a great Romanian history precisely in the period when documentary sources are almost silent concerning the Romanians. It took only a simple shift from the north to the south of the Danube, and a whole Romanian imperial phase was inscribed in the history of the world. The tactic of claiming Byzantine inheritance goes in the same direction; once Byzantium had disappeared, the Romanians appear as its legitimate successors (the idea behind Iorga's well-known work *Byzance après Byzance*). Looking further back, it could be demonstrated that later Roman history is also dominated by the Romanian or pre-Romanian element. According to Hasdeu, Philip the Arabian was a Dacian (despite his name!), as were other Roman emperors. The logic of "Romanianizing" Roman history was taken to the extreme (in the opposite direction to Latinism, but with the same Romanian–Roman identification) by Iosif Constantin Drăgan, who discovered an "imperial millennium of Dacia", illustrated by the fact that no less than forty out of the eighty emperors of Rome were "Thraco–Illyro–Dacians".[28] Finally, let us not forget the Burebista episode, on which communist propaganda capitalized so much around 1980; under his rule a veritable Dacian empire took shape, quite capable of rivaling that of Rome.

With such an imperial inheritance, Dacian, Roman, Romanian–Bulgarian and Romanian–Byzantine, the Romanians should, in more favorable conditions, have been destined to remake the Latin empire of the East. Some historians heavily underline this possibility, which was repeatedly missed as a result of envy and betrayal. If Michael the Brave, writes August Treboniu Laurian, "had not had to deal with men like Basta, Sigismond Báthory, and Ieremia Movilă, the Turks would have deserted Europe, the Dacian provinces would have taken on a quite different aspect, the Romanians would have raised themselves up even then, and their state would have flourished".[29] Hasdeu expresses himself even more categorically in referring to Ioan Vodă the Terrible: "Just then, in a little Romanian land, there appeared a prince whom only the blackest betrayal could have prevented from giving Europe a different aspect, founding a new Latin empire in the Balkan peninsula."[30]

Things become even more remarkable when some writers start to imagine that such a history actually happened! In 1885 a voluminous book appeared in Galați, with the title *The History of the Political Economy, Commerce, and Navigation of Romania*. Its author, Romulus Scriban (doctor of law in Turin, advocate, professor of political and commercial economy), demonstrated the primacy which Romania had always enjoyed in the East: "[...] the wealthiest state in the East, and the envy of all its neighbors, from the most ancient to the newest." What the author frequently calls the "Romanian Empire" appears as a unitary state in the Middle Ages, even larger than the modern Romanian state, at a time when "the center of world trade was the Mediterranean and the Black Sea, whose shores were occupied by Romania from the mouth of the Bug to Mangalia, giving it the title of Queen of the Black Sea". The domination of the Romanian lands by the Turks is transformed by Scriban into a Romanian–Ottoman "confederation", which lasted from 1511 to 1877. In other words, the Romanians and the Turks shared their empire. The future can only be an imperial one too, in keeping with the past: "The Romanians aspire to renew the old Romanian empire of the East, to which they have a right as the legitimate successors in the East of the great Roman empire of the whole world."[31] And, as we are in 1885, the year of the colonial conference in Berlin, the theoretician of Romanian imperial power does not forget to call for Romania to have colonies too!

A century later, a few historians are still flirting with the imperial idea. The latest discovery in the field promotes Vlad Țepeș from the modest rank of Prince of Wallachia to the glittering title of Emperor of the East![32] Even if it is not true it is "patriotic", and that is sufficient.

It is clear that in the modern period Romania sought national unity. This does not mean that there was no room in Romanian politics for intermittent lapses into imperial illusion and a dose of expansionism. The weight of the Romanian–Bulgarian Empire in the historical discourse is associated around 1900 with a very active Balkan policy. This is the period when Romania aspired to the role of principal regional power and arbiter of the Balkans. It is understandable in this context that the Romanian government in 1912 to 1913 could not accept the creation of a greater Bulgaria, which would have threatened Romanian priority. The determining role played by Romania in the second Balkan war, the conclusion of the Treaty of Bucharest, and the acquisition of the Quadrilateral were taken as confirmation of Romanian "hegemony" (consolidated also by the Romanian element in the Balkans, and even, it was hoped at one point, by the installation in Albania of a sovereign related to the queen of Romania).

The same tendency to look beyond strictly ethnic borders can be seen during the First World War. The treaty concluded by the Romanian government with the Entente powers provided for the westward extension of Romania to a line lying some twenty to thirty kilometers beyond the present Romanian–Hungarian border, joining the Tisza at its confluence with the Mureș before following it south to its confluence with the Danube, thus incorporating the Serbian Banat. The mythology of natural frontiers came into play here more than ethnic limits (which are, in any case, far from easy to define): "From the Dniester to the Tisza."[*] Indeed, there was nothing strange in such pretensions—that was how

---

[*] *"De la Nistru pîn'la Tisa"*: the opening line of Eminescu's *"Doina"*. Trans.

they thought at the time. France, likewise, was seeking to shift its eastern border to the Rhine, and not only in Alsace, which would have meant the annexation of territories populated exclusively by Germans. Even if there were islands of Romanian population as far west as the Tisza, the space claimed would have brought Romania more Hungarians and Serbs than Romanians.

The case of Romania in the Second World War is even more complex. The aim acknowledged by Antonescu was the making whole again of Greater Romania, which had been mutilated in 1940. For all that, in the eastern campaign the Romanian troops did not stop at the Dniester. The territory between the Dniester and the Bug (Transnistria) came under Romanian administration. It was, in fact, the bait that Hitler held out to the Romanians to persuade them to give up the lost part of Transylvania (although Antonescu did not see it this way). In any case the "crusade against Bolshevism" sought the destruction of Soviet power and the damming of Slav pressure. In the event of victory Romania would certainly have extended its territory and influence. The expansionist philosophy had been generalized at a European level (with Romania itself falling victim in 1940). It seemed that a new world was being born, and in this context it was not illogical to believe that perhaps Romania's time had come—a Romania for which Cioran, expressing long-accumulated frustration, in accordance with the dynamism of a whole generation, had wished "the destiny of France and the population of China".

The imperial temptation, I repeat, is not dominant in the Romanian historical–political imaginary, but when its fantasies do occasionally come to the surface they cannot be made to go away by the imposition of a historiographical *taboo*. Circumstances forced the Romanians to stay on the defensive rather than going after foreign territories. But all this is explained by history, not by any particular spirit of the nations. It is simplistic to divide the world into peaceful and aggressive peoples, and to put ourselves alone in the first category while we push the "others" into the second. It is likewise simplistic to judge the past through the prism of current norms of international law. If Romania at the beginning of the century had pretensions to more territory and influence than it would ultimately acquire, this happened within the framework of the normal political game— everyone was doing the same thing. Why do things have to be forced so that only the Romanians seem to have proceeded differently? As for Burebista, let us allow him to be a great *conqueror*—it is not this that will damage the image of Romania in the present.

COMPETING RIGHTS: NATIONS, BORDERS, MINORITIES

At this point a theoretical clarification becomes necessary. Two series of arguments have been invoked in the process of the national–territorial restructuring of the last two centuries: on the one hand, an ethnic criterion— "natural" right, or the "right of the peoples" as it used to be put; and on the other, a political criterion corresponding to state configurations which were considered original—historical right. To these may be added geopolitical considerations. The principles in question may be combined, or they may be completely contradictory. Neighboring nations appeal to different arguments, each, in its own way, being in the right before the others. According to historical right, the Sudetenland belongs to the Czech Republic; in terms of ethnic coloring it was German, and so on.

Modern Romania was built primarily on the ethnic principle, but also, when it seemed opportune, by the use of the other criteria: historical and geopolitical. In the case of the areas ruled by Hungary until 1918, the predominant criterion was ethnic; they had never belonged to Romania or the Romanian principalities, but they were inhabited by a majority Romanian population. In the case of the Banat, as we have seen, the historical argument was also made use of, to support the joining of the whole province to Romania as an indissoluble historical entity, regardless of the predominantly Serbian population of its western part. Bukovina invited a twofold approach: ethnic right in the first place for the southern half, which was indisputably Romanian; but also historical right for the whole—as a part of Moldavia until 1775—allowing the fact that the Romanians were, or had become, a minority in the northern half to be passed over. This combination of ethnic and historical right also applied in the case of Bessarabia. A strictly demographic approach would have left a question mark over the northern part of the province (Hotin) and the southern counties (Cetatea Albă and Ismail), where Romanians were a minority in 1918. In the case of Dobrogea, ethnic motives were only subsidiary—regardless of the official arguments—as were historical considerations (it had been part of Wallachia in the time of Mircea the Old). The determining factors were undoubtedly geopolitical in character (the mouth of the Danube and the Black Sea coast). The annexation of the Quadrilateral was also essentially a matter of geopolitical considerations, as was the demand for a western border pushed, in part, as far as the Tisza.

The neighbors of Romania used, and still use, similar arguments, combining the ethnic and the historical in their own way. The issue is complicated by the fact that there are many historical sequences which can be valorized in this sense, and by the many modifications which have taken place in linguistic borders and ethnic composition (usually slowly, but sometimes brutally, as was the case with the deportations and displacements of population during and after the Second World War, or more recently in Bosnia). Every nation has its "ideal map", which does not perfectly match the "ideal maps" of others. Each seeks to consolidate its less obvious rights. As a minority in Transylvania, the Hungarians have come to dream of a remote historical period when the Romanians were not there. Equally, the Romanians, deprived for centuries of a Romanian state in Transylvania, are tempted to separate it retrospectively from the Hungarian crown and from any Hungarian historical and political project and to bring it closer to the two Romanian principalities, integrating it into a general Romanian history.

As the arguments are of the same order, to an observer with no sentimental involvement in the national confrontations of the region the problem of the

Hungarian minority in Transylvania and that of the Romanian minority in northern Bukovina appear in a similar light. In both cases the invocation of a historical right (Transylvania previously belonged to Hungary and Bukovina to Moldavia and later Romania) cannot be used to override the wishes of the present majority (Romanian in Transylvania, Ukrainian in northern Bukovina). All this must be made clear, so that the process of normalizing relations with our neighbors and of European integration will not be blocked by confrontations of a sort characteristic of the divided Europe of yesterday and incompatible with the projected united Europe of tomorrow.

Of course in some areas where they were formerly in the majority the Romanians have lost ground to the "others", especially during the last hundred years. This is the case of Bessarabia and Bukovina, and is no less true of the Romanian element in Serbia and Bulgaria. But it must be sincerely recognized that in other areas, and in the same interval of time, the Romanians have also gained at the expense of the "others". In 1880 the Romanian population of Dobrogea was no more than 28 percent of the total; by the time of the census of 1930 the proportion of Romanians there had increased to 65 percent (not counting the largely non-Romanian Quadrilateral; if it is included the proportion falls to 44.2 percent). A few decades later, in 1992, Dobrogea seemed almost fully Romanianized, with Romanians representing 91 percent of the population. In Transylvania (including all the territories beyond the mountains), according to the 1910 census, Romanians represented 53.8 percent, Hungarians 31.6 percent, and Germans 10.8 percent. By 1930 the proportion of Romanians had risen to 57.8 percent and by 1956 to 65 percent. At present, if we go by the figures in the 1992 census, they represent 73.6 percent (a gain of 20 percent in three-quarters of a century), while the proportion of Hungarians has fallen to around 21 percent and that of Germans to scarcely more than 1 percent, which means that they have almost disappeared as an ethnic reality. There can be no doubt that a process of Romanianization has taken place, in provinces previously characterized by a high degree of ethnic mixing.

The *cosmopolitan town*, formerly so characteristic of the Romanian space, is also a thing of the past. In 1895, out of 10,419 inhabitants of Constanța, 2,519 were Romanian, 2,460 Greek, 1,060 Bulgarian, 2,202 Turkish or Tatar, 855 Jewish, and so on. Nowadays Romanians make up 93 percent of the town's population. At the other end of the country, the demographic structure of Timișoara in 1930 comprised 30 percent Germans, 30 percent Hungarians, and 26.5 percent Romanians. Nowadays, 82 percent of the population of Timișoara is Romanian. Even in Bucharest in the interwar period (according to the same census data of 1930), 20 percent of the population were still of non-Romanian origin; at present 97.6 percent of the inhabitants of the capital are of Romanian nationality. With the exception of the Hungarian presence in a number of Transylvanian cities, and the rising number of Gypsies, the ethnic coloring has become almost pure Romanian, with other shades becoming lost in the whole.[33]

The responsibility for such an evolution belongs to the national state. The national state has proved to be assimilatory *everywhere* (albeit to varying degrees and with varying methods: we cannot equate genocide or deportation with the gradual erosion of minorities). Within the borders of Romania this rule has worked to the advantage of the Romanians; outside, according to the same logic, it has worked against them.

The self-pity which is so frequent in the discourse of the Romanians is not sufficiently justified in this respect. The Romanians have lost, but they have also won. Others (it is sufficient to mention the Germans) have certainly given up far more. It is probable that, if we add up the pluses and minuses, the Romanians have won more than they have lost. Romanian-ness is today in a stronger position than it was a century ago, and, although within somewhat narrower state borders, it is more homogeneous than in interwar Romania, with its high proportion of minorities.

It remains, of course, to be seen how the Europeans themselves, in a future united Europe, will judge the process of ethnic and cultural homogenization which has been characteristic of the last two centuries.

THE FOURTH WORLD POWER

National communism introduced a new note into the relationship, apparently hard to reconcile, between the proclaimed defensive spirit of the nation and its aspiration to the status of a great power. As far as the first part of the equation was concerned, the taboo was categorical: the Dacians, and later the Romanians, had never had pretensions to anything that did not belong to them. At the same time, however, Ceauşescu's megalomaniac policy suggested, and actually made it seem in the eyes of some people, that the dream of greatness which had been nursed by the national subconscious was about to be realized. Neither the times nor the ideology were suited to dreams of empire. Romania could become great not by expansion but by efficiency, by achieving maximum density in a limited space. Thus a small country was transfigured into a great country; a country at the margin of the great political-economic ensembles became a nucleus of the world.[34] The all-encompassing process enveloped, at least at the level of discourse, all aspects of the national life and, by its inevitable projection into the past, the totality of the historical process.

A key role in this project was played by foreign policy, where Romania had to appear to be an indispensable part of international relations, especially as a mediator between the rival blocs (NATO and the Warsaw Pact, China and the Soviet Union, Israel and the Arab states, the developed North and the Third World, etc.). The oppressive demographic policy, in which an increased birthrate was sought at any price, pointed in the same direction: raising Romania among the states of the world by increasing the number of its inhabitants. As far as the economy was concerned, Romania was to become a great industrial power (with fantastic pretensions, such as the prediction that by 1990, some 95 percent of Romanian products would be of world standard and the rest above world standard!). In 1989, agricultural production reached a (fictive) level of 60 million tons, with a per hectare yield far superior to that of any other producer. The urbanization process again placed Romania among the world's leading nations: the demolition of villages was to make way for settlements of urban type, while, much more conveniently, villages became towns and towns became cities by simple command.

As far as military power was concerned, the application of the principle of "the struggle of the entire people" allowed the Romanian army to be raised to something between 4,680,000 and 6,245,000 combatants[35], which would have made it, beyond doubt, one of the leading armed forces of the world. It is interesting to observe that the fictive amplification of the Romanian army was also projected back into history. From a traditional mythology in which the Romanians, although few in number, had almost always succeeded in defeating superior forces, the logic was now reversed. The Romanian nation, though small, had always disposed of powerful armies thanks to the principle of the mobilization of the entire people. From this point of view, Burebista had proceeded exactly like Ceaușescu, which enabled him to raise an army of 200,000 fighting men, a force almost as numerous as that of the Roman Empire (if the improbable figure advanced by Strabo was accepted without the slightest critical reserve). In the Middle Ages, according to the *Military History of the Romanian People*, the Romanians could count on 120,000 to 140,000 armed men; the non-existence of Romania itself at that time did not seem to have caused the authors any difficulty in calculating the size of the Romanian army, even though part of the total belonged to Transylvania, in other words, to the kingdom of Hungary... According to the same calculations, Hungary could call on no more than 14,000 fighting men, the ratio being, therefore, ten to one in favor of the Romanians. This explained the victories, which were won by *small Romanian lands*, but *large Romanian armies*.[36]

In this way the Romanian space was transfigured, acquiring unsuspected densities. Ceaușescu had discovered the recipe for the metamorphosis of a small country into a great power. Some believed him. Among them was Dan Zamfirescu, who does not hesitate to claim that "from the Declaration of April 1964 to the Revolution of December 1989, Romania was indubitably the fourth political power in the world, after Israel (the state and the universally spread ethnic community), the U.S.A., and the U.S.S.R."[37]

What the "Others" Say about the Romanians

Up until now I have talked about the others, and about the relations between the Romanians and the others, from the Romanian perspective. What the *others* think about the Romanians is outside the scope of this book. All I can allow myself are a few suggestions in order to underline the inevitable discrepancy between the image received outside and the Romanians' own representation of themselves. It is a haphazard selection, not a thorough study of the issue.

Leaving to one side Romania deformed by communism and deliberately cut off from Western civilization, let us go back to the years immediately leading up to the Second World War, in other words, to the end of a century of "Europeanization" of Romanian society. At no other time, in its entire history during the last two hundred years, was Romania more integrated in the European family and in the system of European values than it was then.

For this period we have the testimony of two, very different, Western writers: Paul Morand, an urbane Frenchman closely integrated in Romanian social circles; and Olivia Manning, a young Englishwoman, withdrawn and frustrated, and consequently little inclined to look favorably on things. The former published his essay-volume *Bucarest* in 1935, while the latter's *Balkan Trilogy* (the first two volumes of which, *The Great Fortune* and *The Spoilt City*, are set in Romania in the period between 1939 and 1940) appeared somewhat later, in the 1960s. The first author treats the country sympathetically, while the other cannot conceal her antipathy.[38]

What is remarkable, however, given the differences between the two writers, is their fundamental agreement on the character of Romanian civilization. To both visitors, who otherwise have little in common except for the mere fact of belonging to Western culture, Romania presents itself as a country only partially integrated in European civilization, a country of the margins, characterized by a still pronounced store of primitivism, a strange amalgam of modern urban life and rustic survivals. In Bucharest, Paul Morand noted with amusement, Ford automobiles shared the road with ox carts. So much for the "Little Paris"! Olivia Manning sees the citizens of Bucharest as a sort of peasants, some of them authentic peasants and others more evolved peasants, dressed up in city clothes. It is a fluid, insecure world, where nothing is really taken seriously. For Morand, on the other hand, the quite un-Western mentality is a positive quality, a lesson which the Romanians can offer the Westerner: adaptability, indulgence, optimism, the ability to pass through history without caring. The same things only irritate Olivia Manning.

What we remain with in the end is the fact that the Romanians are perceived as *something else* (and I repeat, this is their phase of maximum European integration), a people animated by a different spirit to that of the Western nations—a certain "lightness" in living separates them from the responsible seriousness of others. Our autochthonists may rest content: for Westerners, too, the Romanians are *different*—even if not necessarily in a positive sense—the product and exponents of another type of society. While the West defines itself as an ordered and predictable world, Romania belongs, on the contrary, to a vague and unpredictable space.

The tale of Dracula fits perfectly with this image. When the famous novel first appeared Transylvania belonged to Hungary, and Count Dracula himself is not a

Romanian but a Magyar aristocrat. However, Romania inherited the myth when it acquired the territories over the mountains in 1918. Dracula's home could not have been placed in the Alps (too close to the heart of Europe), or in Tibet (too far away). The Carpathians offered just the right setting: on the edge of Europe, where Western civilization opens on an already different world. We Romanians represent the first circle of otherness, sufficiently close for our curious configurations and disturbing forms of behavior to be highlighted all the more strongly by contrast.

Communism in general, and the transforming megalomania of Ceauşescu in particular, deepened both the real gulf and its projection in the imaginary. If even the "Little Paris" of the 1930s seemed "other" to Westerners, what impression can they have of the Bucharest of today, a city dominated by a pharaonic palace and covered in garbage? Anyway, for any self-respecting foreign tourist the principal objectives of a journey in Romania are Ceauşescu's palace and Dracula's castle, the great symbols of Romanian singularity. The fog surrounding the December Revolution, the brutal and uncontrolled spasms of an as yet unsettled society, "original democracy", the incredible assaults of the miners on Bucharest, street children and orphans with AIDS, etc. Here are only a few of the themes which are likely to confirm the prejudices of the foreign visitor.

I shall cite a few more examples, taken from the French zone, which is considered, rightly or wrongly, to be the least blind to authentic Romanian values. Visiting Bucharest right at the time of the miners' incursion in June 1990, the writer Emmanuel Carrère remains with the impression of a remote and strange land. The glance he casts from the sophisticated "Latin Quarter" of Paris, giving a perspective in which real distances are amplified even more in the imaginary, is expressed even in the title of his essay on a country which had astounded him: "In Romania, that is to say, nowhere".[39]

In 1991 another French writer, Renaud Camus, undertook a rapid tour of all the regions of the country, armed with a summary bibliography and a large stock of prejudices. He does not like Romania, he tells us repeatedly and firmly. He does not like the people, but nor does he like the landscape, whether the hills, the mountains, or the plains. What characterizes the Romanians is "mental confusion". They do not even know their own history. Renaud Camus, convinced that he knows it well, tries to teach them a little during his short stay in Romania.[40]

According to the reader's state of mind, the extravagant impressions of this author may arouse either indignation or hilarity. But the issue is more serious. Once again, it is a question of the perception of Romania, positive or negative it does not matter, as a space of definite otherness, lying outside normal European civilization.

A school textbook can help us to complete the picture. French pupils in their final year of high school are presented with the political map of Europe in 1924.[41] Again the period in question is that between the wars, the time when Romanian democracy was in its maturity. From the French perspective, however, Romania is characterized by "a right-wing authoritarian regime"—like Hungary, in fact, and unlike the democratic societies of the West. Romanian textbooks present Hungary as subject to a fascist-type dictatorship from the coming to power of Horthy in 1920 (which, let it be said in passing, is not strictly true), and Romania as an essentially liberal and democratic country, more resistant than most European states to the assault of totalitarian ideologies. The Hungary/Romania contrast is marked in Romanian historical culture, which makes it all the more interesting that the French textbook puts them in the same category. It is clear that Romania is not recognized as having an authentic democratic tradition; from this point of view, too, the East and the West present different types of civilization.

Faced with such images—and I do not intend to discuss here whether they are fair, distorted, or untrue—the Romanian reaction goes in two principal directions: either immersion in contemptuous autochthonism (we are different from the others, and so much the better!), or, on the contrary, an amplification and exaltation of all notes of modernity and Europeanism. A more balanced and critical approach would certainly create more bridges between ourselves and the West. Westerners will never convince us that there was an authoritarian regime in interwar Romania, but nor can we convince them that it was democratic. There is a way out of the impasse, which probably also brings us closest to the truth: to take into account the amalgam of authoritarianism and democracy which characterizes the period in question. Mythology operates on a register of contrasts; the only way to attenuate it is by a history of nuances.

CHAPTER SIX

The Ideal Prince

HEROES AND SAVIORS

An inexhaustible mythical constellation is made up of the category of *mythologized figures*. The process we are dealing with here is not typically Romanian. On the contrary, nothing could be more universal, more archetypal, than the personalizing of history and of sociopolitical mechanisms. Exceptional figures, mediators between gods and people, between people and destiny, or between people and history, have imposed themselves from the beginning of the human adventure down to the present day, even in the most efficient and apparently skeptical technological and democratic societies. No community can dispense with "heroes" and "saviors", either in contemporary life or in the commemoration of historical tradition. A presidential campaign, whether American, French, or Romanian it matters little, offers a basic idea as to what this process of personalization means to anyone who cares to look. This is the moment when the "saviors" take the platform, just as much in ordinary times, when there is nothing exalting to construct and nothing essential to save, as in difficult situations, when the need for them is strongly felt. Regardless of the context, the archetype functions. These people "other than us" belong to the mystical zone of the imaginary; they are caught in the structures of the sacred. Even in the modern world's secularized version, their action retains something of its original transcendent sense.

An approach to history which deconstructs myths runs the risk of affecting the position of these symbolic figures. When we speak of myth deconstruction in Romanian culture, we instinctively turn to Junimea. Among the representative historians of the current, however, Dimitrie Onciul does not seem at all ready to give up the great figures of the past, or even to diminish their importance. Indeed, his synthesis *From the History of Romania* organizes the whole subject in terms of rulers, from Trajan, through the line of medieval voivodes, to Cuza and Carol I. Quite different is the attitude of Ioan Bogdan. Thanks to him, Junimea remains true to form, offering us the non-conformist point of view that we have come to expect. In his *Romanian Historiography and its Current Problems* (1905), the great

Slavicist quite simply denies that the personalities of Romanian history are of any interest. "Our early history", he states, "does not know great individualities capable of imprinting a certain character on a period or a century." We know too little about rulers like Mircea or Stephen, a little more about Petru Rareş or Michael, "but rulers of this sort were few".[1] This is what decides Bogdan to urge his colleagues no longer to insist on personalities and political actions, since the researching of "Romanian culture", of Romanian civilization, would be more worthy of interest.

The radical solution proposed by the Junimist historian had few chances of success. A Romanian history without the significant involvement of great personalities seemed hard to conceive. It is worth mentioning, however, for the interwar period, the sociologizing approach adopted by Ştefan Zeletin, in his *Social History: How History can become a Science of Causality* (1925). The author proposes a history of structures and collective acts, relegating personalities and events to a subordinate role. However, Zeletin was not a historian, at least not a professional historian. Historians by trade, even those committed to research into socioeconomic and cultural phenomena—like G. I. Brătianu, who came close to the *Annales* school—had no intention of going so far. Brătianu replied promptly to Zeletin, declaring himself against the sociologizing of history (in *New Theories in the Teaching of History*, 1926). The heroes of the past could continue their career!

The evolution of communist ideology and historiography is interesting in this respect. History as seen by Marx was a matter of problems, laws, and socioeconomic mechanisms; in any case, personalities were not in the foreground. In fact the communist project needed heroes in order to justify and illustrate its own historical schema. Energies could not be mobilized merely by a set of abstract philosophical principles. Living examples were needed, and so were symbols. The more so as Marxist economic determinism ended up yielding to Leninist political voluntarism. Communism was built not by the illusory action of socioeconomic laws, but by acts of will and of power. Once the political was installed in the commanding position, a cult of the great makers of history was inevitably generated. Indeed, far from giving up the pantheon, communism only "repopulated" it. In a first phase, princes were replaced by the great rebel leaders and intransigent revolutionaries, from Spartacus to Robespierre. Once the dictatorship of the proletariat had become more and more openly the dictatorship of the great leader (Stalin, Mao, or Ceauşescu), the providential figure found an unassailable position at the very heart of the communist system. And since every leader needs precursors to announce and legitimize him, the communist pantheon was enriched with figures whom the principle of class struggle should not have allowed to return so easily to center stage. The rise of Stalin brought Ivan the Terrible and Peter the Great to the foreground, and Ceauşescu annexed for himself the whole constellation of Dacian kings and medieval voivodes. In general, the nationalist variant of the system amplified the pantheon and gave personalities a role which they had not enjoyed at all in the theories of Marx. Having set out to limit drastically the importance of the "great men", communism ended up amplifying it: it is an excellent illustration of the strength and persistence of the archetype.

THE COMPOSITION OF THE NATIONAL PANTHEON

There is, then, nothing specific in the Romanian case. Investing in the great individuals of the past and the present is not a vocation particular to the Romanians any more than to anyone else. But if the archetype is universal, the modality and intensity of its operation depend on the historical context. Potential saviors are always available; however, the figure of the savior imposes itself as an unavoidable necessity when the community is passing through times of crisis. Great restructurings oblige history to produce exceptional individuals. The Romanian case is no different from any other in the essence of the phenomenon, but it is certainly characterized by an exceptional intensity. For almost two centuries Romanian society has been in crisis. For almost two centuries, since they first decided to enter Europe, the Romanians have been passing through an endless phase of transition. The impact of modernization seems to explain the remarkable position of providential figures in Romanian historical–political culture. In a fluid world, where structures are ceaselessly taken apart and remade, the "father of the nation" seems to be the only firm reference point and is invoked with much more conviction than any political system or vague and uncertain abstract principles. Even the liberal ideology of the nineteenth century adhered, with not very significant hesitations and exceptions, to the standard portrait of the single ruler, the harsh but fair parent, the defender of tradition and order, the savior of the wholeness and independence of the country.

Contrary to Ioan Bogdan's claim that we did not have rulers capable of making a decisive mark on their age, the Romanian pantheon of the nineteenth century was made up almost without exception of princely figures. The selection, adaptation, and establishment of a hierarchy naturally reflected the major reference points of the time. The predominant criteria were Romanian national sense, European values, and the effective exercise of authority. The ideal prince thus fitted into the ideology of the time: he had to be an exponent of Romanianism, a European spirit, and a firm ruler, capable of ensuring the social equilibrium and prosperity of the country.

The national (but also European) dimension of the pantheon[2] finds its first embodiment in the person of Trajan, the central figure of the great foundation myth of the birth of the Romanian people. Decebalus, as we have seen, remains in the shadow of the emperor. The founders of Wallachia and Moldavia occupy a less important position than might have been expected. The shift towards first origins and towards the general Romanian phenomenon may explain the relative discretion where particular foundation myths are concerned. In addition, the status of the individuals in question is equivocal: Negru Vodă or Radu Negru, a well-outlined figure around the middle of the nineteenth century, subsequently underwent a crisis of credibility and ended up being excluded from history in favor of Basarab, who is himself hard to approach, apart from the glorious episode of Posada. In Moldavia there was a similar lack of clarity concerning the Dragoş-Bogdan duo. What is certain is that it is not the founders so much as the voivodes, who illustrated the history of the principalities in their age of glory, who are placed in the highest levels of the pantheon.

The most symbolic figure, after Trajan, is offered by the double image of Stephen the Great and Michael the Brave. They are the most frequently and extensively evoked rulers in school textbooks, in political speeches, and in historical literature (the greater part of Dimitrie Bolintineanu's *Historical Legends* centers on them). They express the glory of anti-Ottoman resistance, the defense of their own country and concomitantly of European Christendom, and likewise the idea of Romanian solidarity—through the union of 1600, the bridge between Dacia Traiana and modern Romania, and through the efforts of the Moldavian ruler to attract Wallachia into a common action. Michael's tragic end places him in the ranks of the martyrs of the Romanian people and demands, as a matter of duty, that his great project be renewed. The long, authoritarian, and flourishing reign of Stephen presents the model of an exceptional and durable Romanian political construction.

Slightly behind the two great symbolic figures of the Middle Ages we find Mircea the Old, the perseverant and independent defender of Romanian territory and its unifier by the acquisition of Dobrogea. Vlad Ţepeş, Petru Rareş, and Ioan Vodă the Terrible also illustrate the vigor and will to independence of the Romanian lands. The more discreet invocation of Iancu of Hunedoara is explained by his equivocal Romanian–Hungarian position. Another ruler much appreciated in the nineteenth century was Matei Basarab, associated by conflict with Vasile Lupu; his exceptional political, military, and cultural merits are recognized, and especially his vocation as defender of autochthonous values in face of the Greek offensive. It is as an exponent of "Romanian resistance" that he is invoked by Mihai Eminescu.

Unfavorably regarded, on the other hand, are rulers, such as Petru Aron, who surrendered the land to the Turks without a fight (even if Stephen the Great had to submit in the end, it was after a series of wars). It is the same with rulers of foreign origin—Despot Vodă, for example (who was moreover a Protestant in an Orthodox land), and of course the Phanariots, with a few exceptions such as Grigore Ghica, who was killed by the Turks for his opposition to the seizure of Bukovina.

The privileged position of warrior heroes seems indisputable. To submit after a fight is more praiseworthy than to submit without a fight, regardless of the price paid. The attitude can easily be explained by the historical canons of the time, by Romanian national–political objectives (independence, unity, affirmation as a regional power), which were inseparable from the military factor, and, in general, by the complexes of a small country, proud that it had once held great European powers in check and aroused the admiration of the world.

The peaceful rulers are not forgotten, however, especially when they give examples of wisdom in governance, the preservation of social peace, or great cultural achievements, which, like military glories, are capable of marking a place for the Romanians on the map of Europe. Alexander the Good, Neagoe Basarab and Constantin Brîncoveanu, and to no less a degree Matei Basarab and Vasile Lupu, the "founders" of Romanian culture in the Romanian language, owe their important place in the pantheon to such achievements.

For the modern period, the principal names retained are those of Tudor Vladimirescu, "Master Tudor", who, in 1821, re-actualized the Romanian national principle, followed by Alexandru Ioan Cuza, the prince of the union, prior to the installation of King Carol I towards the end of the century as the dominant personality in the Romanian pantheon. The great animators of the national idea and of modern culture, Lazăr, Asachi, Heliade Rădulescu, the revolutionaries of 1848 and the unionists of 1859, occupy a second rank compared with the holders of power. Romanian history appears highly personalized, but not in any random way: it is personalized at the very top.

The question is how these shades of the past manage to live a new life, often very intense, in the consciousness of each generation. School, and school textbooks, undoubtedly play an essential role. It is here that the selection, hierarchy, and signification are fixed with maximum rigor. But literature with historical subjects has proved no less important in the effective resurrection of heroes (continued and complemented in the present century by cinema and television). The current image of certain periods or personalities is shaped more often in pure historical fiction than in historical works or textbooks. When we hear the names of Louis XIII, Anne of Austria, Richelieu, and the Duke of Buckingham, we automatically think, even if we are historians, of *The Three Musketeers*, before turning to some specialized monograph on the subject.

So it is with the Romanian rulers. The romantic literature of the nineteenth century conferred on them a force and a presence which the history textbook alone could not guarantee them. Many emerged in this way from anonymity. What would Alexandru Lăpuşneanu be without Negruzzi's short story, Mihnea Vodă the Bad and Lady Chiajna without Alexandru Odobescu; Despot Vodă without Alecsandri; Răzvan and Vidra without Hasdeu; Vlaicu Vodă and Lady Clara without Alexandru Davila? It is no wonder that prose writers and dramatists are attracted towards the secondary figures, who are often controversial and even negative, situated in any case outside the "heroic" zone where they can be evoked freely with all their passions, ambitions, treacheries, and hesitations.

However, the great heroes of the Romanian people also have a distinct place in literary evocations. They do not acquire a banal surplus of ordinary life but a surplus of symbolic charge, an existence of a different nature to that of ordinary mortals. We find them more often sung and glorified in verse than "dissected" in prose. Michael the Brave expresses himself heroically in Bolintineanu's lines:

I do not wish you life, O my captains,
But on the contrary, death: that is what I ask!
[...]
Those who bear the yoke, and still want to live,
Deserve to bear it to their shame!
[...]
This is the Romanian's way, and a Romanian am I,
And under the barbarian yoke I will not bow my head
          ("The Last Night of Michael the Brave")

And in Coşbuc, the same voivode appears transfigured into a cosmic phenomenon:

The savage voivode is clad in mail and in iron,
And harsh is the ringing of his mail.
He wears a giant dome above his forehead,
And his words are thunder, his breath an icy wind,
While the axe in his left hand reaches to the heavens
          And the voivode is a mountain.
          ("Pasha Hasan")

What more is there to add? The textbook becomes useless; poetry says all there is to say. The symbolic figure of Michael is a condensation of the highest potential of Romanian heroism.

Mircea the Old, as evoked by Eminescu in "Epistle III", sinks into the realm of archetype. This "old man, so simple in his speech and in his dress", who teaches the arrogant Bayazid a well-deserved lesson, takes up again the dialogue of Dromichetes and Lysimachus a millennium and a half earlier. In each case the simplicity, wisdom, and patriotism of a people who seem to be outside history are set in opposition to the conquering greed of the great empires. Of Dromichetes and Mircea themselves, nothing but a symbolic essence remains.

No less "trans-historical" is the image of Stephen the Great, as Eminescu summons him to reintegrate the country within its borders and restore its values:

Stephen your Highness,
Do not stay in Putna
[...]
Rise up from your grave
That I may hear your horn sounding
And Moldavia gathering.
If the horn sounds once,
You will gather all Moldavia,
If it sounds twice,
The woods will come to your aid,

If it sounds three times,
All the enemies will perish
From border to border.
     (*"Doina"**)

In Barbu Delavrancea's play *Sunset* (1909), the same Stephen speaks out from beyond the grave and beyond history to confirm the communion of generations in the spirit of the eternal Romanian ideal: "Keep in mind the words of Stephen, who was your shepherd far into his old age [...], that Moldavia was not my ancestors', was not mine, and is not yours, but belongs to our descendants and our descendants' descendants to the end of time." The words are those of the great orator Delavrancea and in no way those of the old ruler, but what does it matter? The image of Stephen the Great that is imprinted in public consciousness owes much more to this play than to any document of the time or scholarly monograph.

Painting complements, and often illustrates, historical literature. The genre reached its peak in the work of Theodor Aman, who, like Bolintineanu, showed a preference for the heroic anecdote. His favorite hero is Michael the Brave, whom he painted in a long series of compositions and portraits (mostly between 1864 and 1870). Vlad Țepeș also features in a painting of 1862–63, pinning down the terrified Turkish envoys with his proud and fearless look. It was exactly the moment when Cuza was imposing a new style—of relative independence—in relations with the Ottoman Empire. But the figure who owes most to the painter is Tudor Vladimirescu. It is hard to say how much likeness there is in the portrait painted by Aman in 1874–76, but what is certain is that that was how Tudor was to remain in the consciousness of the Romanians, called to a new life by the act of artistic transfiguration.

Thus the voivodes were taken out of history and raised above it, acquiring permanence in an eternal time. They became symbolic fictions. Nothing is more powerful in the life of peoples than a national symbol. Mircea, Stephen, and Michael are in this sense makers of modern Romania and of Greater Romania. In them a belief was concentrated, without which nothing would have been possible.

DEATH TO THE BOYARS: THE FILE ON IOAN VODĂ

The words, admiring overall but not without a critical edge, in which Grigore Ureche set down his assessment of the reign of Stephen the Great, are well known: "This Stephen Vodă was a man of no great size, furious, and quick to spill innocent blood; often he would kill at feasts, without a trial [...]."[3] It is beyond doubt the viewpoint of a great boyar of the seventeenth century, not wholly prepared to accept the arbitrary rule of an authoritarian prince. But over and

---

Doina: a variety of Romanian folksong, typically concerned with longing, grief, etc. *Trans.*

above the expression of specifically boyar interests, it is basically a judgement of good sense, transcending "class" borders. It is not normal that a ruler, even Stephen the Great, should kill whenever he thinks fit, especially without a trial. A wave of European humanism and of modern political spirit flows through the words of the old chronicler.

In 1828 the already-mentioned history of Moldavia from a boyar point of view (*Nouveau tableau historique et politique de la Moldavie*) still insists along the lines of Ureche, even amplifying his critical judgement, on the cruelties of Stephen the Great, so that they tend to cancel out the splendor of his warlike deeds (which include the massacre of prisoners). According to the same author, even the victories of the great ruler contributed in the end to the exhaustion and decline of his country. It is a historical interpretation which upholds, clearly enough, the project of a boyar oligarchy better able to run the country than a single man,[4] but it also, I repeat, shows the application of free judgement to one of the great figures of the past.

What is striking in the modern period is the attenuation, and sometimes even renunciation, of such critical assessments, with acts of power being justified through the prism of the higher interest of the nation. The prince knows what he is doing, and what he does is good for the country: this argument, explicit or implicit, gains more and more ground. Paradoxically, Grigore Ureche proves to be closer to a liberal spirit than the modern historians.

The "slaughter of the boyars" comes to enjoy the favor of historians and of public opinion. The balance of right continually shifts in the direction of the rulers, with variations, it is true, from one case to the next, telling for the intensity with which the principle of authority is manifested. Criticism of Stephen the Great becomes rarer and rarer, and finally disappears, while Ştefăniţă is condemned by most historians of the pre-communist period for the unjustified killing of Luca Arbure (only to be approved after 1944 precisely because he liquidated the boyars, the "betrayers of the country"). A. D. Xenopol is not afraid to characterize the rulers with all their failings, but in general the conclusions he reaches are more favorable than the premises would suggest: thus he notes the cruelty of Stephen the Great, but makes it clear that "the blood was shed in the interests of the country".[5] Iorga, in his turn, is ready to pass judgement on anyone, including the rulers, but in his case, too, the principle of authority functions, justified by the necessity of putting a stop to the anarchy of the boyars, which was harmful to the general interest. C. C. Giurescu goes even further. He gives up "inconvenient" assessments (showing not the slightest reservation concerning Stephen the Great, for example) and justifies practically any arbitrary act of power by invoking state interest. Thus, referring to Vlad Ţepeş: "The tortures and executions which he ordered were not out of caprice, but always had a reason, and very often a *reason of state*".[6] If we compare the two "typical syntheses" provided by Xenopol and Giurescu, we can see the progress made by the authority principle between 1890 and 1940, consistent with the erosion of the liberal spirit in Romanian political culture.

The list of rulers left to do whatever they thought best is variable, but once included on this list the ruler could get away with anything. In contrast, weakness in face of the boyars (the boyars being the only people who were in a position to affirm divergent points of view) is treated with contempt. Of particular significance is the case of Petru Șchiopul, a ruler much appreciated by Ureche but despised by almost all the Romanian historians of the last two centuries, in comparison with the great slaughterer of boyars, Ioan Vodă the Terrible.

Ioan Vodă represents one of the most striking cases of ideological transfiguration. His position in the Moldavian chronicles is that of the bad governor par excellence. Azarie attributes to him "the ways of a wild beast" and recounts his wrongdoings in macabre detail: "And some he decapitated and took their wealth, so that his own grew by unfair accumulation, and others he skinned like sheep, others he chopped in four and others he buried alive as if they were dead."[7] We find the same cliché with Grigore Ureche, and the explanation is the passion for wealth of a usurping adventurer: "[...] he shocked all with his enmity and with the horrible deaths he inflicted. And wanting to take the savings of everyone, by no other method but the shedding of blood, every day he invented new sorts of tortures. He put Gheorghe the bishop in the fire alive and burned him, accusing him of sodomy because he had heard that he had assembled great wealth [...]."[8] Even much later, in 1828, the boyar version of Moldavian history sees in Ioan Vodă a ruler hated by all social categories, which, more than his conflict with the Turks, led to his downfall.

The motive of personal enrichment and pathological cruelty, interpretations which have certainly passed through the filter of a boyar and ecclesiastical ideology, give way in the nineteenth century to a portrait no less ideologized, but diametrically opposite to the original version. The "new" Ioan Vodă owes almost everything to Hasdeu, including the well-known portrait, which is no more than a Hasdeian fabrication. In 1865, Hasdeu saw in him a statesman of striking modernity, "a great administrator, a great politician, a great general"[9]—and above all a personality who had seen the need to reform the society of his time against the dominant class and taking into account the interests of the many.

The Junimist reaction came through P. P. Carp, who took the opportunity to launch into one of his few historical–literary polemics. For Carp, Ioan Vodă remains "an adventurer, a condottiere, courageous and brilliant like all condottieri, whose only target was the throne and not the good of Moldavia, and whose only means were tyranny and cruelty". Carp draws attention to the fact that the boyars and monks whom the prince persecuted were positive classes at the time, whose annihilation threatened the foundations of Romanian society: "[...] those very monks who are indeed dangerous nowadays when they are powerful and do wrong all the time, then kept alive that sense of religiosity, which, more than anything else, contributed to giving us the necessary strength to defend our ancestral hearths against the Turkish invasion, so that by shaking the foundations of that establishment, Ioan Vodă was threatening our nationality itself; it is clear that democratic ideas can only be of use where a powerful *tiers état* is able to neutralize the despotic aspirations either of a class or of a single man. In the time of Ioan Vodă, the liberation of the common people from the yoke of the clerical and lay aristocracy could have no other consequence than to put the same people under the yoke of the throne, and, if there must be a yoke, I prefer the yoke of 1,000 to the yoke of one man."[10]

However, it was Hasdeu who emerged victorious in the case of Ioan Vodă, not Carp. It is worth noting that A. D. Xenopol, who repeatedly came in for rough treatment at the hands of Hasdeu, broadly follows the same line of argument. "I have observed", he writes, "that such accusations of cruelty, brought by the chroniclers against a prince, should always be treated with caution, to see if the feelings or aristocratic interests of the class to which the Romanian chroniclers generally belonged are not pushing them to distort the truth. In the case of Ioan Vodă, we shall see that this fear is indeed very well founded, and that if any prince was unfairly judged by the chroniclers of the land it was certainly him."[11]

Hasdeu and Xenopol are the two great historians of liberal orientation of the later nineteenth century (they were even militantly involved in politics), and their logic is easy to decipher. They are adversaries of the boyars and partisans of social reform and of progress in general. A political action on the scale they desired could not, however, be achieved without an authoritarian government. The ends were liberal, but the means less so. It is true that their historical judgement concerned a period that had long passed, but it is informed by a certain political mentality: the cult of the "savior" and the imperative of social order and national solidarity.

I do not propose to follow the posthumous career of the controversial prince in detail. It is certain that, on this occasion, even the great Junimist historians did not go against the current. Ioan Bogdan limited himself to noting the exaggerations, motivated by clerical interests, of the chronicler Azarie, while Onciul, in a few lines, mentions the cruelty but also the "courageous resistance" of the voivode in the face of the Ottoman onslaught.[12] The return to the foreground of the peasant problem with the rising of 1907 served Ioan Vodă well; he now became the hero of the play *Chronicles* by Mihail Sorbul, a faithful rendering of the cliché, in which loyal peasants are protected by the prince and boyars are treacherous. Some time later, C. C. Giurescu, consistent with his historical–political conception, absolved the prince of any hint of gratuitous or interested cruelty; the executions which he ordered "must have had a justification", the historian decided, and so as to lay aside any ambiguity he renounced the epithet "the Terrible", accredited by Hasdeu, speaking instead of Ioan Vodă the Brave.[13]

The triumph of Ioan Vodă in Romanian historical consciousness provides an interesting index of the extent and intensity with which the principle of authority was affirmed.

"WHY DO YOU NOT COME BACK, LORD ȚEPEȘ...?"

The symptom par excellence of the need for authority is seen in another myth, as curious as it is significant, which was woven around Vlad Țepeș. Where this ruler is concerned, the chronicles of Wallachia did not even offer the dark image of Ioan Vodă. He appeared as a quite ordinary prince, about whom it was known only that he had built the citadel of Poienari and the monastery of Snagov; this summary information was supplemented by the anecdote of the people from Tîrgoviște who were obliged to work at Poienari "until their clothes burst", a tale which gives an idea, but no more, of the sadistic originality of the ruler.[14] Otherwise, the information about Țepeș is not Romanian: it comes either from Byzantine historians, especially Chalcocondylas, where the conflict with the Turks is concerned, or from various German chronicles and a Slavonic chronicle, especially concerning the acts of sadism which are attributed to him. It is from these foreign sources that the modern version of the story of Vlad Țepeș has been constructed, a story centered equally on the anti-Ottoman struggle and on the uncompromising justice symbolized by the impaler's stake. The macabre stories of a human monster thirsty for blood lie at the origin of the well-known Dracula myth, which originated in the English-speaking world (invented by Bram Stoker in his famous novel of 1897). The same stories, filtered through another national sensibility and another ideology, were also the source of the Romanian myth. The vampire Dracula and the great patriotic ruler have a common origin; they start from the same point and provide a remarkable illustration of the capacity for transformation which is characteristic of the imaginary. We do not need to discuss the accuracy of the information in the German chronicles (which is present also in a somewhat attenuated form in the Slavonic chronicle). Even if Țepeș was not responsible for a single one of the dreadful deeds attributed to him, the Romanian myth was constructed precisely from this bloody image of his reign. The *stake* has become a political symbol, the symbol of an authoritarian prince who was harsh, because that was what the times required, but fair and devoted to the two supreme principles: order within the state and independence in external affairs.[15]

Everyone sees, of course, what they want to see when they look at the face of the voivode in one of the best-known images of a Romanian ruler. But few know that the famous portrait in the Castle of Ambras in Innsbruck is part of a corridor of horrors, where it hangs alongside other monstrosities. On the basis of one of the engravings, Hasdeu attempted a "philosophy of the portrait of Țepeș". Applying the "physiognomic" method of Lavater, the ingenious historian likens the Muntenian ruler to Cesare Borgia and, even more surprisingly, to Shakespeare.[16] Ioan Bogdan does not fall back on such subtleties. In the case of Țepeș, as in many others, he expresses unconventional opinions. When he comes to the Ambras portrait he notes that "the lost and staring eyes seem tired by a long nervous irritation; the sunken face looks pallid and sick; the disproportionate size of the lower lip betrays an uncontrolled nervous tremor, if indeed it is not the usual mark of degenerates".[17] In *Vlad Țepeș and the German and Russian Narratives about Him* (1896), the great Slavicist agrees with Engel, who had seen in Ţepeş "a cruel tyrant and a monster of humanity". He distances himself from those Romanian historians, from Laurian and Heliade to Xenopol and Tocilescu, who are prepared to transform him "into a great and brave prince, into a military organizer of the country, into a protector of the poor and righteous, and even into a genius of the nation": "We ought to be ashamed of him, not to present him as a model of courage and patriotism", is the final verdict of the incorrigible Junimist.[18]

Ioan Bogdan argued in vain. Vlad Ţepeş found a place in the first rank of the pantheon, with the support of the majority of historians and of public opinion. Şincai considered that the accusations against him were partly "made-up stories".[19] Bolintineanu puts the blame on the boyars: the prince's tyranny was necessary to put a stop to the even worse despotism of the aristocratic class. In this sense, Ţepeş was a revolutionary, a reformer.[20] Xenopol does not minimize the "horrifying cruelty", but he notes that this had "a political aim". In putting a stop to the anarchy generated by the struggles between boyar factions, Ţepeş succeeded in cleansing the land of "evils within".[21] With Giurescu, the discussion comes to a close: Vlad Ţepeş did what he had to do, and his bloody acts are not unique but in keeping with the spirit of the times. The decisive words, however, are those of Mihai Eminescu, words which seem to be engraved in the consciousness of the Romanians: "Why do you not come back, Lord Ţepeş?"* From Eminescu to the present day, all those (and they are many) disoriented by the disorder of Romanian society, by corruption and injustice, have never ceased to invoke Ţepeş with his summary but exemplary and efficient justice.

It is interesting to see the association that could be made, in the historical– political imaginary of the nineteenth century, between Ioan Vodă and Ţepeş on the one hand, and Cuza on the other. *Mutatis mutandis*, and leaving the stake aside, the tales told of Cuza are similar to those of Ţepeş. The resemblance is far from fortuitous, for both rulers are reduced to an archetype. Cuza, too, appears as authoritarian, relentlessly just, no great lover of the boyars, and the defender of the interests of the many. An authoritarian inclination combines with an anti-aristocratic and pro-reform current. Published in 1865, Hasdeu's *Ioan Vodă* echoes Cuza across the centuries.

THE DYNASTIC MYTH

The establishment of the dynasty in 1866, and the imperative of education in the dynastic spirit which had hitherto been absent from Romanian political culture could not fail to affect the arrangement of the national pantheon. The real personality of Carol I, who was indeed a great sovereign and the respected arbiter of half a century of political equilibrium, favored the emergence of the myth. Its purpose, however, regardless of the personality and indisputable contribution of

---

* *"Cum nu vii tu, Ţepeş doamne...?"*: from the closing section of "Epistle III". *Trans.*

the king, lay in the necessity of fixing the political edifice of modern Romania in people's consciousness, and that edifice was constitutional monarchy, symbolized by the royal person.

After a difficult and contested beginning to his reign, Carol consolidated his position following the war of independence and the proclamation of the kingdom in 1881. His long reign (of forty-eight years, one more than Stephen the Great) allowed the myth to come to fruition even within his lifetime. The image of the sovereign, mediocre at first, took on a powerful brilliance in the last years of the century. An educational poster of around 1900 presents "the four pillars of the Romanian people", along with other heroes of Wallachian history. The four are Trajan and Decebalus, Cuza and Carol I. Even Michael the Brave becomes a secondary figure by comparison. Carol appears organically rooted in Romanian history; he represents a new beginning, of course, but a beginning based on much older foundations.

The rulers invoked in association with Carol, sometimes even by the king himself, are Stephen the Great and Michael the Brave; alongside them a special position is occupied by Mircea the Old, with whom Carol carried on a veritable dialogue across the centuries. Indeed, at the battle of Nicopolis in 1396 Carol's ancestor, Frederick of Zollern (the founder of the great Hohenzollern family), had fought alongside the Muntenian voivode. It was a profoundly symbolic association, prefiguring the definitive identification, half a millennium later, of a scion of the famous dynasty with the destiny of the Romanian people. Moreover, Carol I himself had passed through Nicopolis in 1877 (he returned in 1902, on the occasion of the twenty-fifth anniversary of the battles for independence).[22] Finally, Carol, like Mircea, added the territory of Dobrogea to the country, putting the stamp of eternity on what his ancestor's old comrade at arms had done before him. Alongside Mircea, the Danube itself offered the symbol of a predestination. The Danube, down which the prince had traveled in 1866 on the way to his new country; the Danube, which he had crossed in 1877; the Danube, which linked the principality of Sigmaringen, situated near its source, to the land which lay along its lower reaches.

The moment of apotheosis came in the jubilee year of 1906, the fortieth anniversary of the king's accession to the throne. The Romanian pantheon now saw a drastic simplification. Two figures stood out clearly from the rest of the heroes of the Romanian people: Trajan and Carol I. They were the two great founders of the Romanian people and of the kingdom; the others, provisional, incomplete, transitory, only served to connect them. The People and the Kingdom belonged to eternity. The *imperial parallel* and the association with a founding act as important as that of Trajan raised Carol I far above the Romanian voivodes of the Middle Ages.

Dimitrie Onciul's *From the History of Romania*, which was published on this occasion, may give an idea of the scale of the myth. A historian usually prudent and moderate in his assessments but inclined towards a highly personalized history and firm in his dynastic convictions, Onciul reserves almost half of the whole course of Romanian history for Carol I. The reign of Carol, he demonstrates, marks the beginning of "a new era in the development of the Romanian state". This includes the complete union of the principalities, given that at the time of Cuza's abdication "the union was not recognized as a merging of the two lands in a single state but only as a personal and administrative union, admitted on a provisional basis. King Carol was the first ruler to take the title 'Prince of Romania' and the constitution promulgated by the new prince was the constitutive document of the unitary Romanian state."[23] It is significant that the union itself is shifted from Cuza to Carol. Onciul attributed to the sovereign the role of initiator in all the great evolutions of modern Romania. Even the flourishing of Romanian culture is presented largely in terms of the interest shown by the ruling house.

Moreover, in the various accounts devoted to him, Carol I frequently appears as omniscient and gifted with a superior understanding. The great naturalist Grigor Antipa, who wrote an interesting memoir of the first king of Romania, with whom he was in close contact, recounts his first conversation with the sovereign thus: "I had the impression that I was being examined by a true specialist, whose knowledge of the issue was better than my handling of it in the paper I had presented to him."

Seen through the eyes of Antipa, Carol emerges as a quite extraordinary figure, who brings together a formidable set of qualities. He is "careful and unparalleled for thrift", good, fair, mild, understanding, an educator of the people, wise, worthy, a subtle diplomat, a brave soldier, a skilful strategist, "a man of a vast culture and great universal consideration", "one of the wisest and most listened-to sovereigns of the day". He is a "giant", by whose "powerful personality" and "great intelligence" the scholar feels "completely dominated". On the occasion of a trip on the Danube, the great river and the great king reveal their common nature as cosmic phenomena. Antipa quotes Carmen Sylva: "Her Majesty the Danube met His Majesty King Carol I." It was also the queen who said that "even in sleep he wears his kingly crown on his head".[24]

No less inclined towards transfiguration is the account written by the writer-monk Gala Galaction. Here too we are in the presence of a man who is "different", made of other stuff than ordinary people. "The Vodă speaks only seldom and always with substance; the Vodă does not throw money out of the window; the Vodă only stays at table for half an hour; the Vodă does not drink; the Vodă does not like fiddlers; the Vodă lives in the palace like a hermit in his cell." It goes without saying that "he was loved by us far less than he deserved. But what could we do! He was too wise, too virtuous, too guiltless for us."[25]

Basically nothing is false, but everything is hyperbolized and bathed in the light of myth. We cannot imagine Romania around 1900 without the political equilibrium which the dynasty provided, and, in particular, the moderation and sense of duty which characterized Carol himself. But the myth goes further than this, separating the figure of the king from the world of ordinary mortals and organizing the whole of Romanian history around him, reducing the complexity of historical factors to a single or determining impulse. In this way, Carol is raised even higher than Stephen the Great or Michael the Brave, since, it must be recognized, in no other period was so much achieved (the political structures of modern Romania, Dobrogea, independence and the kingdom, railways, and a general flourishing of the economy and trade, the great classics of Romanian culture...). Of course it was not Carol, or not Carol alone, who achieved all these things, but nor did Stephen or Michael do what they did alone: that is our illusion. The further back we look the more the mechanism of power seems to be incarnated in a single person. In all cases myth-making follows the same process: history is personified by its reduction to the deeds and virtues of a central figure.

There followed a period in which, although it was not altogether forgotten, a shadow came over the myth of Carol as a result of the "pro-German" solution favored by the king in 1914, in dissonance with the general orientation, so that his death could only be felt as a relief. It was a sad exit for the bearer of a great myth. Events were turning Romanian history in another direction than that traced by the founder of the dynasty. The way was open for the mythologizing of the second king, Ferdinand, known as "the Loyal" for having the strength to break connections with his country of origin when called to do so by the supreme interests of the nation which had offered him its crown. As the myth-making process followed its customary rules, Ferdinand, in fact a much less powerful personality than his uncle, became the bearer and symbol of the historical achievements of the age. He was the king of the war to make the Romanian people whole, the king of sacrifice and of the Romanian victory in that war, the king of Greater Romania, the king who gave land to the peasants and introduced universal suffrage. To no less a degree than Carol I, he was a *founder*. Faced with this indisputably glorious reign there is no point, given that we are in the realm of myth, asking how much was due to the king and how much to others, to each in part.

The coronation of 1922 was symbolic of a new foundation, but also of the explicit integration of Ferdinand in the long line of makers of Romanian history. Even the choice of the place of coronation, Alba Iulia, directly recalled the great act of Michael the Brave. Meanwhile, Bucharest was the scene of an immense historical procession, featuring Trajan and Decebalus, Dragoş Vodă and Radu Negru, Mircea the Old and Alexander the Good, Stephen and Vlad Ţepeş, Michael together with his captains, Matei Basarab and Vasile Lupu, Cantemir and Brîncoveanu, Horea Cloşca and Crişan, Tudor Vladimirescu, Avram Iancu, Cuza, and, of course, Carol I.[26] The moment marked the full identification of a dynasty that had come from outside with the destiny of the Romanian nation which it had embraced.

The mythologized personality of King Ferdinand is no less singular than that of Carol I. However, it is different, starting from real psychological data as well as from the need to highlight the distinct profile of the new founder. In contrast to the Olympian nature of Carol, Ferdinand is characterized by goodness and humanity, and a closeness to people that helped him to hear and understand the profound voice of the country and its aspiration towards the national ideal and social justice. Carol is a god, Ferdinand a saint. "The completion of our borders and the restoration of our dear land to her true course", comments Gheorghe Cardaş, "have been achieved under the protection of the king with the face and hands of a saint: Ferdinand the Loyal."[27]

The third royal figure to be mythologized was Carol II. His problem proved, from the beginning, to be that of fixing a place for himself in the national mythology, coming after two founding personalities who had largely exhausted the resources of myth. Carol wanted to be a founder too, and as there was nothing left to found in the strict sense of building Romania, the mission which he took upon himself was the making of a *new Romania*. Initially a "consolidator" and "perfecter" of his predecessors' work, as the years went on he established his vocation as that of a new opener of roads, the founder of fundamentally different structures. He set out to raise Romania to the status of a prosperous, civilized, and powerful country. He is the king of youth, the king of the peasants (whom he aspired to raise economically and to illuminate), the king of culture. In his case, regardless of what was really achieved out of this program, we find a coordinated propaganda effort (illustrated by the far from negligible body of poetry exalting his virtues and his historical mission).[28] The reign of Carol II had to appear great from the beginning, by means of projects, even before they were realized. The crowning moment is constituted by the years of royal dictatorship. On the eighth anniversary of his accession to the throne, a dutiful newspaper noted that "the miracle has happened"—the miracle being "after eight years, a new country", and a new country meaning "the work of regeneration" of the king and the multitude of "royal foundations" that were on the way to transforming Romanian society.[29]

The style and "mythic outline" of Carol II are different from those of his predecessors. After the cold solemnity of Carol I and the evanescence of Ferdinand, his image is that of a modern king, dynamic, present in the center of all that was happening in Romanian society, always in the midst of people, with a personal combination of majesty and populist familiarity.

In seeking his own legitimization, Carol was careful to distance himself from previous dynastic mythology, while still leaning on it. Carol I, for whom he had a strong admiration, emerged again from the relative shadow which we have observed. The centenary of his birth in 1939 was amplified into a national event marked with festivals, conferences, volumes of evocations or documentation, philatelic issues, and, not least, the erection of a majestic equestrian statue, the work of Meštrović, on a site between the Royal Palace and the building of the Carol I Foundation.

In any myth-making discourse the remote ancestors have a word to say, and sometimes it carries great weight. The royal dictatorship installed by Carol belongs in fact to a family of authoritarian regimes in the Europe of the time. Autochthonous interpretation, however, proved to have more valorizing power. Thus the new regime could be related to the tradition of the Romanian voivodes. Carol was inaugurating a new historical cycle by returning to a "real exercise of power" along the lines of the rulers of the Romanian lands.[30] Once again mythology proved to be profoundly integrative. Carol and the voivodes belonged together to the eternal Romanian present.

Cezar Petrescu's book *The Three Kings* (1934), evidently written to order and destined for villagers, synthesizes the triple royal myth in its highest and purest form. The coming of Carol I to the country is put, as was only proper, under the sign of cosmic miracle: "For a moment the clouds parted and a patch of blue sky, clear and deep, was lit up. A golden sheaf of light rays burst through. A rainbow raised its arch, translucent and silky, like an ornament for a festival of praise. Beneath it, in the scattered light, an eagle quietly hovered, the same eagle that is on the blazon of the country, on the blazon of Radu Negru, and on the ancient blazon of Sigmaringen [...]."[31] The landing of Carol II, on his return by air from exile in France, becomes, metaphorically, a "descent from the heavens". Carol I is "the maker of the kingdom"; Ferdinand "the maker of Greater Romania"; and Carol II "the maker of eternal Romania" (as well as being "the father of the villages and the workers of the land" and "the king of culture"). What is wholly remarkable in Cezar Petrescu is the splendid isolation of the sovereigns, the sign of the definitive fulfillment of the myth. Politicians completely disappear; the only names mentioned are royal. Everything that has been done in Romania, absolutely everything, is linked, and linked exclusively, with the names of its sovereigns.

Carol II is a special case, however. Where he is concerned the countermyth has proved as strong as the myth. Especially since his abdication in 1940 he has been more and more insistently portrayed as a playboy king, dissolute and unscrupulous, certainly not the builder of a new Romania, but rather responsible for eroding the Romanian democratic system. Even in the monarchist discourse of the present day his personality is passed over rapidly. A distinction can be seen between the complete gallery of four kings and their ideal gallery, in which they are reduced to three: Carol I, Ferdinand, and Michael.

A SECOND DYNASTY?

There was, nevertheless, a second dynasty, not in Cezar Petrescu's book but in other books and other compartments of the collective memory. In contrast to the dynasty that came from outside, this is an indigenous dynasty, and thus the two hypostases of the foundation myth—the exterior and interior versions—are combined in a single synthesis. The transcendent sacrality of the Hohenzollern-Sigmaringen dynasty meets the sacrality springing from national roots of the Brătianu family.[32]

It is, of course, a myth of liberal origin, with an essentially party political purpose. But since the role played by the two great Brătianus—Ion C. Brătianu and Ion I. C. (or Ionel) Brătianu—in the great moments and stages of the construction of modern Romania is beyond dispute, and since for almost a century the Liberal Party was the principal political force in the country, this party myth has become, in a sense, a national myth. In the extreme version, everything is owed to the Brătianus, just as in the royal myth everything is owed to the kings. A liberal leader, I. C. Duca, sums up the political action of Ion C. Brătianu thus: "He wanted the union of the principalities, and it happened. He wanted independence, and he presided over it. He wanted a foreign dynasty, and he brought it into the country. He wanted there to be a kingdom, and he organized it."[33] According to the same system of interpretation, the creation of Greater Romania is owed to Ionel Brătianu, as are the great democratic reforms— universal suffrage and peasant property—and in general the work of consolidating the Romanian state. Compared with Brătianu, the others are mere marionettes. Thus Ionel Brătianu "comes to power when he wants, stays as long as he wants, leaves when he wants, and brings whoever he wants".[34]

As with the kings, symbolic connotations are powerfully highlighted. Ion C. Brătianu was born in 1821, the year of Tudor Vladimirescu's revolution, so that history marked him out for the mission of completing the process of change which was begun then. Nor was Ionel Brătianu born in any ordinary year but in 1864, the year of the great reforms, and even on the very day that the rural law, which he was later to complete, was promulgated. "His word was holy and listened-to", it is said of I. C. Brătianu, and his "grave, Christ-like face" is also commented on.[35] The road to Damascus has its own indigenous political version: "I was going along the street in the company of a colleague when our path was crossed by a man of medium stature, with gray curly hair and beard. A warm face, open and attractive, and eyes that smiled and entered into souls. My colleague said: 'Look, that is Brătianu.' His face remained in my mind and I did not hesitate any longer. I was a liberal."[36]

Is it possible to combine two myths which are each as exclusive as the royal myth and that of the Brătianus? It is, of course, since anything is possible in the mythological logic. But it is no less true that the promoters of the second myth have tended to push the first into the background. With I. G. Duca, the process is flagrantly visible. He presents Carol I as a mediocre sovereign, incapable of understanding the great problems of the age, and achieving in forty-eight years of rule less than Cuza had in a mere seven. He does not even recognize Carol's role in 1877, as it is well known that "the struggle for independence was led by Ion Brătianu". According to Duca, the king was good at very little, even in military matters (a judgement in perfect antithesis with Antipa's amazement at the king's multiple competencies!). As for Ferdinand, lacking will and initiative he could only have become a great king thanks to the merits of his advisers. The ground was thus completely cleared for Brătianu and the great liberal family.[37]

There was no lack of protests at the Brătianist confiscation of history especially on the part of conservatives. Such a disagreement is reflected in P. P. Carp's formula: "the king and the foot soldier." In a speech delivered in November 1886 against those who were attributing to Brătianu the merit of having created Romania, the Junimist leader proposed a quite different founding team: "As far as we are concerned, all this was done by two other people, of whom one is the keystone and the other the foundation of national sovereignty

These two are as follows: first, King Carol; and second, the Romanian foot soldier."[38]

The conservatives disappeared from the political scene after the First World War, with their prestige considerably tarnished (Carp himself had declared that he hoped Romania would be defeated, for her own good), while the Brătianus remained in power and in the pantheon. But not for long!

FEMININE MYTHOLOGY: QUEEN MARIE

Women are not much wanted in Romanian historical mythology. In this respect mythology is only reflecting a current and almost general prejudice. Even today, when a number of Islamic states have women prime ministers, successive governments of Romania are striking for their almost total maleness. It has been observed, not without irony, that even the Romanian delegation to the international women's conference was led by a man.

A woman can enter the mythology, of course, but only in a place fitting for her, in a marginal, subaltern position as witness and moral supporter of the great male enterprises. Gentle Lady Elena, who bore so much from Cuza Vodă, is a significant example of the type of woman who is accepted. In a more heroic version, but equally dependent on great men, we find the women of olden times evoked in Bolintineanu's portrayal of the mother of Stephen the Great, who sends her son to victory or death ("Go to the army, for the country die"), or the mother of Michael the Brave, with her extraordinary reaction to her son's death: "Your news is very sad, / Not that my son has died, / But that even by his death / He has not unbound the Romanians." It remains for the psychologists to give their verdict.

There are a few heroic figures of the second rank in the modern period too: Ana Ipătescu in 1848, and Ecaterina Teodoroiu in the First World War. But the upper reaches of the hierarchy find it hard to accept femininity. Women who want to impose themselves "at the top" are regarded badly. This applies, to take two examples from literature, to Lady Clara and Lady Chiajna. The triad of female "evildoers" of the last half century—Elena Lupescu, Ana Pauker and Elena Ceauşescu—only confirms the apparent rightness of the Romanians' distrust of women in power.

The installation of the dynasty somewhat modified the indigenous feminine typology. A queen is not an ordinary woman, but a figure who shares in the sacredness of the function, regardless of her sex. This is what has allowed a number of great queens to be respected leaders of countries otherwise ruled exclusively by men. In the case of Romania, only two names come into the discussion: Queen Elizabeth/Carmen Sylva, and Queen Marie.

The myth-making process did not go very far in the former case, as it was limited by the powerful personality of Carol I. The space reserved for the queen was limited to the areas of good works, and especially cultural activity, a domain in which her qualities as creator and protector were amplified.

With Queen Marie the situation is quite different. She is the only woman in Romania who has risen to the very heights of myth.[39] Her remote origin may have been a positive asset—she came from another world and was somehow a different being. But what really helped was the war, and, in this context, in contrast to Carol and Elizabeth, the less than convincing image of King Ferdinand, a man with considerable intellectual abilities but timid and equivocal compared with the outgoing character of the queen. A Carol I with his frozen dignity, or a Carol II with his majestic yet familiar style might have been able to carry the whole symbolic charge of the moment, which Ferdinand shared with Queen Marie. It is true that the times called for more. The grandeur of the national ideal which had suddenly become tangible, the disaster of defeat in 1916, the mobilization of energies in the following year, the tragedy of a separate peace, the need to keep up hope in difficult times—all led inevitably to the mythical formula of the *savior*. The Romanians needed a savior, perhaps even more than one figure to share this mission.

We should also take into consideration the real merits of the queen, including what she actually did during the war. Myths are frequently not "undeserved". They isolate, amplify, or invest with a surplus of meaning facts that may be very real. It is certain that the queen did not limit herself to the traditional feminine role of "mother of the wounded", although this was not absent from the mythology (some versions even accredit her with healing powers, like the monarchs of old). She was much more than that; she was (I do not propose to separate the reality from the strictly mythical in this respect) the living consciousness of Romanian unity, the symbol of confidence in final victory.

It is worth noting the account given by a cynic, who was little inclined to admire his contemporaries and who was, on other occasions, far from kind in his appreciation of the queen. Constantin Argetoianu writes thus:

> "Whatever Queen Marie's errors before and after the war, the war remains her page, the page of which she may boast, the page that will seat her in history's place of honor. [...] We find her in the trenches among the combatants, in forward positions; we find her in the hospitals and all the medical units; among the wounded, among the sick; we find her present wherever people met to try to do some good. She knew no fear of bullets and bombs, just as she knew no fear or disgust at disease, or impatience with the often useless efforts provoked by her desire for something better. Queen Marie fulfilled her duty on all the multiple fronts of her activity, but above all in encouraging and raising the morale of those who lived around her and who had to decide, in the most tragic moments, the fate of the country and the people. We may state that during our displacement to Moldavia, Queen Marie was the embodiment, and a fine embodiment, of the highest aspirations of the Romanian consciousness."[40]

By the way in which she influenced Romania's entry into the war in 1916, and again in 1918, when "almost only thanks to her" Ferdinand did not ratify the disastrous Treaty of Bucharest, the queen, Argetoianu concludes, "established herself as a founder of Romania in its new wholeness, and as one of the greatest figures of our national history".[41] A heated characterization, coming from the pen of a skeptic!

Conscious of the role she had had and of the force of the myth which played in her favor, the queen also tried to obtain a suitable role in the years of peace which followed. However, times had changed, and in a more prosaic age, served by conventional politicians, the mythical vocation of the queen could no longer manifest itself. She did not manage to enter the regency either, and Carol II, preoccupied with his own historical stature, pushed her completely to one side. Her death in 1938 proved, however, that the myth was still intact. The displays of grief and gratitude were numerous and sincere, going far beyond the official ceremonial framework. On this occasion Aron Cotruş wrote the significant poem "Lady Marie", in which the queen appears as a providential figure come from far-off shores to infuse the Romanian nation with a new force. Following the well-known mythological procedure she finds her place at the highest point of Romanian history, where she receives the homage of the great heroes of the Romanian people:

Decebalus, if he had known that one day you would come,
through these mountains, over these plains,
would have gathered soldiers in crowds,
and ferocious builders without sleep...
and in his violent princely arrogance,
he would have built, in blood and sweat,
from the hardest stone,
up to the heavens—Sarmisegetuza...

if he had seen you
on the water-beaten shores of the mighty Danube,
He himself, the great Iberian,
Trajan—Emperor,
would have remained on the spot in his iron heel,
amazed, trembling...

Basarab would have pulled up the Carpathians from their roots
to bury under them any foreign army—
if he had felt, across time, that you would come,
one day, on the Jiu rivers...

Stephen the Great
would have halted his stormy armies far off,

to look at you, as you passed thoughtfully
along the bleeding pathways of Moldavia...
he would have ordered to be built without delay
Moldavian monasteries,
on the sites where your deep gaze had rested the most,
and your step of imperial stock...

Before your august sight,
from his proud cavalcades,
with his two eyes like the *puszta*,
revered by all, János Hunyadi would have stopped short...

if Michael the Brave had seen you,
white and alive—
wherever he went
the land would have grown in an instant,
under his iron tread—an empire...[42]

Almost fifty years of communism severely eroded the myth of the queen. The solution chosen, the most efficient of all, was forgetting; in general her name was not even mentioned (though it is interesting that her image was preserved in the sculptural composition of the monument to the "Medical Heroes" in Bucharest, probably due to the sheer ignorance of the authorities!). The few references that were made sought, with the hypocrisy characteristic of dictatorships, to highlight the queen's sexual immorality (again with extracts from Argetoianu, but different passages from those we have just looked at). Today her figure has returned to view, but the myth can no longer have the force of three-quarters of a century ago. Romania lacks a great feminine myth.

INTERWAR SAVIORS

We have seen how the war called insistently for a savior, or more than one, and how the role was played by King Ferdinand and Queen Marie. A third figure must be added, who provides us with a typical case of myth-making: General (later Marshal) Alexandru Averescu. The artisan of the victory of Mărăşti awakened a boundless trust in people's souls, especially in peasants in uniform. His military success, which was in any case only relative, cannot explain everything. Eremia Grigorescu, the hero of Mărăşeşti, never enjoyed anything like the same degree of mythical transfiguration. Quite simply, the form, the look, and the gestures of the general filled many Romanians with the conviction that they were in the presence of a savior. The myth was prolonged and amplified in the first years of peace. Averescu now appeared as the potential reformer of Romanian society, the only one capable of setting the country on a new historical course. The mechanism of myth-making is interesting in his case. The general had, of course, political ambitions, but more in the traditional sense of a career in politics; he lacked the messianic drive, and, unlike candidates for dictatorship, he did not seek contact with a multitude that could be electrified.

Here is what Argetoianu, who was beside him in the crucial years, writes:

> The popularity of General Averescu was a psychosis of the front, and demobilized men brought it back to the villages as they might have brought any illness. The origins of this psychosis must be sought in the fact that whenever things were difficult on one front, General Averescu had been sent to sort them out, and he had managed to do so every time, even in desperate situations. So the soldiers became accustomed to seeing in him a "savior", and they gradually started to call on his protection not only for their needs at the front but also for those at home. [...] Like the spider in the middle of its web, Averescu stayed put and let the flies come to him. He never courted popularity, and at the start of the war it never even entered his head that such a thing might be possible: popularity ran after him, and when it caught him he was the most amazed of all, so amazed that he did not know at first what to do with it [...]. He did nothing to cultivate it or to protect it from the blows of his opponents. While he was in uniform he never went down into the trenches, and after he had taken it off and put on party clothes *he never went down into the villages.* He stayed in Bucharest or Severin, and did all he could to keep people away from him.

Argetoianu also describes one of the general's rare "field trips": "Averescu got out of the automobile, wearing his plain blue wartime coat, and advanced towards the excited, staring crowd; first the mayor, then the priest, then a teacher tried to mutter a speech, but their words stuck in their throats. [...] The general shook their hands, without saying anything, and set off on foot along the rows of people. Men fell to their knees, kissed the hem of his blue coat, nodded, sighed deeply and whispered: 'Preserve him, O Lord, for the sake of our salvation!'"[43]

The purity of the myth is perfect in this case. People's hopes—victory in the war, property rights, the cleaning up of political life—were embodied in a chosen figure, regardless, in the end, of the real qualities and intentions of the person in question. Averescu became prime minister and actually carried out part of the mythical program (the 1921 law granting property rights), but he proved disappointing because what was expected of him was more than that: it was the *transfiguration* of Romania. (France experienced a similar adventure in 1887, with General Boulanger as the hero. Some politicians and a section of public opinion saw in him a new Bonaparte. Pushed by the illusions of others towards dictatorship, the general withdrew at the last minute, to the disappointment of those who had put their trust in him.)

The need for saviors was to become a permanent feature of the interwar period. The notable progress achieved by Romania generated imbalances and frustrations. The traditional political class inspired less and less respect. The aspiration towards a new world and the totalitarian model encouraged the identification of providential personalities everywhere. In the Romania of the 1930s these saviors were three in number: Carol II, with a first saving action in 1930 when he returned to the country and to the throne, followed by a second beginning in 1938, with the installation of the royal dictatorship; "Captain" Corneliu Zelea Codreanu, a charismatic figure whose assassination on the orders of the royal dictatorship regime conferred on him the halo of martyrdom; and Marshal Ion Antonescu, who was called to regenerate Romania after the collapse of 1940. We may notice with all these saviors, so different in other respects, the assuming of a mission involving a radical restructuring of Romanian society and its "restoration to health" by an abandonment of the liberal and democratic pathway on which modern Romania had been built. In contrast to Carol I, Ferdinand, and Brătianu, the new saviors had a totalitarian vocation: it is the sign of an important evolution in the political imaginary.

We return to the great fresco of the Romanian Athenaeum, inaugurated in 1938. Its somewhat official character means that the choice of figures represented is particularly significant. Let us consider the selection.[44] The sequence begins, as we have seen, with Trajan and Apollodorus of Damascus. There follows a space without any named heroes; even the "dismounting", a highly charged historical process involving several real and legendary figures, is symbolized by an anonymous knight being received with bread and salt. The first voivode represented is Mircea the Old, the exponent of the "military state", followed by Alexander the Good, who illustrates the "administrative state". The "Romanian crusade" has its heroes in "Ioan Corvin" (Iancu of Hunedoara), Vlad Dracul and Stephen II (the last being a curious choice, probably arising from the desire to represent Moldavia by a contemporary of the first two); they are accompanied by Vlad Țepeș, "in the middle ground, as a vision", against the background of the citadel of Poienari (a pictorial solution for his ambiguous historical status). Then Stephen the Great stands alone, followed by the "age of peace and faith" personified by Neagoe Basarab and Lady Despina in front of their foundation at Curtea de Argeș, after which Michael the Brave again stands alone. The "ages of culture" are individualized through Matei Basarab, Vasile Lupu, Dimitrie Cantemir, and Constantin Brîncoveanu. The rebirth of Romanianism has as its heroes Horea, Cloșca and Crișan, Gheorghe Lazăr, and, of course, Tudor Vladimirescu, the "great Oltenian". The revolution of 1848 provides no individualized faces in the principalities, but in Transylvania Avram Iancu appears seconded by Buteanu. Cuza and Kogălniceanu represent the union and the great reforms, after which the fresco is reserved for the royal dynasty and its double, the "dynasty" of the Brătianus. Thus, against a background of representative events and monuments, we see Carol I, Queen Elizabeth, and I. C. Brătianu, Ferdinand, Queen Marie, and Ionel Brătianu, Carol II and the great voivode of Alba Iulia.

Prince Michael (the last two associated with scenes illustrating urban life, industry, the army, and cultural effervescence). As well as the dominant "princely" note, we may observe the emphasis placed on the cultural phenomenon (consonant with the culturalizing atmosphere of Carol II's reign), and a more accentuated integration of Transylvania, especially where the period of Romanian national rebirth is concerned (a natural consolidation after the union of 1918).

The Athenaeum fresco represents the pantheon in its completed form, at the end of a century and a half of elaboration and on the eve of the disruptive intervention of the totalitarian regimes. It was a generally accepted pantheon, even in the more delicate contemporary section where Cuza goes hand in hand with Carol I while the kings and the Brătianus avoid casting a shadow over each other. Differences of interpretation and emphasis, such as we find, for example, in the school textbooks, did not affect the overall coherence of the model. We are far from the French model, which was characterized by a high degree of polarization between the historical reference points of the two Frances: revolutionary France, lay and progressive; and conservative France, Catholic and monarchist.[45] For the Romanians, the myth of the providential hero tends to become identified with the myth of national unity around the saving figure, a feature of the Romanian historical and political consciousness which is extremely relevant for all that followed regarding the nation/leader relationship. The search for consensus and for a respected authority were to justify, through history, the turn towards authoritarianism and totalitarianism.

LEGIONARY MYTHOLOGY

The more "different" an ideology, the more different its historical reference points. This was the case in the 1930s with the Legionaries, whose pantheon proved to be appreciably amended compared with the official one.[46] As a revolutionary movement, promoting the purity of autochthonous values and the moral and religious regeneration of the nation, the Legionaries shifted the accent from the zone of power to that of revolt, and from the dominance of the political to the affirmation of Romanian spirituality. Being inclined themselves towards sacrifice, they often preferred the great defeated, those by whose martyrdom a great idea had been perpetuated, to the conquerors. The voivodes are not ignored, but they are valorized more according to how they express the ancestral, somehow atemporal, sense of Romanian purity and solidarity among Romanians: this is what explains the exceptional position of Stephen the Great in Legionary historical invocations (in the spirit of Eminescu's "Doina"). The revolutionaries are highlighted and interpreted from the point of view of the fundamentally national dimension of their actions, which are directed against foreign invasion: Horea, Cloşca and Crişan, Tudor Vladimirescu, Avram Iancu... The Legionary heroes follow in their footsteps; they are men of an ideal for which they are ready to pay with their blood, just like their great predecessors: men like Moţa and

Marin, who fell in Spain in the fight against Bolshevism, and the Captain himself. In the same spirit the defeated Decebalus, in fact victorious in the perpetuation of the Dacian spirit, is preferred to Trajan. Unexpected figures also appear, whose mission is to lead us to the cleanness of times gone by. There is Bucur the Shepherd, for example, the founder of a very different Bucharest to the cosmopolitan and corrupt capital of Greater Romania. The legendary founder features in a drawing in which he is lost among the non-Romanian company names on Calea Victoriei, and wonders: "Lord, am I in my own Bucharest or in Tel-Aviv, Palestine?"[47]

Two forgers of national religion occupy the highest positions in this pantheon: the great Dacian Zalmoxis, who prefigured Christianity; and the prophet of new times, Mihai Eminescu, whose nationalist doctrine was claimed by the Legionaries as their principal ideological reference point. The essence of the national history and of Romanian spirituality is expressed either through the triad Horea–Eminescu–the Captain, or through the succession Zalmoxis–Stephen the Great–Eminescu–the Captain (Zalmoxis being the "greatest precursor of Christ", Stephen "the most Christian defender of Christendom", and Eminescu "the announcer of the Romanian triumph which the Captain bestows in our days and bestows just as our ancient Zalmoxis required". Re-actualizing, decades later, the historical sensibility of the nationalist Right in the 1930s, it was Stephen the Great and Eminescu that Petre Țuțea invoked towards the end of his life, setting them above all the others. The latter he saw as the "absolute Romanian", characterizing him in a striking formula as "the lyrical sum of the voivodes".[48]

However, there are moments when all the national heroes appear insignificant in comparison to the holy shade of the Captain. Then only Jesus remains before him, and history, not just that of the Romanians but that of the world, is summed up in these two great renewers of the human spirit: "The Captain took bodily form in order to change man himself, to spiritualize him, to liberate him as far as possible from the chains of matter. From Jesus Christ to the Captain no one had attempted such a transformation. The Captain was in direct continuity with the Crucified of Golgotha."[49]

Further than that it was not possible to go. But it was possible to go just as far in another direction. And this is what was to happen before long.

FROM BĂLCESCU TO GHEORGHIU-DEJ

In restructuring Romanian society from its foundations and rewriting the history of the country according to completely new criteria, communism, in its first phase proceeded to reorganize completely and give a new meaning to the gallery of national heroes.

The kings, of course, disappeared, being mentioned only as far as was necessary to underline the evil they had done to the country. The Brătianus, too disappeared, as did all the great politicians who had made modern Romania and who were charged with being exponents of the "bourgeois-landlord" regime.

The earlier rulers remained, but in a less glorious position, affected by their condition as representatives of the exploiting feudal class. However significant the merits of Stephen the Great, they could never cancel the fact that "the mass of the peasants, in a state of serfdom, continued to live in misery and to suffer cruel exploitations".[50] With Michael the Brave, things were even clearer. He had "defended the interests of the class of boyars", who had, in their turn, "betrayed the interests of the country", while "the peasantry continued to be exploited".[51]

Some rulers, however, enjoyed a better treatment than others. The best regarded in the 1950s was—could it have been otherwise?—Ioan Vodă the Terrible, the slaughterer of boyars and lover of peasants. Moreover, to his great credit he had been the ally of the Cossacks, who helped him in his campaign of 1574, providing a significant chapter in Romanian–Russian relations. Historians, novelists, dramatists, painters, and composers outdid one another in evoking and actualizing the redoubtable voivode; he even appeared on the stage of the Romanian Opera in Gheorghe Dumitrescu's musical drama *Ioan Vodă the Terrible* (1954).[52]

There was recognition of some of Stephen the Great's merits and deeds too. His firm treatment of the great boyars did not pass unnoticed, and his relations with Kiev and Moscow were another plus point (his own marriage to Evdochia of Kiev and that of his daughter Elena to the son of the grand prince Ivan III of Muscovy).

Dimitrie Cantemir was also promoted, relative to other rulers, by his close relations with Russia. His treaty with Peter the Great, the tsar's visit to Iaşi, the joint anti-Ottoman campaign, and the scholar-prince's Russian exile made up a precious page in the Romanian–Russian chronicle.

But the most representative heroes in this first version of communist mythology are not princes, even those who were Russophiles or slaughterers of the boyars, but the spokesmen of the great class conflicts, the leaders of uprisings, revolutions, and workers' struggles. No names of leaders were available, unfortunately, for the fictive slave revolt in Dacia; a Spartacus of national history could not be found. Even the Bobîlna revolt, which had become one of the great chapters of Romanian history, could only provide a list of names without any biographical consistency. Gheorghe Doja, on the other hand, the minor Szekler noble who became leader of the revolt of 1514, was propelled to the highest zone of the pantheon; initially a mere "revolt", the movement which he had led turned into a "peasant war" on the model of Engels's "German peasant war". Horea, Cloşca and Crişan, and Tudor Vladimirescu were taken over from the traditional pantheon and well integrated in the communist ideology, with a shift of accent from the old, emphatically national, interpretation, to a predominantly social, anti-feudal view of their movements.

The revolution of 1848 provided the supreme myth of history rewritten by the communists: Nicolae Bălcescu.[53] Quite against his will, Bălcescu became the central figure in a large-scale manipulation. He was "helped" in this ascent by his romantic-revolutionary intransigence and the consistency with which he had sought the emancipation and property rights of the peasants (his ideal, a society of small producers, was not exactly the communist ideal for society, but at least it fitted the anti-boyar and pro-peasant demagogy of communism). Above all, he had died young, before he could end up minister or prime minister in a government that would inevitably have been "bourgeois-landlord", as his fellow revolutionaries did. In Bălcescu, the communist regime found the ideal symbol of the absolute revolutionary ideal, against which all other projects and personalities had to be evaluated. As truth was—from the point of view of a totalitarian ideology, and even more in the perspective of the "scientific" ideology of communism—single, indivisible, and indisputable, it followed that only Bălcescu had been right, the others being guilty of hesitation, error, or betrayal according to their distance from the model. Bălcescu served the imposition of the idea that there was only one right way. In fact he became the "leader" of the revolution (which he never was in reality, his position in the provisional government being a secondary one). In order for him not to be left alone he was joined by a few other pure revolutionaries, among them Ana Ipătescu, the "liberator" of the provisional government in June 1848, a hitherto almost unknown figure who suddenly became a celebrity of the moment, and General Magheru, another second-rank figure projected into the limelight. (The association of the three revolutionaries inevitably recalls the great axial boulevards of Bucharest: "Brătianu–Lascăr Catargiu" renamed "Bălcescu–Magheru–Ana Ipătescu".) In the anti-national phase of Romanian communism, Bălcescu also had the merit of having attempted a rapprochement with the Hungarian revolution. In contrast, the heroes of the Romanian revolution in Transylvania, including Avram Iancu and Simion Bărnuţiu (who was treated even more severely), saw their status diminished as the penalty for an orientation which was judged to be too nationalist in the context of the Romanian–Hungarian conflict of 1848–1849. In the 1950s Bălcescu became omnipresent: a pivotal figure in Romanian history, the hero of plays and novels (e.g. the play *Bălcescu* by Camil Petrescu, 1949, and the same author's epic novel *A Man among Many*, 1953–1957), with his face on the principal banknote in circulation (100 lei), his bust displayed in most towns, and his name on the front of a variety of institutions, in particular schools (the high schools previously named after Carol I or Brătianu, and the famous Saint Sava College in Bucharest, all became "Bălcescu", almost no other name being conceivable), he was obliged to place his posthumous glory in the service of the communist project.

In chronological order there followed, of course, the heroes of the working class, socialist and communist heroes, and heroes of the struggle against the "bourgeois-landlord" regime. Here, however, things were complicated from the very beginning, and remained complicated until the end. The history of the Romanian Communist Party was punctuated by mutual accusations, plots, exclusions, and murders. It was not easy to identify the correct way and the personalities who had been right, particularly as the appreciation of one moment might not be valid the next day. Through half a century of communism, everything gravitated towards the living leaders, and especially the great Leader. These succeeded in annexing the history of the Party, regardless of the effective role which had been played by the others. Each political tremor instantaneously produced a corresponding historical tremor. To fall from power meant to drop out of history; and vice versa: the rise to power brought about the amplification of previous biography, even the complete rewriting of an entire segment of history. The fall of Lucreţiu Pătrăşcanu in 1948, followed by that of the Ana Pauker– Vasile Luca–Teohari Georgescu group in 1952, "deprived" history of the respective personalities, who were henceforth mentioned only occasionally in order to be branded. On the other hand, Gheorghiu-Dej, who remained alone, annexed to himself a good part of the history of the past decades.[54] The Griviţa strike of 1933, in which he had been involved, became the key moment of contemporary history. Like Bălcescu, who in fact served to point to and justify him, the party leader rose above the others, with his faithful followers in the second rank, most of them former railway workers (the longest lived being Chivu Stoica). It was, it might be said, the C.F.R.* phase of Romanian history, or, more accurately, of the history of the R.P.R. In 1900 the two great figures of the simplified pantheon were Trajan and Carol I; in the 1950s they were Bălcescu and Gheorghiu-Dej.

Among the names which were more or less highlighted, and which formed a bridge between the two great revolutionary heroes, I might mention Ştefan Gheorghiu (who gave his name to the Party's "Academy") and I. C. Frimu. They maintained a relatively stable position in the communist pantheon, as they had not been implicated in the internal disputes of the interwar period. Constantin Dobrogeanu-Gherea, the "father" of Romanian socialism, was recognized as a forerunner, but remained a controversial figure; he had to pay for his daring theoretical points of view, which were considered deviations by Marxist orthodoxy, especially his opinion that Romania was insufficiently advanced on the road of capitalism and thus unready for the taking of historical initiative by the proletariat.

Where the interwar period is concerned it is worth noting that the principal communist leaders were excluded. This sort of "purging" ensured a comfortable position for Gheorghiu-Dej, with no need to fear competition, even of a retrospective kind. Gheorghe Cristescu, the "founder" of the Party in 1921 and its first secretary general, remained out of history for a long time. Ştefan Foriş, the predecessor of Gheorghiu-Dej, who was killed in 1944 as the result of a settling of accounts, was invariably associated for a long time with the epithet "the traitor", without it ever being made very clear who or what he had betrayed.

Other heroes were promoted from the lesser ranks, who had no aspirations, even posthumously, to the supreme leadership. A special case is that of Vasile Roaită, the teenager killed at Griviţa (C.F.R. mythology again!) while he was

---

* *Căile Ferate Române* (Romanian Railways). *Trans.*

sounding the siren to call the workers to the struggle. The purity of young blood is often invoked in revolutionary myths as a symbol of the justice of the cause and the hope embodied in youth. In the 1950s, Roaită enjoyed a remarkable posthumous celebrity; I shall mention only the famous revolutionary song "Roaită's Siren", and the changing of the name of a seaside resort from Carmen Sylva to Vasile Roaită, truly a radical change. (Its present name, Eforie Sud, should calm the passions!)

We might also recall Ilie Pintilie, a martyr of the communist cause, who died under the fallen walls of Doftana prison in the earthquake of 1940; the heroes who fell in the Spanish civil war or in the French resistance; or the victims (apparently very few if we go by the names listed) of Legionary and Antonescian repression—for example Filimon Sîrbu, executed for treason and sabotage in the interests of the enemy.

The myth of the "illegalist" now took shape, subordinated, regardless of its diverse personifications, to a rigorous typology. The illegalist came from a poor family of workers or peasants (which was not quite true: many communists either had a "classless" marginal background, or originated in petit-bourgeois or even social and intellectual elite circles), experienced hardship and oppression from an early age, was initiated by an older comrade in the secrets of Marxism–Leninism and the revolutionary movement, and, full of self-denial, dedicated his life to the revolutionary struggle, the Party and the People. Prison and torture, even death in many cases, could not defeat him.[55]

By their origins, by the nobility of their ideals and the heroism they demonstrated, the illegalists justified the proletarian revolution and legitimized the new regime. On the other hand, however, they were sufficiently minor figures to pose no threat to the position of the leader. Among them we find a relatively high number of women: fewer, of course, than the men, but well above the usual proportion of women in the sphere of Romanian political mythology. This was the period when the revolutionary woman was affirmed, related to men more often in the comradeship of struggle than in the dialectic of the sexes (which explains the promotion of Ana Ipătescu in the events of 1848).[56] Finally, we may note the relatively high number of illegalists of both sexes who were of non-Romanian ethnic origin (reflecting, indeed, the effective structure of the communist "elite" before 1944). The progressive Romanianization of the Party would be paralleled by the gradual Romanianization of its interwar history, in other words, the reinvention of a history more Romanian than it had been in reality.

Above them all, however, leaving even the leader in a subordinate position, rose the great figures of the communist pantheon: Marx and Engels, Lenin and Stalin. For the first time in Romanian history the supreme heroes no longer belonged to the national storehouse of personalities—a reversal which says much about the initial relationship between Romanian communism and the Romanian nation. The gradual acquisition of a relative autonomy and the orientation of Romanian communism towards nationalism eclipsed, little by little, the gigantic personalities of world (or Soviet) communism, until their invocation became little more than a matter of form, required as part of the strict observation of a ritual. Stalin, accused in his own country, fell from his pedestal. But Lenin's statue dominated the entry into Bucharest until December 1989 (with an inspired setting in front of the Stalinist architecture of *Casa Scînteii**). In a capital which had been left almost without statues, from which the monuments of the kings and the great politicians had disappeared, the survival of Lenin's statue undeniably marked the true reference point of a communism which claimed to be national.

In the shadow of Stalin, other greater or lesser heroes, taken from the history of Russia and the Soviet Union, multiplied in Romania in the 1950s. These were the years when the Romanian pantheon tended to become a mixed, Romanian–Russian–Soviet pantheon. Ivan III made his entry alongside Stephen the Great, and Peter the Great with Cantemir. Bălcescu found his correspondents in the Russian "revolutionary democrats", Herzen, Chernyshevsky, and the others. The Romanian–Russian brotherhood of arms could be seen all through history, culminating in 1877 and in the Second World War. The type of the Romanian illegalist was modeled on that of the Bolshevik fighter. Children and teenagers learned what it meant to be a communist hero according to models which were more often Soviet than indigenous. Aleksandr Fadeyev's novel *The Young Guard* broke all the records for popularity (eight Romanian editions between 1947 and 1963), and the famous teenage heroine Zoia Kosmodemianskaia, a victim of the Nazis in the "great war for the defense of the fatherland", kept company for many years with young Romanians, at least through the fact that one of the main Bucharest high schools bore her name until December 1989.

FROM BUREBISTA TO CEAUȘESCU

In the nationalist phase of communism the pantheon was reorganized, resulting in a hybrid structure in which pre-communist historical tradition was combined with the original communist mythology of class struggle.

Towards the end of the 1950s, with the complete "rehabilitation" of the union of the principalities, Alexandru Ioan Cuza was brought back to his traditional dominant position. Previously, in the "Roller period", reservations had been expressed concerning his "hesitation" and inconsistency in applying the great reforms. Cuza's effigy was to appear, significantly (since nothing is haphazard and non-ideologized in communism), on the 50 lei banknote, between Bălcescu (100 lei) and Tudor Vladimirescu (25 lei), the only ones which remained in circulation

---

* *"Scînteia* House" (*Scînteia,* "The spark", was the Romanian Communist Party's daily newspaper): a massive Soviet-style building of the 1950s which was the center of state publishing during the communist period; now renamed *Casa Presei Libere* (House of the Free Press), it is still home to a number of newspapers and publishing houses, and also to the Romanian Stock Exchange and the Ministry of Culture. *Trans.*

until 1989. The "comeback" of the prince of the union illustrated the (relative) shift of accent from revolutionary to national myths.

The new pantheon was not going to sacrifice the heroes of class struggle, the privileged exponents of classic communist mythology. However, with the increasing affirmation of nationalism they were pushed into the background in comparison with the holders of power, the exponents of the nation and the state, the Dacian kings and great medieval voivodes. Bălcescu remained the great figure of 1848, but he could no longer be the leading personality of Romanian history; he was not eliminated, but others were raised. In the context of 1848 we may note the full valorization of Avram Iancu; his struggles with the Hungarians, not so well regarded in the 1950s, now became fully justified. Horea and Tudor Vladimirescu acquired an ideology more comprehensive than that of simple revolts, exclusively or predominantly anti-noble or anti-boyar. They were affirmed as exponents of the nation and their movements changed from "uprisings", as they were in the 1950s, to "revolutions" (first in the case of Tudor, and rather later, and at the price of some controversy, in that of Horea). The Tudor file is exemplary for the logic of historical mythology. The hero of 1821 passed all ideological examinations con brio, being invoked successively by liberals, Legionaries, "internationalist" communism, and nationalist communism. A major historiographical offensive was launched in the time of Ceauşescu around his relations with the Greek Etaireia movement. After Andrei Oţetea had striven to demonstrate the close links between the two revolutions (*Tudor Vladimirescu and the Etairist Movement in the Romanian Lands*, 1945), the historians of the nationalist phase did all they could to absolve the Romanian revolutionary of any obligation towards the Etairists. An ideology may, with the same effect, invent new heroes or change the image of those already appointed. Unfortunately, Tudor is not able to tell us to which of his admirers he feels closest!

However, the most spectacular rise was, as I have already said, that of the "holders of power". It was somewhat contrary to the ideology of class struggle, but in complete agreement with the new political-ideological demands: the unity of the whole people around the Party and the Leader, separation from the Soviet Union, the marking of Romanian individuality, and the role which Ceauşescu aspired to play in world affairs. It is clear that Ceauşescu, himself the bearer of a (presidential) scepter, was keen to identify himself with the great crowned figures of the past.

Thus the principal voivodes were lined up again at the highest level of the pantheon; their contemporary presence was justified in terms of their importance but also depended on the conjuncture and the succession of commemorations. I seems that Ceauşescu, fed on readings from Bolintineanu and Coşbuc, had a particular admiration for Michael the Brave (although this did not prevent him ordering the demolition of the Mihai Vodă monastery in order to improve the view of his own palace); in any case the maker of the union of 1600 expressed more than any other ruler the idea of eternal Romania, which Ceauşescu wanted to incarnate. Stephen the Great, Vlad Ţepeş and Mircea the Old also received intense coverage in the regime's propaganda.[57] Nor were the "cultural" rulers, like Neagoe Basarab and Dimitrie Cantemir, forgotten; the evocation of their deeds made it easier to support the "protochronist" theses. Even Constantin Brîncoveanu was fully rehabilitated, after his harsh fiscal measures and his oppression of the peasant masses had been condemned in the "class" phase of historiography.

But the most remarkable phenomenon was the massive orientation towards antiquity, the appeal to the Dacian kings. Where Dacia was concerned, the national communists proved to be convinced dynasts! Not only the traditional Decebalus, but Dromichetes, and especially Burebista, were placed in the limelight, making up the originary triad of national history. The commemoration of 1980 served to point out a striking similarity between Ceauşescu and Burebista; even a professional historian like Ion Horaţiu Crişan did not hesitate to write words of homage addressed to the Dacian king in the manner of those addressed to the communist dictator. Thus Burebista was "animated by the burning desire to raise up his folk. To them he dedicated his entire activity, in internal and external affairs, his entire life."[58] This was how Party activists expressed themselves, addressing the great leader, at congresses and plenaries. We may note the successive avatars of the "simplified" pantheon of the Romanians: Trajan and Carol I around 1900, Bălcescu and Gheorghiu-Dej in the 1950s, Burebista and Ceauşescu in 1980.

Much effort was also put into identifying the Dacian kings between Burebista and Decebalus. State continuity required a dynasty. Without going into the details of this thorny question, it is worth recording the amusing adventure of the figure of Scorilo, who overnight became the father of Decebalus. At the origin of this promotion lies the "scholarly joke" of Constantin Daicoviciu, who interpreted the words "Decebalus per Scorilo", stamped on a Dacian pot, as meaning "Decebalus the son of Scorilo" (per presumably meaning "child" in Dacian, by analogy with the Latin puer). A Scorilo, about whom little is known, is also mentioned by the Latin author Frontinus, but his placing in a well-defined dynastic context gave him extra prestige and significance. Now the solemn formula "Decebalus per Scorilo" was even inscribed on the base of a monument to Decebalus; the craftsman who stamped the pot could never have dreamt of the impact his banal gesture would have centuries later!

Cinema production, which was strictly ideologized and carefully controlled, provides a good barometer of the rating of personalities. The historical cinema of the communist era began in 1963 with Tudor, a film which breathes the ideology of the 1950s, albeit in an attenuated manner (Russians: good friends; French and British: supporters of the Turks; boyars: all bad, regardless of nationality; the conflict: strictly social). It was followed, in 1967 and 1968, by the treatment of origins: The Dacians and The Column; then the principal rulers became cinema heroes one after the other, in a highly patriotic and actualized vision: Michael the Brave (1971), Stephen the Great: Vaslui 1475 (1975), Dimitrie Cantemir (1975), Vlad Ţepeş (1978), Burebista (1980) and Mircea the Great (1989).

In 1975 the program of the Communist Party named the following personalities, in a characteristic mixture of Marxist ideology and nationalism: Burebista, Decebalus, Mircea, Stephen, Michael, Gheorghe Doja, Horea, Cloşca and Crişan, Cuza. However, the founders of communism were not forgotten: Marx, Engels, and Lenin (the last of these being mentioned on several occasions).

Towards the end of the communist period, two ideological officials who were qualified in history, Mircea Muşat and Ion Pătroiu, listed the great ages of national history, each bearing the name of the dominant personality, as follows: Burebista, Decebalus, Mircea, Stephen, Michael, Brîncoveanu, Cuza and Ceauşescu. (Their list of great leaders is slightly different: Dromichetes, Burebista, Decebalus, Mircea, Iancu, Stephen, Neagoe Basarab, Michael, Brîncoveanu, and Cuza.) All this only served to point towards Ceauşescu and "the age of dignity and the fulfillment of the great national ideals".[59]

The pantheon is expressed in a more succinct form by the painter Constantin Piliuţă, in his composition *The First President*. Ceauşescu, with scepter in hand, wearing a tricolor sash but with the Party emblem placed in front, appears against a background in which are represented Burebista, Mircea, Michael, Stephen, and Cuza. As we can see, and as in the preceding examples, only sovereigns are present!

For a complete and systematic illustration of the rating of personalities in the last years of the communist dictatorship, we need look no further than the sequence of busts lined up in front of the National Military Museum in Bucharest—an official and competent guide. Here is how the great figures of history are laid out: Dromichetes and Burebista; Decebalus and Trajan; Gelu, Glad and Menumorut; Basarab, Roland Borşa and Bogdan; Mircea the Old and Alexander the Good; Iancu of Hunedoara, Stephen the Great and Vlad Ţepeş; Michael the Brave; Dimitrie Cantemir, Constantin Brîncoveanu and Ferenc Rákóczi II; Horea, Cloşca and Crişan; Tudor Vladimirescu; Bălcescu and Avram Iancu; Kogălniceanu and Cuza.

The selection and grouping of the heroes invites commentary. I shall say no more about the Dacian sovereigns, whose rise in status I have already noted. However, the clever balance between the Romanian provinces is worth noting, with Transylvania situated, as a Romanian land, on the same level as the other two principalities. (In addition, the captions employ the terms: Romanian Land of Muntenia, Romanian Land of Moldavia, Romanian Land of Transylvania). Thanks to the trios of Gelu, Glad and Menumorut, and Horea, Cloşca and Crişan, the Transylvanian heroes are actually more numerous than those of Wallachia or Moldavia, illustrating the obsession with Transylvania and the Hungarophobia that became accentuated towards the end of the Ceauşescu era. Even the Hungarian princes of Transylvania are integrated into the Romanian schema. How many Romanians have heard of Roland Borşa, a Transylvania voivode of the late thirteenth century? Not only can they now hear of him, they can see him too, and even see him hurriedly integrated into the pantheon. Someone had to represent the "Romanian Land of Transylvania" alongside the founding princes Basarab and Bogdan. Like them, Roland becomes—the explanatory plaque informs us—the founder of a Transylvania fighting to win full independence from Hungary (after which it would probably have united with Wallachia and Moldavia... though these were unfortunately not yet in existence at the time).

Also worth noting is the absence of the traditional "couple" Matei Basarab and Vasile Lupu, their punishment, probably, for failing to understand the necessity of Romanian solidarity. The nineteenth-century selection is equally ideologically loaded, shifting the emphasis from "princes" to "revolutionaries", and not just any revolutionaries but the "official" ones: Bălcescu, Avram Iancu and Kogălniceanu.

But what is most striking here, as in any list of providential figures invoked in the Ceauşescu era, is the fact that their sequence closes with Cuza in 1866. Between Cuza and Ceauşescu there is an arid space, productive of secondary heroes but not of exponents of Romanian destiny or creators of history. This "desert" through which the Romanian nation has passed gives meaning to a messianic expectation, highlights the urgency of the saving act, and immeasurably amplifies the stature of the dictator, who becomes comparable not with the little people of his own time but with the heroes of old, those who are already the stuff of epic. Indeed, an express "recommendation" required that the historical portraits in public institutions should stop with Cuza.

A rich illustration of the differentiated treatment applied to the "great men" from one period to the next is provided by the collection *Historical Tales*, published in three volumes (1982–1984) by the prolific popularizer Dumitru Almaş. (This work is adorned with magnificent color illustrations, which are as useful as the text for the purposes of our investigation). The young readers are first presented with the millennial glory of the Dacians and then of the Romanians, though the personalities and faces of ancient kings and medieval voivodes. With the modern period a revolutionary transition takes place, bringing an exclusive concentration on Horea, Cloşca and Crişan, Tudor Vladimirescu, Bălcescu, Avram Iancu, and, of course, Cuza. Then history seems no longer to be made, or even symbolized, by great figures at all, but by heroes of the second or third rank, or even by ordinary characters "from the people", invented ad hoc to make up for the lack of great individuals. The attack on Pleven in 1877 is illustrated by the sacrifice of Majors Şonţu and Constantin Ene, and Captain Valter Mărăcineanu. Somebody seems to be missing; it is like talking about Vaslui without Stephen or Călugăreni without Michael! When we come to 1918, the event appears even more anonymous: the multitude gathers at Alba Iulia, but it is only a multitude with no names (while the large, double-page illustration that is placed before the children's eyes shows an indefinite figure at the rostrum, who does not resemble any of the Transylvanian politicians and churchmen who carried out the union). Socialist and communist leaders are completely eliminated too, for good measure. Only cultural figures seem to be admitted, figures who are, in any case, secondary in a politically oriented pantheon. The ground is thus prepared for an apotheotic finale: the last tales have Ceauşescu as hero, and he is presented in pictures too, alone or with his wife, against a background of the great achievements of socialism and surrounded by shining-faced workers or by an enthusiastic multitude.

Thus we can see the sense and limits of the return to the figures of the traditional pantheon, after the phase of rejection in the 1950s. Entry was refused to the dynasty and to the great "bourgeois" politicians. It is true that in the course of Ceauşescu's rule it is possible to detect a certain softening of judgement on the excluded personalities, in line with the general "improvement" of Romanian history. However, their "rehabilitation" was only relative and was limited to passing mentions in textbooks or to specialized texts for a more detailed treatment, not without often vehement notes of criticism.

In this way we may detect a certain recovery of Carol I. Of course, everything is relative; the first king of Romania enjoyed a truly favorable treatment around 1980 if we compare it with the insults directed at him around 1950. Above all, his role in 1877 is at least partially acknowledged, although this does not prevent the school textbook from accusing him of "betrayal" (regarding the events of 1870), and from referring to his "reactionary Prussian spirit".[60] (As a Catholic from the south of Germany, Carol's "Prussianism" is debatable!). When a historian wrote a book about the monarchy, it was not enough to include an abundance of severe judgements (such as Carol's enrichment by "exploiting the masses of working people") and to highlight the fervent republicanism of the Romanians: the book could not have on its cover or title page any reference to kings or to the dynasty; it was thus given the eloquent title *Contributions regarding political life in Romania: The evolution of the form of government in modern and contemporary history*.[61] The Brătianus and other prominent politicians are treated in a similar way. Some are looked on even more negatively, especially if they died in communist prisons, as Iuliu Maniu did. For this reason Maniu's role in 1918 was first refused and then minimized; since a symbolic figure had to be invoked, this had the effect of propelling Vasile Goldiş far above the others (as had happened, on a different scale, with Bălcescu for 1848). Towards the end of the period the assessment of Maniu was "softened", like almost everything else. The semi-rehabilitation of Antonescu, which I have already mentioned, was part of the same strategy involving the relative and discreet insertion of the great statesmen into the national history, but with a sufficiently modest weighting not to challenge the unique position of the Leader.

The communist heroes suffered, even more than in the time of Gheorghiu-Dej, from the hypertrophy of Ceauşescu's stature. Gheorghiu-Dej himself, to whom none of the promised statues were ever erected, fell rapidly and brutally. From the uncontested leader of Romanian communism he was drastically limited to the Griviţa episode of 1933. His place was hardly above that of an ordinary illegalist. Nor were critiques of the 1950s slow to appear, designed to emphasize Ceauşescu's "communism of humanity" by comparison with the less humane communism of his predecessor. The descent of Gheorghiu-Dej was accompanied by the ascent—prudently stopped before the summit—of Lucreţiu Pătrăşcanu who served to symbolize the national face of Romanian communism and to assist Ceauşescu in his settling of accounts with "Dej's people" and even with the memory of the late leader. There was a "Pătrăşcanu moment" around 1970, when the victim of Gheorghiu-Dej came near to overshadowing, to some extent, the glory of the leader who admitted no rival; the moment was rapidly left behind. The position of Petru Groza was more secure, perhaps due to the fact that he had never been more than a very valuable "fellow traveler" who was not implicated in the scandals of the Party hierarchy. Groza was also the beneficiary of one of the rare statues erected by the communists in memory of their own revolutionaries— it was pulled down at the same time as that of Lenin.

As the years passed, the illegalist heroes were left more and more in the shadows. The picturesque case of Vasile Roaită deserves a mention. At a certain point the teenage hero actually disappeared (his photograph was eliminated from the history textbooks). Rumors were not slow to spread: either there had never been a Roaită at Grivița in 1933, or the not-so-innocent little siren-sounder had actually been a Siguranță informer... Regardless of who Roaită was or was not, the reason for his disappearance could not be more obvious: the "boy hero" was now Ceaușescu himself, and there was no room for two! Indeed, Ceaușescu installed himself in the leading position in the communist movement which Gheorghiu-Dej had previously occupied. The only difficulty—but mythology does not recognize difficulties—lay in the fact that Gheorghiu-Dej had been an adult in the period of the "great struggles", while Ceaușescu was only a child or a teenager. All the same, it was possible to learn that he had begun his revolutionary career, provoking the amazement and admiration of others, at the age of fourteen or even earlier. More and more heroic communist deeds of the 1930s came to be attributed to him. Among them was the episode of 1 May 1939; the celebration on that occasion, which had actually been organized through the trade corporations by the royal dictatorship regime, was transformed into the greatest anti-fascist and anti-war demonstration in Europe, while its principal organizer became Ceaușescu, in close collaboration with his future wife. A photomontage was even put together in which the head of the future dictator appeared in the midst of the multitude, its somewhat unnatural position betraying a certain negligence in the faking of the image. A few more steps back in time and Ceaușescu could have shaken hands with Cuza, putting an end to the relative discontinuity in the recent history of Romania.

In an age almost empty of "heroic" substance, the only figure whom it was considered useful to make a myth of, around the end of the 1960s, was Nicolae Titulescu. Animated by an ideology of absolute values, the Titulescu myth, rather like the Bălcescu myth of the preceding period but on a smaller scale, served to eclipse or inculpate the other actors of the period in question, who were judged against the truth embodied in the mythologized figure. Uninvolved (at least in the mythological variant) in internal political conflicts; the promoter of an active European and world diplomacy, more in the spirit of a world power than that of a small or medium-sized state (and thus the precursor of Ceaușescu's planetary ambitions); the denouncer of fascist aggression, but moderate (not to say naive) in respect to communism, and in particular the Soviet Union, Titulescu offered a seductive array of qualities suitable for recuperation or myth making. But—not enough to make him the equal of Burebista, Cuza, or Ceaușescu!

With Ceauşescu everything seems lacking in proportion—his pretension to found a totally other Romania (going as far as the complete modification of the urban and rural landscape and even of geographical equilibria), concomitant with an obsessive reference to the great exponents of an immutable Romanian destiny, a confusing dialectic in which he *identified* with history at the same time as he tried to *cancel* it out. The discrepancies in his case are impressive—between the idealized past and the real present, or simply between the vulgarity of the presidential couple and the mythical figures invoked. The massive scale of the propaganda—the "brainwashing" by a torrent of pseudo-history which flooded Romanian consciousness—is also impressive.

But the mechanism itself is one that is well known. We have seen it with Gheorghiu-Dej, in spite of the reputation for wisdom and modesty which some want to weave around him. We have seen it with the kings of Romania, in a different context of course, maintaining a different sense of measure and referring to other real models, but no less faithful to the immutable rules of operation. Each time we find the twin hypostases, past and present, of the providential figure, the guarantor of social stability and the interests of the nation, its guide on the difficult road of history. The princes of olden times support the princes of today (a mythological continuity which becomes all the more necessary as the real society passes through phases of rupture). History is an instrument of power.

The concomitant personalization of the past and the present finds a favorable echo in Romanian opinion. In the end, it may be that the Romanians have not been, and are not, monarchists or republicans in reality. Many of them feel the need to put their trust in the "Person at the Top", regardless of name or title. This may be one key to the contradictory evolutions of Romanian politics over the past century.

CHAPTER SEVEN

After 1989

RUPTURE OR CONTINUITY?

The years that have passed since 1989 have seen a remarkable adaptation of historical and political mythology, and especially of the contemporary section of the national pantheon, to the political pluralism that was so vigorously affirmed after the collapse of communism. Political conflicts are extended into historical conflicts. Thus the spectacular confrontation between the two contradictory myths—King Michael and Marshal Antonescu—transposes into historical and mythological terms a fundamental fissure which divides the Romanian society of today.[1]

King Michael, who was driven out by the communists on 30 December 1947, has become a symbol for many upholders of anti-communism and democracy. He seems to be invested with the sacred mission of the savior ("Monarchy saves Romania!"), the one destined to bring the country back to the normal course of its history. The visit to Romania which he undertook on the occasion of Easter in April 1992 highlighted, both by the scale and fervor of the public manifestations and by the high symbolic and religious charge of the event, a quite remarkable degree of mythologizing of his person, function, and historical mission.[2]

The case of Marshal Antonescu is much more complicated. Having been considered in the early days of communism as a traitor to national interests and a war criminal, he underwent, as we have seen, a process of relative rehabilitation in proportion to the nationalist commitment of the communist regime and its separation from Moscow. After 1989 opinions could be expressed fully and freely. According to an opinion poll published in May 1995, some 62 percent of Romanians seem to have had a good opinion of the marshal (placing him above any other leader in the Second World War: Hitler enjoyed the favorable opinion of 2 percent, Stalin and Mussolini 5 percent, Churchill 26 percent, and Roosevelt 31 percent: the last two are paying, of course, for the "betrayal" of Yalta).[3] Those who appreciate Antonescu certainly include anti-communists (in line with the ideology expressed by the marshal), as well as people who simply want to restore a history which has long been obscured. The hard core of supporters, however, those who manifest their admiration vehemently and even aggressively, is made up—and this is the extraordinary paradox!—of the successors of those who sent the marshal before the firing squad in 1946. The former national-communists, those who launched the rehabilitation process before 1989, are now ostentatious admirers of the nationalist and authoritarian virtues of Antonescu. For *România Mare**, for example, Antonescu and Ceauşescu belong to the same sacred corps of "apostles of the Romanian people, who perished by violent deaths, sacrificed on the altar of the fatherland".[4]

The king/marshal antithesis is exacerbated by the latter's unconditional supporters. For them, King Michael was a traitor, as demonstrated by the fact that he was decorated by Stalin.[5] A high point of this denigration was the "documentary" montage shown on the official television channel, *in the name of the government*, on 30 December 1993, in which an idealized image of Antonescu as a fighter and martyr was contrasted with King Michael, pro-Soviet traitor and murderer! The posthumous role of Antonescu is multiple; he upholds authoritarian, autochthonist, and xenophobic tendencies (without anyone having sought his consent), and serves also as a powerful instrument against the king, who replaces the communists as the figure principally responsible for the marshal's execution.

The great political orientations cultivate their own heroes: the kings, the Brătianus or Iuliu Maniu. The last of these is joined by Corneliu Coposu, much wronged in his lifetime, whose death in 1995 produced, as if by magic, a moment of national solidarity, an exceptional mythical sequence to be explained, in as far as myth can be explained, by the "unreal" disinterestedness of the deceased in a world of petty interests.

Among the traditional heroes, Avram Iancu has seen a significant ascent in the context of the Romanian–Hungarian confrontations which have been carefully reanimated and sustained after 1989. (Internal difficulties and debatable government solutions call for an "other" to justify them.) In Cluj there has been an unprecedented war of the statues: Avram Iancu vs. Matthias Corvinus (the latter is threatened by the excavation of the presumed Roman forum, another symbol of Romanian-ness). The festivities in Ţebea in September 1996, organized against the background of the signing—at last!—of the Romanian–Hungarian treaty, gave rise to bitter polemics around Avram Iancu's grave; all sectors of the opposition denounced the official confiscation of the hero, while the diehards of the Party of National Unity accused their former government colleagues (who had decided in the meantime to play the European card) of betraying the national ideals symbolized by the great fighter of 1848.

However wide the current range of heroes and symbols, it is clear that *official discourse* (especially detectable in the frequent historical evocations on official television as well as in school textbooks) continues, and sometimes even amplifies,

---

* "Greater Romania", a weekly newspaper of extreme nationalist orientation, associated with a political party of the same name. *Trans.·*

the fundamental elements of pre-revolutionary discourse. Titulescu has never been invoked so frequently and so admiringly; his contemporaries, Brătainu and Maniu, not to mention King Ferdinand, have come out into the daylight again, but they remain in the background compared with the media attention given to the great personality of Romanian foreign policy. The case of Carol I is likewise significant: he seems to be the victim of an insoluble contradiction between the recognition of his historical dimension, which is hard to avoid (and which even the communism of the last decades partially accepted), and the fact that he symbolizes a monarchy that officialdom has no reason to present in too favorable a light. Rehabilitation in his case, as in that of Ferdinand, has stopped far short of the old dynastic myth, and Cuza remains unrivalled as the official emblematic figure of the making of modern Romania.[6]

A walk through the rooms of the Museum of National History in Bucharest illustrates the extent of resistance to change. Despite the years that have passed, everything looks just as it did before 1989; only the contemporary section (post-1918) has been closed, resolving any controversy for the time being, and a few cases have been added dealing with Kings Carol I and Ferdinand, Queen Marie, and Marshal Averescu. Otherwise there is not the slightest modification to a discourse structured in terms of class struggle (an incredibly long series of peasant uprisings) and of full unity from the earliest times.

A careful analysis of the official discourse reveals the persistence of deeply rooted isolationist attitudes beneath the apparent adherence to European values. The reconstruction of the past which continues to be practiced is one which amplifies autochthonous factors at the expense of European dynamics and influences. To give one example, in 1993 Romania joined the community of Francophone states, but no young Romanian could find out from their history textbook about the origins of this Francophony (which is relative, anyway). The "single" school textbooks published after 1989 (just like those published under communism, but in contrast to those in use before) avoid speaking about French influence, although in the nineteenth century this radically transformed Romanian culture, and even the Romanian language. Modernization is explained exclusively in terms of internal factors, which does not correspond to real history but corresponds very well to certain obsessions prior to 1989. A similar approach can be seen in the definition of medieval Romanian culture, where the Slav–Byzantine model fades in favor of a particular indigenous synthesis, seen as a bridge between East and West.

It is in the light of this continuation of the thread of pre-revolutionary mythology that we must understand the polemic surrounding P. P. Panaitescu's textbook *The History of the Romanians*, which was published before the installation of the communist regime and reintroduced in 1990 to replace the textbooks of the Ceaușescu period. It was withdrawn in the end in response to a wave of protests. Its incompatibility with recent research was the reason invoked, but the real motive was the *type of discourse*, which was quite different to that practiced by national-communist mythology. Although it was published in a period profoundly marked by patriotic spirit (the sixth edition, reproduced in 1990, dates from 1943, from the time of the war and of Antonescu), and although Panaitescu had let himself be seduced by the Legionary ideology (which could not be accused of a lack of nationalism!), the textbook is striking for its demythologizing attitude. The author situates the formation of the Romanian people on both sides of the Danube, draws attention to the Slav influence in the Middle Ages, treats Vlad Ţepeş as a degenerate, does not accept that Michael the Brave had a national consciousness, insists on the nineteenth-century French influence, and so on—all the points which we do not find in the new textbooks introduced in 1992 to 1993, which show an inclination to sacrifice critical spirit with ease in favor of autochthonism and the old mythical clichés.

ALWAYS UNITED?

Unity and *authority* are principles no less in circulation at present than before 1989. From Vlad Ţepeş to Antonescu, the gallery of authoritarian heroes is strongly highlighted. Due to tradition and custom, but also to insistent propaganda, the Romanians seem to be more attracted by symbols specific to national cohesion and authority than to those characteristic of democratic life. It is significant that, at least according to opinion polls (the accuracy of which I shall not discuss), by far the most respected institutions of the country are the army and the Church, with scores of 92 percent and 89 percent respectively in April 1996, compared with Parliament at the other extreme with only 28 percent.[7] This is not the place to discuss the merits, shortcomings, or share of blame of these institutions. The only thing that interests us here is the political imaginary, and from this point of view the orientation of the majority towards institutions which are not necessarily specific to democracy (even if they undoubtedly have their place in it) cannot fail to be striking, as is the massive rejection of the democratic institution par excellence, Parliament. Between pluralism and democracy on the one hand, and cohesion and order on the other, the majority seem inclined towards the latter values (or if they do not incline that way of their own accord, they are urged to do so).

    The return in force of the Church calls for comment. How many Romanians dared to declare themselves believers before 1989? How many dare to declare themselves atheists or skeptics today? The Orthodox Church is always involved in the ritual of historical commemorations; the system of *parastases* for the dead has become generalized, even extending to the commemoration of heroes who lived centuries ago. The canonization of Stephen the Great and Constantin Brîncoveanu in 1992 marked an important date in the process of joining national history with Orthodoxy. The canonization of Michael the Brave is under discussion too; indeed there is said to have been a miraculous apparition of his face (the commandant of the National Military Museum himself was among those who commented on the incident on television). Thus the pantheon and the

Church calendar are tending to fuse. Religious discourse about history is occupying the ground left free by the defunct totalitarian ideology. The involvement of Orthodoxy consolidates national historical values whose credibility was at risk of being affected by the depreciation of communist propaganda and the ideological confusion which followed. The somewhat summary identification of Romanianism with Orthodoxy (which is liable, in the end, to offend or marginalize Romanians of other confessions) seems today to be a privileged means of affirming national cohesion.

From the side of those in power, there can be heard a historical-political discourse which insistently sublimates the idea of national unity and even unanimity around certain values, political attitudes, and personalities. It is often stated that "in the great national problems the Romanians have always shown solidarity", a clever formula, seemingly hard for a true patriot to contest, but completely untrue! In the Middle Ages, as I have already shown, the Romanian principalities were often in confrontation. In the present century Romanian society has proved to be more often divided than united. A crucial decision, leading to the creation of Greater Romania, was the entry of Romania into the First World War in 1916, against the Central Powers. Contrary to the myth of a Romanian quasi-unanimity in the action aimed at liberating Transylvania, it can be observed that a far from negligible section of the political and intellectual elite were not in favor of this political orientation, while some voices were even raised decisively against it (even if all shared, though each in their own way, the "national ideal").[8] And what about the Second World War? Is it possible to claim that all Romanians were enthusiastically in favor of entering the war alongside Germany in 1941, and that again all Romanians, equally enthusiastically, were in favor of turning the guns against Germany in 1944? Then there is the installation of communism. Was it supported by all Romanians? Or did all Romanians fight against it? In fact, during the years of communism an older fracture line was deepened; the old elite was crushed, and a new elite rose from the lower layers of society. It was a process which divided Romania in two, so that we can talk today (in a political and cultural sense) of "two Romanias", just as there has been talk of "the two Frances" since the revolution of 1789.

Indeed, there is nothing particularly remarkable in all this. National unanimity is only a political myth, which has not existed and does not exist anywhere. Divergences appear, as it is only natural they should, in the *great problems*, not in the small ones. The world policy of the United States is the variable resultant of the permanent confrontation of isolationists and interventionists, two completely opposed ideologies. The Maastricht agreement, which sets out the future of the European nations, was ratified in some countries, by referendum, with a minimal majority (in France the "two Frances" again manifested themselves on this occasion, with percentages only slightly above and below 50 percent). We are duty-bound to recognize that Romania has no vocation to be any more unitary than other countries. I limit myself to two recent examples concerning foreign policy and European integration. In 1990, while the opposition staked everything on relations with the West, those in power, already rallying behind the slogan "We won't sell our country!", placed Romania in a singular position even among the former communist countries by hastening to sign a treaty with the Soviet Union, which they evidently expected to have a long life ahead of it! There followed a gradual Europeanization of the forces in power, which provoked dissension right at their heart. The Romanian–Hungarian treaty concluded in September 1996 proved once again that there is no such thing as unanimity; the nationalist parties, who had participated in government until a short time before, were strongly opposed to it.

The ideology of unanimity, illustrated with false historical examples, is no more than a strategy of government; in this way an authoritarian inclination, skillfully insinuated by the appeal to the past (a tactic more efficient than the explicit enunciation of the message), makes itself manifest in a society which affirms, or at least mimics, the values of democracy and pluralism.

THE METHODOLOGY OF FORGETTING

Another characteristic tendency, likewise noticeable in the official zone, is the *concealment of communism*. It might have been expected that historians would "dive" into this completely unexplored territory, which is more essential for the understanding of today's Romania than any other period or historical process. But this is not what happened. The majority of specialists in contemporary history— who represented the largest contingent of Romanian historians in 1989— preferred to "squeeze themselves" into the interwar period, a space of only two decades, or the Second World War, an even more restricted field but highly valorized mythologically speaking, through the contrasting images of Marshal Antonescu and King Michael. More recently, some progress has been made in research, but it remains slow and insufficient in relation to the scale and importance of the problem.

Thus it is that the most interesting contributions, particularly concerning communist repression, have come from non-specialists more than from historians in the universities and research institutes. We are indebted to those outside the nucleus of the profession for the collection and processing of oral information,[9] while for the typical Romanian historian the oral enquiry remains an exotic procedure. The historical professionals continue to give a higher level of credibility to written documents than to the living people who have experienced the history in question. This methodological backwardness intersects with an ideological reasoning. It is not a good idea to write about communism—according to a widespread opinion—first of all because we lack information, and second because we do not have the necessary perspective and risk being subjective. Our descendants and our descendants' descendants will write about it. The systematic evasion of the subject is evident. (It is interesting that for the same category of historians this timidity in research does not apply where Bessarabia is concerned;

in this case there is no problem in going right up to 1989. The difference is that there it is a matter of denouncing Soviet communism, while back here it is the Romanian variety that would have to be denounced.)

As usual the school textbook, especially when it is official and unique, says all there is to say. We are offered—in 1992—*ten pages* on the *half century of communism*, a pallid and ambiguous résumé, compared with over a hundred pages devoted to the quarter century of interwar Romania and the Second World War.[10] The literature textbook proceeds in the same spirit, and indeed goes even further; it generally makes abstraction of communism in the name of the "autonomy of the aesthetic".[11] Who would dare to interpret Dante, Shakespeare, or Balzac outside their ages? It seems that only Romanian writers transcend their terrestrial condition and rise into the absolute sphere of art. The authors of the world history textbook take an even more radical initiative: they quite simply evacuate Marx and Engels from history, along with the whole socialist and communist ideology and movement,[12] at the risk that pupils will understand nothing of the evolution of the last two centuries and, above all, of the period through which we have all lived.

If the textbooks say little about communism in general, about the anti-communist struggle they tell the pupils next to nothing. At least here something could have been learnt from the communists themselves: out of much less they managed to put together a whole series of heroic episodes and "illegalist" heroes. Opposition to communism could have found its exemplary deeds and its heroes too. Peasants killed because they defended their land (certainly more than in 1907, a year which continues to be invoked along with its false death toll of 11,000 victims—at least ten times the true figure); resistance fighters in the mountains (still not rehabilitated by post-revolutionary justice); intellectuals, priests, and politicians who died in prison: the material for a new mythology abounds, but it is almost completely ignored in the official discourse and the history proposed to the young generation.

The present political (and to some extent intellectual) elite was formed in the years of communism. It would not have existed without communism. That is a fact, not a value judgement. It is a fact which explains the reticence which I have mentioned. On top of this there is the need for legitimization, characteristic of any regime, but even more of a regime installed as a result of an overthrow. And legitimization, as we have seen, always presupposes insertion in history. The Romania of today, its people, its institutions and its realities, inevitably have their origins to a greater extent in those fifty years of communism than in the previous history of the country. However, ideologically and mythologically speaking, reference could not be made to a communism that has been overthrown and discredited. It is made to earlier traditions, and especially to the Greater Romania of the interwar period (with less emphasis on what is not convenient, that is to say, *monarchy*).

It is thus curious, but also understandable (and perhaps even laudable, in as much as the procedure illustrates a real will to normalize things), that the army is retying the threads, brutally cut in the post-war years, which bind it to the old Romanian army, while the S.R.I.* invokes the previously much abused Siguranţă, even if it is no secret that a good part of its staff come not from the Siguranţă but from the Securitate. It is the same with the press—a whole series of publications that have appeared since 1989 have borrowed old titles, letting it be understood that with the title they have also obtained a certificate of experience. What more can I say? Romania is the only ex-communist country where the Communist Party has vanished into thin air, where former communist activists remain in power (again a unique case) without having anything to do with a party which no longer exists, and, if it does not exist, almost seems never to have existed.

This is the direction in which we are being urged to go in the end: towards *forgetting*. Communism did not exist! Or at least we have to behave as if it never existed.

There is also another strategy, complementary to forgetting. It can be summed up in the words: "Still, something was achieved." Communism was as it was, but people still worked and created. Such a line of argument—which is indeed true—has the virtue of diverting those who are less skillful in the tricks of dialectic. Any measuring of "achievements" ought to be based on an overall and comparative view. The Danaids, too, worked in their day, perhaps even more than the Romanians. According to this sort of judgement we should appreciate the achievements of Hitler: the greatest motorway network in Europe, the eradication of unemployment... In fact, Romania nowadays is on the margins of Europe from all points of view. While in the West even an isolated house in the mountains will have electricity and running water, in Romania, at the end of intense communist industrialization, hundreds of villages remain without electricity and the network of sewage disposal does not even cover the whole of the capital city. Let no one say this is all just the result of a centuries-old delay. Until a few decades ago there were backward areas—at a similar level to the Romanian villages—in the West too; today they no longer exist. On the eve of the Second World War the ratio of the gross national product per head of population of the most developed countries to that of Romania was no more than three to one. Today, even an estimate of ten to one would be too small. Greece was then at about the same level as Romania; now its performance is several times better. And I have only underlined the strictly material dimension of the problem, which is perhaps less serious than the complete disruption of social structures and mechanisms.

No field escaped the ill-boding impact of an oppressive and deforming system. We like to make much of the literary effervescence of the period—and with some justice. However, literary production swung between adherence (more or less nuanced, more or less transfigured) to the communist project, and escape from reality. With the exception of some subtle games, *à clef*, it did not speak to people about the real preoccupations of the time. The lack of a European audience (which the Romanians felt as an injustice) has its fundamental explanation in this

---

* *Serviciul Român de Informaţii* (Romanian Information Service). *Trans.*

sort of opting out. As for historiography, the contributions were numerous and sometimes interesting, but they did not change the overall fact that, while the little historical school of around 1900 was perfectly synchronous with the European phenomenon, today, regardless of individual merits, the conceptual and methodological discrepancies could not be more evident. (A factual-descriptive and romantic-nationalist line of thought is prolonged here, which no longer carries weight in the West, at least in the university environment.)

People did create sometimes, in spite of communism, as much as they could. But let us not imagine that they could create outside communism, as if the system were just a simple façade, an innocent unleashing of Romanian folklore.

THE FREEDOM TO SAY ANYTHING

In some respects we can observe today the exacerbation of certain themes dear to the national-communist ideology. The explanation is simple: Liberty. Communism did not allow complete freedom even to its own inventions. Initiative, originality, and humor were not its characteristics. Sobriety and boredom seemed indispensable. Moreover, even if Marx had been left far behind, his judgements could not be explicitly contradicted. The forms, at least, had to be saved. Now there is nothing to save.

As we have seen, the Dacians had come right into the heart of the national-communist system. Burebista's Dacia was essentially Ceauşescu's Romania. The present discourse continues—in its dominant autochthonist note—to maintain a certain priority for the Dacian factor in relation with the Roman. But such an interpretation seems almost balanced in comparison with what is going on in the area of extremist Dacianism. In the best tradition of Densuşianu and the Institute of History of the Party, the Dacians are now invading the market with the most varied and ingenious solutions, all of which promote the idea of Romanian anteriority and excellence. At a time when Europe looks at us with suspicion and keeps us outside the door, it can be truly tonic to note that the Romanians, through their ancient ancestors, are at the origins of European civilization. We are not at the margin, but right at the center of the world, and if the others do not see things that way, then the loss is theirs, not ours.

Even more remarkable is the literary phenomenon which goes by the name of Pavel Coruţ: a high-ranking counter-information officer before 1989, today the prolific author of little novels which a large public can never get enough of, based around an actualized Dacian mythology in which Zalmoxis rubs shoulders with the Securitate agent. Trans-historical autochthonism, political–religious fundamentalism, demonization of the foreigner who is ever plotting against the Romanian nation, whence the need for vigilance and for a powerful state—this is the ideological substratum of a literature which prolongs in a new, and ultimately more subtle, manner the manipulation formerly practiced by the Securitate.[13] It was a curious political police, this Securitate, haunted by Dacian phantasms and consequently capable of judging as suspect any less orthodox opinion about the ancestors; indeed the paradox can be explained by the historical–political amalgam specific to the Ceauşescu period, which the Romanians have not completely cast off.

The same bursting of the floodgates can be observed too in the obsessive—for the Romanians—definition of the *national fact*. The "nation" is one of those elastic historical concepts (which ultimately make a rigorous and universal historical terminology impossible), applicable to a number of very different realities; as I have already said, the only clear concept with which it is possible to operate remains that of the "nation-state". Otherwise there is nothing to prevent historians from applying the term to whatever context they like. The problem is not the word in itself, but what is sought by using it. And what is sought is evidently the highlighting of a *national type of unity*, characteristic of Romanian history from the remotest beginnings.

A historian much involved in this sort of trans-historical meditation maintains that, as a result of his defense of such a point of view, he had to face all sorts of unpleasantness in his professional life before 1989.[14] Here it is necessary to make the distinction, essential in the communist ideological game, between substance and form. In pure Marxist–Stalinist orthodoxy, the nation had to be defined as a historical phenomenon of relatively recent date. But if we consider the substance of the issue, even if the use of the term was avoided, in Ceauşescu's time "national unity" extended over the whole of Romanian space and historical time. It would have been an ideological heresy to say that Burebista had headed a national state. But it would have been an even more serious political heresy to present Burebista as a conqueror who brought together territories lacking in cohesion and populations little animated by the awareness of a common destiny. It is not the terms that interest us here, but the substance. And the substance of the ethnically homogeneous, "unitary" and "centralized" state of the Dacian king is the same as that of today's national state.

What has intervened in interpretations of this sort since 1989 is the evacuation of the previous Marxist or Stalinist jargon, and, of course, the freedom of historians (not to mention the ever larger category of amateurs) to argue in whatever terms suit them. Thus we have a "Dacian nation", but, once again, this changes nothing essential in the configuration of the myth of unity, which was fully crystallized before 1989.

A MOMENT WHICH WE MUST GET BEHIND US:
MYTHOLOGICAL BLOCKAGE

The Romanian society of today is animated by powerful mythical pulsations. Out of a complex mythological constellation Raoul Girardet has isolated four fundamental political myths characteristic of the contemporary world: Conspiracy, the Savior, the Golden Age, and Unity.[15] Romania appears at present to be an ideal laboratory where these meet, interweave, and split into countless variants.

Examples are readily at hand. About *unity*, so often invoked, I shall say no more. *Conspiracy* brings onto the stage a multitude of actors, who can be used by all political orientations: the invisible (and surely non-existent) terrorists of December 1989, the "hooligans" of the demonstrations in University Square and those manipulating them from the shadows, the ever-present former Securitate, the Hungarians, of course, the king and the landlords, the great powers, Yalta and Malta, the CIA and the KGB... In such a confused context the *Savior* becomes a necessity. The archetype is a single one, but its faces are very diverse. Ultimately each Romanian has his or her own Savior: President Iliescu, potential presidents Emil Constantinescu or Petre Roman, King Michael... It is interesting to observe how the presidential function, the attributes of which are relatively wide ranging but limited by the constitution, is reserved in the public imaginary for a Savior capable of resolving by his own will and power the serious problems facing today's Romania.

Just as everyone has their own Savior, and their own conspirators, and their own meaning for unity, so everyone stubbornly directs their gaze towards the *Golden Age* which suits them. For many this is interwar Romania, Greater Romania, prosperous and democratic; although it only lasted two decades it seems to be the model in relation to which previous and subsequent history is judged— including the issue of territorial extension. The same Romania understandably offers a powerful argument for the partisans of the idea of monarchy. Others prefer to go back further into the past, in which case the Golden Age merges with the primordial time of the Geto–Dacians, the time when the center of the world was *here*. Others, certainly more numerous than those who dare to admit, are content in their hearts with the Golden Age of communism; those who did not like Ceauşescu can invoke Gheorghiu-Dej, and vice versa. Through the game of alternating these two leaders they hope to save at least part of the communist memory. Thus against the background of an imaginary age without cares, when the cost of living was low and life was without surprises (except for the surprises reserved by the apparatus of repression), we see the outline of an attempt to remake the myth of Gheorghiu-Dej, seen as a great politician and a great patriot, who freed the country of Soviet troops and whom only death prevented from setting Romania on the road to democracy and prosperity.[16] Of course good things can be heard about Ceauşescu too. In fact the Romanian society of today is divided into those who profited from communism, or who imagine that they profited (which is the same thing), and those who lost or consider that their lives would have been better without communism.

History has always been an instrument of power too. Whoever controls the past has good chance of also controlling the present. Since 1989 the conditioning of public opinion through history has proved to be a constant part of the strategy of those in power, a method which is all the more clever as most people do not even notice it. Civil society has to learn to defend itself from "intoxication" by history. Civic education presupposes not only the traditional heroic type of valorization of the events of national history, the virtues of which for a sense of identity I do not contest; it also presupposes the critical and responsible acceptance of the past, as well as skill in "decoding" the historical message, which, like any message, is aimed at "something".

It is clear that the Romanians easily allow themselves to be subjugated by history, or rather by the mythologies constructed upon history. A divided society is reflected in divergent reference points, which, by the characteristic power of the imaginary, only serve in their turn to deepen the divisions. The solution is not to forget history, which would not be possible, let alone desirable, but to attenuate it and modify the criteria of selection. The great decisions which Romanian society has to take today represent a break with the past, with any past. The challenge of modernity and European integration cannot be referred to a mythology with traditionalist emphases. The dominant note of the Romanian historical imaginary still remains autochthonist and authoritarian, while the world towards which we are heading is structured around democratic and European values. It remains to be seen how far the mythological blockage will continue to affect the process of integration and modernization (which it has already delayed), and, conversely, how this process will ultimately lead to a more or less radical re-elaboration of the national mythology.

Note: It should be clear that the political references in this chapter relate to the situation prior to the elections of November 1996. *L.B.*

Conclusion

We have now reached the end of this attempted decoding of a number of mythical structures which are powerfully imprinted in modern Romanian culture. I do not propose to identify alternative solutions which might be more "true" than those I have discussed. Even if, finding myself faced with fabrications or extreme distortions, I have on occasion felt the need to make my own point of view clear, the essence of my argument concerns not History but the historical discourse and its inevitable ideological and mythological charge. Even a completely different type of discourse would have invited a similar approach. History can break loose neither from the constraining structures of the imaginary nor from the equally constraining imperatives of the present. From the perspective of my project it has been used as a source for the present, a disguised source (dressed up as objective truths), but no less eloquent for all that.

The present problem of Romanian society does not lie in the mere fact of implication in the game of the historical imaginary. The figures of this historical imaginary, though adapted to the local climate, are far from being unique. There is no society without foundation myths,[1] heroes, or symbols of unity. The problem is that the way in which the structures of the historical imagination take shape among us today is highly "out of step" with Western European culture and mentality. Communism took over and exacerbated a nineteenth-century mythology, which it then left to us as an inheritance.

Public opinion only knows the accepted "vulgate" of history (if it knows even that). But even in professional circles it is proving hard to break with old clichés. The official discourse only serves to complicate things, in as much as it can be felt to be served by a nationalist, unanimist, and authoritarian interpretation of the events of the past. The hostile reception of the volume *Romanian Historical Myths* (which appeared under my direction in 1995) seems to me to be eloquent; it was attacked virulently for the simple reason that it proposed a critical interpretation of the historical discourse in place of the endless and always self-equivalent "patriotic" litany. On the national television channel one vigilant historian did not miss the occasion to denounce a "Masonic plot", while an autochthonist sociologist launched an unusual summons to scholars to align themselves with an apparently infallible popular intuition, and a military man did not hesitate to enrich the already broad palette of our original democracy with the supposed mission of the army to defend, in peacetime, the values of national history. Various critics even asked the question (habitual in the years of communism), "Whom does such an approach serve?"—in the understanding that it served the "others"

(Hungarians, CIA, KGB, Freemasons, etc.). Whom it serves—apart from the far from unimportant fact that it serves the truth and the standards of a profession—I can say without hesitation: it serves Romania. Jingoistic speeches are, at the most, for "internal use only", if anyone still hopes that in this way they can cover the lamentable state in which Romanian society finds itself. But they are of no use outside. On the contrary, it is precisely this sort of discourse which discredits one nowadays. In history, as in any other field, you must have something to offer your own time and you must speak the same language as your interlocutors. If not, you are out of the discussion, however patriotic your intentions. Nowadays, patriotism in history means rebuilding a historical school of European standard, such as we had in the first part of the century. It is not an improved and amplified version of the events of the past that will promote us in the world, but our own quality as historians, as people capable of intelligently discussing the problems that are discussed *today*.

It is clear that the Europe in which we want to be integrated is not being constructed on the basis of nationalism and autochthonism, but by leaving behind these states of mind. Nationalism had its constructive aspect, which was called for in a certain phase of historical evolution. It is by virtue of it that the modern nations, the national states, coalesced. But the same nationalism—and no other—has stained Europe with blood for two centuries. There is not a good nationalism and a bad nationalism; there is simply nationalism, with all the manifestations that follow from its premises. Today we have to choose. "Le nationalisme, c'est la guerre"—François Mitterand's words on his departure from the political stage perfectly define the historical moment at which we find ourselves. And the symbolic illustration that a history of confrontation has been left behind is offered by the image of President Mitterand and Chancellor Kohl, hand in hand on the battlefield of Verdun. It is the starting point of a new mythology, in any case an overturning of the old one; a "place of memory" invested with a strong conflictual significance becomes a symbol of rediscovery within the same space of civilization.

If nationalism means the acceptance of inextricable conflicts, autochthonism, its privileged variant in the Romanian environment, leads in a no less worrying direction. Nationalism implies the affirmation of primacy over the others. Autochthonism almost ends up ignoring them, sinking into a world of its own, practically out of history.

Neither confrontation nor isolationism are acceptable solutions. We know that only too well, but it seems that history drags us back. Not real history, but the history we imagine. This history, in which the Romanians are different from the others and subject to persecution by the others, a paradoxical combination of illusory superiority with an obsessive complex of inferiority, illustrates a state of mind which is inappropriate to our time. Insistent actualization of a glorified past and abandonment in its trap perpetuate confrontation in relation to others and immobility in relation to ourselves. We do not need to wipe the battlefields from our memory. But perhaps we can succeed, as the French and Germans have succeeded, in giving them a new significance.

March–October 1996

Notes

Three Years on: an Introduction to the Second Romanian Edition

. Simion, Eugen. "Mit, mitizare şi demitizare" (Myth, mythologizing, and demythologizing). *Curentul* (22 July 1999).

. Boia, Lucian. *Jocul cu trecutul. Istoria între adevăr şi ficţiune.* Bucharest: Humanitas, 1998.

. Ştefănescu, Alex. "O jucărie la modă: demitizarea". *România Literară* (21–27 October 1998).

. For the demythologizing of the poet, see the highly controversial issue of the weekly paper *Dilema* (27 February–5 March 1998); and for the upholding of the myth, see the investigation in *Caiete critice* 5–8 (1998), under the title "Eminescu—un model depăşit?" (Eminescu—an outdated model?).

. An interesting collection of articles on this theme can be found in *Dilema* (27 November–3 December 1998): "Vîrsta de aur dintre cele două războaie" (The golden age between the two wars).

. These strongly traditional features of a society still insufficiently in gear with modernity are illustrated by the numerous statistics assembled in the chapter on the Romanian population in *Enciclopedia României* (The Encyclopedia of Romania). Vol. 1. Bucharest, 1938, 134–160.

. Barbu, Daniel. "Destinul colectiv, servitutea involuntară, nefericirea totalitară: trei mituri ale comunismului românesc" (Collective destiny, involuntary servitude, totalitarian unhappiness: Three myths of Romanian communism). *Miturile comunismului românesc.* Under the direction of Lucian Boia. Bucharest: Nemira, 1998, 175–197.

Boia, Lucian. "Sîntem o naţiune, nu o naţiune ortodoxă" (We are a nation, not an Orthodox nation). *Curentul* (24 February 1999).

Boia, Lucian. "'Ameninţarea' federalistă" (The federalist "threat"). *Curentul* (21 December 1998).

). Vulpe, Alexandru. "Geto–Dacii?". *CICSA* 1–2 (1998): 2–11.

. Pop, Ioan-Aurel. *Naţiunea română medievală. Solidarităţi etnice româneşti în secolele XIII-XVI.* Bucharest: Editura Enciclopedică, 1998, 145.

2. *Ibid.*, 72–73 (my emphases).

. *Ibid.*, 141–142.

. Boia, Lucian. *Două secole de mitologie naţională.* Bucharest: Humanitas, 1999.

. Published in the magazine *Oameni în Top* 1 (June 1999): 13.

. *Oameni în Top* 4 (October 1999): 93–97.

. Regarding the present-day individuality and possible future autonomy of Transylvania see Gabriel Andreescu and Gusztáv Molnár, ed. *Problema transilvană* (The Transylvanian problem). Iaşi: Polirom, 1999. Gusztáv Molnár maintains that Transylvania belongs to the "other Europe" (that of "Western Christianity", Catholic and Protestant), and as such is clearly distinguished from the "Old Kingdom" of Romania. Sorin Mitu, in his article "Transylvanian Illusions and Realities", underlines the mythic charge of such a

"Transylvanian entity": Romanians and Hungarians in Transylvania have never had a common project of autonomy, and indeed Transylvania has ended up very similar to the rest of Romania. I would like to add the following observation concerning the religious aspect of the problem: from 1700 to 1948, the Orthodox were in the minority in Transylvania (as many of the Romanians were Uniate); nowadays three-quarters of the population of Transylvania is not only Romanian but also Orthodox!

Chapter One: History, Ideology, Mythology

1   Cazimir, Ştefan. *Alfabetul de tranziţie* (The alphabet of transition). Bucharest: Cartea Românească, 1986.

2. For the somewhat less than bourgeois ideology of the nascent Romanian middle class, see Boia, Lucian. "Réception et déformation: La Révolution française dans la chronique de Dionisie l'Ecclésiarque" (Reception and deformation: The French Revolution in the chronicle of Dionisie the Ecclesiarch). In *La Révolution française et les Roumains* (The French Revolution and the Romanians). Bicentenary studies, ed. Al. Zub. Iaşi, 1989, 279–284.

3. Lovinescu, E. *Istoria civilizaţiei române moderne* (The history of modern Romanian civilization). 3 vols. Bucharest: Ancora, 1924–25; Zeletin, Ştefan. *Burghezia română. Originea şi rolul ei istoric* (The Romanian bourgeoisie: Its origin and historical role). Bucharest: Cultura Naţională, 1925.

4. *Enciclopedia română* (The Romanian encyclopedia). Ed. C. Diaconovici. Vol. 3. Sibiu, 1904, 810 ("România"); Vol. 2, 1900, 762 ("Iaşi"); Vol. I, 1898, 606 ("Bucureşti").

5. The phenomenon of the "refusal of capitalism" in Romanian culture is analysed by Ştefan Zeletin in the chapter "Valoarea şi sensul culturii române reacţionare" (The value and sense of reactionary Romanian culture) in op. cit., 244–255. Similar considerations can be found in Ioan Petru Culianu, who discusses the anti-capitalist mentality of Orthodoxy in contrast to the capitalist spirit of the Protestant ethic (according to Max Weber's thesis). See his essay "Mircea Eliade necunoscutul" (Mircea Eliade the unknown). In *Mircea Eliade.* Bucharest: Nemira, 1995. In the chapter "Enemies of capitalism" (pp. 169–174) he concludes that: "In Romania, at the beginning of the twentieth century, there were no friends of capitalism, other than the capitalists themselves."

6. Georgescu, Vlad. *Mémoires et projets de réforme dans les principautés roumaines (1769–1830)* (Memoranda and projects of reform in the Romanian principalities, 1769–1830). Bucharest, 1970, 170; *Mémoires et projets de réforme dans les principautés roumaines (1831–1848).* Bucharest, 1972, 185.

7. Panu, G. *Amintiri de la "Junimea" din Iaşi* (Recollections of the "Junimea" of Iaşi). Vol. 1. Bucharest: Editura Remus Cioflec, 1942, 99–100.

8. For more on the myth of Michael the Brave, see the following articles by Mirela Luminiţa Murgescu: "Figura lui Mihai Viteazul în viziunea elitelor şi în literatura didactică (1830–1860)" (The figure of Michael the Brave in the vision of the elites and in didactic literature 1830–1860). *Revista istorică* 5–6 (1993): 539–550; "Mythistory in Elementary School: Michael the Brave in Romanian Textbooks (1830–1918)." *Analele Universităţii Bucureşti, Istorie* (1993–1994): 53–66; "Trecutul între cunoaştere şi cultul eroilor patriei. Figura lui Mihai Viteazul în manualele şcolare de istorie (1831–1994)" (The past between knowledge and the cult of the heroes of the country: The figure of Michael the Brave in school history textbooks, 1831–1994). *Mituri istorice româneşti* (Romanian historical myths). Under the direction of Lucian Boia. Bucharest: Editura Universităţii Bucureşti, 1995, 42–71.

9. Costin, Miron. *Opere* (Works). Ed. P. P. Panaitescu. Vol. 1. Bucharest: Editura pentru Literatură, 1965, 15–21.

10. *Cronicari munteni* (Muntenian chroniclers). Vol. 1. Bucharest: Editura pentru Literatură, 1961, 329.

11. Micu, Samuil. *Scurtă cunoştinţă a istoriei românilor.* Bucharest: Editura Ştiinţifică, 1963, 112; the same idea is developed by Micu in *Istoria şi lucurile şi întîmplările românilor* (History and matters and events of the Romanians), recently published as *Istoria românilor* (History of the Romanians). Ed. Ioan Chrindriş. Vol. 1. Bucharest: Editura Viitorul Românesc, 1995, 97.

12. Kogălniceanu, Mihail. *Historie de la Valachie, de la Moldavie et des Valaques transdanubiens* (History of Wallachia, Moldavia, and the Transdanubian Vlachs). Reprinted in *Opere.* Vol 2. Scrieri istorice (Historical writings). Ed. Al. Zub. Bucharest: Editura Academiei, 1976, 177, 184.

13. Bălcescu, Nicolae. *Românii supt Mihai Voevod Viteazul.* Reprinted in *Opere.* Vol. 3. Ed. Daniela Poenaru. Bucharest: Editura Academiei, 1986, 165, 197, 265.

14. Bălcescu, Nicolae. *Despre starea socială a muncitorilor plugari în principatele române în deosebite timpuri* (On the social status of the workers of the land in the Romanian principalities in various periods). Reprinted in *Opere.* Vol. 2. Ed. G. Zane. Bucharest: Editura Academiei, 1986, 151–162.

15. Heliade Rădulescu, Ion. *Echilibrul între antiteze* (Equilibrium between antitheses). Vol. 1. Bucharest: Editura Minerva, 1916, 85, 133.

16. Catargiu, Barbu. *Discursuri parlamentare* (1859–1862) (Parliamentary speeches, 1859–1862). Bucharest: Editura Minerva, 1914, 152–153, 220, 342.

17. On Russo's "Cîntarea României", see G. Zane's comments in N. Bălcescu. *Opere.* Vol. 2, 231–237.

18. Brătianu, Ion C. *Acte şi cuvîntări* (Documents and speeches). Vol. 1, part 1. Bucharest: Editura Cartea Românească, 1938, 21-22.

19. *Ibid.,* 161–162.

20. *Ibid.* Vol. 8, 1941, 163–164.

21. *Ibid.* Vol. 8, 178.

22. *Ibid.* Vol. 4, 1932, 31.

23. *Ibid.* Vol. 8, 213.

24. For the content and historical exploitation of the Chronicle of Huru, see Asachi, G. *Nouvelles historiques de la Moldo-Roumanie* (Historical tales from Moldo-Romania). Iaşi, 1859; and Heliade Rădulescu, Ion. *Elemente de istoria românilor* (Elements of the history of the Romanians). Bucharest, 1860 and 1869. Supplementary information on the controversy can be found in Zub, Al. *Mihail Kogălniceanu istoric* (Mihail Kogălniceanu historian). Iaşi: Editura Junimea, 1974, 749–752; and in Ştefan Gorovei's afterword and notes to Constandin Sion's *Arhondologia Moldovei.* Bucharest: Editura Minerva, 1973.

25. Heliade Rădulescu, Ion. *Echilibrul între antiteze.* Vol. 2, 52.

26. Kogălniceanu, Mihail. *Fragments tirés des chroniques moldaves et valaques* (Fragments drawn from the Moldavian and Wallachian chronicles). *Opere.* Vol. 2, 415–416.

27. Bălcescu, Nicolae. *Puterea armată şi arta militară de la întemeierea principatului Valahiei pînă acum.* Opere. Vol. 2, 50, 61.

28. Zub, Al. *op. cit.,* 751–752.

29. Hasdeu, B. P. *Scrieri literare, morale şi politice* (Literary, moral and political writings). Ed. Mircea Eliade. Vol. 2. Bucharest, 1937, 164 (an article originally published in *Românul,* 11 January 1868).

30. Maiorescu, Titu. "În contra direcţiei de astăzi în cultura română". *Critice* (Critical writings). Vol. 1. Bucharest: Minerva, 1908, 150–151.

31. *Ibid.* Vol. 2, 236.

32. *Ibid.* Vol. 1, 125.

33. *Ibid.* Vol. 1, 128–129.

34. Panu, George. "Studii asupra atîrnării sau neatîrnării politice a românilor în deosebite secole". *Convorbiri literare* (1872): 151–157, 193–203, 233–248, 262–272, 309–319.

35. Murărașu, Dumitru. *Naționalismul lui Eminescu* (Eminescu's nationalism). 1934. Bucharest: Editura Pacifica, 1994, 79.
36. Maiorescu, Titu. *op. cit.* Vol. 2, 224.
37. For Eminescu's nationalist doctrine, see Murărașu, Dumitru. *op. cit.*
38. Maiorescu, Titu. *op. cit.* Vol. 1, 152–153.
39. Iorga, N. *Lupta pentru limba românească* (The struggle for the Romanian language). Bucharest, 1906, 41–42, 52.
40. Iorga, N. "Două concepții istorice" (Two historical conceptions). In *Generalități cu privire la studiile istorice* (Generalities concerning historical studies). Bucharest: Imprimeria Națională, 1944, 98.
41. Iorga, N. *Istoria poporului românesc* (The history of the Romanian people). Vol. 1. Bucharest: Editura "Casei Școalelor", 1922, 9 (originally published as *Geschichte des Rumänischen Volkes*. Gotha, 1905).
42. *Ibid.* Vol. 2, 112.
43. Pârvan, Vasile. *Getica. O protoistorie a Daciei* (Getica: A protohistory of Dacia). Bucharest: Cultura Națională, 1926, 173.
44. Giurescu, Constantin C. *O nouă sinteză a trecutului nostru.* Bucharest: Editura Cartea Românească, extract from *Revista istorică română* (1931–32): 23.
45. Panaitescu, P. P. *Mihai Viteazul.* Bucharest: Fundația "Regele Carol I", 1936, 85–86.
46. "Cuvînt înainte" (Foreword). *Revista istorică română* 1 (1931): 4.
47. Giurescu, C. C. *Pentru "vechea școală" de istorie. Răspuns dlui N. Iorga.* Bucharest, 1937, 47–61.
48. Giurescu, C. C. *Istoria românilor.* Vol. 2, part 1. 4th edition. Bucharest: Fundația Regală pentru Literatură și Artă, 1943, 258.
49. Giurescu, C. C. *Istoria românilor. Din cele mai vechi timpuri pînă la moartea regelui Ferdinand I* (The history of the Romanians from the earliest times to the death of King Ferdinand I). Bucharest: Editura Cugetarea–Georgescu Delafras, 1943, 6.
50. P. P. Panaitescu's historical conception is concentrated in his collection *Interpretări românești* (Romanian interpretations). 1947 New edition. Bucharest: Editura Enciclopedică, 1994; and in his school textbook *Istoria românilor*, which has gone through many editions (most recently Bucharest: Editura Didactică și Pedagogică, 1990).
51. Panaitescu, P. P. "Noi suntem de aici" (We are from here); and "Închinare" (Worship). *Cuvîntul* (20 and 30 November 1940). See also Ciaușu, Milviuța. "Panteonul mișcării legionare" (The pantheon of the Legionary movement) in *Mituri istorice românești*, 199–219.
52. For the historical discourse of the communist period in general, see Georgescu, Vlad. *Politică și istorie. Cazul comuniștilor români. 1944–1977* (Politics and history: The case of the Romanian communists, 1944–1977). Edition prepared by Radu Popa. Bucharest: Humanitas, 1991.
53. Roller, Mihail, ed. *Istoria R.P.R.* Bucharest, 1952 edition, 373.
54. *Ibid.*, 525–529.
55. For details on the canonizations, see Păcurariu, Mircea. *Sfinți daco-romani și români* (Daco-Roman and Romanian saints). Iași: Editura Mitropoliei Moldovei și Bucovinei, 1994.
56. Boia, Lucian. *La mythologie scientifique du communisme* (The scientific mythology of communism). Caen: Paradigme, 1993, 85–87.
57. Lovinescu, E. *Istoria civilizației române moderne.* Ed. Z. Ornea. Bucharest: Editura Științifică 1972, 37.
58. Petric, Aron and Gh. I. Ioniță, *Istoria contemporană a României* (The contemporary history of Romania). 10th grade textbook. Bucharest: Editura Didactică și Pedagogică, 1989 edition, 68.
59. For the interwar period (treated favorably in general), the standard work is that of the official historians Mircea Mușat and Ion Ardeleanu. *România după Marea Unire* (Romani

after the Great Union). 2 vols. (1918–1933 and 1933–1940). Bucharest: Editură Științifică și Enciclopedică, 1983–1988. The relative rehabilitation of Antonescu begins with Marin Preda's novel *Delirul* (The delirium, 1975), and continues, on the historiographical level, with Aurică Simion, *Preliminarii politico-diplomatice ale insurecției române din august 1944* (Political-diplomatic preliminaries of the Romanian insurrection of August 1944). Cluj: Editura Dacia, 1979, becoming fully "officialized" in *Istoria militară a poporului român* (Military history of the Romanian people). Vol. 6, 1989. As for the contribution of Romania to the defeat of Nazism, the plea of Ilie Ceaușescu, Florin Constantiniu, and Mihail Ionescu received intense media coverage: *200 de zile mai devreme: rolul României în scurtarea celui de-al doilea război mondial* (200 days earlier: The role of Romania in shortening the Second World War). Bucharest: Editură Științifică și Enciclopedică, 1984 and 1985. (For the assessment to have been an honest and complete one, the equation should also have taken account of the greater number of days of fighting which resulted from the war waged by Romania alongside Germany, a period four times longer than that which the authors took into consideration.)

60. The Burebista episode is discussed by Florentin Dragoș Necula. "Comunism în Dacia. Burebista—contemporanul nostru" (Communism in Dacia: Burebista our contemporary). *Analele Universității București. Istorie* (1993–1994): 37–51. For the ritual commemoration of 2050 years, see *Scînteia* (6 July 1980).

61. The problem of the capitulations is given an extensive treatment by Mihai Maxim in *Țările române și Înalta Poartă. Cadrul juridic al relațiilor româno-otomane în Evul Mediu* (The Romanian lands and the Sublime Porte: The legal framework of Romanian-Ottoman relations in the Middle Ages). Bucharest: Editura Enciclopedică, 1993. Although the author presents the main lines of the history of the issue, he omits the relationship between the Ceaușescu regime and the capitulations. He opts for a compromise solution, according to which the capitulations were unilateral acts from the perspective of the Porte, but fully fledged treaties from the Romanian point of view.

62. Katherine Verdery has discussed the motivation and avatars of protochronism in detail in *National Ideology under Socialism: Identity and Cultural Politics in Ceaușescu's Romania*. Berkeley: University of California Press, 1991.

63. Anghel, Paul. "Colaj și elaborare originală la Neagoe Basarab" (Collage and original elaboration in Neagoe Basarab). *Neagoe Basarab. 1512–1521. La 460 de ani de la urcarea sa pe tronul Țării Românești* (Neagoe Basarab: 1512–1521: On the 460th anniversary of his accession to the throne of Wallachia). Bucharest: Editura Minerva, 1972, 79.

64. Zamfirescu, Dan. *Războiul împotriva poporului român* (The war against the Romanian people). Bucharest: Editura "Roza Vînturilor", 1993 (text dated 1987), 282.

65. Verdery, Katherine. *op. cit.*

Chapter Two: Origins

1. The thesis is developed by Adolf Armbruster in *Romanitatea Românilor. Istoria unei idei* (The Romanity of the Romanians: The history of an idea). Bucharest: Editura Academiei, 1972 (new edition, Editura Enciclopedică, 1993).

2. Maior, Petru. *Istoria pentru începuturile românilor în Dachia*. Buda, 1812, 8–22. (See also the edition edited by Florea Fugariu. Bucharest: Editura Albatros, 1970, 98–109.)

3. Kogălniceanu, Mihail. *Opere*. Vol. 2, 57, 67.

4. Bălcescu, Nicolae. *Opere*. Vol. 3, 13.

5. Șincai, Gheorghe. *Hronica românilor și a mai multor neamuri*. Vol. 1. Bucharest: Editura pentru Literatură, 1967, 13–14.

6. Russo, Alecu. *Scrieri*. Ed. Petre V. Haneș. Bucharest: Editura Minerva, 1908, 88.

7. Kogălniceanu, Mihail. *Opere*. Vol. 2, 390.

8. Russo, Alecu. *op. cit.*, 172.
9. On the reception of the Dacians in Romanian culture, see also Babu-Buznea, Ovidia. *Dacii în conştiinţa romanticilor noştri. Schiţă la o istorie a dacismului* (The Dacians in the consciousness of our romantics: Sketch for a history of Dacianism). Bucharest: Editura Minerva, 1979.
10. Brătianu, Ion C. *Acte şi cuvîntări* (Documents and speeches). Vol. 1, part 1. Bucharest: Editura Cartea Românească, 1938, 163–176.
11. Hasdeu, B. P. "Pierit-au dacii?". In *Scrieri istorice* (Historical writings), ed. Aurelian Sacerdoţeanu. Vol. 1. Bucharest: Editura Albatros, 1973, 78–106.
12. Bolliac, Cezar "Despre daci" (About the Dacians). *Românul*, 14–26 July and 24 July–5 August 1858; "Excursiune arheologică din anul 1869" (Archaeological excursion in the year 1869). *Scrieri* (Writings). Vol. 2. Bucharest: Editura Minerva, 1983, 307. See also Babu-Buznea, Ovidia. *op. cit.*, 76–81.
13. Regarding Eminescu's "Dacianism", see Călinescu, G. *Opera lui Mihai Eminescu* (The works of Mihai Eminescu). Vol. 2. Bucharest: Fundaţia pentru Literatură şi Artă "Regele Carol II", 1935; Murăraşu, Dumitru. *Naţionalismul lui Eminescu* (Eminescu's nationalism). 1934. Bucharest: Editura Pacifica, 1994; and Sorin Antohi's considerations in *Civitas imaginalis*. Bucharest: Editura Litera, 1994, 111–115.
14. Tocilescu, Grigore. *Manual de istoria românilor.* Bucharest, 1899, 22, 34.
15. Onciul, Dimitrie. "Dacia". *Enciclopedia română.* Vol. 2. Sibiu, 1900, 87.
16. Xenopol, Alexandru D. *Istoria românilor din Dacia Traiană.* Vol. 1. Iaşi: H. Goldner, 1888, 163, 307.
17. Iorga, Nicolae. *Istoria românilor pentru poporul românesc* (History of the Romanians for the Romanian people). Vol. 1. Bucharest: Editura Minerva, 1993, 16, 22. (This edition reproduces that of 1935. Earlier editions had appeared in 1908–1931.)
18. Odobescu, Alexandru. *Ateneul Român şi clădirile antice cu dom circular* (The Romanian Athenaeum and ancient buildings with a circular dome). *Opere complete*, Vol. 3. Bucharest: Editura Minerva, 1908, 330, 332.
19. For details on the conception of these paintings, see the text and illustrations of *Ateneul Român din Bucureşti. Marea frescă* (The Romanian Athenaeum in Bucharest: The great fresco). Bucharest, 1938.
20. For a survey of the images in which Trajan is placed alongside Carol I, see Tănăsoiu, Carmen. "Carol I şi iconografia sa oficială" (Carol I and his official iconography). *Mituri istorice româneşti* (Romanian historical myths). Under the direction of Lucian Boia. Bucharest: Editura Universităţii Bucureşti, 1995, 151–152.
21. Pârvan, Vasile. *Dacia.* English translation. Cambridge: Cambridge University Press, 1928, 189.
22. Pârvan, Vasile. *Dacia.* 5th edition. Bucharest: Editura Ştiinţifică, 1972, 155. (This passage was crossed out in Pârvan's manuscript and does not appear in the English version of 1928; however it was included in the first Romanian edition in 1937. See note 449, p. 229, of the edition cited.)
23. Giurescu, C. C. *Istoria românilor.* Vol. 1. 5th edition, 1946, 123, 173.
24. Istrati, C. I. "Nic. Densuşianu. Viaţa şi opera sa" (N. Densuşianu: His life and work). *Dacia preistorică.* By N. Densuşianu. Bucharest, 1913, cxiii.
25. Eliade, Mircea. "Către un nou diletantism" (Towards a new dilettantism). In *Profetism românesc* (Romanian prophetism), ed. Alexandru V. Diţă. Foreword by Dan. Zamfirsescu. Bucharest: Editura "Roza Vînturilor", 1990, 29. (Originally published in *Cuvîntul*, 11 September 1927.)
26. Portocală, N. *Din preistoria Daciei şi a vechilor civilizaţiuni.* Bucharest: Institutul de Arte Grafice "Bucovina", 1932, 213, 245.

27. Brătescu-Voinești, Ioan Al. *Originea neamului românesc și a limbii noastre*. Bucharest: Editura Cartea Românească, 1942, 39.

28. Concerning the avatars of this mysterious figure, see Petre, Zoe. "Le mythe de Zalmoxis" (The myth of Zalmoxis). *Analele Universității București. Istorie* (1993–1994): 23–36.

29. Eliade, Mircea. "Introducere". *Scrieri literare, morale și politice*. By B. P. Hasdeu. Vol. 1. Bucharest: Fundația pentru Literatură și Artă "Regele Carol II", 1937, lxxvii.

30. Eliade, Mircea. *The Romanians: A Concise History*. Trans. Rodica Mihaela Scafeș. Bucharest: "Roza Vînturilor" Publishing House, 1992, 13.

31. Ciaușu, Milviuța. "Panteonul mișcării legionare" (The pantheon of the Legionary movement). *Mituri istorice românești*, 204–207.

32. Nițulescu, Horia. "Prolegomena la o anumită durată românească" (Prolegomena to a certain Romanian duration) *Dacia Rediviva* no. 1 (April 1941): 2.

33. Ionescu-Nica, G. *Dacia sanscrită. Originea preistorică a Bucureștilor* (Sanskrit Dacia: The prehistoric origin of Bucharest). Bucharest: Tipografia Carpați, 1945. The tone of the lectures included in this brochure is vehemently anti-Hungarian (at a time when the destiny of Transylvania was at issue, a territory claimed by the author using Dacian arguments). Apart from this, it is claimed that the Dacians founded Rome and that the Orthodox patriarchate of Bucharest is the oldest in Europe, naturally "if we take into account the continuity of the religious-spiritual monotheism of the Geto-Daco-Romanians".

34. Roller, Mihail, ed. *Istoria R.P.R.* Bucharest, 1952 edition, 43.

35. See, in this connection, Tudor, Dumitru. *Istoria sclavajului în Dacia Romană* (The history of slavery in Roman Dacia). Bucharest: Editura Academiei, 1957; and *Răscoale și atacuri "barbare" în Dacia Romană* (Revolts and "barbarian" attacks in Roman Dacia). Bucharest: Editura Știinţifică, 1957.

36. Berciu, Dumitru. "Lupta băstinașilor din Dacia împotriva cotropitorilor romani" (The struggle of the natives of Dacia against the Roman invaders). *Studii și cercetări de istorie veche* 2 (July–December 1951): 73–95.

37. *Programul Partidului Comunist Român de făurire a societății socialiste multilateral dezvoltate și înaintare a României spre comunism* (Program of the Romanian Communist Party for the forging of the multilaterally developed socialist society and the advance of Romania towards communism). Bucharest: Editura Politică, 1975, 27.

38. "Începuturile istoriei poporului român". *Anale de istorie* 4 (1976): 142–152. Although the article is unsigned, I consider it my elementary duty to mention at least the names of Ion Popescu-Puțuri and Gheorghe Zaharia, the director and deputy director of the Institute and the principal architects of its historical fantasies.

39. *Istoria militară a poporului român*. Vol. 1. Bucharest: Editura Militară, 1984, 182.

40. Crișan, Ion Horațiu. *Burebista și epoca sa*. 2nd edition. Bucharest: Editura Științifică și Enciclopedică, 1977, 446.

41. Belcin, Dr. Corneliu (lawyer). "Elemente introductive la problema: Originea, vechimea și importanța poporului român în lume" (Introductory elements to the problem: The origin, age, and importance of the Romanian people in the world). *Noi, tracii* 12 (August 1975): 8–11. ("Even a mere 100,000 years of existence on this earth, and we are still led to the conclusion that we are the oldest people of Europe.")

42. Hasdeu, B. P. *Istoria critică a românilor* Vol. 1. Bucharest, 1873, 278-281.

43. See Hasdeu, B. P. "În ce constă fizionomia unei limbi?" (In what does the physiognomy of a language consist?). Chapter 3 of "În loc de întroducere" (By way of introduction). *Etymologicum Magnum Romaniae*. Vol. 1. Bucharest: Editura Academiei, 1886 (new edition, Bucharest: Editura Minerva, 1972).

44. Bogdan, Ioan. *Istoriografia română și problemele ei actuale* (Romanian historiography and its current problems). Bucharest, 1905, 21.

45. Bogdan, Ioan. *Însemnătatea studiilor slave pentru români* (The importance of Slav studies for Romanians). Bucharest, 1894, 17–19, 25.

46. Bogdan, Ioan. *Românii și bulgarii* (The Romanians and the Bulgarians). Bucharest, 1895, 15.

47. Iorga, N. *op. cit.* Vol. 1, 33.

48. Giurescu, C. C. *op. cit.* Vol. 1, 247, 260.

49. Giurescu, C. C. "Slavii au venit în Dacia în calitate de cuceritori" (The Slavs came to Dacia as conquerors). *op. cit.* Vol. 1, 268–278; Panaitescu, P. P. "Problema originii clasei boierești". *Interpretări românești.* 1994 edition, 31–64.

50. *Istoria R.P.R.,* 54–56.

51. Roller, Mihail. "Cu privire la unele probleme din domeniul cercetărilor istorice" (Concerning some problems in the field of historical research). *Studii. Revistă de istorie și filozofie* (July–September 1952): 152–153.

52. *Istoria militară a poporului român.* Vol. 1, 208.

53. Bloch, Marc. *Apologie pour l'histoire ou Métier d'historien* (Apology for history or the trade of historian). Paris, 1964, 15. ("Les hommes ressemblent plus à leur temps qu'à leurs pères.")

Chapter Three: Continuity

1. Șincai, Gheorghe. *Hronica românilor și a mai multor neamuri.* Vol. 1. Bucharest: Editura pentru Literatură, 1967, 282–283, 289.

2. Hasdeu, B. P. *Istoria critică a românilor.* Vol. 1. Bucharest, 1873, 306–308.

3. Xenopol, A. D. *Teoria lui Roesler. Studii asupra stăruinței românilor în Dacia Traiană.* Iași: Tipografia Națională, 1884, 224.

4. Onciul, Dimitrie. "Teoria lui Roesler. Studii asupra stăruinței românilor în Dacia Traiană de A. D. Xenopol. Dare de seamă critică". *Scrieri istorice.* Ed. Aurelian Sacerdoțeanu. Vol. 1. Bucharest: Editura Științifică, 1968, 244.

5. Philippide, Alexandru. *Originea românilor.* Vol. 1. Iași, 1923, 854; Vol. 2. Iași, 1927, 569.

6. Densușianu, Ovid. *Histoire de la langue roumaine* (History of the Romanian language). Vol. 1. Paris, 1902 (reprinted Bucharest, 1929), 288–289: "Un point où nous tombons d'accord avec Rösler c'est que le centre de la formation du roumain doit être placé au sud du Danube."

7. Brătianu, G. I. *O enigmă și un miracol istoric: poporul român* (An enigma and a historical miracle: The Romanian people). Bucharest: Fundația pentru Literatură și Artă "Regele Carol II", 1940, 60.

8. Panaitescu, P. P. *Istoria românilor.* Reproduction of the 1943 edition. Bucharest: Editura Didactică și Pedagogică, 1990, 60.

9. Pârvan, Vasile. *Începuturile vieții romane la gurile Dunării.* 2nd edition. Bucharest: Editura Științifică, 1974, 130.

10. Iorga, N. *Istoria românilor pentru poporul românesc.* Vol 1. Bucharest: Editura Minerva, 1993, 35.

11. *Ibid.,* 51.

12. Giurescu, C. C. *Istoria românilor.* Vol. 1. 5th edition, 1946, 269.

13. *Istoria României.* Vol. 1. Bucharest: Editura Academiei, 1960, 776, 808.

14. *Istoria României.* Ed. Miron Constantinescu, Constantin Daicoviciu, and Ștefan Pascu. Bucharest: Editura Didactică și Pedagogică, 1969, 103–106.

15. *Istoria poporului român.* Ed. Andrei Oțetea. Bucharest: Editura Științifică, 1970, 108.

16. Bârzu, Ligia. *Continuitatea creației materiale și spirituale a poporului român pe teritoriul fostei Dacii.* Bucharest: Editura Academiei, 1979, 82.

17. *Ibid.,* 86; Bârzu, Ligia and Stelian Brezeanu. *Originea și continuitatea românilor. Arheologie și tradiție istorică.* Bucharest: Editura Enciclopedică, 1991, 213.

18. Manea, Mihai, Adrian Pascu and Bogdan Teodorescu. *Istoria românilor. Din cele mai vechi timpuri pînă la revoluția din 1821* (The history of the Romanians: From the earliest times to the revolution of 1821). Bucharest: Editura Didactică și Pedagogică, 1992, 173.

19. Significant for the limits within which the discussion could evolve is the work of Kurt Horedt (a German archaeologist of Romanian origin, professor at the University of Cluj, later settled in Germany): *Siebenbürgen im Frühmittelalter* (Transylvania in the early Middle Ages). Bonn, 1986. Horedt, whose familiarity with the early medieval archaeology of the Romanian area is beyond question, considers that in the seventh century Transylvania was completely Slavicized, that the Slav period continued into the tenth century, and that the Romanian element only appeared from the ninth century. I mention his work not to claim that he is right, merely to show that the problem is too complicated to be dealt with in categorical judgements without appeal. The most recent contribution on the matter is the article "Dridu" by Eugenia Zaharia, in *Enciclopedia arheologiei și istoriei vechi a României* (Encyclopaedia of the archaeology and early history of Romania). Coordinated by Constantin Preda. Vol. 2. Bucharest: Editura Enciclopedică, 1996, 81–83. This repeats the interpretation of the culture as strictly Romanian and perfectly unitary over an area larger than that of present-day Romania. Ion Nestor is mentioned, but Constantin Daicoviciu and Kurt Horedt are not. Probably they did not merit a response, since they did not think as one *ought* to think!

20. *Programul Partidului Comunist Român de făurire a societății socialiste multilateral dezvoltate și înaintare a României spre comunism*. Bucharest: Editura Politică, 1975, 28

21. Tagliavini, Carlo. *Originile limbilor neolatine*. Editura Științifică și Enciclopedică, 1977, 300.

Chapter Four: Unity

1. Kogălniceanu, Mihail. *Opere*. Vol. 2, 394.
2. Xenopol, A. D. *Istoria românilor din Dacia Traiană*. Vol. 1. Iași: H. Goldner, 1888, 19–20.
3. *Ibid*. Vol. 3, 1890, 399–400.
4. Onciul, Dimitrie. *Din istoria României*. Bucharest: Editura Socec, 1908, 76.
5. Sîrbu, Ioan. *Istoria lui Mihai Viteazul*. Vol 2. Bucharest: "Carol Göbl", 1907, 5–6.
6. Iorga, Nicolae. *Istoria românilor pentru poporul românesc*. Vol 1. Bucharest: Editura Minerva, 1993, 210–211.
7. *Ibid.*, 214.
8. Xenopol, A. D. *op. cit.* Vol. 2, 1889, 292.
9. Murgescu, Mirela-Luminița. "Galeria națională de personaje istorice în manualele de istorie din școala primară (1859–1900)" (The national gallery of historical characters in primary school history textbooks, 1859–1900). *Mituri istorice românești*. Under the direction of Lucian Boia. Bucharest: Editura Universității București, 1995, 40.
10. Lupaș, Ioan. *Istoria unirii românilor*. Bucharest: Fundația Culturală Regală "Principele Carol", 1937, 43, 148.
11. Brătianu, G. I. *Origines et formation de l'unité roumaine* (Origins and formation of Romanian unity). Bucharest, 1943, 10–13.
12. *Ibid.*, 138.
13. *Ibid.*, 158–159.
14. Roller, Mihail, ed. *Istoria R.P.R.* Bucharest, 1952 edition, 230.
15. *Ibid.*, 367.
16. *Istoria militară a poporului român*. Vol. 2. Bucharest: Editura Militară, 1986, 308: "As lord of Moldavia, protector of Wallachia, and supported and followed by the Transylvanians, he was seen at the time, both by Romanians and by foreigners, as the political leader of the entire Romanian space." Adina Berciu Drăghicescu and Florea Stănculescu, in *Temeiurile istorice ale primei uniri a românilor* (The historical foundations of the first union of the

Romanians). Bucharest, 1993, 125–126, no longer even feel the need for any explanation, stating simply and categorically: "Stephen the Great may be considered, without exaggeration, lord of all the Romanians."

17. Dogaru, Mircea. *Dracula, împăratul Răsăritului* (Dracula, emperor of the east). Bucharest: Editura Globus, 1995.

18. Cristea, Ovidiu. "Frontul românesc antiotoman în secolele XIV–XV: realitate istorică sau mit istoriografic?" (The Romanian anti-Ottoman front in the fourteenth and fifteenth centuries: Historical reality or historiographical myth?). *Miturile comunismului românesc.* Under the direction of Lucian Boia. Bucharest: Editura Universității București, 1995, 166–171.

19. Bodea. Cornelia. *Lupta românilor pentru unitatea națională 1834–1849* (The struggle of the Romanians for national unity, 1834–1849). Bucharest: Editura Academiei, 1967.

20. *Istoria românilor. Epoca modernă și contemporană* (The history of the Romanians: The modern and contemporary period). 8th grade textbook. Bucharest: Editura Didactică și Pedagogică, 1992, 45.

21. A remarkable achievement from this point of view is the "portrait of France" minutely reconstructed by Emmanuel Le Roy Ladurie, in collaboration with Paul Dumont and Michel Demonet, in "Anthropologie de la jeunesse masculine en France au niveau d'une cartographie cantonale (1819–1830)" (Anthropology of masculine youth in France at the level of district cartography, 1819–1830), reproduced in *Le territoire de l'historien* (The territory of the historian). By Emmanuel Le Roy Ladurie. Paris: Gallimard, 1978, 98–175. Where physical build is concerned, for example, there are *départements* where deficiencies of height (under 1.57 m.) affect over a quarter of the male population, while in others they affect less than 1 percent. From the cultural point of view, the literacy rate in some *départements* is over 80 percent, while in others it falls below 10 percent.

22. Cîmpeanu, Pavel. *De patru ori în fața urnelor* (Four times at the ballot box). Bucharest, 1993.

23. Drăghicescu, Dumitru. *Din psihologia poporului român.* 1907. 2nd edition. Bucharest: Editura Albatros, 1995, 141.

24. *Ibid.*, 138, 400.

25. *Ibid.*, 345, 353, 356, 361.

26. Blaga, Lucian. *Spațiul mioritic.* 1936. Bucharest: Humanitas, 1994, 165–166.

27. Ornea, Z. *Anii treizeci. Extrema dreaptă românească* (The 1930s: The Romanian extreme Right). Bucharest: Editura Fundației Culturale Române, 1995, 91–95.

28. Blaga, Lucian. *op.cit.*, 164.

29. Vulcănescu, Mircea. *Dimensiunea românească a existenței.* Editura Fundației Culturale Române, 1991, 130–149.

30. Călinescu, George. *Istoria literaturii române de la origini pînă în prezent* (The history of Romanian literature from its origins to the present day). Bucharest: Fundația Regală pentru Literatură și Artă, 1941, 886.

31. Noica, Constantin. *Sentimentul românesc al ființei.* Bucharest: Editura Eminescu, 1978, 62.

32. *Ibid.*, 11.

33. Ceaușescu, Nicolae. *Istoria poporului român* (The history of the Romanian people). Ed. Ion Popescu-Puțuri. Bucharest: Editura Politică, 1983, 118, 121.

34. Zamfirescu, Dan. *Cultura română, o mare cultură cu destin universal* (Romanian culture: A great culture with a universal destiny). Bucharest: Editura "Roza Vînturilor", 1996.

35. Patapievici, H.-R. *Politice* (Political essays). Bucharest: Humanitas, 1996, 63.

36. Lovinescu, E. *Istoria civilizației române moderne.* Vol. 1. Bucharest: Ancora, 1924, 118.

Chapter Five: The Romanians and the Others

1. Proverbs offer a synthetic expression of traditional opinions. See Zanne, Iuliu A. *Proverbele românilor* (The proverbs of the Romanians). Vol. 6. Bucharest: Editura Socec, 1901, 11–14.

23–28, 131–137, 308–310, 429–430; also the articles "Armean" and "Arţibur", in Hasdeu's *Etymologicum Magnum Romaniae*, vol. 2.

2. Brătianu, Ion C. *Acte şi cuvîntări* (Documents and speeches). Vol. 4. Bucharest: Editura Cartea Românească, 1932, 241.

3. Panaitescu, P. P. "De ce n-au cucerit turcii ţările române?" (Why did the Turks not conquer the Romanian lands?). *Interpretări româneşti.* New edition. Bucharest: Editura Enciclopedică, 1994, 112.

4. Murăraşu, Dumitru. *Naţionalismul lui Eminescu.* 1934. Bucharest: Editura Pacifica, 1994, 118

5. Drăghicescu, Dumitru. *Din psihologia poporului român.* 1907. 2nd edition. Bucharest: Editura Albatros, 1995, 252, 256.

6. *Ibid.*, 262.

7. On the Western model, and especially French and German influence, see my study "Sur la diffusion de la culture européenne en Roumanie (XIXe siècle et début du XXe siècle)" (On the diffusion of European culture in Romania: Nineteenth century and early twentieth century). *Analele Universităţii Bucureşti. Istorie* (1985): 51–69.

8. Drăghicescu, Dumitru. *op. cit.*, 81.

9. Brătianu, I. C. *op. cit.* Vol 1, 31–32.

10. Argetoianu, Constantin. *Pentru cei de mîine. Amintiri din vremea celor de ieri* (For those of tomorrow: Reminiscences from the time of those of yesterday). Vol. 2, part 4. Bucharest: Humanitas, 1991, 105.

11. Eliade, Pompiliu. "Introduction". *De l'influence française sur l'esprit public en Roumanie* (On French influence on the public spirit in Romania). Paris, 1898, i-xi.

12. Maneca, Constant. *Lexicologie statistică romanică* (Romance statistical lexicology). Bucharest, 1978.

13. Drăghicescu, Dumitru. *op. cit.*, 86, 88.

14. Caragiale, I. L. *Scrisori şi acte* (Letters and papers). Ed. Şerban Cioculescu. Bucharest: Editura pentru Literatură, 1963, 19–29: letter of Caragiale to Alecu Urechia, 7/20 July 1905. Delavrancea's opinion of Germany: "Administration, army, arts, sciences, letters, trams, railways, cabs, waiters, barbers, public, general stores, houses, monuments, food, beer, all, all, all, foolish, stupid, imbecile!"

15. Kogălniceanu, Mihail. *Opere.* Vol. 2, 609.

16. Boia, Lucian. *op. cit.*, 55–56.

17. Iorga, Nicolae. *Războiul nostru în note zilnice* (Our war in daily notes). Vol. 1. Craiova: Editura "Ramuri", n.d., 18.

18. *Ibid.* Vol. 2, 170.

19. The installation of the Soviet myth is discussed at greater length by Adrian Cioroianu: "Lumina vine de la Răsărit. Noua imagine a Uniunii Sovietice în România postbelică, 1944–1947" (Light comes from the East: The new image of the Soviet Union in postwar Romania, 1944–1947). *Miturile comunismului românesc.* Under the direction of Lucian Boia. Bucharest: Editura Universităţii Bucureşti, 1995, 68–112.

20. For the industrial mythology of communism, including the obsession with engineering, see Boia, Lucian. *La mythologie scientifique du communisme* (The scientific mythology of communism). Caen: Paradigme, 1993.

21. The first representative text is Mihail Kogălniceanu's *Esquisse sur l'histoire, les mœurs, et la langue des Cigains* (Sketch of the history, the customs, and the language of the Gypsies), 1837 (reproduced in *Opere.* Vol. 2, 354–385). For an overview of the issue, with a rich bibliography, see Potra, Gheorghe. *Contribuţiuni la istoricul ţiganilor din România* (Contributions to the history of the Gypsies in Romania). Bucharest: Fundaţia "Regele Carol I", 1939.

22. Iancu, Carol. *L'Emancipation des Juifs de Roumanie (1913–1919)* (The emancipation of the Jews of Romania, 1913–1919). Montpellier, 1992. The author considers that Romania was "at the forefront of the countries which professed a systematic state anti-Semitism" (p. 32).

23. Drăgan, Iosif Constantin. *Istoria românilor*. Bucharest: Editura Europa Nova, 1993, 267.

24. Volovici, Leon. *Ideologia naţionalistă şi "problema evreiască". Eseu despre formele antisemitismului intelectual în România anilor '30* (The nationalist ideology and the "Jewish problem": An essay on the forms of intellectual anti-Semitism in 1930s Romania). Bucharest: Humanitas, 1995, 208.

25. Scurtu, Ioan and Constantin Hlihor. *Complot împotriva României, 1939–1947*. Bucharest: Editura Academiei de Înalte Studii Militare, 1994.

26. See the mythological résumé of the issue in Drăgan, Iosif Constantin. *op. cit.*, 255–266.

27. A significantly titled book is Titu Georgescu's *România între Ialta şi Malta* (Romania between Yalta and Malta). Bucharest: Editura "Şansa", 1993.

28. For the list of emperors of Thraco-Dacian origin see Drăgan, Iosif Constantin. *op. cit.*, 46–47. See also the same author's *Mileniul imperial al Daciei* (The imperial millennium of Dacia). Bucharest, 1986.

29. Laurian, August Treboniu. *Istoria românilor*. 4th edition. Bucharest, 1873, 425.

30. Hasdeu, B. P. *Ioan Vodă cel Cumplit*. Bucharest: Imprimeria Ministerului de Resbel, 1865, xxi.

31. Scriban, Romulus. *Istoria economiei politice, a comerţului şi a navigaţiunei României*. Galaţi, 1885, 73–76.

32. Dogaru, Mircea. *Dracula, împăratul Răsăritului*. Bucharest: Editura Globus, 1995.

33. I have reproduced (or calculated as percentages) demographic data from the following sources: Ionescu, M. D. *Dobrogea în pragul veacului al XX-lea* (Dobrogea on the eve of the twentieth century). Bucharest: Socec, 1904, 905; Ionescu, M. D. *Cercetări asupra oraşului Constanţa* (Researches on the town of Constanţa). Bucharest, 1897, 88; *Recensămîntul general al populaţiei României din 29 decembrie 1930* (General census of the population of Romania on 29 December 1930). Published by Sabin Manuilă. Vol 2. Bucharest: Imprimeria naţională, 1938; *Recensămîntul populaţiei şi locuinţelor din 7 ianuarie 1992* (Census of population and dwellings on 7 January 1992). Vol. *Structura etnică şi confesională a populaţiei* (Ethnic and confessional structure of the population). Bucharest, 1995.

34. Boia, Lucian. "Destinul mare al unei ţări mici" (The great destiny of a small country). *Miturile comunismului românesc*. Under the direction of Lucian Boia. Vol. 2. Bucharest: Editura Universităţii Bucureşti, 1997, 19–30.

35. Ceauşescu, Ilie. *Războiul întregului popor pentru apărarea patriei la români. Din cele mai vechi timpuri pînă în zilele noastre* (The war of the entire people for the defense of the fatherland among the Romanians: From the earliest times until our days). Bucharest: Editura Militară, 1980, 409.

36. *Istoria militară a poporului român*. Vol. 2, 1986, 39–41. ("The application of the principle of the defense of the fatherland by the entire people led to the creation of an impressive Romanian military power with few equals on the European continent in terms of the number of soldiers assembled.")

37. Zamfirescu, Dan. *Războiul împotriva poporului român*. Bucharest: Editura "Roza Vînturilor", 1993, 145.

38. Morand, Paul. *Bucarest*. 1935. Paris: Plon, 1990; Manning, Olivia. *The Great Fortune*. London: Heinemann, 1960; and *The Spoilt City*. London: Heinemann, 1962.

39. Carrère, Emmanuel. "En Roumanie c'est-à-dire nulle part." *La Règle du Jeu* 2 (1990): 152–173.

40. Camus, Renaud. *La Guerre de Transylvanie* (The war of Transylvania). Paris: P.O.L., 1996.

41. Vauréal, François and Laurence Bonfighli. *Histoire* (History). Under the direction of Robert Frank. Paris: Belin, 1995, 11.

Chapter Six: The Ideal Prince

1. Bogdan, Ioan. *Istoriografia română și problemele ei actuale*. Bucharest, 1905, 19.
2. On the national pantheon see Murgescu, Mirela-Luminița. "Galeria națională de personaje istorice în manualele de istorie din școala primară (1859–1900)". *Mituri istorice românești*. Under the direction of Lucian Boia. Bucharest: Editura Universității București, 1995.
3. Ureche, Grigore. *Letopisetul Țării Moldovei* (The chronicle of the land of Moldavia). Ed. P. P. Panaitescu. Bucharest: Editura de Stat pentru Literatură și Artă, 1955, 111.
4. "Nouveau tableau historique et politique de la Moldavie". *Mémoires et projets de réforme...* (Memoranda and projects of reform...). By Vlad Georgescu. 1972, 193–194.
5. Xenopol, A. D. *Istoria românilor din Dacia Traiană*. Vol. 2. Iași: H. Goldner, 1889, 415–417.
6. Giurescu, C. C. *Istoria românilor*. Vol. 2, part 1. 4th edition. Bucharest: Fundația Regală pentru Literatură și Artă, 1943, 44.
7. Panaitescu, P. P. *Cronicele slavo-române din secolele XV–XVI publicate de Ioan Bogdan* (Slavo-Romanian chronicles of the fifteenth and sixteenth centuries edited by Ioan Bogdan). Bucharest, 1959, 149.
8. Ureche, Grigore. *op. cit.*, 184.
9. Hasdeu, B. P. *Ioan Vodă cel Cumplit*. Bucharest: Imprimeria Ministerului de Resbel, 1865, xxi.
10. Lovinescu, E. P. P. *Carp, critic literar și literat* (P. P. Carp: Literary critic and man of letters). Bucharest: Socec, [1942], 42–45.
11. Xenopol, A. D. *op. cit.* Vol. 3, 104.
12. Bogdan, Ioan. *Letopisetul lui Azarie* (The Chronicle of Azarie). Bucharest: 1909, 30; Onciul, Dimitrie. *Din istoria României*. Bucharest: Editura Socec, 1908, 68.
13. Giurescu, C.C. *op. cit.* Vol. 2-1, 209.
14. *Cronicari munteni*. Vol. 1. Bucharest: Editura pentru Literatură, 1961, 85, 242.
15. On the development of the Țepeș political myth, see Constantinescu, Daniela. "Vlad Țepeș și imaginea prințului ideal în societatea românească a secolului al XIX-lea" (Vlad Țepeș and the image of the ideal prince in nineteenth-century Romanian society). *Analele Universității București. Istorie* (1993–1994): 67–78.
16. Hasdeu, B. P. "Filosofia portretului lui Țepeș" (The philosophy of the portrait of Țepeș). *Scrieri literare, morale și politice*. Vol. 2. Bucharest: Fundația pentru Literatură și Artă "Regele Carol II", 1937, 7–20.
17. Bogdan, Ioan. *Vlad Țepeș și narațiunile germane și rusești asupra lui* (Vlad Țepeș and the German and Russian narratives about him). Bucharest, 1896, xviii.
18. *Ibid.*, vi, x.
19. Șincai, Gheorghe. *Hronica românilor și a mai multor neamuri*. Vol. 2. Bucharest: Editura pentru Literatură, 1967, 60.
20. Bolintineanu, D. "Vlad Țepeș Vodă". *Viața lui Vlad Țepeș și Mircea Vodă cel Bătrîn* (The life of Vlad Țepeș and Mircea Vodă the Old). 2nd edition. Bucharest, 1870, 5–63.
21. Xenopol, A. D. *op. cit.* Vol. 2, 278, 293.
22. The king himself spoke about all this in his historical address to the Romanian Academy, "Nicopole. 1396–1877–1902". *Cuvântările regelui Carol I* (The addresses of King Carol I). Ed. C. C. Giurescu. Vol. 2. Bucharest: Fundația pentru Literatură și Artă "Carol I", Bucharest, 1939, 306–322.
23. Onciul. Dimitrie. *op. cit.*, 117.

24. Antipa, Grigore. "Cîteva amintiri despre regele Carol I" (A few memories of King Carol I). *Din viaţa regelui Carol I* (From the life of King Carol I). Contemporary accounts and unpublished documents collected by Al. Tzigara-Samurcaş. Bucharest, 1939, 26–27, 30–31.

25. Galaction, Gala. "Aşa cum mi-l aduc aminte" (As I remember him). *Ibid.*, 68–69.

26. Gorun, I. (Al. Hodoş). *Încoronarea primului rege al României întregite la Alba Iulia şi la Bucureşti* (The coronation of the first king of Romania made whole in Alba Iulia and in Bucharest). Bucharest: Editura I. G. Herz, n.d., 11–17.

27. Cardaş, Gh. *Regele Carol al II-lea preamărit cu slavă şi credinţă de cîntăreţii neamului.* (King Carol II exalted with praise and faith by the singers of the Romanian people). Bucharest: Biblioteca pentru toţi, n.d., 5–6.

28. See, for example, the anthology collected by Gh. Cardaş (*op. cit.*). Among the better-known poets included in the volume of verses dedicated to Prince, and later King, Carol II from his birth to 1936 may be mentioned George Coşbuc, Octavian Goga, and Adrian Maniu.

29. Petrescu, Cezar. "Ctitorii regale" (Royal foundations) and "Minunea totuşi s-a împlinit" (Yet the miracle has happened). *România* (4 and 9 July 1938).

30. Giurescu, C. C. "Influenţe ale tradiţiei naţionale în noua noastră organizare de stat" (Influences of national tradition in our new state organization). *Zece ani de domnie ai Maiestăţii Sale Regelui Carol al II-lea* (Ten years of reign of His Majesty King Carol II). Vol. 1. Bucharest, 1940, 74.

31. Petrescu, Cezar. *Cei trei regi* (The three kings). 2nd edition. Bucharest: Editura Abeona, 1993, 17.

32. An excellent analysis of the mythologizing of this "dynasty" can be found in Şerban, Sorin. "Brătienii" (The Brătianus). *Mituri istorice româneşti*, 154–170.

33. Duca, I. G. *Portrete şi amintiri* (Portraits and memories). 5th edition. Bucharest: Humanitas, 1990, 36.

34. Diamandi, Sterie. *Galeria oamenilor politici.* (The gallery of men of politics). 1935. Bucharest: Editura Gesa, 1991, 94.

35. Şerban, Sorin. *op. cit.*, 163.

36. Bacalbaşa, Constantin. *Bucureştii de altădată* (Bucharest of past times). Vol. 1. Bucharest: Editura Ziarului "Universul", 1927, 101.

37. Duca, I. G. *Memorii* (Memoirs). Vol. 1. Bucharest: Editura Expres, 1992, 26–27, 100–120, 140.

38. Lovinescu, E. *op. cit.*, 92.

39. Bizomescu, Maria. "Un mit feminin: Regina Maria" (A feminine myth: Queen Marie). *Mituri istorice româneşti*, 171–198.

40. Argetoianu, Constantin. *Pentru cei de mâine. Amintiri din vremea celor de ieri.* Vol. 3, part 5. Bucharest: Humanitas, 1992, 15, 109.

41. *Ibid.* Vol. 5. Bucharest: Editura Machiavelli, 1995, 157. We find the same appreciation with Alexandru Marghiloman: the queen was "the only being who believed that the end of the war would be as it was. It is true: everybody doubted, *everybody*, without exception." *Note Politice* (Political notes). Vol. 3. 2nd edition. Bucharest: Editura Machiavelli, 1995, 364.

42. Cotruş, Aron. *Maria Doamna.* Bucharest. 1938, 14–16.

43. Argetoianu, Constantin. *op. cit.* Vol. 6, 1996, 44–46.

44. See the brochure *Ateneul român din Bucureşti. Marea frescă.* Bucharest, 1938. The final part of the fresco has been modifed: Carol II and Michael are missing.

45. The "divided" pantheon of the French has been investigated by Christian Amalvi: *Les Héros de l'Histoire de la France. Recherche iconographique sur le panthéon scolaire de la Troisième République* (The heroes of French history: Iconographical research on the school pantheon of the Third Republic). Paris, 1979; *De l'art et la manière d'accommoder les héros de l'histoire de*

France (On the art and manner of accommodating the heroes of French history). Paris, 1988.

46. Ciauşu, Milviuţa. "Pantonul mişcării legionare." *Mituri istorice românești*, 199–219.

47. *Porunca vremii* (The commandment of the time) (28 March 1935).

48. Ţopa, Ovid. "Rostul revoluţiei românești. De la Zalmoxe prin Ştefan Vodă şi Eminescu la Căpitan" (The purpose of Romanian revolution: From Zalmoxis through Stephen Vodă and Eminescu to the Captain). *Buna Vestire* (The annunciation) (8 November 1940); Ţuţea, Petru. *Între Dumnezeu şi neamul meu* (Between God and my people). Bucharest: Editura Arta Grafică, 1992, 110–111.

49. "Noul întrupat" (The new incarnate). *Buna vestire* (8 November 1940).

50. Roller, Mihail, ed. *Istoria R.P.R.* Bucharest, 1952 edition, 138.

51. *Ibid.*, 182.

52. Bizomescu, Maria. "Ioan Vodă—un mit antiboieresc" (Ioan Vodă: an anti-boyar myth). *Mituri istorice românești*, 116.

53. Drăguşanu, Adrian. "Nicolae Bălcescu în propaganda comunistă" (Nicolae Bălcescu in communist propaganda). *Miturile comunismului românesc*. Under the direction of Lucian Boia. Bucharest: Editura Universităţii Bucureşti, 1997, 131–165.

54. In 1947–48, the early editions of Roller's textbook kept a balance between Gheorghiu-Dej, Ana Pauker, and Vasile Luca, who are mentioned to an equal extent and with relative discretion. In the 1952 edition the last two disappear, while Gheorghiu-Dej is mentioned repeatedly, becoming the central figure of contemporary history. Moreover, the textbook is full of quotations from his articles and speeches (which were not there before). Three portraits of him are reproduced, compared with a single presence, in a group photograph, in the previous editions.

55. Şerban, Sorin. "Ilegaliştii" (The illegalists). *Miturile comunismului românesc*, 45–58.

56. For feminine mythology in communism, see Petre, Zoe. "Promovarea femeii sau despre destructurarea sexului feminin" (The promotion of woman, or the destructuring of the female sex). *Miturile comunismului românesc*, 22–38.

57. The career of Mircea the Old under communism is discussed by Cristiana Dineaţă: "Mircea cel Bătrin. De la comemorări religioase la mari adunări populare" (Mircea the Old: From religious commemorations to great popular assemblies) and "Rovine—o ecuaţie cu mai multe necunoscute" (Rovine: An equation with many unknowns). *Mituri istorice românești*, 72–102.

58. Crişan, Ion Horaţiu. *Burebista şi epoca sa.* 2nd edition. Bucharest: Editura Ştiinţifică şi Enciclopedică, 1977, 495.

59. Muşat, Mircea and Ion Pătroiu. "Epoca demnităţii şi împlinirii marilor idealuri naţionale" (The age of dignity and the fulfillment of the great national ideals). *Marele Mircea Voievod* (The great voivode Mircea). Coordinated by Ion Pătroiu. Bucharest, 1987, 518–525.

60. Hurezeanu, Elisabeta, Gheorghe Smarandache, and Maria Totu. *Istoria modernă a României* (The modern history of Romania). 9th grade textbook. Bucharest: Editura Didactică şi Pedagogică, 1985 edition, 94, 96.

61. Scurtu, Ioan. *Contribuţii privind viaţa politică din România. Evoluţia formei de guvernămînt în istoria modernă şi contemporană.* Bucharest: Editura Ştiinţifică şi Enciclopedică, 1988.

Chapter Seven: After 1989

1. Drulă, Leonard. "Ion Antonescu şi Mihai I. Între istorie şi politică" (Ion Antonescu and Michael I: Between history and politics). *Mituri istorice românești* (Romanian historical myths). Under the direction of Lucian Boia. Bucharest: Editura Universităţii Bucureşti, 1995, 220–254.

2. The confrontation, which was made evident on the occasion of this visit, between the royal myth and the anti-monarchist countermyth is analyzed by Mihai Coman in "La Ritualisation de la visite du Roi Mihai Ier à l'occasion des Pâques" (The ritualization of the visit of King Michael I on the occasion of Easter). *Analele Universității București. Istorie* (1993–1994): 79–89.

3. *Evenimentul zilei* (9 May 1995).

4. *Almanahul România Mare*, 1996; the cover features the faces of the twelve apostles of the Romanian people: Decebalus, Vlad Țepeș, Ioan Vodă the Terrible, Michael the Brave, Constantin Brîncoveanu, Grigore Ghica, Horea, Tudor Vladimirescu, Ecaterina Teodoroiu, Nicolae Iorga, Ion Antonescu, and Nicolae Ceaușescu.

5. Drăgan, Iosif Constantin. *Istoria românilor.* Bucharest: Editura Europa Nova, 1993. Among the chapter titles are: "Marshal Antonescu and the holy war, 1941–1944", and "The treachery of King Michael and his decoration by Stalin". (The decoration received by the king is even reproduced on a whole page!)

6. See also, in this connection, Scurtu, Ioan. *Monarhia în România, 1866–1947* (Monarchy in Romania, 1866–1947). Bucharest: Editura Danubius, 1991, which is no more favorable to the institution of monarchy than the same author's volume of 1988, which it summarizes (see above, chapter six, note 61). Curiously, but significantly, the first pages of the book deal with... the republican tradition. At the end the reader is offered a statistical table showing the evolution of European political regimes from 1866 to the present day (21 monarchies and 2 republics in 1866, and 11 monarchies and 22 republics in 1991; and in the whole world, still in 1991, 118 republics and 44 monarchies). The implicit conclusion is that monarchical regimes are falling out of fashion. However, another statistical approach also seems legitimate, since, whatever anyone may say, we cannot compare Albania with Sweden or Somalia with Japan. The only model of development today is represented by the Western world. And the western half of Europe is equally divided between republics and monarchies. In fact the balance rather inclines towards the monarchical principle, if we add the non-European states that are highly industrialized and have indisputably democratic regimes: the United States (republic), Canada, Japan, Australia, and New Zealand (monarchies). All this does not give the dynastic system any additional historical chance. It is just that that is how the statistics are!

7. Poll published in *Evenimentul zilei* (12 April 1996). In October 1996, however, the army fell to 76 percent and the Church to 83 percent.

8. Among the politicians, those who opted for the "other" solution included P. P. Carp, Titu Maiorescu, Alexandru Marghiloman, and Constantin Stere. The gallery of great historians of the day consisted of six names: A. D. Xenopol, Dimitrie Onciul, Ioan Bogdan, Nicolae Iorga, Constantin Giurescu, and Vasile Pârvan. Of these, only Iorga actively campaigned for entry into the war (Xenopol would have done the same but was prevented by illness); the behavior of the others may be considered "reserved". Among writers, the two great Transylvanian classics, Ioan Slavici and George Coșbuc, paradoxically did not join the struggle for political union. Even more, Slavici published "pro-German" articles in the press during the occupation, as did Tudor Arghezi, Gala Galaction, D. D. Pătrășcanu, and others. Among scientists, Grigore Antipa collaborated with the German authorities, Simion Mehedinți was a minister in the Marghiloman government, and Victor Babeș incurred rebuke for a certain type of "accommodation". As we can see it is not a matter of a limited and marginal group, and certainly not of "traitors" or even "indifferents". Quite simply, part of the Romanian elite had a *different* idea of the national interests.

9. It is worth drawing attention here to the rich memorialistic literature—from which I limit myself to citing the exceptional epic of prison life published by Ion Ioanid under the title *Închisoarea noastră cea de toate zilele* (Our daily prison). 5 volumes. Bucharest: Editura

Albatros, 1991–1996—and numerous radio and television programs, among which the outstanding document remains *Memorialul durerii* (The memorial of pain), an oral enquiry carried out with perseverance by Lucia Hossu-Longin, and running to over fifty episodes.

10. Manea, Mihai and Bogdan Teodorescu. *Istoria românilor. Epoca modernă și contemporană* (The history of the Romanians: The modern and contemporary period). 12th grade textbook. Bucharest: Editura Didactică și Pedagogică, 1992, 206–325 (for 1918–1947) and 326–335 (for 1947–1989); there are no important modifications in later editions.

11. *Limba și litratură română* (Romanian language and literature). Coordinated by Nicolae I. Nicolae. 12th grade textbook. Bucharest: Editura Didactică și Pedagogică, 1993.

12. Mureșan, Camil, *et al. Istoria universală modernă și contemporană* (Modern and contemporary world history). 10th grade textbook. Bucharest: Editura Didactică și Pedagogică, 1991, and later editions.

13. For a succinct but pertinent analysis of Coruț's writing, against the general background of Dacian mythology, see Petre, Zoe. "Le mythe de Zalmoxis." *Analele Universității București. Istorie* (1993–1994): 23–36.

14. Iscru, G. D. *Formarea națiunii române* (The forming of the Romanian nation). Bucharest: Casa de editură și librărie "Nicolae Bălcescu", 1995.

15. Girardet, Raoul. *Mythes et Mythologies politiques* (Political myths and mythologies). Paris: Éditions du Seuil, 1986.

16. See, in this connection, Betea, Lavinia. *Maurer și lumea de ieri. Mărturii despre stalinizarea României* (Maurer and the world of yesterday: Testimonies about the Stalinization of Romania). Arad: Fundația "Ioan Slavici", 1995 (inteviews with Ion Gheorghe Maurer, Gheorghe Apostol, Alexandru Bârlădeanu, and Paul Sfetcu). Favorable opinions of Gheorgiu-Dej can also be found in Brucan, Silviu. *Generația irosită* (The squandered generation). Bucharest: Editura Univers-Calistrat Hogaș, 1992. There is eulogistic characterization in Popescu, Dumitru. *Am fost și cioplitor de himere* (I was also a carver of chimeras). Bucharest: Editura Expres, n.d. For a demythologizing analysis, on the other hand, see Tismăneanu, Vladimir. *Fantoma lui Gheorgiu-Dej* (The ghost of Gheorghiu-Dej). Bucharest: Editura Univers, 1995. For more detail, see Boia, Lucian. "Un mit Gheorghiu-Dej?" (A Gheorghiu-Dej myth?). *Miturile comunismului românesc*. Under the direction of Lucian Boia. Bucharest: Editura Universității București, 1997, 173–182.

Conclusion

1. In 1996, on the occasion of the visit to France of Pope John Paul II, the "two Frances" once again affirmed their mythological divergences, against the background of an ad hoc debate around the issues of freedom of conscience and church-state relations. Two founding myths were set face to face: the conversion of Clovis at the end of the fifth century (the Catholic version); and September 1792 and the proclamation of the republic and the battle of Valmy (the lay version).

Selected Bibliography

The present work is based on a variety of historiographical, literary, and iconographic sources, and on numerous contributions concerning the various aspects of the problem; all of these are mentioned in the text and in the notes. I shall not list them again here, but shall limit myself to works of a more general character, mentioning only those which were effectively used in my argumentation.

To a large extent the theoretical premises are my own. They are synthesized in my forthcoming *Pour une histoire de l'imaginaire*.* Hayden White's *Metahistory* (The Johns Hopkins University Press, 1973) has the great merit of demolishing the myth of historical objectivity. The connections between history and ideology are analyzed, with reference to the French case but with wider conceptual and methodological implications, by Christian Amalfi in *Les Héros de l'Histoire de France. Recherche iconographique sur le panthéon scolaire de la troisième République* (The heroes of French history: Iconographic research on the school pantheon of the Third Republic), Paris: Phot'œil, 1979; and *De l'art et la manière d'accommoder les héros de l'histoire de France. Essai de mythologie nationale* (On the art and manner of accommodating the heroes of French history: Essay in national mythology), Paris: Albin Michel, 1988.

A number of essential points of references for the issue of foundation myths and of origins in general can be found in Mircea Eliade's *Aspects du mythe* (Aspects of myth), Paris: Gallimard, 1963. For traditional societies, an indispensable source is the volume prepared under the direction of Marcel Détienne: *Tracés de fondation* (Lines of foundation), Louvain-Paris: Peeters, 1990. A remarkable analysis of a set of modern foundation myths is provided by Elise Marienstras in *Les Mythes fondateurs de la nation américaine* (The foundation myths of the American nation), Paris: Maspero, 1994.

For the imaginary of the nation, an essential point of reference is Dominique Schnapper's essay *La communauté des citoyens. Sur l'idée moderne de nation* (The community of citizens: On the modern idea of nation), Paris: Gallimard, 1994.

For political myths, which are inseparable from those of history, two fundamental works should be mentioned: André Reszler's *Mythes politiques modernes* (Modern political myths), Paris: Presses Universitaires de France, 1981; and Raoul

---

* Boia, Lucian. *Pour une histoire de l'imaginaire* (For a history of the imaginary). Paris: Les Belles Lettres, 1998. *Trans.*

Girardet's *Mythes et Mythologies politiques* (Political myths and mythologies), 1986. New ed. Paris: Seuil, 1990.

The three volumes published under my direction and under the aegis of the Center for the History of the Imaginary in the History Faculty of the University of Bucharest—*Mituri istorice românești* (Romanian historical myths). Bucharest: Editura Universității București, 1995; and the two volumes of *Miturile comunismului românești* (Myths of Romanian communism), Bucharest: Editura Universității București, 1995–1997—represent stages in the preparation of the present book.

No historiographical reconstruction or analysis can do without the fundamental contributions of Alexandru Zub, outstanding for the quality of their documentation and for their balanced interpretations. Among these I mention: *Mihail Kogălniceanu istoric* (Mihail Kogălniceanu, historian), Iași: Editura Junimea, 1974; *Vasile Pârvan: efigia cărturarului* (Vasile Pârvan: The image of the scholar), Iași: Editura Junimea, 1974; *Junimea: implicații istoriografice* (Junimea: Historiographical implications), Iași: Editura Junimea, 1976; *A scrie și a face istorie* (Writing and making history), Iași: Editura Junimea, 1981; *De la istoria critică la criticism* (From the critical school to criticism). Bucharest: Editura Academiei, 1985; *Istorie și istorici în România interbelică* (History and historians in interwar Romania), Iași: Editura Junimea, 1989.

For the still insufficiently researched communist period, the key work of reference remains Vlad Georgescu's *Politică și istorie. Cazul comuniștilor români. 1944–1977* (Politics and history: The case of the Romanian communists, 1944–1977), Edition prepared by Radu Popa. Bucharest: Humanitas, 1991. Katherine Verdery offers a pertinent analysis of the Romanian mythical pulsations of the same period in *National Ideology under Socialism: Identity and Cultural Politics in Ceaușescu's Romania*, Berkeley: University of California Press, 1991.

There is an attempt at a synthesis (up to 1944) in my own *Evoluția istoriografiei române* (The evolution of Romanian historiography), Bucharest: Tipografia Universității București, 1976. I have taken a number of facts, ideas, characterizations from this work. However, my interpretations have evolved considerably in certain respects, and the differences between the two books are also due to the disruptive factors present in 1976: the awareness of a limit that could not be crossed (self-censorship) and actual censorship, then termed "press direction", which imposed a long series of modifications to the initial text (including: the amplification of the chapter dealing with Marxist historiography, "dissociation" from Onciul's theory of ad migration, and the elimination of C. Giurescu's argument regarding the capitulations).

For the origins of the Dacian myth, see Ovidia Babu-Buznea's *Dacii în conștiința romanticilor noștri. Schiță la o istorie a dacismului* (The Dacians in the consciousness of our romantics: Sketch for a history of Dacianism), Bucharest: Editura Minerva, 1979—a demonstration which is itself to some extent "contaminated" by the ambient Dacianism of the time.

Sorin Antohi proposes an interesting exploration of various compartments of the social imaginary and of Romanian utopian constructions of the last two centuries, in *Civitas imaginalis*, Bucharest: Editura Litera, 1994.

An essential work on Romanian ideology at the beginning of the modern period (including aspects relating to historical consciousness) is Vlad Georgescu's *Ideile politice și iluminismul în Principatele române, 1750–1831* (Political ideas and enlightenment in the Romanian principalities, 1750–1831), Bucharest: Editura Academiei, 1972, complemented by the documentary annexes *Mémoires et projets de réforme dans les principautés roumaines* (Memoranda and projects of reform in the Romanian principalities), 1769–1830, Bucharest, 1970, and 1831–1848, Bucharest, 1972.

Regarding the succession and interference of ideologies, seen especially from a literary perspective but inserted into a broader cultural framework, the minute researches of Zigu Ornea are notable and ever useful. I limit myself to citing, from among his earlier contributions, *Sămănătorismul* (Sămănătorism), Bucharest: Editura Minerva, 1970; and from his recent work, *Anii treizeci. Extrema dreaptă românească* (The 1930s: The Romanian extreme Right), Bucharest: Editura Fundației Culturale Române, 1995.

For a clear and balanced synthetic presentation of the various ideologies and models of development, I refer the reader to the two volumes by Keith Hitchens, *The Romanians, 1774–1866*, Oxford: Clarendon Press, 1996; and *Rumania 1866–1947*, Oxford: Clarendon Press, 1994.

Finally, there is a survey—which I have made use of in the present work—of the models invoked in the process of modernizing Romanian society in my article "Les Roumains et les Autres. La quête des modèles dans la societé roumaine des XIXème et XXème siècles" (The Romanians and the Others: The quest for models in the Romanian society of the nineteenth and twentieth centuries), in the Institut Français de Bucarest collection *L'Etat des lieux en sciences sociales*. Texts collected by Alexandru Duțu and Norbert Dodille, Paris: L'Harmattan, 1993, 39–48.

Glossary

Compiled for the English version by James Christian Brown

Note on the pronunciation of the Romanian names:
The vowels *a, e, i, o* and *u* should generally be pronounced approximately as in Italian, with the exception of a final *i*, which is usually silent; *i* or *e* before another vowel sounds like English *y* (e.g. *Ion* resembles the English *yon*). The vowel *â* or *î* resembles the *i* in *fill*, and *ă* sounds like the *a* in *about*. The consonants *ş* and *ţ* are pronounced like English *sh* and *tz* respectively. When immediately followed by *i* or *e*, the letters *c* and *g* are pronounced as English *ch* in *church* and *g* in *gem*. In all other cases (including *ch* and *gh* before *e* and *i*) they are pronounced as in the English *coat* and *goat*.

Adrianople (Edirne), Treaty of (1829): treaty concluding the Russian–Turkish war of 1828 to 1829; under its terms the Turkish right of intervention in Moldavia and Wallachia was limited and the autonomy of the principalities was increased; in the meantime they remained under Russian military occupation and administration until 1834.

ALECSANDRI, Vasile (1818–90): one of the principal Romanian poets of the nineteenth century. A participant in the revolution of 1848 in Moldavia and in the movement for the union of the principalities, he served Cuza's government as a diplomat and was later Minister Plenipotentiary in Paris from 1885 to 1890.

ALEXANDER the Good: prince of Moldavia 1400 to 1432; a faithful ally of King Wladyslaw Jagiello of Poland, whose suzerainty he acknowledged. His reign saw consolidation of the Moldavian state, and the recognition by the Patriarch of Constantinople of an independent metropolitan see of Moldavia, based at Suceava.

AMAN, Theodor (1831–1891): painter, a founding figure of modern Romanian visual art. His works include a number of paintings on historical themes.

ANTONESCU, Ion (1882–1946): general (marshal from August 1941) and politician. Having been marginalized by Carol II, he was appointed prime minister in September 1940; the king abdicated a few days later. Antonescu established a dictatorial regime, initially in collaboration with the Legionaries (whom he later suppressed). The influence of Nazi Germany was strong, but actual German occupation was avoided. In June 1941 he led the country into war against the Soviet Union in alliance with Germany, seeking the liberation of Besarabia and northern Bukovina. Although these aims were achieved at first, the course of the war later turned against Romania. Antonescu was removed from power by a coup d'état led by the young king, Michael, in August 1944, and was subsequently sentenced to death by a communist court and executed.

ARGETOIANU, Constantin (1871–1952): diplomat before the First World War and politician in the interwar period, active in various parties; he was interior minister in General Averescu's 1920–1921 government, shared leadership in the Iorga-Argetoianu government of 1931–32, and later supported the royal dictatorship of Carol II, under which he served briefly as prime minister in 1939. He was imprisoned by the communists in 1950 and died in prison in 1952.

Aurelian withdrawal: the withdrawal of Roman civil and military organization from Dacia under Emperor Aurelian in 271; the imperial border was re-established at the Danube.

ASACHI, Gheorghe (1788–1869): a leading promoter of modern Romanian education, the press, and the theatre in Moldavia.

AVERESCU, Alexandru (1859–1938): general (later marshal) and politician. After organizing, in his capacity as war minister, the suppression of the 1907 peasant uprising, and directing operations against Bulgaria in the second Balkan war of 1913, he became a hero of the First World War, in which he led the Romanian army to victory at Mărăşti in 1917. He was briefly prime minister in 1918, again in 1920–21 as leader of the People's Party, and in 1926–27. His second term was marked by the introduction of the important land reform of 1921.

BĂLCESCU, Nicolae (1819–1852): revolutionary and historian. He was among the founders of the secret reformist society Frăţia ("The brotherhood") in 1843, and played a leading role in the revolution of 1848 in Wallachia. He was a member of the provisional government set up in June 1848. In 1849 he attempted unsuccessfully to negotiate a peaceful settlement between Avram Iancu and the Hungarian revolutionary government. After the failure of the revolution he continued to work in exile for collaboration among revolutionaries of different nations.

BĂRNUŢIU, Simion (1808–1864): a leading figure in the Romanian revolution of 1848 in Transylvania, subsequently professor of public law and philosophy at the University of Iaşi in Moldavia.

BASARAB I: prince of Wallachia c. 1310 to 1352, who unified the lands to the east and west of the River Olt, so establishing the core territory of the principality. He defeated an invading Hungarian army at the battle of Posada in 1330.

BETHLEN, Gabriel (Bethlen Gábor): prince of Transylvania 1613 to 1629. Taking advantage of Emperor Ferdinand II's engagement in the Thirty Years' War he took control of much of Hungary in 1620 and was briefly nominated as king of Hungary, in opposition to the Catholic emperor, but he gave up his claim in return for guarantees of liberty for Hungarian Protestants. In 1627 he launched the project of a "kingdom of Dacia", which would have united Transylvania and the Romanian principalities.

BLAGA, Lucian (1895–1961): poet and philosopher. His principal philosophical works consist of three trilogies, of Knowledge, Culture and Values. Perhaps the most widely known element of his thinking is the notion of the "Mioritic space", according to which the character of the Romanian people is determined by its origins in a land of rolling hills and valleys.

Bobîlna Uprising (1437): a rising, largely of peasants, in western Transylvania, finally suppressed in 1438 after fierce fighting.

BOGDAN: prince of Moldavia in the 1360s; regarded as the founder of the principality, having "dismounted" there after crossing the mountains from Maramureş to escape Hungarian rule.

BOLINTINEANU, Dimitrie (1825–1872): poet, the author of several volumes of historical legends in verse.

BRĂTIANU, Gheorghe (1898–1953): liberal politician and historian, son of Ion I. C. Brătianu. He died in a communist prison in 1953.

BRĂTIANU, Ion C. (1821–1891): liberal politician. A member of a boyar family, he participated in the 1848 revolution in Wallachia and was later a leading figure in the movement to unite the principalities, and subsequently in the replacement of A. I. Cuza as their ruler by Karl of Hohenzollern–Sigmaringen (later King Carol I). In 1875 he was one of the founders of the National Liberal Party. He served as prime minister almost continuously from 1876 to 1888, thus playing a key role in the war of independence and the proclamation of the kingdom.

BRĂTIANU, Ion I. C. (1864–1927): son of Ion C. Brătianu, leader of the National Liberal Party, and prime minister during much of the period 1908 to 1927 (including the years of the First World War, the Paris peace conference, and creation of Greater Romania).

BRÎNCOVEANU, Constantin: prince of Wallachia 1688 to 1714. He tried to strengthen the autonomy of the principality from the Turks, developing closer links with the Habsburg Empire, but he and his five sons were finally beheaded in Constantinople (having refused to convert to Islam in return for their lives), and the principality was subsequently brought under closer Turkish control through the Phanariot regime. He is also noted for his support of the Orthodox Church and for the cultural achievements of his reign. The style of architecture seen in his palaces and churches was revived as a national style at the end of the nineteenth century. He is now considered a saint by the Romanian Orthodox Church.

Bucegi: mountain range in the southern Carpathians, close to Sinaia and the royal palace of Peleş. Unusual rock formations in the mountains have fuelled speculations on the wilder fringes of Dacianism that they were the center of a mysterious lost civilization

Bucharest, Treaty of (May 1918): treaty ending hostilities between Romania and Germany, Austria–Hungary, Bulgaria and Turkey, leaving Romania apparently defeated and with considerable losses of territory. Although ratified by Parliament it was never signed by King Ferdinand.

BUCUR the Shepherd: the legendary founder of Bucharest.

BUREBISTA: Getic ruler who united many of the Thracian tribes north of the Danube into a single kingdom in the mid-first century BC, and launched attacks on the Roman territories in the Balkans. He was finally killed in a rebellion around 40 BC and his kingdom divided.

BUTEANU, Ioan (1821–1849) and DRAGOŞ, Ioan (1810–1849): Ioan Buteanu was one of the leaders of the Romanians fighting against Hungarian troops in the Apuseni mountains in 1848–49. Ioan Dragoş, on the other hand, was a supporter of the Hungarian revolution and a member of the Parliament in Pest, who negotiated with Avram Iancu on behalf of the Hungarian government. During the negotiations, Buteanu was captured and killed in the course of a Hungarian assault. Dragoş was considered a traitor by Avram Iancu's Romanians, who killed him in reprisal.

Călugăreni: battle, 1595, in which Michael the Brave was victorious over an Ottoman force commanded by Sinan Pasha (though he was unable to follow up the victory, and was forced to withdraw).

CANTEMIR, Dimitrie (1673–1723): prince of Moldavia 1710 to 1711, the author of a number of scholarly works, including a history of the Ottoman Empire and a description of Moldavia. He joined Peter the Great in his war against the Turks, and went into exile in Russia when their campaign ended in failure; he later served Peter as a counselor.

CARAGIALE, Ion Luca (1852–1912): writer and journalist; his social comedies and prose sketches of life in late-nineteenth-century Romania are among the best-known classics of Romanian literature.

CARMEN SYLVA: pen name, as poetess, of Queen Elizabeth.

CAROL I (1839–1914): prince of united Romania 1866 to 1881, and king 1881 to 1914. Following the abdication of A. I. Cuza in 1866, Karl of Hohenzollern–Sigmaringen was persuaded by Ion C. Brătianu to accept the throne of the united principalities. Shortly after his arrival he promulgated a new constitution based on that of Belgium, which affirmed the permanent union of the principalities under the name of Romania and made no mention of foreign guarantors or Ottoman suzerainty. He gained in popularity by his role at the head of the army in the war of independence of 1877–78, as a result of which Romania was internationally recognized as an independent kingdom in 1881. His sympathies in foreign affairs were pro-German, leading him to sign a secret alliance with Germany and Austria–Hungary in 1883, and to seek Romania's entry into the First World War on their side in 1914.

CAROL II (1893–1953): king of Romania 1930 to 1940, son of Ferdinand I. As crown prince he was notorious for his scandalous private life. Having renounced his right to the succession and gone into exile in 1925, he returned to claim the throne in 1930. In 1938 he established a corporatist dictatorship, replacing the political parties with his own Front for National Rebirth. He was forced to abdicate in September 1940, following the humiliating loss of Romanian territory earlier in the year.

CARP, Petre (1837–1919): conservative politician and a founder of the Junimea group. In 1914 he was one of the few Romanian political leaders to favor entry into the Great War on the side of the Central Powers.

CEAUȘESCU, Elena (1919–1989): wife of Nicolae Ceaușescu, holder of various academic titles, none of which she seems to have had any entitlement to; executed with her husband in December 1989.

CEAUȘESCU, Nicolae (1918–1989): communist leader. As a communist activist in the 1930s he was twice imprisoned. He later held various offices in the postwar communist regime. In 1965 he was elected first secretary of the Central Committee of the Romanian Communist Party, and went on to become president of the Council of State in 1967, and the first president of Romania in 1974, turning the office into a personal dictatorship. Initially his rule brought a period of relative liberalization within Romania, and he was admired abroad for his defiance of the Soviet Union over the invasion of Czechoslovakia in 1968. In the 1970s and 1980s, however, repression increased, and the destructive effects of his policies became evident. He was overthrown in December 1989 and executed after a summary trial.

CIORAN, Emil (1911–1995): philosopher, much preoccupied with themes of alienation and despair. He obtained a scholarship to study in France in 1937, and settled there permanently after the Second World War. He wrote thereafter in French, and is considered one of the great twentieth-century French stylists.

CODREANU, Corneliu Zelea (1899–1938): founder of the Legionary Movement. He was imprisoned in 1938 and assassinated on the orders of King Carol II.

COŞBUC, George (1866–1918): one of the best known Romanian poets, associated particularly with traditionalist, rural themes.

CRAINIC, Nichifor (1889–1972): poet of Orthodox religious inspiration and editor of the journal *Gîndirea* (The thought), close in his thinking to the Legionary Movement. He was imprisoned by the communists from 1947 to 1962.

CREANGĂ, Ion (1837–1889): writer, one of the founding fathers of Romanian prose, best known for his literary folktales and childhood reminiscences. His story *Ivan Turbincă* tells of a Russian soldier who terrorizes the devil and tricks Death, who takes revenge on him by allowing him to live for ever.

CRISTESCU, Gheorghe: the first general secretary (1921–1924) of the Communist Party of Romania, which was founded in 1921 as a result of the secession of the extreme Left from the Socialist Party.

Cucuteni culture: a culture of the Neolithic period, named after a site in Moldavia dated to the centuries around 3,000 BC.

CUZA, Alexandru Ioan (1820–1873): first ruler of the united provinces of Wallachia and Moldavia 1859 to 1866. Having been elected prince in both principalities, he worked to integrate them administratively into a single state, which from 1862 was commonly referred to as Romania. His reforms included the emancipation of the peasantry and major land redistribution. He was forced to abdicate in 1866.

DECEBALUS: ruler of the Dacians 87 to 106 AD, and adversary of the Roman emperor Trajan in two wars. He committed suicide after the final Dacian defeat at Sarmizegetusa.

DELAVRANCEA, Barbu Ştefănescu (1858–1918): writer and politician, renowned for his oratory.

DESPINA: wife of Neagoe Basarab, who shared in his religious and cultural activities.

DESPOT Vodă: prince of Moldavia 1561 to 1563. He was Lutheran, and declared religious toleration in Moldavia. The heavy taxation required to finance his project of an anti-Ottoman crusade provoked discontent, and he was killed by rebellious boyars.

Dismounting (*Descălecat*): the term used in the traditional history of Moldavia and Wallachia for the founding event of the arrival of princes from Maramureş or Transylvania (Dragoş, Bogdan, and Negru Vodă).

DOBROGEANU-GHEREA, Constantin (1855–1920): socialist leader and ideologist, and literary critic.

DOJA, Gheorghe (Dózsa György, 1470–1514): Szekler noble, leader of an army raised in Transylvania to fight the Turks, which turned into a peasant rebellion against landlord abuses when the planned crusade was suspended. He was finally defeated at Timişoara, and brutally executed.

DRAGOŞ (fl. mid-fourteenth century): voivode from Maramureş who was granted territory in northern Moldavia by the king of Hungary. His descendants were later ousted by Bogdan.

DRAGOŞ, Ioan (1810–1849): see BUTEANU, Ioan.

DROMICHETES: head of a Getic kingdom north of the Danube around 300 BC, who resisted attacks by the Macedonian ruler of Thrace, Lysimachus.

DUCA, Ion G. (1879–1933): liberal politician, prime minister in 1933, assassinated in the same year by a group of Legionaries.

ELIADE, Mircea (1907–1986): writer and historian of religions. In his youth he was sympathetic to the ideals of the Legionary movement. He served as Romanian Cultural Attaché in London and later Lisbon during the Second World War, and settled in Paris in 1945. He subsequently moved to the U.S.A., and from 1957 was Professor of the History of Religions at the University of Chicago.

ELIZABETH, Queen (Elizabeth of Wied, 1843–1916): wife of King Carol I, also known as a poetess under the pen name Carmen Sylva.

EMINESCU, Mihai (1850–1889): poet and journalist, a member of the Junimea group. Generally regarded as the national poet of Romania, he is commemorated by countless statues, busts etc. throughout the country, and has become a symbolic representative of Romanian culture. As well as his concern with the national past and present, his poetry is characterized by a late romantic air of melancholy and a rich musicality of language.

EUTROPIUS: fourth-century historian, author of a history of Rome from its foundation.

FERDINAND I (1865–1927): king of Romania 1914 to 1927, nephew of Carol I. He and Queen Marie were crowned as sovereigns of Greater Romania in Alba Iulia in 1922.

FORIŞ, Ştefan: general secretary of the Communist Party of Romania 1940 to 1944, assassinated on the orders of Gheorghiu-Dej and the other leaders of the Party in 1944.

FRIMU, I. C. (1871–1919): socialist leader.

GELU, GLAD, and MENUMORUT: voivodes in western Transylvania, the Banat, and Crişana, reported by the twelfth-century Hungarian chronicler Anomymus to have resisted the Hungarian invasion at the end of the ninth and beginning of the tenth centuries.

GHEORGHIU, Ştefan (1879–1914): socialist leader.

GHEORGHIU-DEJ, Gheorghe (1901–1965): communist leader. A railway worker, imprisoned in the 1930s for his communist activities, he became general secretary of the Communist Party of Romania in 1945 and was instrumental in gaining control of the government for the communists. Having eliminated his rivals, he was sole head of the Communist Party from 1952 until his death.

GHICA, Grigore III: prince of Moldavia 1764 to 1767 and 1774 to 1777, and of Wallachia 1768 to 1769. He protested against the Austrian annexation of Bukovina in 1775, and was put to death by the Turks as a consequence

Great Union: the union with Romania, in 1918, of territories previously under foreign rule, thus creating Greater Romania. Bessarabia was the first to unite (in March), followed by Bukovina (in November). Finally, Transylvania, along with the formerly Hungarian territories of the Banat, Crişana and Maramureş, united with Romania by the decision of a great assembly gathered in Alba Iulia on 1 December 1918 (confirmed by the Treaty of Trianon in 1920).

Greater Romania: the Romanian state at its largest extent, in the period 1918 to 1940. Created by the Great Union of 1918, it was dismembered in 1940 by the annexation of northern Transylvania to Hungary, northern Bukovina and Bessarabia to the Soviet Union, and southern Dobrogea to Bulgaria. Of these, only northern Transylvania was restored to Romania after the Second World War.

Grivitsa: fortification captured by the Romanian army in the course of the siege of the Turkish stronghold of Pleven in 1877, during the war of independence.

Griviţa strike: 1933 strike of workers at the Griviţa railway workshops in Bucharest, later considered a key moment in the history of the communist movement.

GROZA, Petru (1884–1958): politician, leader of the Ploughmen's Front, a satellite party of the communist movement. In May 1945 he formed the first government dominated by communists. He was prime minister until 1952.

From 1952 to 1958 he was president of the Presidium of the Great National Assembly (the collective presidency of the Romanian People's Republic).

HELIADE RĂDULESCU, Ion (1802–1872): writer, linguist, and politician, founder of the first Romanian newspaper, *Curierul Românesc* (The Romanian courier) in 1829, a participant in the revolution of 1848 in Wallachia, and a promoter of Western influence in Romanian culture.

HOREA, CLOŞCA, and CRIŞAN: leaders of the peasant uprising of 1784 in Transylvania, against oppression by the nobility. After initially gaining control of large areas of western Transylvania, the rising was suppressed by an imperial army. Horea and Cloşca were brutally executed in 1785; Crişan committed suicide in prison.

IANCU, Avram (1824–1872): revolutionary leader in Transylvania in 1848. As a result of the Hungarian revolutionary government's decision to unite Transylvania to Hungary and its refusal to accept the demands of the Transylvanian Romanians, Avram Iancu led an army of Romanian peasants against the Hungarians in the Apuseni mountains. Peace was finally reached in 1849, thanks to the mediation of Nicolae Bălcescu, but the Hungarian revolution was suppressed by Russian forces shortly after. Iancu withdrew to live among the mountain peasants.

IANCU of Hunedoara (Hunyadi János or John Hunyadi, c. 1407–1456): Hungarian nobleman of Romanian descent, who rose to become prince of Transylvania in 1441. In 1443–44 he led a massive and partially successful campaign against the Turks in the Balkans. From 1446 to 1453 he was governor of Hungary during the minority of László V. He died in 1456 shortly after inflicting a defeat on the Turks at Belgrade. His son, Matthias Corvinus, later became king of Hungary.

IOAN Vodă the Terrible: prince of Moldavia 1572 to 1574, who suppressed rebellions on the part of the Moldavian boyars.

IONESCU, Nae (1890–1940): philosopher, professor at the University of Bucharest, promoter of an existentialist philosophy which stressed "personal experience". He was a formative influence on the young Romanian intellectuals of the interwar period, Mircea Eliade and Mircea Vulcănescu being among his disciples. He supported Carol II at first, and was later sympathetic to the Legionary Movement.

IONIŢĂ (Kaloyan): ruler of the second Bulgarian tsardom, 1197 to 1207. He was the younger brother of its founders Petru and Asan (also known as Peter and Ivan Asen).

IORGA, Nicolae (1871–1940): historian, professor at the University of Bucharest, and an exceptionally prolific writer of historical books and articles, a key figure in the development of Romanian historiography. As a politician before and during the First World War he militated for the Romanian national idea. He became prime minister in 1931–32. He was assassinated by the Legionaries in 1940.

IPĂTESCU, Ana (1805–1875): heroine of the 1848 revolution in Wallachia. In June 1848 she played a leading role in the release of the members of the Provisional Government, who had been arrested by opponents of the revolution.

KISELEFF (Kiselyov), Pavel Dmitriyevich: Russian general, charged with the administration of Wallachia and Moldavia from 1829 to 1834 (after the Treaty of Adrianople). He later served as a reforming minister in Russia and as Russian ambassador to Paris.

KOGĂLNICEANU, Mihail (1817–1891): historian, an active participant in the Revolution of 1848 and advocate of the union of Moldavia and Wallachia; prime minister of the United Principalities 1863 to 1865.

LAZĂR, Gheorghe (1779–1823): scholar and educationalist, founder of Romanian-language education in Wallachia, head of the Saint Sava School in Bucharest.

Legionary Movement: political movement of the extreme Right, nationalist and anti-Semitic, with a strong element of Orthodox mysticism. The Legion of the Archangel Michael was founded by Corneliu Z. Codreanu in 1927. The movement was constituted as a political party, initially known as the Iron Guard, in 1930. Repressed by the Carolist regime in 1938–39, it came to power with Ion Antonescu in 1940. It was finally suppressed after a rebellion in 1941.

LUPESCU, Elena: mistress of Carol II. Their relationship was the cause of his exclusion from the succession in 1925. She returned to Romania with him in 1930, despite the general disapproval of the Romanian political class.

MAIORESCU, Titu (1840–1917): literary critic and conservative politician, a leading figure in the Junimea movement; prime minister 1912 to 1914.

MANIU, Iuliu (1873–1953): politician. Before the First World War he was a campaigner for Romanian rights in Transylvania and served as a member of the Budapest Parliament from 1906. He played an important role in the events leading to the union of Transylvania with Romania in 1918, and was president of the interim governing council there from 1918 to 1920. Later, as leader of the National Peasant Party, he was prime minister of Romania three times between 1928 and 1933. He was a consistent opponent of the dictatorial regimes established in Romania from 1938 onwards. Having been arrested after the communist takeover, he died in prison in 1953.

Mărăşeşti: battle in August 1917 in which a massive German advance on the Moldavian front was halted by the Romanians, under Eremia Grigorescu, after fourteen days of fighting.

Mărăşti: battle in July 1917, in which a Romanian army commanded by General Averescu successfully pushed back the forces of the Central Powers.

MARGHILOMAN, Alexandru (1854–1925): conservative politician. Having been one of the advocates of friendship with Germany, he was appointed prime minister in the spring of 1918, when Romania was forced to sue for a peace settlement with the Central Powers.

MARIE, Queen (Marie of Edinburgh, 1875–1938): wife of King Ferdinand I. She influenced Romania's entry into the First World War on the side of Britain and France.

MATEI Basarab: prince of Wallachia 1632 to 1654; his reign saw the development of printing in Wallachia and the introduction of the Romanian language in the Church.

MATTHIAS Corvinus: king of Hungary 1458 to 1490, son of Iancu of Hunedoara. He is renowned for his military and diplomatic achievements and as a patron of the arts.

MICHAEL I (b. 1921): king of Romania 1927 to 1930 and 1940 to 1947 (interrupted by the return of his father Carol II in 1930). He played a central role in the coup d'état of August 1944, by which the Antonescu regime was overthrown and Romania switched its allegiance from the Axis to the Allied side. Having attempted to resist the communist takeover he was finally forced to abdicate in 1947 and went into exile. After the fall of communism he was initially refused permission to enter the country. He was allowed to visit at Easter 1992, but was again refused entry two years later. This obstruction ended with the change of government in 1996.

MICHAEL the Brave (1558–1601): prince of Wallachia 1593 to 1601, and briefly also of Transylvania and Moldavia in 1600. Rebelling against Turkish suzerainty in 1594, he joined the campaign of the Holy League of European powers against the Ottoman Empire. After being forced to withdraw after his victory at Călugăreni in 1595, he finally drove the Turks out of Wallachia with the aid of Sigismond Báthory of Transylvania, who had likewise rebelled. Although Michael had been forced to accept Transylvanian suzerainty as the price of Báthory's support, he regained autonomy by an alliance with Emperor Rudolf II in 1598. When the new prince of Transylvania, Andreas Báthory, renewed the claim of suzerainty over Wallachia, called for Michael's removal, and undertook to renew the payment of tribute to the Turks, Michael invaded Transylvania in 1599 and took control of the principality. In 1600 he invaded Moldavia and ousted Ieremia Movilă, whose Polish allies favored peace with the Turks. He briefly succeeded in getting imperial recognition as prince of all three territories. However, the Habsburg general Giorgio Basta took advantage of a noble revolt against Michael in Transylvania in 1600 to regain control of the principality for the emperor. Meanwhile, Polish forces invaded Moldavia, restoring Ieremia Movilă to the throne, and went on to set his brother Simion Movilă on the throne of Wallachia. By the end of 1600 Michael had lost all three territories and was obliged to regain the support of Rudolf II. When Sigismond Báthory returned to power in Transylvania in 1601, Rudolf supported Michael's invasion of the principality, this time in collaboration with Basta. Báthory was defeated, but Michael was assassinated at Basta's instigation before he could take advantage of this new opportunity.

MIRCEA the Old (or the Great): prince of Wallachia 1386 to 1418, in whose reign the principality reached its greatest extent, with the incorporation of Dobrogea. After defeating the Turks in his own territory at Rovine in 1394, he participated in King Sigismund of Hungary's unsuccessful crusade which ended at the battle of Nicopolis in 1396. (His epithet "the Old" actually has nothing to do with his age: he was referred to in this way by later chroniclers to distinguish him from more recent rulers of the same name.)

NĂSTASE, Ilie (b. 1946): a leading international tennis player in the 1970s, put forward in the local elections of June 1996 by the Romanian Party of Social Democracy (then in government) as candidate for mayor of Bucharest: he lost the election.

NEAGOE Basarab: prince of Wallachia 1512 to 1521; the founder of the famous church at Curtea de Argeş, and author of the Slavonic work *The Teachings of Neagoe Basarab to his son Teodosie.*

NEGRU VODĂ (Radu Negru): legendary founder of Wallachia, where he is said to have "dismounted" in the late thirteenth century, coming from Transylvania.

NOICA, Constantin (1909–1987): philosopher. After being imprisoned from 1958 to 1964 he worked as a researcher in Bucharest, before moving, in 1975, to the mountain resort of Păltiniş, near Sibiu. There he continued to be visited by younger Romanian intellectuals, on whom he had a profound influence.

Paris, Congress of (1856): Congress leading to the treaty which ended the Crimean War. The final treaty ended the Russian protectorate in Wallachia and Moldavia, leaving them under Turkish suzerainty with the European powers as guarantors. The southern part of Bessarabia (annexed by Russia in 1812) was restored to Moldavia. As a result of the deliberations of the Congress, it was decided that future constitutional arrangements in Wallachia and Moldavia should decided by an ad-hoc assembly in each principality, thus beginning the process which was to lead to the union of the principalities in 1859.

PĂTRĂŞCANU, Lucreţiu (1900–1954): communist leader, one of the few intellectuals in the leadership of the Communist Party. He played an important role, as Communist Party representative, in the change of regime in August 1944, and was minister of justice from 1944 to 1948. As a promoter of a more national and less authoritarian version of communism, he was arrested in 1948 and executed in 1954.

PAUKER, Ana (1893–1960): communist leader, of Jewish origin, representative of the Muscovite wing of the Party. She played an important role in the early years of the communist regime, and was foreign minister from 1947 to 1952. In 1952 she was removed from all positions of power by Gheorghiu-Dej.

Peleş: castle, mainly in German style, built as a summer palace for King Carol I and Queen Elizabeth between 1875 and 1914, outside the mountain resort of Sinaia in the southern Carpathians

PETRU Aron: prince of Moldavia three times between 1451 and 1457.

PETRU Rareş: prince of Moldavia 1527 to 1538 and 1541 to 1546, an illegitimate son of Stephen the Great. He played an active part in the struggle between János Zápolyai and Ferdinand of Habsburg for control of Transylvania. Much of the famous external mural painting of the northern Moldavian monasteries dates from his reign.

PETRU Şchiopul (the Lame): prince of Moldavia three times between 1574 and 1591.

Phanariots: the name given to a series of Greek princes of Wallachia and Moldavia in the eighteenth and early nineteenth centuries, so called because many of them came from the Phanar district, a Greek area of Constantinople.

Quadrilateral: the southern part of Dobrogea, annexed by Romania in 1913 after the second Balkan war, and returned to Bulgaria in 1940.

RADU Negru (see NEGRU VODĂ)

RÁKÓCZI, Ferenc II (1676–1735): Hungarian nobleman, a leader of resistance to Habsburg dominance. He was elected prince of Transylvania in 1704 and continued his anti-Austrian campaign there; after Habsburg rule in Hungary and Transylvania was established by the Treaty of Szatmár (1711) he went into exile, finally settling in Turkey.

Règlement Organique: constitution adopted in Wallachia (1831) and Moldavia (1832) under the Russian protectorate of 1829 to 1834 and subsequently ratified by the Turkish government. It provided for the election of princes from among the local aristocracy, and for the setting up of legislative assemblies dominated by the boyar class.

ROLAND Borsa: prince of Transylvania three times between 1282 and 1293

Rovine: battle fought in 1394; traditionally seen as a great victory of Mircea the Old over the superior forces of the Turkish sultan Bayazid I.

RUSSO, Alecu (1819–1859): Moldavian writer, best known for his "Cîntarea României" (Song of Romania).

SADOVEANU, Mihail (1880–1961): one of the best-known Romanian novelists, and an active collaborator in the postwar communist takeover.

Sarmizegetusa: Dacian citadel in southwestern Transylvania (near the town of Orăştie), the capital of Decebalus's kingdom and the site of his final battle with the Roman invaders.

Securitate: political police of the communist regime from 1948 until the revolution of 1989. Under Ceauşescu it permeated Romanian society through an extensive network of informers, and served as one of the principal bases of his power. It was replaced in 1990 by the Romanian Information Service (SRI).

Siguranţă: under the law of 1929 concerning the organization of the Romanian police, that part of the police responsible for observing and combating actions directed against the safety of the public and the state. It was abolished in 1948 and replaced by the Securitate.

ŞTEFĂNIŢĂ: prince of Moldavia 1517 to 1527, initially as a minor, with real power being in the hands of his tutor, the prominent boyar Luca Arbore. On reaching his majority he removed Arbore from his privileged position and subsequently had him executed.

STEPHEN the Great: prince of Moldavia 1457 to 1504. Although he was initially an ally of Vlad Ţepeş of Wallachia, in 1462 he laid siege to the Wallachian port of Chilia, ostensibly to prevent it falling into Turkish hands, and so further weakened Vlad's then precarious position. In 1475 the Turks invaded Moldavia. Stephen defeated Mehmet II's army at the battle of Vaslui, and, despite a subsequent Turkish victory at Războieni, the Turks were forced to withdraw. Stephen was named the "athlete of Christ" by Pope Sixtus IV for his resistance to Ottoman expansion, but he received little help from other European rulers. He withstood a further Turkish invasion in 1484, but at the cost of the ports of Chilia and Cetatea Albă, and finally agreed to pay tribute to the Turks as the price of Moldavian independence. His daughter Elena married Ivan, son of Ivan III of Muscovy, in 1483. Stephen is now regarded as a saint by the Romanian Orthodox Church.

TEODOROIU, Ecaterina (1894–1917): heroine of the First World War. After taking part in the defense of Tîrgu Jiu in 1916, she became an officer in the Romanian army and was killed in battle the following year.

TITULESCU, Nicolae (1882–1941): politician and diplomat. He was finance minister in 1917–18 and 1920–21, and foreign minister in 1927–28 and 1932–

36. From 1920 to 1936 he represented Romania at the League of Nations, and he was president of the League in 1930 and 1931. He settled to France in 1936.

Union of the Principalities: the union of Wallachia and Moldavia in 1859, achieved through the election of the same prince, A. I. Cuza, in both territories, and followed by the administrative integration of the principalities during his reign.

VĂCĂRESCU, Ienăchiţă (c. 1740–1797): author of naïve verses, a precursor of the modern Romanian poetry which emerged in the nineteenth century.

VASILE Lupu (the Wolf): prince of Moldavia 1634 to 1653. He invaded Wallachia several times, seeking to gain control of it by placing his son on the throne in the place of Matei Basarab.

VLAD Dracul (the Dragon, or the Devil): prince of Wallachia 1436 to 1442 and 1443 to 1447. He was initially an ally of Iancu of Hunedoara in his wars against the Turks, but Iancu later turned against him and supported the boyar rebellion which led to Vlad's assassination in 1447. His nickname comes from the Order of the Dragon, with which he was invested by Emperor Sigismund of Luxemburg.

VLAD Ţepeş (the Impaler): prince of Wallachia, briefly in 1448, then from 1456 to 1462, and again briefly in 1476. He was the son of Vlad Dracul, hence the name "Dracula" by which he is best known outside Romania. He rebelled against Turkish suzerainty and attacked the Turkish territories south of the Danube, provoking a retaliatory invasion in 1462, led by Mehmet II in person. Vlad successfully harassed the Turkish army and horrified the sultan with the spectacle of a forest of impaled Turkish prisoners on the road to the capital Tîrgovişte, but he was forced to withdraw into Transylvania, leaving Wallachia under Turkish control. After a long period of captivity in Hungary he returned to his throne in 1476, but was quickly killed, probably by resentful boyars.

VLADIMIRESCU, Tudor (c. 1780–1821): leader of a revolutionary movement in Wallachia, in alliance with the Etairist movement in Greece. In 1821 he raised a peasant army in Oltenia and took effective control of the government of Wallachia. Meanwhile, an Etairist force under Alexander Ypsilantis arrived from Moldavia. When a Turkish army entered Wallachia to restore order, Tudor's continuing negotiations with the Turks and refusal to help the Etairists earned the hostility of Ypsilantis, who had him executed.

Vodă: title given to the princes of Wallachia and Moldavia, later sometimes used of the kings of Romania.

VULCĂNESCU, Mircea (1904–1952): philosopher, sociologist, and economist, a disciple of Nae Ionescu. He served as an undersecretary of state in the Finance Ministry in Antonescu's government. He died in a communist prison in 1952.

Index

Giurescu, Constantin C., 64, 66–68, 75,
79, 96, 108, 120, 134–135, 196, 198,
200, 244, 246, 248, 253–254, 256, 260
Giurescu, Dinu C., 75
Glad, Transylvanian voivode, 124, 222,
270
Goethe, Johann Wofgang von, 56, 80
Goga, Octavian, 177, 254
Goldiş, Vasile, 224
Gorbachev, Mikhail, 167, 176
Grigorescu, Eremia, 210, 273
Groza, Petru, 225, 270
Guizot, François, 30
Gusti, Dimitrie, 63

Hasdeu, Bogdan Petriceicu, 52–53, 55–
57, 59, 63, 88, 90–93, 97, 99, 105–
107, 115–116, 124–125, 178, 193,
197–200, 243, 246–248, 251–253
Havel, Vaclav, 8
Heliade Rădulescu, Ion, 43, 48–49, 193,
200, 243, 271
Herder, Johann Gottfried, 33, 132, 143
Herodotus, 68, 83, 99
Herzen, Alexandr Ivanovich, 219
Hitler, Adolf, 173, 180, 227, 234
Hodoş, Nerva, 84, 254
Hohenzollern-Sigmaringen, dynasty,
201, 205, 265, 267
Homer, 81
Horea, 56, 69, 80, 81, 97, 203, 212–215,
220, 222–223, 256, 271
Horthy, Miklós, 187
Hunyadi János: see Iancu of Hunedoara
Huru, fictional character, 47–48, 124,
243

Iancu, Avram, 203, 212–213, 216, 220,
222–223, 228, 264, 266, 271
Iancu of Hunedoara, voivode of
Transylvania, 15, 135, 192, 212, 222,
271, 273, 277
Ibrăileanu, Garabet, 150
Ieremia Movilă, ruler of Moldavia, 178,
273–274
Iliescu, Ion, 10, 21–22, 24, 106, 174, 237

Ioan Vodă the Terrible, ruler of
Moldavia, 52–53, 178, 192, 195, 197–
200, 215, 252–253, 255–256, 271
Ionescu, Nae, 61, 146–147, 154, 271,
277
Ionescu, Nicolae, 52
Ionescu-Nica, G., 100, 247
Ioniţă, king of the Bulgarians and
Romanians, 38, 115, 244, 271
Iordan, Iourgu, 126
Iorga, Nicolae, 17, 53–54, 60, 64–68,
75–76, 93, 108, 119–124, 134, 138,
158, 164–165, 178, 196, 244, 246,
248–249, 251, 256, 264, 271
Iorgulescu, Mircea, 2
Ipătescu, Ana, 207, 216, 218, 272
Ipsilanti, Alexandru, ruler of Wallachia,
84
Istrati, Constantin I., 97–98, 246
Iunian, Grigore, 76
Ivan III, grand prince of Muscovy, 215,
219, 276
Ivan the Terrible, tsar of Russia, 190

Jesus Christ, 214
Jordanes, 104, 118
Julian the Apostate, Roman emperor, 55
Jullian, Camille, 100

Kaloyan: see Ioniţă
Kiseleff, Pavel, 159, 272
Kogălniceanu, Mihail, 40–41, 49–50, 55,
58, 88–89, 115, 131, 154, 164, 212,
222–223, 243, 245, 249, 251, 260,
272
Kohl, Helmut, 240
Kosmodemianskaia, Zoia, 219

Lahovari, Ion, 161
Lapedatu, Alexandru, 64
Laurian, August Treboniu, 46–47, 55,
87, 106–107, 115, 178, 200, 252
Lavater, Johann Kaspar, 199
Lazarus, Moritz, 144
Lazăr, Gheorghe, 193, 212, 272
Lenin, Vladimir Ilich, 218–219, 222, 225

The Păltiniş Diary
A Paideic Model in Humanist Culture

Gabriel Liiceanu, Professor of Philosophy, University of Bucharest

"This wonderful book describes an initiation, an awakening, and a form of spiritual fraternity. That such experiences could take place in the stifling atmosphere of Ceauşescu's Romania is a powerful argument against the thesis of absolute totalitarian control over human mind." - **Vladimir Tismaneanu,** Director of the Center for the Study of Post-Communist Societies, University of Maryland

The intellectual resistance to totalitarian regimes can take many forms. This remarkable volume portrays one such story of resistance in Romania during the reign of Ceauşescu: that of Constantin Noica, one of the country's foremost intellectuals.

Noica was an original thinker belonging to the remarkable intellectual generation of important figures such as Mircea Eliade, E. M. Cioran and Eugene Ionescu, but he chose to stay in Romania after the communist takeover when many others fled. Harassed and jailed for six years, Noica retreated to the mountains and gathered around him some brilliant young minds and future talent to challenge and nurture them in a time when communism denied them the materials of true intellectual importance.

The author of this volume Liiceanu, himself a brilliant philosopher, was Noica's closest disciple and during every meeting he noted every conversation in a diary which came to be known as *The Păltiniş Diary*. The volume is a wonderful homage to an intellectual master and to the power of intellect and freedom.

2000, 228 pages
963-9116-88-2   cloth $49.95 / £31.00
963-9116-89-0   paperback $22.95 / £13.95

**AVAILABLE TO ORDER AT ALL GOOD BOOKSHOPS
OR CHECK OUT OUR WEBSITE WWW.CEUPRESS.COM
FOR FULL ORDERING DETAILS**

Coming Winter 2000

National Identity of Romanians in Transylvania

Sorin Mitu, Babes-Bolyai University of Cluj, Romania

"It is the most thorough and authoritative investigation of modern Romanian identity in Transylvania yet undertaken." **Keith Hitchins,** University of Illinois

"One of the latest results from a Romanian historian who was able to cope with the totalitarian heritage of Romanian communism... highly recommended." - **Ambrus Miskolczy,** Department of Romanian Studies, Eötvös Loránd University, Hungary

This meticulously researched and elegantly written book is an unparalelled study of the emergence of modern Romanian identity in Transylvania during the eighteenth and nineteenth centuries. Based upon a plethora of contemporary published sources, Mitu approaches national identity from a variety of perspectives.

The author sheds new light on the problems of self-evaluation using a method he describes as "functional analysis" to examine a complex set of ideologies and propaganda. This approach helps the reader to understand the intricate web of contemporary Romanian nationalism.

450 pages
963-9116-95-5 cloth $55.95 / £34.95